Wodehouse

with

New Friends

Ellery Cobbold: An Illustration of Capital in a Labour paper

Wodehouse

with

New Friends

by

TONY RING

and

GEOFFREY JAGGARD

with illustrations by

Bernard Canavan

PORPOISE BOOKS

© Tony Ring and Geoffrey Jaggard 2001
who assert their rights as authors
....

Cover & Illustrations by Bernard Canavan © Porpoise Books 2001
Other illustrations reproduced from original magazine appearances.
Information requested about copyrightholders.
....

Printed by Antony Rowe Limited, Chippenham, England
A CIP for this book is available from the British Library

Porpoise Books
68 Altwood Road Maidenhead SL6 4PZ
....

ISBN 1 870 304 21 7

Contents

List of Illustrations

INTRODUCTION TO *WODEHOUSE WITH NEW FRIENDS*

As regular subscribers will be aware, each of the first six volumes of the *Concordance* concentrated on a group of linked or themed stories. That left a plethora of material to be covered by the last two books whose links would in some cases inevitably prove somewhat obscure. The decision was taken to divide the remaining almost thirty novels and more than a hundred short stories according to whether one or more characters were in action on more than one occasion.

Volume 7 covered works which dealt with characters, such as members of the Drones Club, who appeared in more than one story. Volume 8 is thus a residual volume covering books and stories in which no active characters appeared more than once (subject to a few exceptions, where their reappearance was not expected!).

One possible exception to this approach needs some explanation, for *The Indiscretions of Archie* has been treated for this purpose as a single novel. Not all readers of this book may be aware that it started life as a series of eleven self-contained short stories which first appeared in the *Strand* from March 1920 to February 1921, excluding the Christmas 1920 issue. In the USA, ten of the stories appeared in *Cosmopolitan* from May 1920 to February 1921, and one did not appear at all.

From these stories, the book evolved and was published on both sides of the Atlantic in 1921. In its conception and evolution it can thus be likened to *The Inimitable Jeeves*, published in 1923 but based on 13 stories appearing in magazines between 1918 and 1922. In both cases, the order of the stories was changed substantially, and most were converted into two or more chapters for book purposes. *The Indiscretions of Archie* was perhaps edited more than *The Inimitable Jeeves*, with new introductory material appearing in a number of stories, and it is noticeable that about half the first four chapters did not appear in the magazine versions at all.

Despite the extensive reworking, very few changes in detail relevant to this *Concordance*, and those all minor, can be found on a close comparison of the magazine and book texts. Accordingly, the principal references have been to the UK book version, with chapter number where appropriate. On the few occasions where a reference to an original magazine proved necessary, a standard magazine reference with a unique three-lettered reference assigned to that magazine story has been used. Readers will therefore find a mixture of references to a novel and to individual stories within magazines.

A comparison of the equivalent chapters in book and the two magazines, for those who are interested, is:

Story Title (Strand Version)	Book	Strand	Cosmopolitan
The Man Who Married a Hotel	1-3, part 9, part 11, 16	3/20	5/20
Archie and the Sausage Chappie	part 18, 20	4/20	6/20
Dear Old Squiffy	7-8	5/20	7/20
Doing Father a Bit of Good	part 9-10	6/20	8/20
Paving the Way for Mabel	17, part 18, 19	7/20	9/20
Washy Makes His Presence Felt	21-22	8/20	10/20
A Room at the Hermitage	12-13	9/20	11/20
First Aid for Looney Biddle	14-15	10/20	12/20
Mother's Knee	23-24	11/20	1/21
Strange Experiences of an Artist's Model	5-6	1/21	Did not appear
The Wigmore Venus	25-26	2/21	2/21

The remainder of this book is relatively straightforward, but attention should be drawn to the four *Appendices* and the two *Series Notes* which appear after the main text. The first *Appendix* has sought to draw together the various dedications which PGW made in respect of his books, and where the dedication is not excessively long, it has been reproduced.

The second describes the evolution of *Laughing Gas*, which was originally written as a 30,000 word novella for a magazine, before being rewritten as a full-length novel. The appendix explains how the plot was enhanced and new characters introduced into the novel.

Appendix 3 relates to the manuscript of *The Girl in Blue* and uses it to illustrate the writing style of Wodehouse, pointing out that even a highly amended manuscript which appears complete must have been rewritten subsequently, as a number of plot elements had changed in the published book

Appendix 4 uses research from a French Wodehousean, Anne-Marie Chanet, to explore the extent to which Wodehouse drew on the French author Georges Courteline's work in two of his novels, but particularly in *French Leave*.

As this is the final volume in a series which has taken eight years to publish, readers will not be surprised that further information has appeared in respect of matters covered in earlier volumes. The opportunity has been taken to add two updating notes, one about the Earldom of Blandings and the other about another revised version of *The Prince and Betty* (see *Volume 7)* which appeared in 1931, and which can virtually be described as a new, unpublished Wodehouse novel. Unfortunately, at the time of writing the notes, not all the instalments of the magazine in which the new version appeared in serial form had been traced, so the notes are not as comprehensive as they otherwise could be.

THE REFERENCE SYSTEM USED IN THE
WODEHOUSE MILLENNIUM CONCORDANCE

One of the main purposes of this concordance is to encourage readers, by the different references, allusions and comments in this work, to read, or reread the stories to which they refer. To facilitate this, the source of a character, place, quotation or other reference has been identified as specifically as feasible.

Most Wodehouse stories, particularly before the second world war, appeared in magazines in the US and the UK, as well as in book form in both countries. On occasion the book versions differed in a subtle, or even substantial manner; differences could also be found between them and the magazines. Whilst sometimes such changes would be important to the story, more often they were editorial omissions for space reasons or minor changes in the name of a character or location. So difficult to trace are some of the magazines there can never be any certainty that all relevant issues have been reviewed and the author would be pleased to hear from readers who may be aware of additional items which could be included in any future revision.

In providing references, the principal source has been the first UK book publication. Where a change has been made in a later edition of which the author is aware, or in a story is published for the first time in book form in an omnibus edition, that is made clear. Only entries unique to US books (again principally to the first editions) or to magazines in either country are mentioned with their own references, and these will be found even where the story itself appears in a UK book.

The following summarises the material reviewed in preparation of this volume of the concordance.

UK BOOK COLLECTIONS WITH FEATURED STORIES

TMU	The Man Upstairs	Methuen	1914
MLF	The Man with Two Left Feet	Methuen	1919
IOA	Indiscretions of Archie	Herbert Jenkins	1921
NSE	Nothing Serious	Herbert Jenkins	1950
PLP	Plum Pie	Herbert Jenkins	1966

US BOOK COLLECTIONS WITH FEATURED STORIES

USIOA	Indiscretions of Archie	Doran	1921
MTL	The Man with Two Left Feet	Burt	1933
USNSE	Nothing Serious	Doubleday	1951
USPLP	Plum Pie	Simon & Schuster	1967

In addition, stories not previously published in book form in the USA were included in anthologies produced after Wodehouse's death. Reprints of stories covered by this volume can be found in:

THS	The Swoop and Other Stories	Seabury	1979
TUW	The Uncollected Wodehouse	Seabury	1976

REFERENCES FOR MAGAZINE TITLES

Ainslee		Ainslee
Aldin	**	The Cecil Aldin Book
Answers		Answers
ASCW		All Star Cavalier Weekly
BurrMcK		The Burr McKintosh Monthly
Century		Century Magazine
Colliers		Colliers
Cosmo		Cosmopolitan
Ellery		Ellery Queen
Escapade		Escapade
Grand		Grand Magazine
Household		Household Magazine
JohnBull		John Bull
LHJ		Ladies' Home Journal
McClure		McClure
Nash		Nash's Magazine
PallMall		Pall Mall
Pan		Pan
Pearson		Pearson's
PicRev		Pictorial Review
Playboy		Playboy
Red		Red Book
SatEvePost		Saturday Evening Post
Strand		Strand Magazine

Sunday	Sunday Magazine
ThisWeek	This Week
Throne	The Throne and Country
VanFair	Vanity Fair (US edition)
WHC	Women's Home Companion
Windsor	Windsor

** An anthology of many authors' works published in 1932 by Eyre & Spottiswoode

UK NOVELS COVERED FULLY BY THE TEXT

WTT	William Tell Told Again	A&C Black	1904
NGW	Not George Washington	Cassell	1907
JTR	Jill the Reckless	Herbert Jenkins	1921
IOA	Indiscretions of Archie	** Herbert Jenkins	1921
GOB	The Girl on the Boat	Herbert Jenkins	1922
TAS	The Adventures of Sally	Herbert Jenkins	1922
HOW	Hot Water	Herbert Jenkins	1932
LAG	Laughing Gas	Herbert Jenkins	1936
SUM	Summer Moonshine	Herbert Jenkins	1937
QUS	Quick Service	Herbert Jenkins	1940
SPF	Spring Fever	Herbert Jenkins	1948
TOR	The Old Reliable	Herbert Jenkins	1951
FRL	French Leave	Herbert Jenkins	1956
DBB	Do Butlers Burgle Banks	Herbert Jenkins	1968
TGI	The Girl in Blue	Herbert Jenkins	1970

** For a discussion of the 'novel' status of *Indiscretions of Archie*, see the *Introduction to Wodehouse with New Friends* (page ix).

US NOVELS COVERED BY THE TEXT

TLW	The Little Warrior	Doran	1920
USIOA	Indiscretions of Archie	Doran	1921
TMM	Three Men and a Maid	Doran	1922
MOS	Mostly Sally	Doran	1923
USHOW	Hot Water	Doubleday, Doran	1932
USLAG	Laughing Gas	Doubleday, Doran	1936
USSUM	Summer Moonshine	Doubleday, Doran	1937
USQUS	Quick Service	Doubleday, Doran	1940
USSPF	Spring Fever	Doubleday	1948

USTOR	The Old Reliable	Doubleday	1951
USFRL	French Leave	Simon & Schuster	1959
USDBB	Do Butlers Burgle Banks	Simon & Schuster	1968
USTGI	The Girl in Blue	Simon & Schuster	1971

In addition, one novel not previously published in book form in the USA was included in an anthology produced after Wodehouse's death. It can be found in:

| NGW | Not George Washington | Continuum | 1980 |

SERIALISED NOVELS COVERED BY THIS VOLUME

UK Book Ref	US Book Ref	Magazine Reference	Story Title	Date
JTR	TLW	Grand	Jill the Reckless	9/20 to 3/21
		Colliers	The Little Warrior	10-4 to 28-8/20
GOB	TMM	Pan	Three Men and a Maid	2/21 to 9/21
		WHC		10/21 to 12/21
TAS	MOS	Colliers	Mostly Sally	8-10/21 to 31-12/21
		Household		11/25 to 4/26
HOW	USHOW	Colliers	Hot Water	21-5/32 to 6-8/32
LAG	USLAG	ThisWeek	Laughing Gas	24-3/35 to 28-4/35
		Pearson		7 to 12/35
SUM	USSUM	SatEvePost	Summer Moonshine	24-7/37 to 11-9/37
		Pearson		9/37 to 4/38
QUS	USQUS	SatEvePost	Quick Service	4-5/40 to 22-6/40
TOR	PTR	Colliers	Phipps to the Rescue	24-6/50 to 22-7/50
FRL	USFRL	JohnBull	French Leave	12-11/55 to 3-12/55

SHORT STORIES COVERED BY THIS VOLUME

UK Book Ref	US Book Ref	Magazine Reference	Story Ref	Story Title	Date
TMU	TUW	Strand	MUP	The Man Upstairs	3/10
		Cosmo			3/10
TMU	THS	Strand	STW	Something to Worry About	2/13
TMU	TUW	Strand	WDD	When Doctors Disagree	12/10
TMU		Strand	BAC	By Advice of Counsel	7/10
TMU		Strand	MWD	The Man Who Dislikes Cats	5/12
		LHJ	FKA	The Fatal Kink in Algernon	1/16
TMU	TUW	Strand	RIE	Ruth in Exile	7/12
		Ainslee			8/12

IOA	TIO	Strand	PWM	Paving the Way for Mabel	7/20
		Cosmo			9/20
IOA	TIO	Strand	WMP	Washy Makes His Presence Felt	8/20
		Cosmo			10/20
IOA	TIO	Strand	ARH	A Room at the Hermitage	9/20
		Cosmo	ABA	A Bit of All Right	11/20
IOA	TIO	Strand	FAL	First Aid for Looney Biddle	10/20
		Cosmo			12/20
IOA	TIO	Strand	MOK	Mother's Knee	11/20
		Cosmo			1/21
IOA	TIO	Strand	SEA	Strange Experiences of an Artist's Model	1/21
IOA	TIO	Strand	TWV	The Wigmore Venus	2/21
		Cosmo			2/21
NSE	USNSE		HTU	How's That, Umpire?	
PLP	USPLP	Playboy	GCS	A Good Cigar is a Smoke	12/67
	TUW	Answers	WPS	When Papa Swore in Hindustani	24-8/01
	TUW	Grand	TDH	Tom, Dick and Harry	7/05
	TUW	Nash	MIS	Misunderstood	5/10
		BurrMcK			5/10
	TUW	Strand	BSA	The Best Sauce	7/11
		PicRev	DOH	A Dinner of Herbs	2/13
	TUW	Pearson	EDO	The Education of Detective Oakes	12/14
		ASCW	HMY	The Harmonica Mystery	13-3/15
		Ellery	DAE	Death at the Excelsior	5/78
		VanFair	AAI	Aubrey's Arrested Individuality	5/17
		Strand	BTG	Back to the Garage	7/29
		Cosmo	FFD	Franklin's Favorite Daughter	7/29
		Grand	COL	The Colour Line	4/20
		McClure	GOF	The Golden Flaw	3&4/20
		Strand	COI	Creatures of Impulse	10/14
		McClure			10/14
		Windsor	CPB	Cupid and the Paint Brush	4/03
		Sunday	IDK	The Idle King	5/03
		Strand	JOW	A Job of Work	1/13
		Colliers			6-9/13
		PallMall	MLB	Mike's Little Brother	10/13
		Ellery	MBD	Mr McGee's Big Day	11/50
		Throne	KHE	The Kind-Hearted Editor	5-12/08
		Strand	TSF	The Spring Frock	12/19
		SatEvePost	TSP	The Spring Suit	12-7/19
		Aldin	GOW	Gone Wrong	1932

ACKNOWLEDGEMENTS

With this volume, the *Millennium Wodehouse Concordance* reaches its conclusion. To review all of P G Wodehouse's fiction has been a mammoth task, and there will inevitably have been some inconsistency in the extent to which characters, real and fictional, places and other matters have been included in these eight books. Despite this, the mistakes which will have undoubtedly crept in, and the omissions which readers will not find, the *Concordance* represents as complete a reference work as is practically possible.

It could not have been written without help. The principal debt is due, of course, to the late Sir Pelham Grenville Wodehouse, without whose consistently brilliant work it would neither have been necessary or possible. Linked to this is the substantial thank you due to his literary representatives for permitting its publication.

Next, I should refer to the late Geoffrey Jaggard, whose concept caused him to start gathering information in the 1950s, and to publish two pioneering volumes in the 1960s, *Wooster's World* and *Blandings the Blest*. His unpublished notes on the remainder of Wodehouse's output to that date formed a useful starting point for the *Concordance* and a check on some of the entries to be included. Jaggard, of course, did not have that invaluable tool, the word processor, to help him collate the immense amount of raw material, and it is true to say that without the development of the last decade's technology the *Concordance* could not have been produced.

Thirdly, I must pay tribute to the publisher, John Fletcher of Porpoise Books. A series of this type requires a publisher of many talents, not least the stamina to keep going over a nine-year gestation period. Not only was John responsible for the task of physically guiding the book through from text to publication, but he acted as a self-appointed editor, raising hundreds of queries, both minor and critical, on aspects of my drafts. His intellectual grasp of the English language, his familiarity with the Wodehouse canon, and thorough and patient attention to detail, generated many constructive suggestions which were incorporated into the text.

After often painstaking discussions, John commissioned the original illustrations (including the dust jackets) by Bernard Canavan which appear throughout the eight volumes, although another Wodehousean friend, Tim Andrew, suggested that Amber Sanchez be invited to produce the *Pub Signs of Market Blandings* in *Volume 5*. We could make no progress towards discovering the present ownership of any copyright in relation to the illustrations reproduced from old magazines which appeared in the later volumes, and invite notification from those affected.

Because the scope of the *Concordance* was deliberately set as wide as possible, so that it would pick up alternative references in both UK and US editions of the books, and the magazine publication of serials and short stories, it was essential to have access to the latter. I know of no complete collection (either of original copies, photocopies or microfilms) of the vast range of magazines in which the relevant material has appeared, indeed I do not believe such a collection will ever be possible, but I was materially assisted in my task by the generous assistance of an American friend, Len Lawson. Len spent considerable time arranging for copies from library sources of many elusive American titles. Other suppliers of magazine appearances include the Wodehouse specialist dealers Nigel Williams and Charles Gould: thanks to them and many others also for helping me to expand my own collection of original magazines.

Others have drawn attention to particular matters, and their contribution has generally been noted as part of the relevant *Concordance* entry. Jan Piggott, Archivist at Dulwich college, added authority to *Wodehouse Goes to School* with two erudite essays, and in this volume there have been contributions from Anne-Marie Chanet and Neil Midkiff. If I have inadvertently omitted any other acknowledgement I can only apologise and plead sheer volume of paper.

Our proof-reading has been in the capable hands of two enthusiastic members of the Wodehouse community. The late Charlotte Murphy undertook the exercise for most of the volumes with great enthusiasm, and her daughter Helen fulfilled this role with equal care for the last three volumes.

Producing the *Concordance* has been a fascinating exercise, particularly when one has come across an explanation for a difference in text. To regard the *Concordance*, as one journalist recently did, as an exercise in literary anorakism, is wholly to misunderstand its purpose, which has been to remind the world of the enormous number of characters and locations P G Wodehouse created, to remind the reader of his felicity with the English language, and to encourage people to return to the books and enjoy the plots, the characters and the language for themselves. If at the same time it provides answers to the memory-challenging thoughts and questions which come into one's head from time to time, so much the better.

TONY RING
Great Missenden
July 2001

WODEHOUSE WITH NEW FRIENDS

(In this, the last volume in the Millennium Concordance, we meet the characters about whom Wodehouse wrote on just one occasion.)

1920: a trying year for inhabitants of the United States, with every boat arriving from England bringing a fresh swarm of British lecturers. **(WHC-TMM; Pan-TMM)**

ABBOTT, Alice, Lady: born **Alice "Toots" Bulpitt**, the châtelaine of Walsingford was large, blonde and of a monumental placidity which not even earthquakes on the terrace or a roof falling in would unduly disturb. And if such stoicism seems strange in one who once earned her living demonstrating underclothing and then in the chorus of musical comedy, it must be remembered that it was only in the restless days of the thirties that the term 'chorus-girl' came to denote a small, wiry person with india-rubber legs and flexible joints. In the era of her professional engagements, the personnel of the ensemble were tall, stately creatures shaped like hourglasses, who stood gazing dreamily at the audience, supporting themselves on long parasols. Sometimes they would emerge from the coma for an instant to bow slightly to a friend in the front row, but not often. As a rule they just stood, statuesquely. And of all these statuesque bystanders, none ever stood with more complete statuesque immobility than Toots Bulpitt. But things change, and as her life progressed she developed new talents for making fudge and doing crosswords, and a new appreciation of the joy of dramatic intervention, best illustrated when she presented her husband, **Sir Buckstone** (whom had she met when in the chorus of *The Pink Lady*) with a bouncing new brother-in-law, **Sam. (SUM)**

ABBOTT, Sir Buckstone, Bart: of **Walsingford Hall**, Berkshire, a retired Lt. Col in the Berkshire Territorials and member of the **Overseas Club**. Husband of **Alice** and father of **Jane**, he was surprisingly broad-minded and phlegmatic: he liked Americans enough to marry one, and having realised he had insufficient grey matter for the Diplomatic Service, accepted that he could not even be a simple country gentleman. As he put it, fate had other views and made him the "greasy proprietor of a blasted rural doss-house". The sunshine and fresh breezes to which he was exposed had given his face a healthy redness which deepened to mauve when emotionally stirred. His book *My Sporting Memories*

1

Sir Buckstone Abbott looks at his daughter Jane as King Lear did at Cordelia

recollected his big-game-hunting binges but had, alas, to be printed at the Bart's own expense by **J Mortimer Busby**. (SUM)

ABBOTT, Imogen ('Jane'): a delightful archetypal Wodehousean popsy, a small, slim, pretty girl of about twenty, with fair hair (ginger, according to **Joe Vanringham**), eyes of cornflower blue, an attractive laugh and a boyish jauntiness of carriage. On occasion the eyes became suffused with that tender refracted light which appears when women are called on to deal with refractory children or misguided parents. A somewhat more imaginative description of Jane came from Joe, who stared at her like a bear at a bun, and likened her to a **Fournier** picture in *La Vie Parisienne* come to life. Her judgment of character can justifiably be questionned, for she had become secretly engaged to **Adrian Peake**, one of the worst bounders in the whole of Wodehouse. Fortunately for the sanity of the reader, she emerged from the spell just in time when she learned that Joe would be off to California without her. (SUM)

ABBOTT, Sir Wellington, Bart (the late): attired only in pyjamas after nipping smartly from his blazing bedroom, this brazen bart had once stood and watched his venerable Elizabethan pile, **Walsingford Hall**, go up in flames. Like **Sheridan**, he had warmed his hands at his own fireside, and had forgotten the cold wind blowing round his ankles as he realised that here was a chance to put into practice the concepts of architecture with which he had unsuccessfully been trying to impress his advisers. There was then no obstacle to the scope of his originality and the result was a new Walsingford, in inglorious technicolour. (SUM ch2)

ABBOTT'S FOLLY: the name given by many to **Walsingford Hall**. (SUM ch2)

***ABC OF MODERN DANCING, The*:** by 'Tango', the fifty cent manual used as a basic guide by **Henry Mills**. (MLF-TLF)

ABEDNEGO: needed to mop his forehead when leaving the fiery furnace. (TOR ch19)

ABERCROMBIE AND FITCH: **Jane Shannon** was convinced that **Joe Davenport** and **Kay Shannon** would hit it off like ... . (Colliers-PTR)

3

ABERDEEN TERRIER: when approaching **Stiffy** in **Beverley Hills**, one member of the species was met with Aristocratic Disdain. **(Aldin-GOW)**

ABOU BEN ADHEM: woke from a deep dream of peace, offering a model for **Hodger**. **(TOR ch15; NSE-HTU)**

ABRAHAMS, David: one of four children of **Isadore** and **Rebecca**; he appreciated goulash. **(TAS ch14)**

ABRAHAMS, Isadore: the founder-proprietor of that deservedly popular dancing resort the **Flower Garden**, who dwelled in the bosom of his admirable family, consisting of wife and four offspring, at Far Rockaway, NY. **(TAS ch14)**

ABRAHAMS, Jacob 'Jakie': the second of the four children, who not only appreciated goulash but gobbled it. **(TAS ch14)**

ABRAHAMS, Morris: the third of the four. **(TAS ch14)**

ABRAHAMS, Rebecca: the wife of **Isadore**, who boasted of a comfortable plinth of chins and four children. **(TAS ch14)**

ABRAHAMS, Sadie: the original and correct spelling of **Saide**. **(Colliers-TAS pt10)**

ABRAHAMS, Saide: the said fourth child of **Isadore**. It is quite extraordinary that the book editions in both the UK and the US (first edition, hard cover and paperback) repeat this spelling of the name 'Sadie', which surely appears nowhere else. To find the correct spelling it is necessary to refer to the magazine version! **(TAS ch14)**

ABSALOM: the son of Saul, who would have approved of **Beatrice Bracken**'s suggestion that **Packy Franklyn** should have a haircut. **(HOW ch2)**

ACHMED (or AHMED) IBN ABDALLAH OF BAGHDAD: the views on time of ... gave **Purbach** and **Regiomontanus** the laugh of their lives but also caused their first quarrel. **(TOR ch17)**

ACTORS WHO HAVE DIED ON THE STAGE: one of eleven articles by **James Orlebar Cloyster** which were rejected by three magazines in two weeks. **(NGW ptII ch2)**

ADE, George: wrote fables which **James Cloyster** almost knew by heart, but which **Malim** did not find amusing. **(NGW ptII ch8)**

ADONIS: **Mervyn Spink**, a cork-drawing ..., sought to play the serpent in **Lord Shortland**'s Garden of Eden. **(SPF ch11)**

4

ADVENTURE OF THE FIVE ORANGE PIPS, The: **Jerry West** wondered whether **Crispin Scrope** would try to intimidate **Barney Clayborne** by using orange pips in a similar manner to that described in *The Five Orange Pips*, a Sherlock Holmes title permitted an extra three words by the publishers. **(TGI ch12)**

[ADVENTURE OF] THE SPECKLED BAND, [The]: another Sherlock Holmes title, this time deprived of its first three words. **(IOA ch8)**

ADVENTURES OF SHERLOCK HOLMES, The: the choice of bedtime reading for **Lord Seacliff**, which proved to be a bad choice as he had just reached *The Adventure of the Speckled Band* at the time when he was about to receive a visit from **Peter**[2]. **(IOA ch8)**

ADVICE TO THE LOVELORN: a column in the evening paper in the name of **Heloise Milton** which was promised to **Elizabeth Herrold** after the previous editor, a man, resigned. **(Red-BCL)**

AFFINITIES: the zero on the roulette-board of life. **(TMU-RIE)**

AFRICA: where **Jill Willard** might be expected to go if **Mike Bond** turned her down when she proposed. **(DBB ch2)**

AGEE, Emma Lucille: wrote a dirty novel selling in its millions in the US and had a literary luncheon in her honour. **(TGI ch11)**

ALADDIN:

I couldn't have been more surprised if I had been Aladdin just after rubbing the lamp.

(LAG ch14)

Jane Opal had similar feelings on the occasion that she thought wistfully of **Packy Franklin** wished he was with her and, looking up, saw that he was. **(HOW ch7)**

ALBANY: where **Sir Godfrey Tanner** lived, attended by his butler, **Jevons**. **(Strand-COI)**

ALBERT: a lad on the *Lechton*. **(NGW ptII ch14)**

ALBERT MEMORIAL, the: would have gone along with **Beulah Brinkmeyer** had she attached herself to its wrist as she did to **RH(JC)** and pulled. **(Pearson-LAG)**

ALCALA: a New York apartment block with cheap rooms at the top and bottom, sandwiching a chorus-girl belt. **(TMU-INA)**

ALCATRAZ: Smedley Cork thought he would prefer ... to his home, as he would not be forced to drink yoghurt. **(TOR ch1)**

ALEXANDER[1]: a fat cat belonging to a fat American woman, wrapped in silk and fur (the f.c., not the f.A.w.). He was flung aside by **Priaulx Jnr** by the tail and finally lost all credibility with his owner when he produced six kittens. **(TMU-MWD)**

ALEXANDER[2]: a Persian cat owned by **Matilda Robinson** which **Marion Ringwood** coveted after seeing it at a cat show, though it did not become available for sale until it, like its namesake, presented its owner with six kittens. **(LHJ-FKA)**

ALEXANDER, Mr: a critic of the [*New York*] *Times*, who told **Wally Mason** that *The Rose of America* was the best musical piece he had ever seen, and that his fellow-critics felt the same. **(JTR ch18)**

ALEXANDER'S RAGTIME BAND: a steam melodeon made a spirited plunge into ... **(MLF-CRH)**

ALFRED: a brigand of **Peter**'s young imagination, who with **Dick** and **Ted[1]** kidnapped him and took him to the woods before being bitten by **Fido**. **(MLF-BIS)**

ALGIERS: according to **Mr Johnson**, a hell on earth. **(MLF-OTN)**

ALICE BLUE GOWN: the sort of tune to which **Sam Bulpitt** would think out his best coups. **(SUM ch15)**

ALICE IN WONDERLAND: a book which **Barney Clayborne** had probably read, for she knew how to react when **Jerry West** sneezed. Its plot was as nothing compared to musical comedy, thought of as one Mad Hatter's Tea-Party. When **Soup Slattery** read it, he could not believe that the White Rabbit would be wearing a business suit and carrying a clock, even though he was having tea with the Queen. See also **Mae West**. **(JTR ch15; LAG ch24; HOW ch16; TGI ch12)**

ALLENBY: one of six acquaintances of **Joe Vanringham** not known to **Jane Abbott**. **(SUM ch5)**

ALL FOR HER: a Nosegay Novelette in which the hero, anxious to win the esteem of a lady, had bribed a tramp to simulate an attack upon her in a lonely road. **(GOB ch16)**

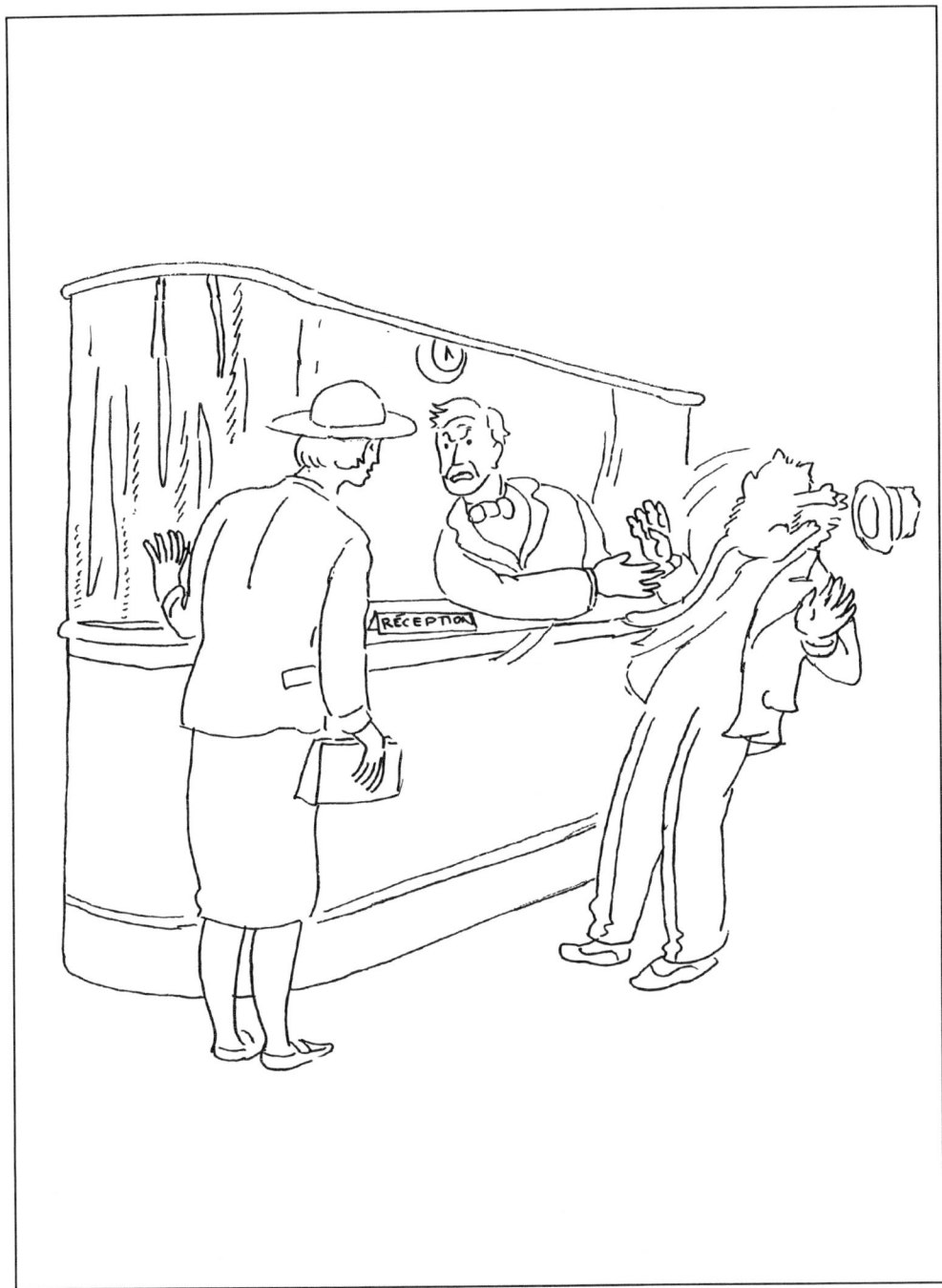

Alexander sent flying by M. Priaulx

ALL QUIET ON THE WESTERN FRONT: an example of a film which proved the theory that if the story line was strong enough a film did not need a love interest. **(LAG ch24)**

ALMANAC(H) DE GOTHA: a volume available from any French bookstore, this eminent work would have revealed the **Vicomte de Blissac**'s Christian name, and proved that **Old Nick** really was a Marquis. **(HOW ch13; USHOW ch13; FRL ch5; USFRL ch5)**

ALPHONSO:

> Alphonso, who for cool assurance all creation licks,
> He up and said to Emily who has cheek enough for six:
> 'Miss Emily, I love you. Will you marry? Say the word!'
> And Emily said: 'Certainly, Alphonso, like a bird!'

(GOB ch4)

ALSATIAN: an animal owned by **Mabel Steptoe** which received an uppercut from **Howard S. (QUS ch19)**

AMALGAMATED DYES: Freddie Rooke bought a pile of ... shares on margin and lost £200 in an awful slump on the Stock Exchange. **(JTR ch1,6)**

AMERICA AND ITS PEOPLE: the book which **Lord Wildersham** felt competent to write after spending a fortnight in the United States with **J Ringwood Macklin** in the spring of 1907. **(LHJ-FKA)**

AMERICAN BEAUTY: the type of rose in the bouquet presented to **Mr Saltzburg** on the New York opening night of *The Rose of America*. **(JTR ch18)**

AMERICAN LEGION STADIUM: the **Hollywood** venue where the tar was whaled out of **Mugsy Steptoe** by **Wildcat Wix**. **(QUS ch7)**

AMERICAN MILLIONAIRES: there are, it seems, two distinct kinds. A typical member of one group has a mauve face and an eighteen-stone body, and grinds the face of the poor in a diet of champagne and lobster à la Newburg, whilst a recognisable specimen of the other is small and shrivelled, about 7 stone 4 pounds, who fortifies himself with a light repast of hot water, triturated biscuit and pepsine tabloids, before, of course, clubbing the stuffing out of the widow and the orphan **(Strand-JOW)**.

APOLLO THEATRE 3ᴰ·

Licensed by the Lord Chamberlain to THOS. DAWB & WM. COOPER.

LESSEE & MANAGER   -   EDWARD LAURILLARD.

PHYLLIS NEILSON-TERRY'S & CECIL KING'S SEASON·

THE ANGEL IN THE HOUSE

by

Joseph Vanringham

Programme

The programme for the show which so upset the Princess von und zu Dwornitschek

AMERICANS: the suggestion that ... frequently have daughters seemed to disconcert **Lady Underhill**. **(JTR ch1)**

ANANIAS: acted a lie, to the disgust of **Augustus Robb**. **(SPF ch16)**

ANAXIMANDER (c610-546BC): apparently held the primary cause of all things to be the Infinite. **(NGW ptI ch2)**

ANDERSON, Blinky: the proprietor of **East Side Delmonico's**, to whom **Freddie Bowen** was no stranger. **(Strand-JOW)**

ANDERSON'S PARISIAN CAFÉ AND RESTAURANT: ie **East Side Delmonico's**. **(Strand-JOW)**

ANDREWS, Mary Raymond Shipman: an illustrative example of the reason why **Adelaide Brewster Moggs** declined to add to her burden by taking her husband's surname as well. **(VanFair-AAI)**

ANDROMEDA: see **Perseus**

ANGEL IN THE HOUSE, The: the play by **Joe Vanringham** about his stepmother which was forecast to run at the **Apollo** for a year, until the rights were bought by the stepmother in question and the piece closed. **(SUM ch13,21)**

ANGELINA: female party in **James Cloyster**'s *Society Dialogues*, imitated in real life by a good-looking girl round whose waist lay **Sidney Price**'s arm. **(NGW ptII ch13)**

ANGLIN, Margaret: like **Ellen Terry**, she had nothing on **Gladys Winch** when it came to delivering the line: "Yes, madam". **(MOS ch10)**

ANTELOPE: a steam-packet on whose deck approaching **St Rocque Oily Carlisle** stood, disguised as **M le Duc de Pont-Andemer**, and on which he made the acquaintance of both **Julia Gedge** and **Lady Beatrice Bracken**. **(HOW ch7,11)**

ANTIGUA:

> Is it my face you object to, or my manners, or my figure? There was a young bride of Antigua, who said to her mate, 'What a pig you are!' Said he, 'Oh, my queen, is it manners you mean, or do you allude to my fig-u-ar?"

(JTR ch1)

ANTI-TOBACCO LEAGUE: two anonymous aunts of **Lancelot Bingley** were members. **(PLP-GCS)**

APOLLO: his clean-shaven bust offered **Joe Vanringham** scope for artistic endeavours on which he sought **Jane Abbott**'s approval. See also **Moffam, Archie**. (SUM ch17; IOA ch3; Colliers-JOW)

APOLLO THEATRE: featured *The Angel in the House*. (SUM ch13)

APOLLYON: his straddle-across-the-way technique was imitated by **Oily Carlisle**. (HOW ch15; QUS ch3)

APPLEBY GANG: headed by **Horace**, it included **Basher Evans**, **Charlie Yost** and **Ferdie the Fly**. (DBB ch1)

APPLEBY, Horace: after an apprenticeship with the **Duplessis** mob (during which he helped to clean out a house in Cannes to which it became his ambition to retire), he became head of the **Appleby gang** of gun-free criminals whose favourite technique was to obtain a post as butler and organise an inside job. When visiting **Wallingford** he was himself held up and robbed, but his wallet was recovered by **Ada Cootes**, to whom he went on to be engaged. When not buttling he lived in a semi-detached residence at **Resthaven** (or **Restharrow**), Croxley Road, Valley Fields. His final job was planned to involve **Bond's Bank**, and he went as far as to fire decoy shots to draw the police to **Mallow Hall** before investing £50,000 in a gamble on the Bank's future. (DBB; USDBB ch4)

APPLEBY, Josiah: a late member of the firm of **Marlowe, Thorpe, Prescott, Winslow and Appleby**, whose portrait, it is to be hoped, did not do him justice. (GOB ch13)

ARBUCKLE, Roscoe ('Fatty') (1887-1933): did not handle pastry with a surer touch than did **J L T Smith**. (IOA ch20)

ARCHBISHOP OF CANTERBURY: would not have been able to persuade the reformed **Basher Evans** to crack a pete, but he could provide a special licence for the purposes of matrimony. (GOB ch17; DBB ch7)

ARCHILOCHUS (fl c650BC): when handed his hat by the lady of his affections he consoled himself by writing satirical verse about her in a new metre. (GOB ch8)

ARCHIMEDES (c287-212BC): historians recorded his reaction to solving an intricate problem. Had **Soup Slattery** been in a bath when he heard about the location of **Julia Gedge**'s diamonds, and had he known the meaning of the expression 'Eureka!', it is highly probable that Soup's reaction would have been the same. **(HOW ch1)**

ARDMORE: where **Archie Moffam** went for a bite to eat after **Salvatore**'s dismissal. **(Cosmo-MMH)**

ARISTOPHANES (c448-388BC): **Cloyster**'s contributions to St Gabriel's College musical festivities had demonstrated the true panache of ... Whilst at Dulwich, PGW and his elder brother Armine had appeared on the same stage during a production of *The 'Frogs'*, by this author; Armine accompanying the cast on the piano and PGW himself being part of two Choruses: of Worshippers and of Frogs. **(NGW ptII ch3)**

ARISTOTLE (384-322 BC): wrote about the art of exciting the reader's pity and terror, and his *Ethics* was a big hit. His pocket editions were the sort of thing that **Roland Bean** would read. **(NGW ptII ch3; GOB ch15; TMU-MMM)**

ARMAND: the floor waiter at the Hotel Magnifique, St Rocque. **(FRL ch4)**

ARMITAGE, His Honour Sir Roger: sentenced **Ginger Moffat** to five years. **(DBB ch2)**

ARMY, the: an American football team which did not include a Berserk Senator in its ranks. **(HOW ch2)**

ARNOLD OF MELCHTHAL: of the light-yellow hair, he was the third person who made up the group elected to visit **Hermann Gessler** and later **William Tell**. His supposed knowledge of the law did not prevent him from having the first finger on his left hand dipped in boiling oil. **(WTT ch1,4)**

ARNOLD OF SEWA: a Swiss citizen who was disappointed not to have been selected among the delgation to **Gessler** to complain about **taxes**. But when he did visit, independently, he suffered from a burnt finger. He expressed the opinion that guile, rather than brute force, was needed to overcome the problem, but after being piked by **Leuthold**, he retired to bed for two days and missed the subsequent excitement. **(WTT ch2,4,9)**

ARNOLD, Benedict (1741-1801): would probably have cancelled a dinner date with **Jane Hunnicutt**. **(TGI ch11)**

GREEK SPEECH.

"The 'Frogs' of Aristophanes." [Originally produced in Athens at the Festival of the Lenaea, 405 B.C.] .

Dramatis Personæ.

Dionysus	SHELLEY, M. B.
Xanthias	RIPPMANN, C. H.
Heracles	CLARKE, G. T. K.
Charon	AINSWORTH, A. R.
Aeacus	RICHARDS, R. C.
A Maid-servant of Persephone	CULLIS, H. T.
An Inn-keeper	BRIGHT, W. A.
Another Inn-keeper	PRATT, R.
A Dead Man	CROSS, R. B.

Servants of Aeacus, Attendants, &c.

Chorus of Frogs	HALL, E. S. LEGG, G. T. SMITH, C. J. WODEHOUSE, P. G.
Leader of the Chorus	BROCK, L. G.
Chorus of Worshippers	BROCK, L. G. DOUGLAS, S. M. INGLIS, A. L. KING, E. C. SMITH, C. J. WODEHOUSE, P. G.
Accompanist	WODEHOUSE, E. A.

The Incidental Music was expressly composed for the occasion by E. D. RENDALL, Esq., M.A., Mus.Bac.

ARSENIC AND OLD LACE: **Smedley Cork** might ask how much an angel would have made if he or she had invested in ... **(TOR ch21)**

ASCOT: **Lady Beatrice Bracken** never failed to attract attention in its Royal Enclosure. **(HOW ch2)**

ASHLEY: the town in Maine from where **Charles Ferris** had come. **(MLF-ATG)**

ASK DAD: the title of a Wodehouse/Bolton/Hirsch musical comedy which opened its try-out run in Toronto in 1918. Although its name was changed to *Oh, My Dear* by its New York opening on 26 November, 1918, five of the show's songs were published under *Ask Dad* wrappers before being reprinted as part of the renamed show's music. It was revived twice: first in a Jeeves/ Wooster story as a show written by George Caffyn (see *Volume 6*) and secondly as a successful **Pottinger and Abeles** show in which **Pearl Delahay** appeared. **(Strand-BTG)**

ASK DAD **NUMBER TWO COMPANY**: touring production of the musical comedy in which **Pearl Delahay** and the **narrator**[3] were members of the cast. It opened at the Harmanus-Bleecker in Albany before moving on to other locations such as Eulalia and **Franklin**. **(Strand-BTG)**

ASTAIRE, Fred (Frederick Austerlitz, 1899-1987): the trouser buttons of ... had been known to change hands for considerable sums. His movies had even reached the small American town of Cicero. **(DBB ch8)**

ASTERISK: a magazine which accepted work from **Smith**. **(Strand-PAW)**

ASTHORE: a song sung by **Owen Bentley** to the discomfort of **Mr Prosser**, resulting in the decimation of the Infant Samuel. **(TMU-POM)**

ASTOR: the hotel where **Fillmore Nicholas** stayed after becoming a theatrical manager. **(TAS ch9)**

ASTOR, Vincent: a poor man by comparison to **Reggie van Tuyl**. If the man referred to was not Vincent at all, despite the evidence offered by two book publishers and two magazines, but *Viscount*, he would most probably have been William Waldorf Astor, the first Viscount, (1848-1919). **(IOA ch14)**

ASTORIA: the home of **Mr McGee**. **(Ellery-MBD)**

ATHENAEUS (fl 2nd cent): one of his gems was *The Deipnosophists*, which had been translated into English, and proposed that every investigation which was guided by principles of Nature fixed its ultimate aim entirely on gratifying the stomach. **(NGW ptI ch2)**

ATKINSON, Rupert: aged fourteen, dared **Thomas Billing** to eat bread. **(Strand-COI)**

ATLANTIC: **Billie Bennett, Mortimer Bream, Eustace Hignett, Jane Hubbard** and **Sam Marlowe** were all returning from New York on this White Star liner. **(GOB ch1)**

ATLANTIC CITY: a seashore resort, the birthplace of so many musical plays. It was a great place to play in the summer and for a couple of weeks round Easter. **(JTR ch16; TLW ch17)**

ATLANTIC LINERS: staterooms on ... are curious things. When you see them on the chart in the passenger-office, with the gentlemanly clerk drawing rings round them in pencil, they seem so vast that you get the impression that, after stowing away all your trunks, you will have room left over to do a bit of entertaining – possibly an informal dance or something. When you go on board, you find that the place has shrunk to the dimensions of an undersized cupboard. And then, about the second day out, it suddenly expands again and you find yourself quite comfortable.

Ships' concerts are given in aid of the Seamen's Orphans and Widows and, after one has been present at a few of them, one seems to feel that any right-thinking orphan or widow would rather jog along and take a chance of starvation than be the innocent cause of such things. They open with a long speech . . . This done, the amateur talent is unleashed and the grim work begins. **(GOB)**

ATTENBOROUGH: looked after **James Cloyster**'s evening clothes when they were unlikely to be required. **(NGW part II ch23)**

ATTILA THE HUN (c406-453): never managed to create the sort of havoc caused by French civil servants asking for time off for funerals. However, like **Joss Weatherby** and unlike **George Holbeton**, he would have stood his ground and investigated further the phenomenon of a densely moustached stranger galloping up shouting "Hey!" **(FRL ch2; QUS ch10)**

ATTWATER, Cyril: the son of **John B**, he received wealth beyond his wildest dreams when acceding to **Adrian Peake**'s suggestion that he should become a temporary postman at a salary of 2s 6d per letter. **(SUM ch18)**

ATTWATER, John B: father of **Cyril** and formerly butler at **Walsingford Hall**, Berks, he became the landlord of the **Goose and Gander, Walsingford Parva**. **(SUM ch7)**

ATTWATER, Miss: **John B**'s brother's daughter, who was the temporary barmaid at the **Goose and Gander**, disliking it and considering it to be a 'dog's island'. She happily participated in a plot to serve the papers on **Tubby Vanringham**, and confused **Adrian Peake** thoroughly with stories of **Sam Bulpitt**'s practical jokes. **(SUM ch16,18)**

AUBREY: like **Fido**, is a name which a dog may be able to get over, but which makes him start with a handicap. **(MLF-BIS)**

AUGUSTUS: the name given by **Wally Mason** to a worried stage-hand, though in one instance he was renamed **Rollo**. **(JTR ch3; TLW ch3)**

AUNT: **Jane Hunnicutt**'s, living in Bournemouth, who had a birthday coming up on Friday, thought that all artists painted Russian princesses lying in the nude on tiger skins and didn't approve of smoking. **(TGI ch2,6)**

AUNT BETSY: **Homer Pyle**'s and **Barney Clayborne**'s, who came to grief shoplifting during the autumn sale at **Gimbels'**. **(TGI ch1)**

AUNT CLARA: see **Lady Mannering**

AUNT FANNY: **Chipperfield**'s supposed ... would have spent most of her life up a gum-tree if anyone had followed his exhortations. **(TGI ch13)**

AUNT GERALDINE: one of **Ginger Kemp** and **Bruce Carmyle**'s minor relatives, who was baffled by Bruce's attempts to win **Sally Nicholas**'s hand. **(TAS ch4,15)**

AUNT GWENDOLYN: see **Blinkhorn, Gwendolyn**

AUNT LOUISA: **George Balmer**'s, married to his **Uncle Robert** and mother of three. **(TMU-TTM)**

AUNT LOUISE: another of **Ginger Kemp** and **Bruce Carmyle**'s minor relatives. **(TAS ch4)**

AUNT MARY: yet another of **Ginger Kemp** and **Bruce Carmyle**'s minor relatives. **(TAS ch4)**

AUNT MYRTLE: **Chippendale**'s, living in East Dulwich, who pawned his father's (her brother's) false teeth in order to contribute to a mission for propagating the gospel among the unenlightened natives of West Africa. She also wore false teeth, the first pair of which were ill-fitting, so she used them as the basis for a mouse-trap. When she caught her own toe in it, it was nearly severed and had to be amputated. She served a thirty day term for battery when the police closed in on **Uncle Reggie**'s bettery. **(TGI ch13)**

AUNT PHYLLIS: a fat man in his 50s with a passion for lager and a ribald outlook on life, who wrote the ... column on *Advice for the Lovelorn* on a weekly London paper. **(TGI ch6)**

AUNTS:

> "Rapidly he diagnosed her as a mother or aunt. She looked more like an aunt."

(TMU-TTM)

> "And there are people," he remarked sardonically, "who say that blood is thicker than water! I'll bet they never had any aunts."

(GOB ch17)

AUREATA: Fifth Avenue restaurant where **Henry**[1] called the head waiter a fat-headed vampire. **(Red-ROM)**

AUSTRIA, the Emperor of: owned Switzerland in the days before it had a hotel, and appointed **Hermann Gessler** as its Governor. He was assassinated by the Lords of **Eschenbach** and **Tegerfelden** as he rode from Stein to Baden. **(WTT ch1,15)**

AUTHENTICS, The: a cricket team, a tour with which would have been more attractive to **Tom Ellison** than the prospect of playing in the forthcoming match. **(TUW-TDH)**

BAAL, the priests of: when he realised how much it cost to publish a book at his own expense, **Sir Buckstone Abbott** was crushed and miserable, and gashing himself like ... **(SUM ch1; TOR ch7)**

BABCOCK, Henry: a messenger, not rested before his return journey but arrested in connection with a bond robbery, and according to **Cassidy**, a squealer. **(IOA ch5)**

BABE: a chorus girl in the line up for *She's All Right*, who claimed to have been mistaken on the street for **Peggy Hopkins**. **(Grand-COL)**

BABE: a pretty girl who was employed in the ensemble of *The Rose of America*. **(JTR ch11)**

BABES IN THE WOOD: **Jill Mariner** falling asleep on **Wally Mason**'s shoulder after an all-night rehearsal made them appear to be a couple of ... **(JTR ch16)**

BABYLON: on the New York State road near **Sally** and **Ginger Kemp**'s apartment. **(TAS ch18)**

BACHELORS' CLUB, the: one of its members swore he knew a fellow who met a man whose cousin worked. **Freddie Rooke** had a moody and silent dinner there with **Derek Underhill**. **(JTR ch8; TMU-TGP)**

BAERMANN, Isadore ('Izzy'): introduced the **Love-r-ly Silver Cup** competition, and was more than a little upset at having to present it to **Mrs Francis** instead of **Miss Roxborough**. **(MLF-ATG)**

BAGSTER, Ellabelle: the cashier at the **Hotel Cosmopolitan** hairdressing salon, who shared an apartment with **May Gleason** and wore her hair peroxided. **(Grand-COL)**

BAILEY, 'Gentleman': a broken-down feller from 'Eton or 'Arrer, who tramped with **Roach** and was a friend of **Jerry Moore**. An inveterate talker, he expressed his philosophies on life in general and Woman in particular, and put his personal interests to the forefront when contemplating the romance of Jerry and **Jane Tuxton**. **(TMU-BAC)**

BALL, Neal: Cleveland shortstop who had made the only unassisted triple play in the history of baseball, and whose glove was in the possession of **Daniel Rackstraw**[2]. **(Colliers-PAP)**

BALMER, George Albert: spirited individual who went to **Roville** because **Harold Flower** called him a vegetable. Until then, he had been a neatly-dressed, mechnical, unenterprising young man, blessed with an **Uncle Robert**, an **Aunt Louisa** and three cousins, **Percy**[3], **Eva** and **Geraldine**. He was engaged at a modest salary by the **Planet Insurance Company** and had the good fortune to inherit one thousand pounds at the age of 24. When he met **Julia Waveney's companion**, he mistook her for Lady J W herself, and sought to recover her supposed winnings at the casino by a piece of elementary private enterprise. After he had restored the pickings to her, and caused her to be dismissed from her post, the two agreed to marry and emigrate to Canada, but only after they exchanged names. **(TMU-TTM)**

BALTIMORE: *The Rose of America*'s opening in ... was that of a wholly revised show, largely written by **Wally Mason**. It was the sort of theatre town which preferred pieces with a New York reputation to new pieces. **(JTR ch16; TLW ch17)**

BAND OF HOPE, the: promoted temperance. **(TGI ch11)**

BANDOLERO, The: **Sam Marlowe** seemed to think he was ... **(GOB ch4)**

BANKHEAD, Tallulah (1903-68):

> "Poor Lord Topham," said Bill. "You get about as much chance to talk in this house as a parrot living with Tallulah Bankhead."

(TOR ch15)

BANKS, Henderson: **George Marlowe**'s literary agent, a serpent wriggling into George's Eden, who kept chasing him for an overdue serial story. His conversation – he was one of nature's monologists – concentrated on writers, editors, publishers and prices per thousand words. He became the accredited agent for **Grace Pemberton**, arranging three novels and a series of short stories for her, whilst almost causing her to have a nervous breakdown. **(Strand-PAW)**

BANKS, Otis Elmer, PhD: the author of *The Will and its Training*, on which **George Mellon** unsuccessfully sought to rely when asking his boss for a rise. **(Strand-TSF)**

BANNISTER, Ann: a former fiancée of **Reggie Swithin** (later **Lord Havershot**), she had been a newspaper girl before earning her living as the nanny-governess to **Joey Cooley**, the dental doorkeeper to **I J Zizzbaum** and briefly as the beleaguered press agent to the despised **April** (or **Hazel**) June. Small, brisk, energetic, and abundantly supplied with buck and ginger, she nevertheless succumbed to the temptation of becoming engaged to **Eggy Mannering** not through the workings of the love god but as

19

a challenge, to see if she could wean him away from the other god, alcohol. When he decided to attend to the problem for himself, she resigned her post and returned to her first choice. **(LAG; Pearson-LAG; ThisWeek-LAG)**

BANQUO: his ghost was a model for **Roland Bean**, and, like that spectre, **Gladys** had no speculation in her eyes. See **Macbeth**. **(JTR ch17; TMU-MMM,INA)**

BARCLAY'S BANK: that and the **National Provincial** were not thought to be the only banks worth busting. **(DBB ch4)**

BARKER, Ellen: the wife of **Horace** and cook-housekeeper to the **Rooke. (JTR ch1)**

BARKER, Horace: the valet to **Freddie Rooke**, and a discerning judge of the quality of his employer's port wine and Havanas. He also accurately judged the relative merits of **Jill Mariner** and **Derek Underhill**, approving of the first with an unerring eye and disliking the second. For one of his few errors, see **Parker**. **(JTR ch1,18)**

BARKER, Mrs: the mother of **Horace**, to whom **Ellen** had taken straight away, and vice versa. **(JTR ch2)**.

BARLOW, Mrs: the bridge-playing housekeeper to **Mrs Steptoe** at **Claines Hall**, Sussex. **(QUS ch7)**

BARREL CLUB, the: a home-from-home at 153 York Street, Covent Garden, from which **James Orlebar Cloyster** wrote to **Margaret Goodwin**. It was the only club in England that allowed, indeed urged, its members to sit on a barrel. The **Rev John Hatton** was a member and he proposed Cloyster's election. **(NGW ptI ch3; ptII ch8,9)**

BARRIBAULT'S HOTEL: London's favourite haunt of the wealthy. Since the wealthy were almost uniformly repulsive, its lobby around one-thirty was always almost full of human eyesores and **Terry Cobbold**, sitting in her new hat at a table near two financiers who shared four chins, raised the tone considerably. **Jerry West** arranged to have dinner with **Jane Hunnicutt** there on a Friday three days hence, postponed it to the Saturday and managed it on the Wednesday. **(SPF ch4; TGI ch2)**

BARRYMORE, Lionel Blythe (1878-1954): Howard Steptoe could remember either him or **Adolph Menjou** pining for a woman he had loved and lost, and wanting a portrait of her so he could sit

The Barrel Club

and look at it and dream of what might have been. See also **Eddie**. **(QUS ch10)**

BARTLETT, Augustus: had an intensely subordinate job with **Kahn, Morris & Brown** (or possibly only **Morris & Brown**), and consequently affected the brisk, incisive manner of speech befitting one in close touch with the great figures of finance. **(TAS ch1; Colliers-TAS pt1))**

BASIL: see **Rathbone, Basil**

BASSETT, Captain: Scots Guards, loved **Marion Henderson**, to whom he gave **Alexander**[1] in an attempt to speed his wooing. **(TMU-MWD)**

BASSETT, Chester Bellington: the reader is in two minds about this bright, alert, able, ambitious young Bostonian who was the first secretary to the American Embassy in London. Instinct tells us that we want him to come a cropper and fall on his face, but honesty compels us to acknowledge that he, rather than his rival **Algy Wynbrace** (whom he regarded as a boob, excrescence and pest), was the proper mate for **Marion Ringwood**. It is fitting that it was his umpteenth gift, of the cat **Alexander**[2], which eventually won the match. **(LHJ-FKA)**

BASSINGTON-BASSINGTON: a family related to the Kent B-Bs, with a charming daughter considered by his family to be a suitable mate for **Bruce Carmyle**. **(TAS ch15)**

BATES: one of five acquaintances of **Jane Abbott** not known to **Joe Vanringham**. **(SUM ch5)**

BATES, Bill: admitted to being a millionaire from either Glasgow or Pittsburgh, but only a hereditary one, before he became **Alan Beverley**. **(TMU-MUP; Cosmo-MUP)**

BATTERSBY: crashed in such a way as to wipe out **Beatrice Chavender**. **(QUS ch12)**

BATTERSEA CATS' HOUSE: where **Alexander**[2] was sent by **Algy Wynbrace** in the expectation of rapid action. **(LHJ-FKA)**

BATTERSEA DOG'S HOME: a stuffed rat in ... was reported as having a higher chance than **Houndsditch Wednesday** in the Cup Final. **Colonel Reynolds** hoped that they poisoned the animals that they received there. **(TMU-TGP; TUW-WPS)**

BATTERSEA PARK ROAD: the citizens of ... specialised in Brain, not Crime, for they were authors, musicians, newspaper men, actors and artists. **(MLF-RUP)**

BATTLING TUKE: was strongly rumoured to have accepted an invitation to lie down in the seventh round of the heavyweight championship bout against **Benny Whistler**. **(TAS ch1)**

BAUMGARTEN: a friend of **William Tell**'s, who escaped from **Gessler**'s soldiers in a small ferryboat rowed across a lake by Tell during a fierce storm. **(WTT ch3)**

BAXTER, Warner (1891-1951): see **Fred**

BAYARD, Chevalier: **Jill Willard** thought **Appleby** a cross between him and **Sidney Carton**, and became one of Appleby's warmest admirers. **(DBB ch11)**

BBC: see **British Broadcasting Corporation**

BEAK STREET REGISTRY OFFICE: where **Augustus Robb** waited initially in vain for **Alice Punter**, and **Mike Cardinal** and **Terry Cobbold** were to be clients. **(SPF ch16,23)**

BEALE'S ART GALLERIES: on W45th St, which held an auction sale including a **Pongo** who was masquerading as an identical piece of objay dar. **(IOA ch9)**

BEAN, Roland: considered by **Robert Ferguson**, for whom he worked as office-boy, to fit the definition of **Miasma**. He had eyes which shone with quiet, respectful reproof through gold-rimmed spectacles, the manner of a middle-aged saint and a boring fount of knowledge on such varied matters as the Niagara Falls and horsehair sofas, and was to be rewarded by a transfer to the employment of **Raikes and Courtenay** in either Edinburgh or San Francisco. **(TMU-MMM; Cosmo-MMM)**

BEARCAT, Tennessee: the professional name of **Sam Proctor**, a boxer at 133lb whose prospective opponent, **One-Round Smith**, failed to show. See also **Tennessee Bear-Cat**. **(Strand-JOW)**

BEATRICE MAE SOMEONE-OR-OTHER'S ADVICE TO THE LOVELORN: the sort of column in a newspaper behind which dramatic criticisms are likely to duck snuggly. **(Strand-BFL)**

BEAUMONT, Sir Francis (1584-1616) see **Fletcher, John:**

BEAUMONT CO: a London film-maker which signed up **Eileen Stoker** for two pictures. **(SPF ch1)**

BEEFSTEAK CLUB: the scene of the decisive moment when **Archie Moffam** was told by his elder brother **Rupert** to go and seek his fortune in the USA. **(Strand-MMH)**

BEEF STROGANOFF: a likely name for a sinister character who was empowered to expel non-conformist American gangsters from their fraternities. **(DBB ch1)**

BEERY, Wallace (1886-1949): there was a rising demand in **Hollywood** for actors such as ..., with maps like **Howard Steptoe**. **(QUS ch8)**

BEES: the **Trent** variety bit like serpents and stung like adders. **(FRL ch1)**

BEETHOVEN, Ludwig van (1770-1827): one of the victims of virtual murder by the inhabitants of **Battersea Park Road** or **Prince of Wales Road**. **(MLF-RUP; Strand-RUP)**

BEEVOR CASTLE: Kentish seat of the **fifth Earl of Shortlands** with moat, battlements, ivied walls and a disused wing dating back to 1259. **(SPF ch3)**

BEEVOR, Tony, Viscount: the son and heir of the **fifth Earl of Shortlands**, he was resident on his Kenyan ranch. **(SPF ch1,6)**

BEHRMANN, Sam: his dramatic adaptation of **Jeff d'Escrignon**'s novel was expected by **Russell Clutterbuck** to run for two years. **(FRL ch12)**

BELIAL, sons of: reading from left to right: **Horace Appleby, Ferdie the Fly, Smithy** and **Frank**. **(DBB ch9)**

BELINDA: **Freddie Carpenter**'s yacht. **(FRL ch4)**

BELL, Alexander Graham (1847-1922): his invention of the telephone allowed one brother to remain reasonably strong while in conversation with another. **(TGI ch9)**

BELLA: a boarding-house housemaid. **(MLF-BTB)**

BELL-BOY: at the Hotel where **Freddie Bowen** worked was a red-headed, world-weary and prematurely aged individual whose cousin ran a café on 14th street. **(Strand-JOW)**

BELLEAU WOOD, battle of : **Lancelot Purvis** was not in this first world war battle. **(Grand-COL)**

BELLE DAME SANS MERCI, La: **Kay Shannon** was surprised to learn that **Joe Davenport** had heard of **Keats**, but did not comment on his possible misquotation. The fact that some reference books offer 'Ah, what can ail thee, wretched wight, alone and palely loitering' as Joe did, and not the perhaps more frequently accepted 'knight-at-arms' instead of 'wretched wight', presumably led to her giving him the benefit of the doubt. **(TOR ch2,13; Colliers-PTR)**

BELLE ISLE: Gerald Foster took **Sally Nicholas** in a hired car to ..., but his only conversation was about his unconcealed desire for success. **(TAS ch7)**

BELLE OF WELLS, The: **James Cloyster** wrote the lyrics for a second production of **Stanley Briggs's** ... **(NGW ptII ch22)**

BELLEU WOOD, battle of: neither was **Lancelot Purvis** in the battle with this spelling. **(McClure-GOF)**

BELLPORT: a Long Island location where **Sam Bulpitt** once put the bite on a millionaire at his country home. **(SUM ch14)**

BELSHAZZAR: even the writing at his feast had not been more ominous than **Mike Bond**'s spoken line: "They'll probably need it." in the double context of visits by Bank Trustees and bottles of champagne. **(DBB ch5)**

BENHAM, George: a grave, young friend of **Arthur Moffam**, who wore spectacles and lived to regret the practice of writing plays especially for one actress, when that actress walked out on him in the middle of rehearsals. The incident caused him to reflect that only the prophet **Job** had been really qualified to write plays, and even he would have found the going tough if his leading lady had been **Vera Silverton**. **(IOA ch12)**

BELSEY, Richard: Stanley Briggs's valet at the theatre which bore his name. **(NGW ptII ch25)**

BENNETT, Constance: one of three human ingredients who, mixed together, would produce **Lady Beatrice Bracken**. **(HOW ch2)**

BENNETT, J Rufus: a retired Wall Street operator who had for years been tentatively dipping one foot in the grave but finding it too cold to go in deeper. During the formative years of his great fortune he frequently did things to his competitors which would not have been tolerated in the purer environment of a lumber-camp. He was eventually successful in renting **Windles** for a summer with his part-time friend **Henry Mortimer**. He disliked one of his daughter **Billie**'s fiancés, **Sam Marlowe**, but he arranged, broke off and rearranged her engagement to the unsuitable **Bream Mortimer**. **(GOB ch1,10,11,15)**

BENNETT, Katie: trouble was never far from the unselfish life of this friend of **Genevieve**, who cared for her grandfather and ran his second-hand bookshop on 6th Avenue, near Washington Square. Though not pretty, she had nice eyes, and received a proposal from **Ted Brady**. Her relationship with her grandfather was such as to make her defer her acceptance unitl he had signified his approval. **(MLF-CRH)**

BENNETT, Matthew: a retired bookseller and the grandfather of **Katie**, he was paralysed from the waist down. When not playing draughts, he was promoting his current *alter ego*, variously President Roosevelt, the prophet Elijah and the King of England. In the latter guise, he refused to let Katie marry the commoner **Ted Brady** although his decision was reversed when Ted was crowned King too. **(MLF-CRH)**

BENNETT, MENDELBAUM & CO: firm of lawyers with which **J Rufus Bennett** practised. **(GOB ch17)**

BENNETT, Wilhelmina ('Billie'): the vivacious daughter and principal achievement of **J Rufus**, and devoted mistress of **Pinky-Boodles**. She was blessed with the attractive ivory skin which accompanies red hair, and her colour-scheme also featured green, blue or grey eyes, the whole painted on a canvas of just the right size which highlighted a small nose, a nice, wide mouth and a soft, round, chin. Honestly described by **Sam Marlowe** as the third prettiest girl he had ever seen, she had such an effect on him that he dropped into the drink for her sake. One of her favourite hobbies was getting engaged; one of her second favourites getting unengaged again. To our knowledge, and in quick succession, she played both games with **Eustace Hignett**, Sam Marlowe, **Bream Mortimer**, Bream Mortimer (again), Sam Marlowe (again) and Bream Mortimer (again again), before pulling out halfway through the next round with Sam. **(GOB)**

BENSONBURG: a tiny village on the shore of Great South Bay, Long Island, where the air was bracing, the scenery picturesque and the society mixed. **(FRL ch1)**

BENTLEY, Owen: once an actor, he was engaged for minor parts best suited to young men with names known to the public. His claim was a batting average of 33.07 for Middlesex, but as his average fell, he was employed instead by the London and Suburban Bank, and during his spare time he dramatised *White Roses*. He had one **Uncle**, **Henry**, an independent income of under £200 pa, and his eye on **Audrey Sheppherd**. **(TMU-POM)**

BENYON, John: robbed the **New Asiatic Bank** of $ 100,000 and after being convicted he jumped bail with it to **Algiers**, where he lived for five years. To a man whose addiction to baseball was such that he would risk hell and high water for the sight of a single game, the new life was equivalent to a prison sentence. On hearing that two famous American teams were about to play an exhibition match at **Chelsea Football Ground**, he accepted the risk and attended. **(MLF-OTN)**

BERKSHIRE TERRITORIALS: **Sir Buckstone Abbott** had once been in the ... **(SUM ch22)**

BERLE, Milton: if **John McGee** and **Herbert Higgs** were celebrating a reunion for the benefit of the television cameras, one wanted to know where they were, and where was ...? **Kay Shannon** did not want to feel, when with the man she loved, that she had been wrecked on an island with ... . **(Colliers-PTR; Ellery-MBD)**

BERLIN, Irving (Israel Baline, 1888-1989): was rejected as a possible solution to a crossword clue because his name consisted of twelve letters not nine, began with an 'I' not a 'P', and he was not Italian. **(SUM ch22)**

BERNHARDT, Sarah (Henriette Rosine Bernard, 1844-1923): **Gladys Winch** backed herself in gold, notes or lima beans against the theatrical talents of ... . As a tray-carrier. **(TAS ch10)**

BETTY HUTTON: was **Phipps'** tip in the fourth race at Santa Anita. **(TOR ch17)**

BEVAN, George: had only recently married **Maud**, a friend of **Wally Mason**, with whom George had turned a dying show into a success. (See *Volume 5*, where his principal appearance, in *A Damsel in Distress*, is reported). **(JTR ch4; TLW ch4)**

BEVAN, Maud: the daughter of the **Earl of Marshmoreton** and wife of **George**. (See *Volume 5*). **(TLW ch4, Grand-JTR)**

BEVERLEY, Alan: not only did this blackhearted pipe-smoking knocker on studio floors, thought of as 'The Brute', turn out to have an attractive voice, but also a pleasantly dishevelled exterior with his hair kept in a disordered mop. But he got into trouble with **Annette Brougham** when he sought to improve her lot in an underhand manner after following her from the Embankment via Charing Cross and Sloane Square to the King's Road, Chelsea, and from the 33rd Street Elevated, 8th Street Station and Washington Square. **(TMU-MUP; Cosmo-MUP)**

BEVERLY HILLS: near **Hollywood**, where a householder would employ a 'couple' who proved to be generally incompetent and left the following week, to be succeeded by another couple, equally subhuman. In contrast to Hollywood, it is a good place for dogs, an oasis in a rather depressing countryside where each of the houses has a front lawn running unfenced to the pavement and where, on each lawn, there sits a dog. **(TOR ch1; Aldin-GOW)**

BEVERLY HILLS HOTEL: where first **Reggie Havershot** and then **JC(RH)** and **JC(TF)** stayed. **(Pearson-LAG; ThisWeek-LAG)**

BEVERLY-WILSHIRE HOTEL: the chemist shop in this **Hollywood** doss-house was a haven of temporary relief for the teething problems of an earl. **(LAG ch4)**

BICKLES, Archie: had $200,000 awarded against him for breach of promise, even though he was practically a pauper. **(FRL ch9)**

BIDDLE, Conky: the impecunious nephew of **Lord Plumpton**, whose nickname was derived from the throwaway comment by a distant schoolmaster that his skull was full of concrete. His low IQ was forgiven by those impressed with his spectacular outer crust, for he out-Caryed any **Grant** and beat any Gregory in the **peck**ing order. Though he might be forgiven for his dislike of slugs and his uncle, some will marvel at what they might consider to be his unjustified good fortune in securing immunity from the undeservedly unpopular game of cricket, in the arms of his **Clarissa Binstead**. **(NSE-HTU)**

BIDDLE, Gus 'Looney': the greatest left-handed pitcher the **New York Giants** had had for a decade, who had nevertheless once suffered a bad day against the **Pittsburgh Pirates**. He was a long, strongly-built young man in a grey suit, with a suitably large, freckled face, an india-rubber neck, a dull brick-red face, gold tooth, lips which curled back in an unpleasant snarl, hands like two young legs of mutton and a fiancée with personality. He lost $15.55 playing poker, his cool following a row, and the use of his pitching hand after mistaking a wall for **Archie Moffam**. **(IOA ch14,15)**

BIDDLE, Looney,'s fiancée: was a determined-looking girl with fine brown eyes and a ringing soprano voice. She wore a blue dress, a large hat with daisies, cherries and a feather, and walked out on **Looney** in the middle of her vanilla and maple. **(IOA ch14)**

BIDDLECOMBE HUNT BALL: famed for the extra tremoloes of ecstasy inspired by the comeliness of its feminine revellers, such as **Lady Beatrice Bracken**. **(HOW ch2)**

BIDDLEFORD CASTLE: the Norfolk family seat of the **Havershot**s, complete with battlements and deer, but in reality incomplete, for it was one of the ruins that had been knocked about a bit by **Cromwell**. **(LAG ch2)**

BIG CLOUD: a Red Indian who, according to **Peter**, lived in the rhododendron bushes by the lake. **(MLF-BIS)**

BIGELOW, Constance: told **Jane Opal** it was a mistake to marry anybody but a poor man, because you appreciate the little treats so much. **(HOW ch2)**

BIGGER & BETTER STUDIO: motion picture company where **Isadore Wertheimer** was the production manager, and **Stiffy** and **Clara Svelte** were among the stars employed. **(Aldin-GOW)**

BIJOU DREAM: where **Lancelot Purvis** used to escort **May Gleason** and **Ellabelle Bagster**. **(Grand-COL)**

BILBURY: one of four places of similar names, with stations and trains critical to the construction of the plot of *The Murder at Bilbury Manor*. **(SUM ch16)**

BILDAD THE SHUHITE: see **Job**

BILL[1]: a parrot who shared with **Nellie Bryant** both hardships and lodgings at 9 Daubeny Street, Pimlico, London SW. He spent much of his time pondering on the problem; "Why am I a parrot?" and was sufficiently vexed to bite **'Enry**. **(JTR ch5)**

BILL[2]: a wiry fox-terrier of jaunty, slightly disreputable demeanour, whose attempt to bite off the head of an acquaintance of uncertain breed was interpreted as an invitation to an Irish terrier and two poodles to join the ruck. **(TMU-RIE)**

BILL[3]: a friend of the **Shy Man** and active campaigner against animal rights. **(MLF-HMV)**

BILL[4]: a friend of **Katie MacFarland**, who ate at **Mac's**. **(MLF-MOM)**

BILL[5]: at the **Leicester Theatre**, was invited to 'cummere quick'. **(JTR ch2)**

BILL[6]: see **Wilhelmina Shannon**

BILLING, Mr: long, stringy occupational sunbather who enjoyed a game of bridge. **(SUM ch1,23,25)**

BILLING, Thomas: an eleven-year-old boy at **George Tanner**'s school, who once ate a slice of bread covered with brown boot-polish on a dare from **Rupert Atkinson** and **Alexander Jones**. After having his air-rifle confiscated by the headmaster, he confessed to having used the gun to shoot **Herbert**, the school gardener, in scenes reminiscent first of the action of the Rev Augustine Mulliner's brother (*The Bishop's Move, see Volume 2*) and secondly of Lord Emsworth (*The Crime Wave at Blandings, see Volume 5*), although the latter was the only one of the three mentioned to have actually committed the crime. **(Strand-COI)**

BILLINGTON: an impresario whose new show in New York was to include **Mabel Winchester** as a member of the chorus. **(IOA ch17)**

BILL THE BLOODHOUND: see **Rice, Henry Pifield**

BILLY: an amiable, self-respecting spaniel, who had the misfortune to be billeted on one **Scrymgeour**, and whose ultimate refusal to perform silly tricks for that legal luminary's mere amusement led to romance, though not, alas, for Billy. **(TAS ch2)**

BILTMORE: the hotel where **Freddie Rooke** stayed whilst in America. **(JTR ch13)**

BINGHAM, Freddie: no **Apollo** he, for he was square in shape, bullet-headed with too much chin, and his teeth were not prominent following two seasons of college football. Otherwise, his life story is very similar to that of **Lord Freddie Bowen**, who featured in the UK version of the story. **(Colliers-JOW)**

BINGLEY, Lancelot: a rising young artist, with a private income, an IQ about that of a retarded child of seven and an addiction to tobacco, who was engaged to **Gladys Wetherby**. To overcome opposition to their union, she arranged for him to paint her uncle, but it was catching him in a completely different pose which enabled them to secure his consent. **(PLP-GCS)**

BINGLEY-ON-THE-SEA: a uniquely foul Sussex watering-place of depressing aspect to which **Sam Marlowe** went on losing **Billie Bennett**. **(GOB ch8)**

BINNS, K-Leg: since he had beaten **Mullins** more easily than had **Bugs Butler**, it was suggested that he should have been the contender against **Lew Lucas** for the heavyweight championship. **(TAS ch13)**

BINNS, Porky: presumably a member of either the **Frith Street Gang**, when he was pinched by **P C Keating**, or the **Groome Street Gang**, when **Officer Kelly** did the honours. **(TUW-MIS; BurrMcK-MIS)**

BINSTEAD, Clarissa: a lissom American girl of medium height, with eyes and hair of a browny hazel, a charming voice and the overall appearance of a seraph who ate lots of yeast but she had a serious flaw in her make-up. We are not speaking here of her foundation, her powder, her rouge, her lipstick or her mascara, but of something much more than skin deep. Something so unpleasant that we can scarcely bring ourselves to utter the words, so terrible that we must disguise the truth, and stoop to the font of all evil to tell you that:

Clarissa thought cricket a mere shallow excuse for walking in your sleep

In her campaign of terror against those who appreciated the noble game she resorted to catapulting tin foil at their engrossed forms, but was soon brought to justice before the highest court in the land. **(NSE-HTU)**

BINSTEAD, Mr: the American father of **Clarissa** who ran a gigantic business employing lots of Vice-Presidents. **(NSE-HTU)**

BINSTEAD, Professor: a friend of **Daniel Brewster**, a connoisseur of Art who selected the tapestries for the dining-room of the **Cosmopolis** and various other paintings. He was a small, middle-aged man with tortoiseshell-rimmed spectacles, and was asked by Brewster to bid for **Pongo**, which he succeeded in obtaining at $ 2,300. **(IOA ch2,11)**

BIOSCOPE: would not give **Adela Cork** a job. **(TOR ch20)**

BIRDSEY, J Wilmot: of East 73rd Street, NY. From being a footballer in his youth, he evolved into a baseball fanatic. After becoming the father of **Mae Elinor**, he was sentenced by his wife to exile and transportation to a suite in the **Savoy** in London, courtesy of *RMS Olympic*, and found his only reprieve at **Chelsea Football Ground**. His actions immediately afterwards merely served to reinforce his commitment to the game and his friendship with fellow addicts. **(MLF-OTN)**

BIRDSEY, Mrs J Wilmot: mother of **Mae Elinor** and judge, jury and prosecuting counsel in the case of *Baseball v Proximity to Daughter*. **(MLF-OTN)**

BIRDSEY, Mae Elinor: see **Countess of Carricksteed**

BISHOP, Bruce: **Chris Selby** sat opposite him for over an hour the day before he shelled **Consolidated Pea-Nuts**, sending the price down by twenty points. **(JTR ch12)**

BISMARCK, Otto Edward Leopold, Prince von (Duke of Lanenburg, 1815-1898): he had been portrayed, with the assistance of hats and false hair, at ships' concerts. **(GOB ch6)**

BIVATT, Franklyn: an unpleasant little **American millionaire** of the second type, with a weak digestion, a taste for dogmatic speech, a desirable daughter and an appearance like one of **Conan Doyle**'s pterodactyls. He was arrested at **East Side Delmonico's**, where he received the come-uppance that was undoubtedly due following his refusal to let his daughter **Margaret** marry the man of her choice. **(Strand-JOW)**

BIVATT, Margaret: the daughter of **Franklyn**, who forced her to wait before agreeing that she could take her **Freddie Bowen** to her bosom. **(Strand-JOW)**

BIVATT, Twombley: the son of the millionaire, and brother of **Margaret**, who ran up a poker debt of $1,000. **(Strand-JOW)**

***BLACK FOR LUCK*:** a short story which appeared in *Strand* and *Red Book* in mid-1915 but underwent a wholesale rewrite before its inclusion in *The Man With Two Left Feet* in 1917.

BLACK HAND: **Salvatore** seemed to **Daniel Brewster** to look like something connected with its executive staff. **(Cosmo-MMH)**

> Packy did not reply. He had come into the room and was now closing the door with every circumstance of wariness and caution. It was as if he had been the janitor at an

emergency meeting of the Black Hand to whom had been assigned the task of making sure that the coast was clear.

(HOW ch6)

> One moment, stillness; the next, Joseph hurtling through the air, all claws and expletives, and herself caught in a clasp that shook the breath from her, and kssed so emphatically that it seemed not so much a kiss as a Black Hand explosion.

(Red-BCL)

BLACK ONION GANG, The: in nine cases out of ten, the butler at a country house turned out to be a member of ... **(SPF ch13)**

BLACK RUIN: what **Mabel Prescott** thought **Eggy** was drinking. **(LAG ch9)**

BLAIR, Cosmo: a short, stout, highbrow dramatist, who added to **Lord Shortlands'** heavy depression by extending his stay at **Beevor Castle** indefinitely and becoming engaged to his daughter **Clare Cobbold**. His latest play had run for nine months and a year in London. He inadvertently helped to spike one of **Spink**'s dastardly plots, by the simple expedient of knowing **Roland Winter**, to whom he planned to offer a part in his new play. **(SPF ch3,10,18)**

BLAKE, Ada: **Tom**'s wife, whose cottage at Fenny Stratford was used as a headquarters whilst waiting for cargo. **(NGW ptII ch14)**

BLAKE, Jno: though he owned a small shop on Sixth Avenue, New York City, Jno was English and dispensed to the NY air the atmosphere of one who drove to the Derby in a dogcart. He unwisely agreed to sponsor **Blake's Unknown** in a pie-eating championship, but when that wimp dropped out, he associated himself with the incomparably superior **Washington McCall**. **(IOA ch21)**

BLAKE, Tom: once the energetic leader of the potato-slingers at Covent Garden, he was the brother of **Kit Malim**. In his youth he pinched and popped his father's best trousers, and spent the stamp money on beer. In later years he became the proprietor and skipper of the barges *Ashlade* and *Lechton*, and gave his name to **Cloyster**'s published poetry, before taking over the activity on his own account. **(NGW)**

BLAKE'S UNKNOWN: from London, with an amazing knack of stowing food away in quantity, such as four pounds of steak and potatoes as a starter. After hearing **Mrs McCall** on the subject of *Rational Eating*, however, he announced a treaty of friendship between himself and all the pies in the world. **(IOA ch21)**

BLAMONT-CHEVRY, Prince: a friend of **Old Nick**, to whom he offered the advice that prisons in Paris were bad enough, but then invited him to dinner and left him to pay the bill. He was virtually penniless until he obtained a job as a waiter working for Nick at the **Mazarin**, but in this role he was not proving very satisfactory. **(FRL ch3,12)**

BLANDISH, Myrtle: a cabaret girl who had a habit of never going to bed before five. She was **Packy Franklyn**'s first fiancée of record, but ran off with a fellow named Scott, Pott or even Bott. **(HOW ch2)**

BLANKLEY, Mrs: one of **James Cloyster**'s landladies. **(NGW ptII ch22)**

BLANK'S MAGAZINE: took **Jones**'s work for three years. **(Strand-PAW)**

BLAYTHWAYT: a sportsman and business acquaintance in real estate of **Robert Ferguson**, the latter having some eighteen months earlier been engaged to the girl now acting as **Blaythwayt's** secretary. **(TMU-MMM; Cosmo-MMM)**

BLAYTHWAYT'S SECRETARY: after having been engaged to **Robert Ferguson**, she reentered his life after eighteen months with cake, cocoa and shortly afterwards a shared dislike of **Roland Bean**. She recounted her experiences of being locked in both her New York and London offices all night, having dreamt she had been chasing dill pickles round Union Square, and chocolate éclairs around Trafalgar Square. They celebrated their reunion both at the Savoy in London, and at the restaurant which answered to *0430 Bryant* in America. **(TMU-MMM; Cosmo-MMM)**

BLEAK HOUSE: a novel by **Charles Dickens** in which the Thing and Thing thing ended with all the money going to the lawyers. **(FRL ch1)**

BLEKE'S COFFEE HOUSE: a morgue; a relic of Old London, to which his **Uncle Donald** summoned **Ginger Kemp**. **(TAS ch4)**

BLENKINSOP, Maud Kellog: a writer with red hair and a bad complexion who had been at school with **Grace Pemberton**, and was now said to be earning eight guineas per thousand words (or seven cents a word) thanks to the attentions of **Henderson Banks**. **(Strand-PAW; PicRev-PAW)**

BLENKINSOP'S LIQUID LIFE-GIVER: **Meggs** drank sufficient of this supposed indigestion palliative to float a ship. **(MLF-AST)**

BLIGH, Captain William (1754-1817):   he appeared to have left his less agreeable qualities to **Beulah Brinkmeyer**, and was well-mannered compared to **M Boissonade**. **(LAG ch7; FRL ch6)**

BLINKHORN, Gwendolyn: **Lady Beatrice Bracken**'s aunt, who regarded **Packy Franklyn** as a flippertygibbet, he returning the compliment with interest by referring to her as a cheater-at-solitaire. Generally, she was perceived to be a pre-eminent blister with a searching eye and nasty cracks. **(HOW ch2,17)**

BLISSAC, Maurice, Vicomte de ('Veek'):   the effervescent young heir to the châtelaine of the **Château Blissac** was a willowy Etonian with a pleasant face who believed in living. If he could be said to have had an ambition other than being in the forefront of the action, it could only have been the fulfilment of a wish complex which, briefly summarised, was that there was no point in merely painting a town red if it could be embellished by a vivid and luminous vermilion. According to **J Wellington Gedge** he was France's leading souse. On a rare occasion when he was outwitted by his friend **Packy Franklyn**, he was hampered briefly by the misapprehension that he had murdered a drinking-partner, but the reappearance of the said reveller in his life was a source of considerable cheer. **(HOW; USHOW ch1)**

BLISSAC, Vicomtesse de: the mother of the **Vicomte** who had great influence with the French Government. **(HOW ch1)**

BLOGSON: held a brief but pointed dialogue with Snogson, to the presumed fascination of the readers of *Fireside Chat*. **(TMU-WDD)**

BLOOMER: the boots in which he first played football for England were in **Daniel Rackstraw**'s museum, and were bet against **Meredith**'s ball. **(TMU-TGP)**

BLORE, Eric: **Shorty** resembled an ... rather than a **Robert Taylor**. **(SPF ch4)**

BLOSSOM, Joe: conceded without a fight that **Thomas Kitchener**'s claim on **Sally Preston** should be treated as the stronger. **(TMU-STW)**

BLUE BOAR: an inn at **Windlehurst** where **Sam Marlowe** stayed, but with a false sense of security as far as his standing with his red-headed belle was concerned. **(GOB ch15)**

BLUE BOAR: the only Walsingford hotel of a higher class, at which **Princess von und zu Dwornitzchek** stopped for refreshment on the way to **Walsingford Hall**. **(SUM ch20)**

BLUE CHICKEN: a pub frequented by **Drexdale Drew** and others. **(QUS ch18)**

BLUE LION: an inn on Main Street, **Wellingford** or **Wallingford**, it was the temporary home to **Charlie Yost**. **(DBB ch8; USDBB ch8)**

BLUFFINGHAME: rhymes with **Framlinghame**; which rhymes with **Moffam**; which rhymes with Frome; which rhymes with combe, tomb, and womb; with cwm; with rheum; with whom; with flume, glume, and plume; and with bloom, boom, gloom, groom, loom, room and zoom. **(IOA ch3; MLF-OTN)**

BLUMENTHAL, Maxie: a music publisher who remarked that since the words of *Mother's Knee* were gooey enough to hurt, and since the tune reminded him of every other song hit he had ever heard, there was nothing to stop it selling a million copies. **(IOA ch23)**

BOADICEA (d61): in her girlhood she must have resembled **Jane Hubbard**. **(GOB ch4)**

BOB[1]: **Julia Waveney's companion**'s brother, who wanted his sister to join him in Canada. **(TMU-TTM)**

BOB[2]: a dog belonging to **Fred[2]**, who was poisoned by **Bill[3]**. **(MLF-HMV)**

BODEGA: an English hostelry where **Max Faucitt** passed pleasant hours. **(TAS ch5)**

BODGER: a Kent county cricketer whose finger-spin enabled him to make the ball dip and turn late on a sticky wicket. **(NSE-HTU)**

BODGER, BODGER, BODGER AND BODGER: Horace Appleby's solicitors, and when you got four Bodgers, you got something. **(DBB ch14)**

BODGETT, Arnold H: of Wistaria Lodge, duly received a reply from **Stanley Briggs**. **(NGW ch25)**

BODKIN: an assistant cashier who was prevented from invading **Lady Beatrice Bracken**'s compartment with his family. **(HOW ch2)**

BODKIN, Louise: his sister. **(HOW ch2)**

BODKIN, Miriam: his wife. **(HOW ch2)**

BOGART, Humphrey (1899-1957):

> An impression exists in the public mind that there is some system of rules and regulations, rigidly enforced by the men up top, which compels all American gangsters to look like Humphrey Bogart and when speaking to snarl like annoyed cougars.

(DBB ch1)

BOHEMIANS: when married, lived in Oakley Street, Kings Road, Chelsea. Bearing in mind that *Not George Washington* had been written in 1907, it may reasonably assumed that the location had in it elements of PGW's own exposure to scruffy side streets of the King's Road, such as Markham Square, where he lived when he came from Shropshire to work at the Hong Kong and Shanghai Bank, and the rather more pleasant Walpole Street (which appears under its own name (and even its own number, 23) in the book. **(NGW ptII ch1)**

BOISSONADE, Pierre Alexandre: Commissaire de Police at **Roville-sur-Mer**, with an office in the Rue Mostelle. He was both a great bull of a man with a red, accordion-pleated neck and beetling eyebrows, and a bully. There seem to have been two schools of thought concerning his personality. The one, of which he himself was the only representative, considered him a *bon enfant*, a good fellow. The other, incomparably more numerous, credited him with the disposition of a snapping turtle and manners which would have been considered brusque by **Simon Legree** or **Captain Bligh** of the *Bounty*. He received part of his just desserts when the **Comte d'Escrignon** gave him a black eye while he was breaking into **Terry Trent**'s room, for he suspected Terry of murdering her sister **Jo**. **(FRL ch1,6,10)**

BOLES, BOLES, WICKETT, WIDGERY AND BOLES: Lincoln's Inn Fields legal advisers to **Sir Buckstone Abbott**, who hoped with some desperation that they would sanction his proposal to use dynamite in the matter of **Sam Bulpitt**. **(SUM ch17)**

BOLT, Ben: wrote of Alice, who trembled with fear at a frown. **(QUS ch1)**

BONAPARTE, Napoleon (1769-1821): made the gesture of drawing himself to his full height impressive. He had his successes and his failures, like all of us, but they are of sufficient renown to be used as a comparator for the thoughts and feelings of lesser men (although in terms of height alone, there were few lesser men). Let us review first some of his successes. When he saw an enemy's weak point, he went straight at it, crumpling the enemy and causing him to fly from the field in rout. On one occasion **Archie Moffam** felt as Napoleon might have done after thinking up a hot one to spring on the enemy. And like **Joss Weatherby**, though unlike **George Holbeton**, he would have stood his ground and investigated further the phenomenon of a densely moustached stranger galloping up shouting "Hey!"

If we turn to look at other matters, we find that he was an example of a gifted man who was notoriously unlucky in his love life. The spirits which were lowered at Moscow were neither vodka nor brandy, and while it was unlikely that the retreat he led from that city was conducted in dead silence, his movements at that time may have been the ponderous type adopted by **Bill Shannon** when disappointed. It was of no consolation to **Fillmore Nicholas** to know that Napoleon had experienced the ignominy of being bettered in debate by a woman. Indeed, after **Gladys Winch** explained that she could cook but not act, Fillmore resembled the little man at Elba.

We conclude with a couple of more general pointers. We are confident that if he had ever chosen to conceal his presence by dropping silently to the floor and hiding under the desk, he would have seen to it that his boots, and eighteen inches of trouser leg, were not sticking out, and that, had he wished to sleep while hiding, he would have been able to do so immediately with but a pillow for his head. Overall, he seems to have been a person of interest, in good times or bad, which perhaps explains why he had been portrayed, with the assistance of hats and false hair, at ships' concerts. **(JTR ch2; GOB ch6,12; TAS ch1,10; IOA ch21; HOW ch15; SUM ch21; QUS ch10,11; TOR ch3,8,15; DBB ch1,9; TGI ch12)**

BOND, Sir Hugo: the recently deceased uncle of **Mike**, he had been a rubicund bachelor who had bought **Mallow Hall** and popularity by embezzling from the bank which bore his name on an impressive scale. **(DBB ch2,6)**

BOND, Isabel (or Isobel): an imperious old aunt of **Mike Bond**, who had once been a formidable character. She had a dachsund, two cats, a broken leg, a distaste for cryptic crosswords and a liking for **Jill Willard**. **(DBB ch2,10)**

BOND, Mike: the unfortunate who had drawn the short straw as nephew of **Sir Hugo** and had thus inherited the bankrupt **Bond's Bank** to go alongside the estate at **Mallow Hall** (tel: Wellingford or Wallingford 834). He was slim and wiry, as befitted a Cambridge lightweight boxer of distinction who had ridden in the Grand National. His attempt to redeem the debts caused by his uncle's tangle of frauds was complicated by an insurance policy which provided £100,000 if he was injured with intent to kill, but only £5,000 on his death. He was heroinically supported in his efforts to save the family name by his fiancée **Jill Willard**. **(DBB; USDBB ch9)**

BOND'S BANK: although supposedly as safe as the Bank of England, it had been raided by **Sir Hugo Bond** to pay for popular projects such as a library, to the extent of £200,008 19s 6d. After **Mike Bond** had managed to recover half the deficit, restitution of the remainder was deferred whilst various attempts were made by different individuals to relieve the institution of the need for further security measures. After a young lady had been locked into the somewhat capacious safe, though, the dénouement quickly followed (in a more sentimental manner than common with Wodehouse) with the remainder of the shortfall being contributed as investment capital by **Horace Appleby** (£50,000), **Ferdie the Fly** and **Smithy** (both £25,000). **(DBB ch2,5,6,15)**

BONES, Caesar: transplanted greenbacks from **John Denville**. **(NGW ptII ch5)**

BOOCH, Cosmo: the **Hollywood** press agent to **Joey Cooley** who had thought up the nosegay stunt so disliked by the right-thinking principals of the sketch. He was poked in the snoot by the **Mystery Fiend** while playing checkers with the aptly named **Dikran Marsupial**. **(LAG ch12)**

BOODLE, Mrs Robert: of Sandringham, Mafeking Road, Balham, was advised that **Stanley Briggs** had no opening for her son. **(NGW ch25)**

BOOTH & BAXTER BISCUIT FACTORY: a source of employment in Walsingford, Berks, its posts being suitable particularly for those running more to muscular development than social polish. **(SUM ch19)**

BOOTH THEATRE: ran **Gerald Foster**'s second play for a week before it flopped. **(TAS ch14)**

BOOTLE INTELLIGENCER: its statement in a five-line review that a book is readable has been known to presage an Event; ie an occasion when the public's purse empties in droves to secure copies of a novel such as *Parted Ways*. **(Strand-PAW)**

BORED PALLID: the range of subjects which bored **Algy Wynbrace** pallid included:

- All literature except the sporting papers
- Breakfast
- Cubist paintings
- The Future of Women
- Lawn tennis
- The Movement for the Better Housing of Working Men
- Problem plays, and
- Wagner

Note the omission from the list of 'Cats'. He wasn't bored pallid by cats. He hated them, and they filled him with genuine horror. **(LHJ-FKA)**

BORNEO WIRE-SNAKE: **Jane Hubbard** would know what to do when bitten by a ... **(GOB ch7)**

BOSTON: in the first game of the season, their batters suffered at the hands of **New York Giants' Clarence van Puyster**'s pitching. **(Colliers-PAP)**

BOTTICELLI, Sandro (Alessandro Filipepi, 1444-1510): the way she did her hair made **Terry Cobbold** look like a ... angel. **(SPF ch4)**

BOULE: a game of chance in which the ball is programmed to tease, to rest in the hole you have backed until the end, and then hop into another. **(TMU-TTM)**

BOURKE, Timothy: on release from Ellis Island he had found work helping to construct the New York subway, but an unidentified error which occurred while he was working in compressed air in a casement under water caused him to suffer from the bends and die. He proved not to have been the same person as **Mike Burke**'s brother **Tim**, who like Mike didn't have an 'O'. **(PallMall-MLB)**

BOWEN, Lord Freddie: whilst visiting New York he had met, wooed and won the heart of **Margaret Bivatt** but not, alas, that of her father. He promised that Freddie could claim Margaret once he had earned a total of $500 by physical or mental labour. In pursuit of that target he took a job on a news-stand, another as a waiter and finally a third as a prize-fighter, but it was the threat of becoming a journalist and reporting the misfortunes of his prospective father-in-law which eventually obtained for him his bride. **(Strand-JOW)**

BOYD & CO: the **Boyd** family business, and producer of Excelsior Home-Cured Ham and Boyd's Premier Breakfast Sausage. **(MLF-BFL)**

BOYD, James Renshaw: inherited **Joseph** and renamed him **Reginald**. He was a rough-haired, clean-shaven, square-eyed young man from Chicago who grabbed **Elizabeth Herrold** to her distress when she told him some good news. A playwright, the extent of his incompetence impressed all the critics, especially **One in Authority**, but created the right atmosphere for reconciliation. **(MLF-BFL)**

BOYD, Mr: the sporting father who gave his son **James** the chance to prove himself as a playwright. **(MLF-BFL)**

BRACKEN, Lady Beatrice: the spectacularly beautiful daughter of the **Earl of Stableford**, whose incomparable beauty always added distinction to the **Biddlecombe Hunt Ball** and could even have attracted attention in the Royal Enclosure at **Ascot** or among the revellers parading around **Lord's Cricket Ground** during the lunch interval in the Eton and Harrow match. Her devotion to her fiancé, **Packy Franklyn**, was marred by a Florence-Craye-like tendency to try to mould his appreciation of good books and pictures, and it came no surprise when she took a packet to find him and break the engagement. **(HOW ch2,11,16)**

BRADSTREET: on meeting **Desborough Topping**, he was provided with a rare occasion for raising his hat with a deferential flourish. **(SPF ch3)**

BRADY, Diamond Jim: the old **Hollywood** was considered to have been rather like a combination of **Santa Claus**, **Good King Wenceslas** and ... in its generosity. **(Colliers-PTR)**

BRADY, Ted: of the Glencoe Athletic Club, NY, had brown eyes, a **Charles Dana Gibson** profile, a frankness of character and seriousness of purpose which fortunately required little speech, and a single-hearted devotion to the equally diffident **Katie Bennett** that survived even his enthronement as a king **(MLF-CRH)**.

BRAHE, Tycho (1546-1601): an eminent Dane who measured time by means of altitude, quadrants, azimuths, cross-staves, armillary spheres and parallactic rules. **(TOR ch17)**

BRAID, James (1870-1950): talk about his lofting shots, raised in conversation by **George Marlowe**, was heard absent-mindedly by **Grace Pemberton**. **(Strand-PAW)**

BRAINS: see **Chumps**

BRETHREN OF TRINITY HOUSE: a group of pampered pets for some reason excused from jury duty. **(TGI ch2)**

BREWSTER, Daniel: the immensely proud proprietor of the **Hotel Cosmopolis**, and only incidentally the father of **Bill** and **Lucille**, he was a massive, grey-haired millionaire. He was good at losing things: his daughter's hand, when he wasn't looking, $2.50 at golf to **Archie Moffam** (playing 25 cents a hole and losing 10 and 8), the value of a piece of 'objay dar' to his sacked valet, **Parker**, and the objay itself when it fell to the floor. His first impression of Archie was to demand his head *passant regardant* on a charger, but he was gradually reconciled to him after receiving his assistance in one or two matters of concern, and the reconciliation was completed by the announcement of his impending grandfatherhood. **(IOA)**

BREWSTER, Mabel: the sister of the late **Wilmot**, who considered that any later liaison entered into by his widow could only be to a nobody. **(HOW ch1)**

BREWSTER, Sergeant Herbert: a swarthy bicycling member of the **Wellingford** or **Wallingford** constabulary, who captained the village cricket team and was walking out with **Ivy**. **(DBB ch3,8,15; USDBB ch3,8,15)**

BREWSTER, Lucille: see **Moffham, Lucille**

BREWSTER, William ('Bill'): the Yale-educated son of **Daniel** and sister of **Lucille**, who had but one topic of conversation with which to regale those willing to listen, to wit, the superlative divinity of **Mabel Winchester**, the English chorus girl who had given him her heart. Until, that is, he saw her for what she was, and transferred his attention to **Spectatia Huskisson**. **(IOA ch9,19)**

BREWSTER, Wilmot: the late husband of **Mrs Gedge**, who in his prime had been a multi-millionaire oil man. **(HOW ch1)**

BRICE, Archie: of the Paris office of the *New York Herald Tribune*, he was the friend who put **Jeff d'Escrignon** in touch with **Russell Clutterbuck**. **(FRL ch10)**

BRIGGS, Anthony, JP: the late MP for **Loose Chippings**, in the High Street of which a statue had been erected that struck visitors with awe. **(QUS ch13)**

BRIGGS, Paul Axworthy: known as the 'Boy Novelist', he took over **Joseph/Reginald** on the night he started his new work. **(MLF-BFL)**

BRIGGS, Stanley: played musical comedy at the **Briggs Theatre**, but was not averse to playing straight theatre, such as the part of **James** in *The Girl Who Waited*. **(NGW ptII ch4,22,25)**

BRIGGS THEATRE: the venue for musical comedy and occasional straight plays, named after **Stanley Briggs**. **(NGW ptII ch4,25)**

BRIGNEY, GOOLE AND BUTTERWORTH: in correspondence with **Sir Mallaby Marlowe** *re* **Wibblesley Eggshaw**. **(GOB ch8)**

BRINKMEYER, Beulah: sister of **TP**, she was the heavy, the equivalent of **Simon Legree** as far as **Joey Cooley, Teddy Flower**, **RH(JC)** and **RH(TF)** were concerned. She proved to be allergic to Mexican horned toads, frogs and being poked in the snoot and pushed in the pond by fiends such as **JC(RH)** and **JC(TF)**. As far as experiences like that were concerned, not even her regular attendance at the **Temple of the New Dawn** could be of any assistance. **(LAG ch5f; Pearson-LAG; ThisWeek-LAG)**

BRINKMEYER-MAGNIFICO: a movie studio only nominally under the control of **Theodore Brinkmeyer**, which inserted into its contracts with child stars such restrictive practices as no games, no dogs, no swimming and no **candy**. **(LAG ch5,12)**

BRINKMEYER, Theodore P: the rather stout, billowy, bespectacled president of **Brinkmeyer-Magnifico**. He was under the thumb of the tyrant, his sister **Beulah**, whose attitude towards him would have been no different if he had been a stately home and she **Oliver Cromwell**. He was one of several liable to be poked in the snoot by **JC(RH)** or **JC(TF)**, and as a result of these trials and tribulations, he often wished he had remained where he started, in the cloak-and-suit business. **(LAG ch5,11,12; Pearson-LAG; ThisWeek-LAG)**

BRISTOL COLISEUM: where a grandfather died of a surfeit of paste. **(MLF-HMV)**

BRISTOL HOTEL: one of the good hotels in **Roville-sur-Mer**. **(FRL ch5)**

BRITISH BROADCASTING CORPORATION: it may have been the unfortunate employer of the depressing **Blair Eggleston** but its weather announcer could turn a phrase as well as the next man. **(HOW ch2; SUM ch1)**

BRITISH MUSEUM: the principal source for research into the raw material of **Prof Wilberforce**'s book. **(LHJ-FKA)**

BRIXTON: red-eyed wives in … faced silently-scowling husbands at the evening meal and children were sent early to bed after the wrong team won the Cup Final. It was the home of **Basher Evans**, but not a suburb which went in much for floral displays. **(DBB ch8; TMU-TGP)**

BROADWAY: where the big money was. **(TOR ch21)**

BRODIE:

> ". . . you bust a woman's room and what happens? She wakes up and gets set to scream. And what happens then? You either have to do a Brodie out of the window and prob'ly break your damn neck, or else you've got to go and choke her."

Will Beulah Brinkmeyer escape being poked in the snoot?

In the UK version of the text, the word 'Brodie' was replaced by 'dive', offering rather a good clue to the probable meaning of this American slang. **(USHOW ch11)**

BRONX CHEER, the: after working faithfully and successfully with **Soup Slattery** in the safe-breaking line for years, **Julia** just gave him the ... and disappeared. **(HOW ch15)**

BROOKE-HAVEN, P: the pseudonym under which PGW wrote a number of pieces for *Vanity Fair* including *Aubrey's Arrested Individuality*.

BROOKPORT: a village on Long Island, NY's Great Bay Lagoon which, like the mosquitoes which outnumbered its human population, lived entirely on summer visitors such as **Daniel Brewster**. It was considered by **Jill Mariner** to be a sort of Southend in winter. **(JTR ch7; IOA ch9)**

BROOKS, Alf: on holiday from his Battersea milk round, this gab-gifted choirboy, this prince among men, scented, curled in the best Edwardian tradition and looking beautiful in light flannel, a new straw hat and the yellowest shoes in south-west London, reflected ruefully but resiliently that **Ellen Brown** was not the only mushroom in the omelette. **(MLF-RUP)**

BROOKS, Joe: a Broadway producer who tried to tempt **Henry Rice** away from the **Walter Jeliffe** theatrical company. **(Century-BTB)**

BROTHERLY LOVE: a horse tipped to win at Newmarket, on whose nose **Crispin Scrope** placed £100 after he learned that it was owned by someone he had been at school with and that its jockey's name was **Copper**. **(TGI ch4,8,14)**

BROTHER MASONS: a successful and profitable farce written by **Edgar Trent** for Broadway, the TV rights for which were sold for $2,000 net per daughter. **(FRL ch1)**

BROUGHAM, Annette: a composer of waltzes from a studio in Chelsea or Washington Square, New York, three of which had been published without conspicuous success. She lived in a room beneath **Alan Beverley**, where she kept body and soul together by teaching piano and singing to pupils who shared but a single teaspoonful of grey matter. But all was not what it seemed. **(TMU-MUP; Cosmo-MUP)**

BROWN: the pseudonym adopted by **Clarence van Puyster** when he joined the **New York Giants** baseball team. **(Colliers-PAP)**

BROWN, Arthur: never got engaged to **Sally Preston**, but only because he didn't ask, which, on reflection, probably saved him some trouble. **(TMU-STW)**

BROWN, Delilah: originally destined to be an actress, she emerged as a district visitor with an innocent taste for fun. **(Throne-KHE)**

BROWN, Ellen: known by the milkman **Alf Brooks** as 'Little Pansy-Face', Ellen lived and worked in a second floor flat in York Mansions, (either on **Prince of Wales Road** or **Battersea Park Road**, Battersea) where she attracted the attention of the local flatfoot in more senses than one. She was charged by her employer **Jane** on one occasion with the theft of money, and on another with the theft of money and a brooch, and although not guilty of extracting cash, she did admit to borrowing the trinket. Though she was uncomplaining when arrested by **PC Plimmer**, her tortured, crushed eyes conveyed her helplessness as her thoughts turned to the fate of her hair whilst in prison, but the idea of being able to call her captor Eddie offered some consolation. **(MLF-RUP; Ainslee-RUP; Strand-RUP)**

BROWN, Miss: née **Brougham**, the nominal buyer of *Child with Cat*. **(TMU-MUP)**

BROWN, Phil: a man with dark, restless eyes who played straight for **Joe Widgeon** in the best jazz-and-hokum team on the **Keith Circuit**, rehearsing at the Century Roof and being held over at the **Palace**. **(JTR ch9)**

BROWNING, Robert (1812-1889): his *Pippa*'s statement that God was in his heaven and all was right with the world would have been approved by **Crispin Scrope**, had he been aware of it, after his brother had written out a cheque for an amount equal to his most pressing debts. **(TGI ch4)**

***BROWNS OF BRIXTON, The*:** written by the **Rev Mr Hatton**, it was to be published by **Prodder and Way**, and suggested the style of **James Cloyster** but with improvements. **(NGW ptII ch20)**

BRUCE, Robert the (1274-1329): was not afraid of spiders. **(SUM ch21)**

BRUDOWSKA, Mme: a performer in vaudeville, in partnership with her beloved serpent **Peter**. She was a striking woman of foreign appearance and a sinuous walk, who was reputed to earn $1,000 per week. **(IOA ch7)**

BRUGGENHEIM, Mrs: rented a home at **Brookport** for a summer at a time when she, or anyone else, could have bought it for $105,000. **(JTR ch7)**

BRUNSWICK COLISEUM: where **Nigger**'s grandfather died in the properties room, from a surfeit of paste. **(Red-HMV)**

BRUSSELS: the host city for the meeting of the **Pen and Ink Club**. **(TGI ch1)**

BRUTE, The: see **Alan Beverley**. **(TMU-MUP)**

BRUTUS, Marcus Junius (85-42BC): compared to ..., **Maxwell Faucitt** claimed to be no orator. See also **Julius Caesar**. **(TAS ch1; TOR ch8)**

BRYAN, William J (Jennings, 1820-1925): one of the names given by a male guest in Room 618 of the **Hotel Cosmopolis** following a sing-song and a raid. He was also on **Aubrey Devine**'s list of the seven most prominent men in the United States. **(IOA ch19; VanFair-AAI)**

BRYANT HALL: the New York rehearsal venue, on 6th Avenue close to 42nd Street, for the *Rose of America* team. **(JTR ch10)**

BRYANT, Adonis: a film actor, one of whose efforts was watched by **Looney Biddle** and his girl-friend, although Looney concluded that he was a pill. **(Cosmo-FAL)**

BRYANT, Nelly: a mild, unaggressive, girl with a soft, pleasing voice unspoiled by its rummy American accent. She was in show business, but had been workless since *Follow the Girl* had finished its run at the Apollo. Though unmarried, she shared dingy lodgings at 9 Daubeny Street, Pimlico, London SW with the cheerful extrovert **Bill**[1] until she returned to New York at **Freddie Rooke**'s expense. When he caught up with her there, the love which had been blossoming flowered, and we assume that she fulfilled her ambition of living in the country with chickens and pigs. **(JTR)**

BRYCE, Police Constable Robert: 14 stone of bone and muscle, who stopped the fight between **Shute** and **Welsh**. **(TMU-WDD)**

BUCKSTONE, John Baldwin (1802-1879): in his day at the Haymarket, Bohemians used to meet at the **Café de l'Europe** close by. **(NGW ptII ch8)**

BUFFIN, James ('Spider'): a small, ugly professional pickpocket of just 105lb, whose eyes showed suspicion and secrecy. He sought to pursue his hobby, revenge, after being sent down for sand-bagging both **Kelly**, when he was caught by **PC Keating**, and **'Nigger' Sloan**, when **Officer Kelly** did the necessary. The officers involved both had unexpected reprieves from assault when Buffin reappeared, and on each occasion the latter himself found himself under more urgent threat from another quarter. **(TUW-MIS; BurrMcK-MIS)**

BULGARIAN PEASANTS: apparently drink yoghurt in great quantities to keep themselves rosy. **(TOR ch1)**

BULPITT, Alice ('Toots'): see **Abbott, Alice, Lady**

BULPITT, Sam: the long-lost (although in some people's view not long-enough-lost) brother of **Alice Abbott**, he reappeared on the scene from America via Nice, Cannes and Monte Carlo; a small, round, rosy man dressed in a loose sack suit and square-toed shoes of a vivid yellow. After early careers as road sweeper and singing waiter, this warrior rose to dizzy fame as the foremost **plasterer** in America. Operating under a slogan shared with the Royal North-West Mounted Police, he was man enough to admit to one honourable failure, the case of **Elmer B Zagorin**, from whom he later inherited untold wealth. At least, it remained untold until he explained to his niece **Jane** that he proposed to settle $500,000 on her when she married, and decided to buy **Walsingford Hall** in order to turn it into a country club. **(SUM)**

BULWINKLE, Mr: an experienced film director in whom both **April** and **Hazel June** had expressed full confidence. **(LAG ch21; Pearson-LAG; ThisWeek-LAG)**

BUMSTEAD, Dagwood: the best husband in America, with a loving heart, gentle nature, fondness for dogs and a taste for exotic sandwiches. **(TOR ch2)**

BUNBURY: the bald-headed (though with fringes of orange hair) producer of *The Primrose Way*, which stalled as the result of Spanish influenza. **(TAS ch6)**

BUNT, Sir Percy: a friend of **Hermione Pegler**, a senior civil servant with an austere outlook. **(FRL ch7)**

BUNYAN, Ferret: a great **plasterer** in London who once managed to serve **Sir Buckstone Abbott** with a writ for £2 7s 6d representing a knee-length hosiery bill. **(SUM ch10)**

BURBAGE HOTEL: the New York establishment which had once employed **Jeff d'Escrignon** as a waiter. **(FRL ch8)**

BURKE: had **Derek Underhill** suddenly become engaged to a niece of an individual named in ...'s *Peerage*, he would have had no hesitation in offering her up to his mother for inspection. **(TLW ch1; Grand-JTR)**

BURKE, Dr: a Walsingford doctor. **(SUM ch19)**

BURKE, Michael ('Mike'): journeyed from Skibbereen to New York, where he became a policeman based at Windle Market police station, near Merlin Street. A big, strong man, he proved equal to the task of balancing a sense of justice with a feeling of responsibility towards his family, particularly his kid brother **Tim**. **(PallMall-MLB)**

BURKE, Tim: **Mike**'s brother, he also came from Skibbereen but was spirited away by the excitement on reaching New York. He experienced a spell on Ellis Island, but emerged, a gigantic, red-haired man with a bare head and a desire to teach foreigners Irish jigs. **(PallMall-MLB)**

BURN, Dolly: with whom both **Tom Ellison** and **Dick Henley** were in love. She treated them equally, going unchaperoned up the Char with each and giving each a couple of dances at the Oriel ball. And why shouldn't she? She liked them both, and was safely engaged to **Harry Drew**. **(TUW-TDH)**

BURNS, Robert (1759-1796) emphasised the advisability of budgeting for the possibility of well-laid plans going awry, though he explained his theories in what Jeeves called the 'North British' dialect. He wrote also of 'wee sleekit cow'rin tim'rous beasties' and circumstances were wont to arise where this description could have been equally applied to members of the human race. **(DBB ch9,14)**

BURROWES, Lester: the thrice-married manager of **Bugs Butler**, he was a small man who wore a checked tweed suit and brown bowler hat. **(TAS ch13)**

BURTON, Billy: of the Irish-American, the only athlete who could touch **Ted Brady**. **(MLF-CRH)**

BURTON, James: the pseudonym of **Elliot Oakes**, who adopted the character of a retired ship's chandler. **(TUW-DAE)**

BURWASH, B K: dentist to **Joey Cooley** and **Teddy Flower** who did **RH(JC)** no good turn by handing over to him the extracted tooth. **(LAG ch5)**

BUSBY, J Mortimer: the literary agent who published *My Sporting Memories* for **Sir Buckstone Abbott**, on the basis that the bart would pay costs of £200, but there was confusion over the responsibility for 'incidental expenses connected with the office' of £96 3s 11d. His skin was more sensitive than his soul, and he was badly sunburnt when he failed to seek adequate protection, rather like those of his clients who did not appoint their own lawyers in their dealings with him. The Society of Authors waged an unending, spirited but always fruitless war, but his business approach was described with candour, admiration and relative adverbs by **J J Vanringham** on leaving his service:

> "Those contracts of yours! I always picture the author, having signed on the dotted line, leaping back as a couple of sub-clauses in black masks suddenly jump out of a jungle of 'whereases' and 'hereinafters' and start ganging up on him with knuckledusters."

(SUM ch1,3)

BUSTER[1]: a Boston terrier, which was the pride and joy of **Patrolman Morehouse**. **(TOR ch16)**

BUSTER[2]: **Marlene Hibbs**'s bull terrier-type dog, which bit **P C Simms**. **(TGI ch11)**

BUTLER: to **Sir Mallaby Marlowe** at Bruton Street, an old retainer who had known **Sam Marlowe** as a small boy. **(GOB ch8)**

BUTLER, Bugs: a singularly repulsive individual with a mean and cruel curve to his lips who was in training at White Plains to fight against **Lew Lucas** after he had beaten **Cyclone Mullins** in 15 rounds. **(TAS ch13)**

BUTLER, Edith: the pen-name of that **Prosser** who was the author of the story *White Roses*, subsequently dramatised by **Owen Bentley**. After carelessly losing the letter from Bentley enclosing the play manuscript, he hijacked the script, but willingly paid over the profits when ownership had been established. **(TMU-POM)**

BUTLER, 'Rabbit': had been a member of the **Frith Street Gang** when arrested whilst assaulting **PC Keating**, and of the **Groome Street Gang** when doing the same to **Officer Kelly**. **(TUW-MIS; BurrMcK-MIS)**

BUTTERFLY CLUB: asked **Mrs Hignett** to be the guest of honour at a weekly dinner. **(GOB ch1)**

BUTTERWORTH: one of six acquaintances of **Joe Vanringham** not known to **Jane Abbott**. **(SUM ch5)**

BUTTERWORTH, Charles: see **Eddie**

BYNG-BROWN-BYNGs, the: Lady Teresa Cobbold was connected with ... through her mother. **(SPF ch14)**

CABOT, Chauncey: one of many aliases of **Herbert Higgs**. **(Ellery-MBD)**

CAESAR, Gaius Julius (102-44BC): James Cloyster understood how ... must have felt when on the brink of the Rubicon. His clean-shaven bust offered **Joe Vanringham** scope for artistic endeavours on which he sought **Jane Abbott**'s approval. His disappointment on receiving Brutus's dagger was nothing as compared to **Phipps**' when he heard **Bill** (or **Jane**) **Shannon** reveal his criminal past. **(NGW ptII ch1; SUM ch17; TOR ch8; Colliers-PTR)**

CAFÉ BRITANNIQUE: the fly-infested Soho eaterie where **Harold** introduced **Narrator[1]** to **Jean Priaulx**. **(TMU-MWD)**

CAFÉ DE L'EUROPE: part of the glassless society. **(LAG ch3)**

CAGNEY, James: RH(JC) rather thought that JC(RH) was pulling too much of the ... stuff. **(LAG ch19)**

CAHN: the producer with **Goble** of musical comedies such as *Coralie*. **(Strand-BTG)**

CAIN'S STOREHOUSE: Sally Nicholas disliked **Bruce Carmyle** with an almost Gingerian intensity. "Was it," she wondered, "to be snubbed by an Englishman that her fathers had bled? Did Bruce Carmyle supppose that the Spirit of '76 was in ..." **(MOS ch4)**

CALIFORNIA: where one could throw an outdoor party without needing the consent of the weather monitor. **(QUS ch14)**

CALIFORNIA MOTHERS: a substantial group of ... wished to tar and feather **Joey Cooley** or, as the case may be, **Teddy Flower**, instead of kissing him when they read about his escapades in the *Los Angeles Tribune*. **(Pearson-LAG)**

CALLAGHAN, Mr: the name adopted by **Smithy** when taking dictation from **Jill Willard**. **(DBB ch11)**

CALLENDER, George Barnett: a young playright who fell in love and the sea simultaneously. **(TMU-DEW)**

CAMELOT: the great tournament of the year was called YE WORLD'S SERIES. **(Escapade-RTR)**

CANADIAN MOUNTED POLICE: had their professional pride. **(SatEvePost-SUM)**

CANDIDE: a book (by **Voltaire**, the pseudonym of François Marie Arouet, 1694-1778) which was not on **Chris Selby**'s reading list. **(JTR ch6)**

CANDY: was defined to include ice-creams, chocolate-creams, nut sundaes, fudge, all-day suckers, doughnuts, marshmallows, pies in their season, starchy food and seconds of chicken. **(LAG ch5)**

CANNES: where **Adrian Peake** lapped after the dog **Dwornitzchek**. **(SUM ch1)**

CAPONE, Al (Alphonse, 1899-1947):

> "Personally, I'd sooner be somebody living in Chicago that Al Capone didn't much like than your father's valet."

(HOW ch7)

CAPTAIN, a police: smaller than his subordinates, but unlike them, he didn't want **Archie Moffam**. **(IOA ch6)**

CAPTAIN COE'S FINAL SELECTION: in the **Punter** Stakes, had **Shorty** at shorter odds than **Mervyn Spink**. **(SPF ch4)**

CAPTAIN KIDD: see **Kidd, Captain William**

CARDINAL, Mycroft ('Mike'): in the United States as in Britain it would be bold parents who elected to christen their son after the greatest of all detectives. Yet Sherlock had a no less brilliant brother after whom the Cardinals did pay such a tribute. Geoffrey Jaggard suggested that there were clues to Mike's background to support the conclusion that he might well have been a godson (if not an even closer relation) to the evanescent Mycroft Holmes, though presumably there are good reasons why the relationship could not be openly acknowledged. What is known, however, is that the abbreviation to 'Mike' of an unusual name helped to foil a master criminal named **Spink**. Mike was a friend of **Stanwood Cobbold** and school friend of **Lord Beevor**, had looks like a Greek god, a pleasing personality and the financial comfort which came from being a partner in one of **Hollywood**'s most prosperous picture agencies. His wooing of **Terry Cobbold** hit a number of snags, notably when he appeared to be chasing **Eileen Stoker**, but judicious repair to his appearance by **Augustus Robb**'s tools made a major contribution to settling the matter. **(SPF)**

CARLISLE, Gertrude: known professionally as 'Gum-Shoe Gertie', she had been **Oily**'s partner until a year after their marriage, when an enforced stay in hospital nursing a broken leg gave him the freedom to see another lady friend, and after expressing her opinion with a vase she left, to re-emerge in the *persona* of **Medway**, maid to **Julia Wedge**. **(HOW ch1,10,17)**

CARLISLE, Gordon ('Oily'): a beautifully dressed American confidence trickster of dark, slender, refined and distinguished appearance, who kept hidden the nasty place on his left leg where a disappointed investor in Australian gold-mines had expressed himself. He was a friend of **Soup Slattery** and the husband of **Gum-shoe Gertie** although the latter had left him after a dispute over another woman. He took the name of the **M le Duc de Pont-Andemer**, with supposed estates in Touraine, and the steam-packet *Antelope*, for a visit to **St Rocque**, where he tried to double-cross Soup and use a gun on **Jane Opal** before, to his considerable surprise, Gertie reappeared. **(HOW)**

CARLISLE THEATRE: ran **Gerald Foster**'s second play for a week before it flopped. **(Colliers-TAS pt10)**

CARLTON HOTEL: where **Julia Gedge** stayed when visiting her solicitor about English income tax. **(HOW ch11)**

CARLTON HOTEL: one of the good hotels in **Roville-sur-Mer**. **(FRL ch5)**

CARMEN FLORES PLACE, the: a **Hollywood** Palace, it was once the home of the sizzling Latin star whose name it bore, before being acquired by **Adela Shannon Cork**. It nestled in the mountains where Alamo Drive petered out into a dirt track fringed by cactus and rattlesnakes, and came complete with swimming-

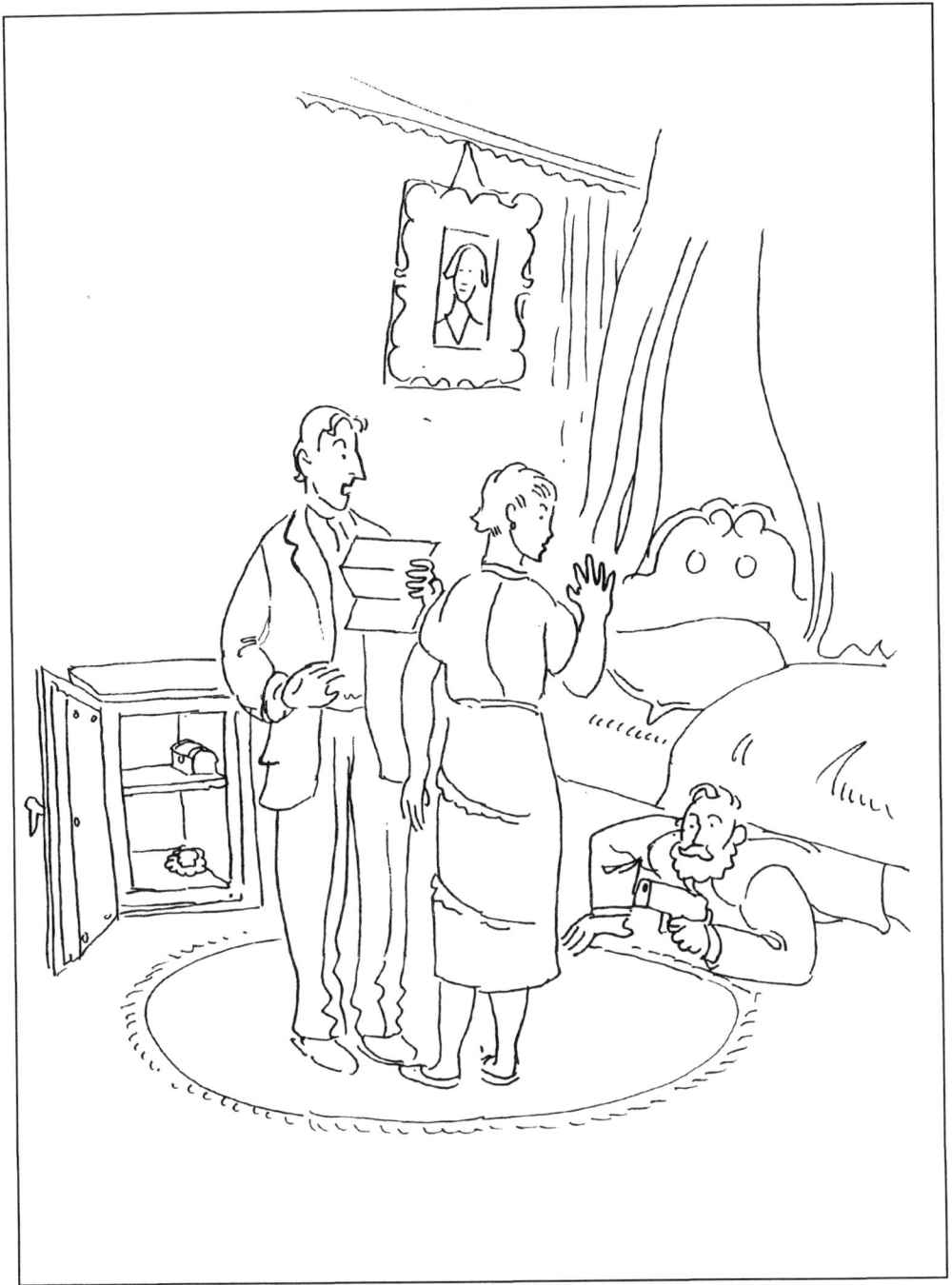

Oily Carlisle confronting Jane Opal and Packy Franklyn

pool, rose garden, orange trees, lemon trees, Jacaranda trees and a stone-flagged terrace. **(TOR ch1)**

CARMYLE, BRENT & CO: operated coal mines in Wales, and had been run by **Bruce Carmyle**'s father until he died and left his son half a million. **(TAS ch10)**

CARMYLE, Bruce: a hard, slightly sinister looking man, tall and dark with a tight, precise mouth and rather high cheek bones. A member of the bar, in his junior days he had devilled for **Scrymgeour**. After meeting the delightful **Sally Nicholas** on a French train, he extracted her New York address by telling downright lies to his cousin **Ginger Kemp**. Quietly and methodically, like a smooth, respectable wolf settling on the trail of Red Riding Hood, he prepared to pursue her, initially failing but apparently achieving his objective in New York until the realisation that she was a professional dancer who entertained men in her rooms made him think again. **(TAS)**

CARNATION HALL: had a doorkeeper informative about **Sidney Price**. **(NGW ptII ch13)**

CARPENTER, Frederick ('Butch') a young American, with freckled face and bright red hair who was the majority shareholder in the celebrated sparkling table-water **Fizzo**. He was rumoured to be worth $20 million including the steam-yacht *Belinda* but neither this wealth nor the physique which came from being a great footballer at Princeton (14 stone and a 44" chest) could prevent him losing his trousers to some enthusiastic **St Rocque** revellers. After he had reached the conviction that he and **Mavis Todd** were soul-mates, his romantic arrangements were complicated by his accepting an invitation to **Terry Trent**'s apartment, where he was discovered leaving her bedroom in his pyjamas. The expected proposal to Mavis was finally made at the fifteenth hole of a local golf course after she had sliced into the undergrowth. **(FRL)**

CARPENTIER: his bout with **Jack Dempsey** was a landmark in pugilistic roughstuff. **(GOB ch17)**

CARRICKSTEED, the Countess of: the American wife of the sixth Earl, née **Mae Elinor Birdsey**, a girl to whom her mother was always very close. **(MLF-OTN)**

CARRICKSTEED, the Rt Hon the sixth Earl of: Hugo Percy de Wynter Framlinghame, whose name was pronounced 'Froom' and his title 'Croxted'. He was a young man with a receding chin and so little forehead that when he frowned his hat flew off but he nevertheless married **Mae Elinor Birdsey** of New York. **(MLF-OTN; McClure-BRF)**

CARTON, Sidney: the character from Dickens's *A Tale of Two Cities*, whose name was spelt 'Sydney', would not have rejoiced at a breach in relations between a couple of folk, but would have done all in his power to heal it. **Jill Willard** thought of **Appleby** as a cross between him and the **Chevalier Bayard**, and became one of Appleby's warmest admirers. **(HOW ch18; DBB ch11)**

CASABIANCA: the name of the title character in a poem by Mrs Hemans, it was also given to the stage door man at the **Leicester Theatre**, who was a slow thinker, perplexed by the consequences of fire. **(JTR ch3; TAS ch13)**

CASANOVA DE SEINGALT, Giacomo Girolamo (1725-1798): Kay Shannon approved of **Joe Davenport**'s claim to be a reformed ... **(TOR ch2)**

CASINO MUNICIPALE: with pillars crimson and cream, tables sky blue and pink, it was the larger of two casinos in **Roville**, the haunt of the gambler who meant business, and numbered **boule** among the attractions which it offered to its clientele. **(TAS ch3; TMU-TTM)**

CASINO MUNICIPALE: the golden-domed edifice which made **St Rocque** a popular resort. **(HOW ch1)**

CASSIDY: a police officer colleague of **Donahue**, who was even larger. **(IOA ch6)**

CASTLE, Mrs: Charlie Ferris's jaw dropped at the end of the dance competition when he saw his wife on the floor, acting like ... and the **Dolly Sisters** rolled into one. **(SatEvePost-ATG)**

CASTLE, Vernon (1887-1918): featured on **Aubrey Devine**'s list of the seven most prominent men in the United States. His name was wrongly attributed to **Charlie Ferris** by the dance hostess **Miss Roxborough** when passing him on to some of her colleagues for further tuition. **(VanFair-AAI; SatEvePost-ATG))**

CAT: an anonymous specimen was the vehicle by which its owner, the dastardly **Captain Muller**, murdered his room-mate **Captain Gunner**, some reports suggesting that the animal, too, expired. **(TUW-DAE; Pearson-EDO)**

CAT CAME BACK, The: a comic vulgar song from the London 'Alls. **(TMU-MWD)**

CATFIELD, Walter: the comic in *Ask Dad*, who disliked **Pottinger**'s suggested gag. **(Strand-BTG)**

CATHERINE II THE GREAT, Empress of Russia (1729-1796): had a personality cloned in **Adela Topping**. **(SPF ch4)**

CATO, Marcus Porcius (234-149BC): the bust at **Walsingford Hall** of this unpleaasant-looking man who suffered from long-nose syndrome, no eyeballs and a bare upper lip, was considerably improved when **Joe Vanringham** got to work on it with a pencil. **(SUM ch12)**

CATS' HOME DIRECTEUR: a courteous, sympathetic official who prolonged **Alexander**'s life. **(TMU-MWD)**

CATSKILLS, the: **Rutherford Maxwell** holidayed in ... **(TMU-INA)**

CAWNPORE: **Vera Upshaw** was as thrilled when she heard **Homer Pyle** ask for a copy of her book *Daffodil Days* in a bookshop as those engaged in the Indian Mutiny would have been on hearing the skirl of the bagpipes at ... **(TGI ch5)**

CAWTHORNE, Joe: see **Fred**

CHAFFINCH: an acting pseudo-butler to **T P Brinkmeyer**, he looked the part with his Englishness, his round stomach and his moon face containing gooseberry eyes. Yet he proved untrustworthy in business, not even being satisfied with the promise of a scandalous commission rate of 50%. **(LAG ch8,17)**

CHAMOIS: the **Tell** family ate one roast the first day, cold for the next four, and minced with sippets of toast on the sixth. **(WTT ch3)**

CHANCELLOR OF THE DUCHY OF LANCASTER: about the only job not tried by **Conky Biddle**. **(NSE-HTU)**

CHANDOS, George: if **James Cloyster** had decided to adopt ... as a *nom de plume*, the fact would soon have reached the public domain. **(NGW ptII ch11)**

CHANEL NUMBER FIVE: **hens** are not ... when it comes to giving off aromas. **(FRL ch1)**

CHANTICLEER: how he flapped his wings and crowed at the sight of the sun acted as a model for **Captain Bassett**. **(TMU-MWD)**

CHAPLIN, Charlie (1889-1977): did not have J L T Smith's speed and control over huckleberry pies. **(IOA ch20)**

CHAR: a river which **Dolly Burn** went up in a Canader separately with **Dick** and **Tom**. **(TUW-TDH)**

CHARING CROSS: a bleak station on a foggy January day, with the air cold, raw and tasting coppery. **(JTR ch1)**

CHARLES: one of the footmen at **Claines Hall**. **(QUS ch9)**

CHARVET, M: the owner of a Paris establishment which sold cambric handkerchieves by the dozen, although when the customer was **Old Nick** the transaction was more one of lend-lease. **(FRL ch11)**

CHÂTEAU BLISSAC: a castle of mouldering stone and spikey turrets near **St Rocque**, built in the late fourteenth or early fifteenth century. Its plumbing was in poor repair, it had a leaky cistern and it had been rented for the season to **J Wellington Gedge** and his wife. Situated on a hill, the ground descended sharply from its terrace through many-coloured gardens and shrubberies to a lake, on the edge of which was a boathouse and, beyond, were sand-dunes and the harbour of St Rocque. **(HOW ch1)**

CHAUCER, Geoffrey (c1340-1400):

> "How well do you know your Chaucer?"
> "My what?"
> "The father of English poetry."
> "Oh, that Chaucer."

(TGI ch3)

CHAVENDER, Beatrice: she was the widow of **Otis**, the late brother of **Mrs Steptoe**, and had once been engaged to **Jimmy Duff** before breaking it off on account of his obsession with ham. Her personal circumstances led her to reverse the role of Haroun al Raschid so that, instead of the customary person of wealth and standing masquerading as a beggar, she was the beggar who successfully maintained the illusion that she still had her millions, even when she had actually lost it all in the **Battersby** crash. Her portrait had been painted by the promising **Joss Weatherby**, and hung at the **Steptoe** establishment, where it reinforced her illusion. She rather injudiciously promised £500 to a girls' school in Brighton where she gave an address. Her condemnation of the quality of the products subsequently offered by **Duff and Trotter** led to a reconciliation with Jimmy and an agreement to try again. **(QUS)**

CHAVENDER, Otis: the late husband of **Beatrice**, he had been in Import and Export. **(QUS ch2)**

CHEERYBLE BROTHERS, the: from Dickens's *Nicholas Nickelby*, were considered just to be elderly Boy Scouts. **(TGI ch3)**

CHELSEA: an area which was home to members of the AB social classes, such as **Annette Brougham** and **Alan Beverley**. **(TMU-MUP)**

CHELSEA FOOTBALL GROUND: the scene of the baseball game which so inspired **J Wilmot Birdsey, John Benyon** and **Waterall. (MLF-OTN)**

CHELSEA POLICE STATION: where **Freddie Rooke** and **Jill Underwood** served their time. **(JTR ch5)**

CHESTER, Sir Portland: impresario given this name, possibly by mistake, as well as the more becoming **Sir Chester Portland** or the mere Sir Chester. **(TLW ch3; Grand-JTR)**

CHEVALIER BAYARD (Pierre de Terrail, 1473-1524): **Crispin Scrope** deserved notices like those of the ..., who would have shaken hands warmly with **Soup Slattery** had he been present to hear Soup observe that "I never choked no woman yet, boy, and I don't aim to begin". **(HOW ch11; TGI ch9)**

CHEZ JIMMY: a Paris establishment which was mourning the loss of both **Gustave** and **Philippe**. **(HOW ch1; FRL ch5)**

CHIBNALL, Sidney: the youngish, sinewy butler to **Mrs Howard Steptoe** at **Claines Hall, Loose Chippings**, who was not to be taken lightly. Outwardly sedate, he was a man of strong passions, particularly given to brooding over his proprietorial rights in **Vera Pym**, barmaid at the **Rose and Crown** (for he felt that his fiancée was prone to overdo the hospitality due to casual customers) and to imprisoning guests in the coal cellar before ascertaining their identity. **(QUS ch1,7,10,13,19)**

CHICAGO: where one changed trains if travelling from New York to Los Angeles, and wished to watch the world heavyweight boxing championship. **(LAG ch1)**

CHICAGO DICK: a kidnapper well known to the police. **(Red-BIS)**

CHICAGO KATE: the woman whom **McGee** thought he recognised proved not to be ... after all. **(Ellery-MBD)**

CHIDERDOSS, Doss: the provider of poetry for the *Sporting Times* represented the limit of **Freddie Rooke**'s appreciation of the art. **(JTR ch14)**

CHILD AND CAT: the clever and original title chosen by **Alan Beverley** for his artistic reproduction of a child holding a cat. "That," he had to explain, "is the cat." But whatever quality it lacked, it still sold for ten guineas to an appreciative **Annette Brougham**. **(TMU-MUP)**

CHILLICOTHE: the Ohio home town of **Joey Cooley** and **Teddy Flower**. **(LAG ch5)**

CHINGACHGOOK: anyone who tried to christen a baby ... would risk being run in for being drunk and disorderly. **(TGI ch13)**

CHINNERY, Elmer: contrived to retain the fortune he had made from the fish-glue business, in which he had been a partner of the first husband of the **Princess von und zu Dwornitzchek**, despite the inroads made upon it by the platoon of ex-wives to whom he was paying alimony. On hearing that his fourth wife was trying to serve him papers he had come to England in an attempt to retain a little of what still remained. A large and spreading man, this Elmer, whose favourite activity after wife-swapping seems to have been devouring waffles.

> "No ordinary purse," Sir Buckstone Abbott told his daughter Jane, "could stand the drain of what he pays out to ex-wives."
>
> "Not to mention ex-waffles, I expect," rejoined that shrewd girl.

(SUM ch1,2,10)

CHIPPENDALE, Mr: the father of **R C**, who was paradoxically attached to his well-fitting false teeth, with which he used to crack brazil nuts. **(TGI ch13)**

CHIPPENDALE, Reginald Clarence: **Crispin Scrope**'s butler, in reality a broker's man. It could be said that the **Goose and Gander** was the temporary centre of his life, for he drank there, he was rude to **P C Simms** there, and he gave the landlord's niece **Marlene Hibbs** bicycle lessons there on a stolen bicycle. He was just 5' 6" tall, with muddy complexion, sticking out ears and the beak and eyes of a farmyard fowl, and, despite his size, an inability to distinguish between miniatures. **(TGI ch8,9,13)**

CHIPPENDALE, ('Tidy') Thomas: a cousin of **Reginald**, who once cleaned out a church down Hammersmith way. **(TGI ch11)**

CHISHOLM, R B: held gloomy views on what would become of us all. **(TGI ch8)**

CHOPIN, Frédéric (1810-1849): one of the victims of virtual murder by the inhabitants of **Battersea Park Road,** or **Prince of Wales Road**. **(MLF-RUP; Strand-RUP)**

CHRISTIE, Dame Agatha Mary Clarissa, (1890-1976): a mutual admiration for her art, and an equally mutual dislike for shrimps, helped break the ice between **Freddie Carpenter** and **Mavis Todd**. But **Adela Cork** asked of the one who shared her initials "Who is Agatha Christie?" **(TOR ch7; FRL ch7)**

CHRISTIE'S: well-known London salerooms. **(IOA ch10)**

CHRONICLE: took quite a lot of **James Cloyster**'s work. (The *Daily Chronicle* took at least 57 pieces by PGW between September 1902 and September 1906.) **(NGW ptII ch3)**

CHUMPS:

> "He *is* a chump, you know. That's what I love about him. That and the way his ears wiggle when he gets excited. Chumps always make the best husbands. When you marry, Sally, grab a chump. Tap his forehead first, and if it rings solid, don't hesitate. All the the unhappy marriages come from the husband having brains. What good are brains to a man? They only unsettle him."

(TAS ch10)

CHURCH OF ABYSSINIA, the: **Bill** (or **Jane**) **Shannon** persuaded **Phipps** that he had hit **Joe Davenport** with a bottle during an argument about the Claims to Apostolic Succession of ... **(TOR ch14; Colliers-PTR)**

CHURCH LADS ANNUAL OUTING, the: the jamboree of the **Mellingham-in-the-Vale** troop would be all the more exciting for the funds raised at the Jumble Sale from the sale of two old pairs of **Crispin Scrope**'s trousers and a cracked teapot. And, of course, of a valuable miniature donated by **Barney Clayborne**. **(TGI ch11,12)**

CHURCHILL, the Rt Hon Sir Winston, KG, PC, MP (1874-1965): there were things up with which he would not put and in this respect he was imitated by **Bill Shannon**. **(TOR ch11)**

CICERO: an American town which hosted bootleggers' conventions. **(HOW ch5)**

CINCINNATI: where people's lives were very drab until **April June** caused a riot. But you had to watch out for your watch, or it might be dropped in the **Soup**. In earlier times, when it came to the theatre, it wanted something special. **(TLW ch17; LAG ch4; HOW ch16)**

CINDERELLA: Appleby had been swept off his feet by the charms of the principal girl playing ... when he had attended his first pantomime at the tender age of twelve. **(DBB ch11)**

CIRO'S: where **Smedley Cork** unbent sufficiently to invite **Joe Davenport** to stay. **(TOR ch6)**

CITY AND HOME COUNTIES BANK: where **George Holbeton** proposed to cash **J B Duff**'s cheque at the earliest opportunity. **(QUS ch17)**

CLAINES HALL: a Tudor mansion in **Loose Chippings**, Sussex purchased by **Mrs Steptoe**. Telephone number: Loose Chippings 803. **(QUS ch1)**

CLARA: the pie-faced girl whom **Percy** loved. **(SUM ch21)**

CLARENCE: like **Fido**, a name which a dog may be able to get over, but which makes him start with a handicap. **(MLF-BIS)**

CLARICE: the 'best little girl in Flatbush', she was happily reconciled to **Phil Brown**. **(JTR ch9)**

CLAYBORNE, Bernadette ('Barney'): the sister of **Homer Pyle**, she was arrested for shoplifting at **Guildenstern's Stores**. She was a middle-aged widow, full of mischief, with a policy of direct action and with plenty of friends such as **Bill Scrope**. She hit **Jerry West** over the head when he sneezed in her cupboard at **Millingham Hall**; she volunteered to take **Crispin Scope**'s role in the watering-local-police-constables sketch; and she took the lead in arranging the forthcoming marriage between herself and **Crispin Scrope**. **(TGI)**

CLAYBORNE, Wally: a late handsome dynamic pet of the sporting set who had married **Barney** for her money. **(USTGI ch15)**

CLAYBOURNE, Wally: both the Barrie and Jenkins and the later Penguin editions insist that **Barney**'s husband was both 'U' and 'non-U'. **(TGI ch15)**

CLEAN DOLLARS:

> [Mrs Hignett] was halfway across the Atlantic with a complete itinerary booked, before ninety per cent of the poets and philosophers had finished sorting out their clean dollars and getting their photographs taken for the passport.

Thus ran the 1961 Digit paperback film tie-in edition, the earlier editions seeming to prefer the more credible 'clean collars'. This presumably represents the true origin of the expression 'money-laundering', a concept which the *Oxford English Dictionary* dates back only to 1973. **(GOB (Digit) ch1)**

CLEAR SPRING: the brand name of the table-water in which **Mavis Todd** and her brother **Chester** held a controlling interest. **(FRL ch5)**

CLEGHORN: one of five acquaintances of **Jane Abbott** not known to **Joe Vanringham**. **(SUM ch5)**

CLERKENWELL: the district of London where **P C Keating** caught **Spider Buffin**. **(TUW-MIS)**

CLEOPATRA (c69-30BC): **Archie Moffam** would have been immune from her charms even if he had had to extract a fly from their eyes. If she, **Helen of Troy, Hedy Lamarr, Lily Langtry** and **La Belle Dame Sans Merci** had paraded together past **Joe Davenport** in one-piece bathing suits, he claimed that he would not even have whistled at them. **(IOA ch13; TOR ch13)**

CLEVELAND, Grover: one of the names given by a male guest in Room 618 of the **Hotel Cosmopolis** following a sing-song and a raid. **(Strand-PWM)**

CLOUSTON, J Storer: the author of *The Lunatic at Large Again*, a story which was serialised simultaneously with **GOB** and which also featured a character hiding in a suit of armour. **(GOB-Preface)**

CLOYSTER, James Orlebar: a self-centred young journalist, some of whose characterictics and adventures resemble those of the young Wodehouse, and others those of the young **Herbert Westbrook**, co-author of the book in which he appears. He had been educated at Cambridge, where he had managed a third class honours in the classical tripos. We first met him as he fell out of a dinghy off the coast of Guernsey and into the path of **Margaret Goodwin**, with whom he fell in love. Deciding to defer marriage until he had made his name as a writer in London, he took a cheap and dingy hotel in York Street, and then moved successively to 93a **Manresa Road** and Walpole Street.

In the first year of his literary career he submitted 53 articles to editors, of which two were published, but became more successful as a poet, being able generally to place two verses a week at a guinea each. After he joined the *Orb*, he met **Julian Eversleigh** and his love for Margaret was put on a back-burner as he fell for Julian's cousin **Eva**. Despite increasing his earnings to over £1,000 per annum he still failed to honour his obligation to Margaret and sought to disguise the extent of his earnings by appointing three agents through whom he submitted his material, a scheme which, though ingenious, was to rebound and require him to become dependent on a woman for true happiness. **(NGW)**

CLUNK: was **J B Duff**'s osteopath. **(QUS ch2,3)**

CLUTTERBUCK, J Russell: an American publisher, of the firm **Winch and Clutterbuck**, with a summer house in **Bensonburg**, who went to Paris searching for **Jefferson d'Escrignon** to confirm a deal after receiving his manuscript for publication. He was one of those Americans who bulged opulently in all directions, with a round face, round eyes and round spectacles, but despite his apparent surplus flesh he had already been able to persuade three individuals to take the name **Mrs Clutterbuck**. **(FRL ch1,7,8,10)**

CLUTTERBUCK, Mrs (the third): though the best little woman in the world, she did not understand her husband, **Russell**. She suffered from mumps, chicken-pox (complete with pink spots) and measles twice. **(FRL ch8)**

COBB, Police Constable: of Millbourne, Hampshire, was verbally routed by the cockney batteries of **Sally Preston** when informing her that her puppy had no collar, contrary to regulations, but he nevertheless had the last word. **(TMU-STW)**

COBBOLD, Lady Adela: see **Topping, Adela**

COBBOLD, Lady Clare: the second daughter of the **fifth Earl of Shortlands**, she was the type of girl who went about the English countryside in brogues and tweeds, stealing her father's grease-stained favourite hat for the vicar's jumble sale and generally meddling so vigorously in the lives of the peasants that one wonders how England escaped a Reign of Terror. It was she who came across the stamp album which caused so much grief to so many, and Clare then compounded her many faults by becoming engaged to **Cosmo Blair. (SPF ch3,4,18)**

COBBOLD, G Ellery: a stout economic royalist of Great Neck, NY, who looked like a cartoon of 'Capital' in a Labour magazine. For a Republican he was inordinately proud of his blue-blooded descent from the same stock as the **Earl of Shortlands**, through a connection in about 1700, and was comparably shocked to hear of his son's proposed *mésalliance* with a celluloid star. Perhaps the period of his life which he would most wish to have hidden was when he employed the putative criminal **Mervyn Spink. (SPF)**

COBBOLD, Stanwood: the son of **G Ellery** was a doughty All-American footballer whose enormous frame, a mass of bone and muscle, concealed a heart of gold but could not conceal a face like a hippopotamus. In his father's view the bone extended throughout his head, although a more charitable view was taken by his friend **Mike Cardinal**. His inability to keep a secret, thought Mike, had been inherited from a mother who had been frightened by a BBC announcer. Stanwood was an old friend of **Terry Cobbold** and actually became engaged to her during a misunderstanding involving his fiancée, **Eileen Stoker**, and Mike. This did not last long, and neither did his aspirations to be an impostor for after having allowed Mike Cardinal to impersonate him at **Beevor Castle**, he went there himself as **Rossiter**, a philatelist, and was discovered immediately. **(SPF)**

COBBOLD, Lady Teresa: the youngest of the **Cobbold** clan, she was an old friend of the distantly related **Stanwood** and on one occasion, to get away from the stifling atmosphere of **Beevor**, she spent a month in the chorus of a musical comedy on the London stage. She resembled in looks her late mother, in her day one of London's prettiest debs. So she was slim, blue-eyed and fair-haired, with the sort of oomph which made strong men quiver and straighten their ties. And her nature was beautiful, kind, gentle, dovelike and sweet, except, it seemed, when rejecting **Mike Cardinal**'s advances on the grounds that he was a flippertygibbet and she did not trust him. She became engaged to him after he kissed her, though, only to become engaged also to Stanwood through a misunderstanding. **(SPF)**

COBO BAY: a prawn-gathering centre of Guernsey. **(NGW ptI ch2)**

COCKBURN, Charlie: at the **St George's Theatre**, would probably become the director of **Cosmo Blair**'s next play. **(SPF ch10)**

CODGER: of Sussex C C C, used a bat, not an umbrella, when making his pretty late cut through the slips. **(NSE-HTU)**

COFFEE-HOUSE: one of the resorts of the artist, author, actor or Bohemian to which **Archie Moffam** was introduced by his new American friends. **(IOA ch4)**

COHAN, George M (1878-1942): featured on **Aubrey Devine**'s list of the seven most prominent men in the United States. **Charlie Ferris** wanted to hear what he had said to **Willie Collier** about the Lambs. **(VanFair-AAI; SatEvePost-ATG)**

COHEN AND CORCORAN: Weatherby and **Chibnall** were said to be like ... **(QUS ch9)**

COHN, Jacob: one of the partners in **Goble and Cohn**, producers of musical comedies such as *Coralie*. **(JTR ch10; Cosmo-FFD)**

COINCIDENCE: the zero on the roulette-board of life. **(TMU-RIE)**

COLEMAN, Eustace: the **Mallow Hall** butler, meagre in size but with a full head of hair, he had become a widower after many stormy years of matrimony. He allowed **Appleby** to deputise for him on payment of £100. **(DBB ch2)**

COLLIER, Willie: Charlie Ferris wanted to hear what **Georgie Cohan** had said to him about the Lambs. **(SatEvePost-ATG)**

COLMAN, Ronald (1891-1958): Joey Cooley was to be taught to speak in an in-between voice, like that of ... In one of his pictures, a wire-haired terrier had made a big hit. **(LAG ch14; Aldin-GOW)**

COLNEY HATCH: to where **Tom Ellison** thought **Farmer Rollitt** should be removed. **(TUW-TDH)**

COLNEY HATCH ARGUS, The: its editor was likely to be the only person to have accepted work of the type submitted in his early career by **James Orlebar Cloyster**. **(NGW ptII ch2)**

COLOSSAL-EXQUISITE: the **Hollywood** studio which was expected to offer $50,000 for the diary of the late **Carmen Flores**. **(TOR ch7)**

COLOSSAL-SUPERHUMAN: another **Hollywood** studio, whose representative thought that **Sergeant Ward** lacked dramatic intensity. **(TOR ch16)**

COLUMBUS ECHO AND VESPUCCI INTELLIGENCER, The: gave the first **Van Puyster** in America a column and a half. **(Colliers-PAP)**

COME ON IN: the first show in which **Pearl Delahay** had appeared but it closed in Schenectady after prospective audiences failed to respond. **(Strand-BTG)**

CONEY ISLAND: **Katie Bennett** had never been to ... with its Dreamland, Luna Park, Scenic Railway and Steeplechase. **(MLF-CRH)**

CONNOLLY, Aloysius: the well-known American labour leader, who called a strike among building operators working on **Dan Brewster**'s new hotel after a man was sacked for loafing. He was a stout, square-faced individual of commanding personality, doubtful of **Archie Moffam**'s capabilities:

> "He says he's the manager of your new hotel," said Mr Connolly. "Is that right?"
>
> "I suppose so," said Mr Brewster, gloomily.
>
> "Then I'm doing you a kindness," said Mr Connolly, "in not letting it be built."

(IOA ch24)

CONNOLLY, Mrs: the mother of **Aloysius**, who had seen her son off to New York from their home-town station some thirty years earlier. **(IOA ch24)**

CONNOLLY, One-Eyed: according to **Tubby Vanringham**, the only person barred from being a paying guest at **Walsingham Hall**. **(Pearson-SUM)**

CONSOLIDATED NAIL FILE AND EYEBROW TWEEZER CORPORATION, the: of Scranton, Pennsylvania, was at a loss to understand the business deal which **Ellery Cobbold** tried to cobble together. **(SPF ch1)**

CONSOLIDATED PEA-NUTS: were down twenty points thanks to the attentions of **Bruce Bishop** and his gang. **(JTR ch12)**

CONSUL, THE ALMOST HUMAN: a nickname given to **Henry Mortimer** by the servants' hall, and to the **second Earl of Havershot**. **(GOB ch10; LAG ch3)**

CONTENTED EXPRESSION:

> Professor Binstead had picked up a small china figure of delicate workmanship. It represented a warrior of pre-khaki days advancing with a spear upon some adversary who, judging from the contented expression on the warrior's face, was smaller than himself.

(IOA ch2)

COOKSON, Charlie: a friend of **Sidney Price** and follower of **Dan Leno**, who got fined if he was late to work. **(NGW ptII ch17,19)**

COOLEY, Joey: a child film star of singular personal beauty, with the ability to sprint and throw oranges but not to engage in unarmed combat. He may have changed his name from **Teddy Flower**, as this was the handle given to the character in the original appearance in *This Week*. He was known for a time as the 'Idol of American Motherhood', and had co-starred with **April (or Hazel) June** in at least one movie. He enjoyed a normal range of juvenile pursuits, such as eating candy until his teeth demanded the attention of **B K Burwash**, painting red noses on statues and inserting toads in the bed of dictatorial tyrants. Such was the confusing nature of the revelations concerning this fourteen-year-old's adventures in the fourth dimension, that we are forced to refer to his actions whilst assuming a second *persona* as **Reggie Havershot** as those of **JC(RH)**, and it was while so disguised that he was able to use his inherited strength and poke a considerable proportion of his enemies in the snoot. **(LAG; Pearson-LAG)**

COOPER, Gary (Frank James Cooper, 1901-1961): **Patrolman Morehouse** and **Sergeant Ward** were destined to be bigger movie stars than ... **(TOR ch20)**

COOPER, (Dame) Gladys (Constance, 1888-1971): **Nigger**'s mother was no ... **(MLF-HMV)**

COOTES, Ada: the loyal secretary to **Mike Bond**, she was short and stocky, keen on detective novels and quick to prevent rannygzoo. Thus she inserted her weapon between the legs of a fleeing crook,

The Earl of Havershot and Joey Cooley prepare for their return to normal life

Adela Cork decides to put the Carmen Flores diary in the safe

hit inebriated citizens with umbrellas and got herself locked in a safe. Though not possessed of a face capable of launching a thousand ships, and having instead the square sturdy figure of a London Scottish scrum-half, she still had the confidence to say "I love to cook. I suppose it's because I'm so good at it." We wish her well with her retired **Horace Appleby. (DBB ch2,5,9,12)**

COOTES, Mr: **Ada**'s father, who had been a butler until his retirement. **(DBB ch2)**

COOTIE:

> "What's the use, Freddie, between old pals?" said Algy, protestingly. "You know perfectly well that Underhill's a cootie of the most pronounced order, and that, when he found out that Jill hadn't any money, he chucked her."

In the book versions, the word 'worm' had been used instead. **(Colliers-TLW ch8)**

COPPER, Bill: the jockey who would be riding **Brotherly Love. (TGI ch8)**

COPPER KETTLE, The: a **Wellingford** or **Wallingford** tea shoppe. **(DBB ch2; USDBB ch2)**

CORALIE: a musical comedy produced by **Goble and Cahn** (or **Goble and Cohn**). It was about the same time, 1928, that *Rosalie*, a show in which Wodehouse had played a significant role, was a Broadway hit. **(Strand-BTG; Cosmo-FFD)**

CORDELIA: see **King Lear**

CORELLI, Marie (Mary Mackay, 1855-1924): a real swell when it came to writing, though she didn't push out something every day. A copy of her complete works was one of the many presents sent to **Marion Ringwood** by **Chester Bassett**. See also **Henry James. (NGW ptII ch13; TMU-POM; LHJ-FKA)**

CORK, Adela Shannon: formidable is the word to describe this former film star of the silent screen, known to the world as the **Empress of Stormy Emotion**. She was tall, dark, large and stately, with slumbrous eyes which could, and did, light up in a baleful blaze, all in all having something of the look of portraits by **Louise de Querouaille**. Each of her three late husbands had curled up before her like carbon-paper, and aging film directors continued to wake in the night, having dreamed that they were back in pre-talkie days, arguing some technical point with the

Empress. Now owner of the **Carmen Flores Place**, she permitted her brother-in-law **Smedley Cork** to live with her, and otherwise displayed occasional human emotions, such as succumbing to blackmail when the threat is one of worms down the back of the neck. **(TOR)**

CORK, Alfred: the late millionaire brother of **Smedley**, who achieved the distinction of marrying **Adela Shannon**, the world-famous film-star of the silent screen days. He won further fame, though posthumous, by being run over by a rubberneck motor-coach and leaving a will in which he enjoined his wife to 'support' Smedley after his death, this term being interpreted by Adela as restricted to a bed, three meals a day and all the yoghurt he did not want. **(TOR ch1,2)**

CORK, Christopher Robin: one of the many aliases of **Herbert Higgs**. **(Ellery-MBD)**

CORK, Smedley: the unhappy brother of the late **Alfred**, he was forced to eke out a miserable existence as a pensioner of his formidable sister-in-law **Adela**. Despite this, he remained a large, stout, elderly man who looked like a Roman emperor who had been doing himself too well on starchy foods and forgetting to watch his calories. Once wealthy, he had made himself **Hollywood**'s leading angel, which had rapidly caused a diminution in his fortunes. His final few thousands had been swallowed by a sweet little whimsical comedy adapted from the French, which ran from a Friday opening until the end of the week. He was now lazy, selfish, idle, encumbered with two chins and as confirmed a bachelor as ever knew **Bill** (or **Jane**) **Shannon** for twenty-five years without proposing. The clause in Alfred's will which enjoined Adela to support Smedley unfortunately did so in language which was equivocal, so that she could and interpret it as meaning that he could do what he liked as long as he did what he was told. **(TOR; Colliers-PTR)**

CORKER, Harry: an old acquaintance of **Augustus Robb**, known as 'Old Suction Pump', who once broke into a house while under the influence, caught hold of the safe as it came round the second time, twiddled the knobs and got dance music from a Continental station. **(SPF ch8)**

CORNED BEEF HASH BETTY GRABLE: a choice dish at the studio commissary. **(TOR ch2)**

COROT, Jean Baptiste Camille (1796-1875): Claines Hall displayed a painting from his Italian period. **(QUS ch7)**

CORTES, Hernando (1485-1547): James Cloyster appreciated his feelings as he stared with eagle eyes at the Pacific.

And so did *Punch*, as Oliver Wise recalled to the writer a short poem in a long-forgotten issue:

> There can't have been an R S P C A
> In Panama, on that auspicious day
> When Cortes, quite the stoutest of his men,
> Stood silent – upon a Peke – in Darien.

(NGW ptII ch1)

COSMOPOLIS HOTEL: see **Hotel Cosmopolis**

COSY CORNER: accepted the first story from **Alexander Tudway**, which set him on his way to what might have been a glittering career had he not tried too hard to encourage budding talent. **(Throne-KHE)**

COURTELINE, Georges: his work was the principal inspiration for the personality of **Old Nick. (FRL preface,** and see **Appendix 4)**

COURTNEIDGE: tried to get **Rice** but failed. **(MLF-BTB)**

COUSINS EVA, GERALDINE and PERCY: George Balmer's, they were children of his **Uncle Robert** and **Aunt Louisa. (TMU-TTM)**

CQD CALL: this seems to have been the plea for help which was made on behalf of damsels in distress in the days before the SOS had been invented. The dictionaries tell us that 'CQ' were the communication letters used at the beginning of radiograms of general information, or safety notices, or by short-wave amateurs on the radio as an invitation to other short wave amateurs to talk. The letters stood for 'Call to Quarters'. **(Pearson-SAG; Colliers-SAG)**

CRACKNELL, Reginald: a young 'Millionaire Kid' with butter-coloured hair, who had been at Harvard with **Fillmore Nicholas,** and was the reputed owner of the largest private collection of alcohol in the world. He also collected actresses, the latest acquisition being blonde **Mabel Hobson** of the Follies whom he planned to star in *The Primrose Way*. **(TAS ch1,6,16)**

CRANE, Sidney: the suspected principal baritone of *The Girl From Brighton* company. **(MLF-BTB)**

CRANE, Mrs Sidney: was suspicious about the principal baritone of *The Girl From Brighton* company, on whom she sicked the detective strength of **Stafford's International Bureau**. She replaced the unpopular **Clarice Weaver** as leading lady in the show. **(MLF-BTB)**

CRAPS: an American gambling game played with dice, also known as 'rolling the bones', during which the use of such evocative and sometimes meaningless expressions as 'Come, eleven', 'Come, little seven' and 'Baby needs new shoes' are mandatory. **(JTR ch6)**

CREMORNE: a mahogany derelict, who spent his youth on the sea when liners were sailing-ships. **(NGW ptII ch6)**

CREOSOTE, a female: **Mrs Barlow** told **Joss Weatherby** that **Mrs Chavender** was ... **(QUS ch13)**

CRIPPEN, Dr (1861-1910): an example of a gifted man who was notoriously unlucky in his love life. **(DBB ch9)**

CRIPPS, Sir (Richard) Stafford (1889-1952): would not let **Lord Topham** take a solitary dashed penny out of the country. Topham's pals told him it was because Sir S was afraid he would only spend it foolishly, and that is presumably what P G Wodehouse himself thought when he reached the USA in 1947 and found that his bank accounts in England were frozen for the duration. **(Colliers-PTR)**

CRŒSUS (fl 6th cent BC): if he had applied to live in the stone apartment house at 18 E57th Street, New York, which **Chris Selby** used as a postal address, the authorities would probably have looked upon him a little doubtfully at first and hinted at the desirability of a month's rent in advance. **Joe Davenport** regarded **Smedley Cork** as a ... . **(JTR ch9; TOR ch3)**

CROMWELL, Oliver (1599-1658): was not renowned as a respecter of other people's property. **George Balmer** felt himself to be a blend of **Sir Galahad**, ... and a Berserk warrior when the croupier declined to pay out on a losing bet. On discovering just who had been attacking **P C Keating**, **Spider Buffin** must have felt as Cromwell did at Dunbar when the Scots left their strongholds on the hills and came down to the open plain. **(LAG ch2; TMU-TTM; TUW-MIS)**

CRUSHED PANSY: the restaurant with a soul (and possibly a sole), where **Lancelot Bingley** suggested to **Gladys Wetherby** that their projected union should go ahead the following week. **(PLP-GCS)**

CRUSOE, Robinson:

> [Mr Bennett] suddenly became aware of something bright and yellow resting beside [his] watch, and paused, transfixed, like Robinson Crusoe staring at the footprint in the sand. If he had not been in England, he would have said it was a patch of sunshine.

(GOB ch10)

CRYSTAL PALACE: the scene of a Cup Final between **Houndsditch Wednesday** and **Manchester United**. **Nigger** asked **Jack** about prizes and ribbons he might have won at competitions held there. **(TMU-TGP; MLF-HMV)**

CRYSTAL PALACE CAT SHOW: if **Algy Wynbrace** had escorted **Marion Ringwood** to the ..., **Chester Bassett** would not have seen **Alexander**, and Marion might well have become Algy's. **(LHJ-FKA)**

CUNARD: ran a fleet of ships which were well spoken of. **(JTR ch6)**

CUPID OR MAMMON: in the *Nosegay Novelette* series, featured a girl who had to choose between the humble suitor or her parents' choice of a wealthy man. **(GOB ch15)**

CURFEW SHALL NOT RING TONIGHT, The: **Robert Ferguson** wondered whether every girl who had recited ... in front of a rustic audience without being lynched had been seized with the prospect of stardom on the stage. **(TMU-MMM)**

CURIOUS FREAKS OF ECCENTRIC TESTATORS: one of eleven articles by **James Orlebar Cloyster** which were rejected by three magazines in two weeks. **(NGW ptII ch2)**

CURIOUS SCENES IN CHURCH: another of the eleven. **(NGW ptII ch2)**

CURSE, the: Freddie Rooke's name for **Lady Underhill**. **(JTR ch1)**

CUTHBERT: was engaged to **Mae D'Arcy**. **(JTR ch16)**

CYRIL: **Young Kelly**'s cousin who was noted for killing rats with his teeth. **(SUM ch14)**

DAFFODIL DAYS: a newly published work by **Vera Upshaw**. **(TGI ch3,5)**

DAILY EXPRESS: **Bill**[1] thought a sheet from the ... might have been substituted for his normal *Daily Mail*, as the bottom of his cage did not taste as good as usual. **(JTR ch5)**

DAILY MAIL: the Paris edition was offered to a fleeing **George Balmer**. The English edition had a superior flavour, and reported **Joe Vanrigham**'s play as "Sparkling satire". **(JTR ch5; SUM ch3; TMU-TTM)**

DAILY MIRROR: carried a photograph of **Lady Beatrice Bracken**. **(HOW ch12)**

DAILY TELEGRAPH: reported **Joe Vanrigham**'s play as "mordant and satirical". **(SUM ch3)**

DALLAS, Reginald: the donor of the unfortunate dog **Tommy** to **Sylvia Reynolds** but he was tactless in the way he showed off his collection of braces. After his proposal of marriage had been scuppered by her father, he was rewarded for his abstemiousness in the matter of providing a replacement pug by Sylvia's disproportionately grateful parent. **(TUW-WPS)**

DALY: made a home-run. **(MLF-OTN)**

DAMOCLES (fl 4th cent BC): might have been expected to jump in fear at a sudden noise. **(SPF ch12)**

DAMON (fl 4th cent BC): like ... and Pythias, **Rufus Bennett** and **Henry Mortimer** had had a friendship which neither woman could mar nor death destroy. Or so Rufus had imagined. **(TMM ch10)**

DANCING:

> "If you want to dance, you've got to provide yourself with a girl, haven't you? How long do you think it would take the management at the Trocadero to bounce a fellow who started pirouetting all over the floor by himself?"

(SPF ch17)

DANGERS OF DIANA, The: a series of moving pictures in which the heroine was in the sort of position **Billie Bennett** imagined herself to be in with **John Peters**. (**GOB ch13**)

DANIEL (fl 6th cent BC): tentatively threaded his way through a den of lions. (**HOW ch12**)

DANTE, Alighieri (1265-1321): did not take kindly to being smirked at. Had he be shown through the *Inferno* by **Virgil**, and had Virgil opened a door in the very heart of the yellow soap zone to reveal a small bedroom and a cracked pitcher he, like **Joss Weatherby**, would have shaken his head. Although most people consider that he had spoken the last word on the *post mortem* arrangements for housing the criminal classes, **Peter Rayner** thought he could have given him a few new ideas after his first week at the **Rastall-Retfords'**. (**HOW ch9; QUS ch7; TUW-BSA**)

d'ARCY, Mae: the languorous chorine of *The Rose of America*, known to her friends as 'the Duchess'. (**JTR ch11,16**)

DATCHET, first Earl of: carried the bag of **William the Conqueror** down the gangway. (**Strand-JOW**)

DATCHET, Earl of: by reputation an average sort of rotter, this son-in-law of **Franklyn Bivatt** specialised in aristocratic idleness, an inherited skill, for his family had never worked. (**Strand-JOW**)

DAUBENY STREET: a Pimlico thoroughfare where the sun never penetrated, and was always dingy and depressing despite the brightness of such inhabitants as **Nellie Bryant** and **Bill**[1]. (**JTR ch5**)

DAVENPORT, Joe: loved the gravely attractive young **Kay Shannon**, to whom he proposed at a number of places including the **Purple Chicken**, and when her eyes were intently fixed upon him, he felt as if some hidden hand had introduced an eggwhisk into his soul and begun to rotate it. Kay's doubts about accepting him revolved in part around the existence of his little red book of telephone numbers, she being unconvinced that they were in reality all chunks of the dead past. After having written cowboy stories for the pulps, and worked and been fired alongside **Bill** (or **Jane**) **Shannon** at **Superba-Llewellyn**, Joe was resting whilst he contemplated what should be his next career, which was likely to be the creation of a literary agency in partnership with Bill (or Jane). **(TOR; Colliers-PTR)**

DAVENPORT-SIMMS, Eustace: though he still played cricket for Essex or Sussex or somewhere, he was emphatically no longer engaged to **Clarissa Binstead. (NSE-HTU)**

DAVID (c1060-970BC): like ... and Jonathan, **Rufus Bennett** and **Henry Mortimer** had had a friendship which neither woman could mar nor death destroy. Or so Rufus had imagined. Yes, dear reader, you have seen these honeyed words before. Try **Damon**.

Goliath could not have made a better target practice for David's throwing skills than did **Orlando Flower** for the oranges hurled by **RH(JC). (TMM ch10; LAG ch16)**

DAVIS, Mrs: the cook at **Mallow Hall**, who sprained her ankle tripping over **Thomas. (DBB ch5)**

DAWKINS: had been the chairman of that smoking-concert at the **Barrel Club** on the occasion when he was debagged by **Druids. (NGW ptII ch8)**

DAWN OF HOPE: a cocktail so named because it cheered one up. **(Strand-JOW)**

DAY DREAMS: the title of a picture which by rights should have been called *Venus*. **(IOA ch25)**

DAY OF JUDGMENT, the: it was not done for a well-bred Londoner to be addressed unexpectedly by a stranger.

> Absolutely it wasn't done. During an earthquake or a shipwreck and possibly on the Day of Judgment, yes. But only then.

(JTR ch2)

DEAR ABBY: an *Advice to the Lovelorn* column on one of the American papers. **(TGI ch6)**

DEBENHAM: the name of the family who came to own the former **Mariner** family home in Worcestershire. **(JTR ch13)**

DELACOUR, George: see **Norcross, Minna**

DELAHAY: one of **Willoughby Scrope**'s partners, who needed a consultation about the ... business. **(TGI ch3)**

DELAHAY, Pearl: the stage and maiden name of Pearl Gooch, who was in the chorus of *Ask Dad* when it opened but was transferred to the second company when it was ready to go on tour. When the show reached her home town of **Franklin**, Pearl was given the chance to play a bigger role but merely proved that she would be better off at home with her husband **Brewster** and young son **Elmer. (Strand-BTG)**

DE LA HOURMERIE, M.: the director of the department at the **Ministry of Dons and Legs** in which **Old Nick** occasionally practised his profession, so occasionally that when a member of staff told him that Nick was in the office M de La H thought he was being trifled with. He was a small, stout man of pug-dog appearance who traced Nick as far as Paris in pursuit of the Dossier **Quibolle** after being hit on the head with a hatchet by another member of his staff, **M Letondu. (FRL ch2,6)**

DELANE, Vera: the fiancée of **Prosser**, who three times received unstamped letters from her bank to her home at Woodlands, Southbourne, Hants. **(TMU-POM)**

DE L'HOURMERIE, M.: an alternative version of spelling **M de la Hourmerie**'s name. **(JohnBull-FRL)**

DELILAH (fl 11th cent BC): it was not she who was the Biblical creature who reminded **Lord Plumpton** of **Clarissa**, for her work was not so raw as that of **Jezebel. (SPF ch21; NSE-HTU)**

DE MILLE, Cecil B (Blount, 1881-1959): the **Carmen Flores Place** creaked at night, dating back to the ... period. **(TOR ch16; USTOR ch16)**

DEMPSEY, Jack (William Harrison, 1895-1983): had once struck a bad patch, but his bout with **Carpentier** had been a landmark in pugilistic roughstuff. **(GOB ch17; DBB ch7)**

DENHAM, Lois: a willowy, blond chorus girl who was the recipient of diamond sunbursts from her boyfriend, **Izzy** of the hat check. **(JTR ch11,15)**

DENVILLE, John: a Johnsonville, Michigan, resident whose house was broken into about midnight by **Caesar Bones. (NGW ptII ch5)**

DEPUTY ASSISTANT LYRIST (or LYRIC WRITER): of *Coralie*, who had a habit of chewing pencils. **(Strand-BTG; Cosmo-FFD)**

DE QUEROUAILLE, Louise, Duchess of Portsmouth (1649-1734): her imperious look, as reproduced on portraits, made the beholder appreciate the steely nerve which **King Charles II** must have had to associate with anything so formidable. **(TOR ch4)**

DER HARRAS, Rudolph: advised **William Tell** to beg for his life. **(WTT ch11)**

DESBOROUGH-SMITH: another acquaintance of **Joe Vanringham** one of six who was not known to **Jane Abbott**. **(SUM ch5)**

d'ESCRIGNON, Jefferson, Comte: the eldest son and heir of the **Marquis de Maufringneuse et Valerie-Moberanne**, by his first marriage, who maintained a modest bed-sitter in the Rue de Jacob, Paris, where he worked with modest success as a purveyor of popular fiction. Jeff was a striking young man, being tall, dark and wiry, with a humorous mouth and quick brown eyes. He had moved to America almost immediately after his father's second marriage until the outbreak of war, when he returned to France and became a member of the Maquis, and was still only fourteen when he received a battlescar on the cheek. Falling in love with **Terry Trent** made him revert to type, for he kissed her and murmured "Je t'aime" and "Je t'adore", but then avoided her as he was under the impression she was rich. On his return from an important meeting with his publisher in Paris, he was subjected to an unprovoked assault with a door by Police Commissioner **Boissonade**, which did his prospects with Terry no harm at all. **(FRL)**

DETECTIVE, a: appointed by **Freddie Rooke** in New York to find **Jill Mariner**, he looked like Freddie's **Uncle Ted**. **(JTR ch13)**

DETROIT: when it came to the theatre, it was a city which would take anything. **(TLW ch17)**

DETROIT DORA: proved not to be the woman whom **McGee** thought he recognised. **(Ellery-MBD)**

DEVEREUX, Janice: a fictional detective who impersonated a maid in order to detect criminals trying to burgle a safe in a country house. **(HOW ch8)**

DEVEREUX, Ronny: a crony of **Freddie Rooke** and **Algy Martyn** with a commendable talent for clocking human ticks. He boxed for the Varsity in his final year at Cambridge, and broke the news of the broken engagement between **Jill Mariner** and **Derek Underhill** to Freddie. **(JTR ch1,8)**

DEVINE, Aubrey Rockmetteller: after marrying **Adelaide Brewster Moggs** he was unable to retain his own personality, being known everywhere simply as 'A... B... M...'s husband', which gave him a feeling of disembodied spirituality. He could not box or fox-trot, but he could and did plunge into the Hudson River to rescue **Genevieve O'Grady**, but it was still A... B... M...'s husband who received public acclaim for the feat. **(VanFair-AAI)**

DEVINE, Matilda: Max Faucitt once played under her banner at the old Royalty in London, and **Elsa Doland** reminded him of her. **(TAS ch5)**

DIALOGUES OF MAYFAIR: an article by **James Cloyster**, published through the medium of **Sidney Price**. **(NGW ptII ch13)**

DICEY, Pauline: roller-skated for an hour with a black-moustached knight while her fiancé floundered in Mug's Alley. **(TMU-WDD)**

DICK: the groom at **Peter's father**'s house, the owner of **Jack**. **(MLF-BIS)**

DICKENS, Charles (1812-1870): his characters had been portrayed, with the assistance of hats and false hair, at ships' concerts. **Chester Bassett** had bought a parrot for **Marion Ringwood** as the two of them slummed it through ...'s London. **(GOB ch6; LHJ-FKA)**

DICKON: a plug-ugly guard who fell out with **Walt** over love for a kitchen-maid. **(TMU-SAG)**

DICK THE SNATCHER: a kidnapper well known to the police. **(MLF-BIS)**

DISTRICT MESSENGER BOYS: were asked by **Jean Priaulx** to take **Alexander** in a hat-box to a Cat's Home. **(TMU-MWD)**

DIX, Dorothy: knew better than to help oneself to the wine of a person you have just insulted, and would have been able to advise **Bill Shannon** as to whether on the evidence **Kay Shannon** loved **Joe Davenport**. **(TOR ch4; FRL ch6)**

DOCTOR: a young man called in by **Mrs Pickett** to inspect the body of the deceased **Captain Gunner**. His suspicion that Gunner had been poisoned proved to be accurate. **(TUW-DAE)**

DOCTOR CUPID: the author of the *In the Consulting Room* column for *Fireside Chat*. **(TMU-WDD)**

DOCTOR JOYCE BROTHERS, the: ran an *Advice to the Lovelorn* column on one of the American papers. **(TGI ch6)**

DODSON, Jacob[1]: a Manchester football museum curator, who owned the **Meredith** ball and was a friend of **Daniel Rackstraw[1]**. **(TMU-TGP)**

DODSON, Jacob[2]: a Detroit baseball fanatic, who owned the bat which **Hans Wagner** had used as a boy, and was a friend of **Daniel Rackstraw[2]**. **(Colliers-PAP)**

DOG: an anonymous example suffered the extreme penalty whilst **Captain Muller** was experimenting with the effects of venom extracted from a cobra. **(TUW-DAE)**

DOGFOOD:

> By the time it was evening I was thoroughly miserable. I found a shoe and an old clothes-brush in one of the rooms, but could eat nothing.

(MLF-HMV)

DOLAND, Elsa: a pretty actress with big eyes, she made a big hit when taking over the leading role in *A Primrose Way*. In her private life she was less successful, however, stealing **Gerald Foster** from his fiancée **Sally Nicholas**, joining **Goble and Kahn** also to the detriment of Sally's fortunes and entering into a marriage which, we learnt on the best authority, went 'blooey'. **(TAS ch1,5,8,10,14)**

DOLLEN: expressed his views on time in 1863 in *Die Zeitbestimmung Vermittelst Des Tragbaren Durchgangsinstruments Im Verticale des Polarsterns*, subsequently made into a musical by **Rodgers** and **Hammerstein** under the title *North Atlantic*. **(TOR ch17)**

DOLLY SISTERS: see **Castle, Mrs**

DONAHUE, Mr: an American gentleman, now alas deceased, who had often travelled on a plane on which **Jane Hunnicutt** was working as an air hostess. He had always appeared to be in a bad temper, but had obviously developed a softer spot for her than he had for the Revenue authorities, as he ignored them for fifteen years and tried to leave her all his money when he died. **(TGI ch2,13)**

DONAHUE, Officer: a taciturn gentleman, he allowed the left corner of his mouth to twitch slightly. **(IOA ch6)**

DONAHUE, Plug: taught **Gordon Carlisle** how to bust safes. **(HOW ch10)**

DORMAN, George: the 10-year-old son of **Mr Dorman** and grandson of **Mrs D** who was clipped over the ear by **Prosser** for blowing a trumpet. **(TMU-POM)**

DORMAN, Mr: a Shropshire farmer who let out rooms for such as **Prosser** and **Owen Bentley** to relax in whilst on vacation. **(TMU-POM)**

DORMAN, Mrs: the aged mother of **Mr Dorman** who had a local reputation as a wise woman. She forecast that **Prosser** would marry, and that **Owen Bentley** would get pots of money. **(TMU-POM)**

DORM OF THE HILLS, Earl: a small, elderly, furtive individual with eyes set too close together and a weak, cunning smile, who sent the last of his six daughters to **Camelot** for help against fiery dragons. **(TMU-SAG)**

DOSTOEVSKY: spellbound by a magazine. **(Colliers-TLW)**

DOSTOIEVSKY, Fyodor Mikhailovich (1821-1881): handled gloomy scenes with relish. **(JTR ch8)**

DREW, Drexdale: in *The Limehouse Mystery*, he darted to the panel between the bars at the **Blue Chicken** with rapid, silent footsteps, an action later imitated by **Vera Pym** at the **Rose and Crown**. **(QUS ch18)**

DREW, Rev Henry ('Harry'): the captain of the local cricket team who acquiesced in the request by **Tom Ellison** and **Dick Henley** that they should be allowed to open the innings to determine which of the pair would first propose to Harry's fiancée, **Dolly Burn**. **(TUW-TDH)**

DREXDALE CASTLE: the home of the aging but capable **Dowager Duchess of Shropshire**. **(LHJ-FKA)**

DRIVER, Mrs: the landlady at 93a **Manresa Road**, Chelsea. **(NGW ptII ch1)**

DRONES CLUB: the members' club to which both **Reggie Havershot** and **Algy Martyn** belonged, but of course, until Algy showed up,

Freddie Rooke could not be served a cocktail. **(JTR ch8; LAG ch1)**

DRUIDS: a double line of ... performed at the smoking-concert at the **Barrel Club. (NGW ptII ch8)**

DRYDEN, John (1631-1700): opined that sweet was pleasure after pain. **(TGI ch4)**

DUCHESS, the: see **d'Arcy, Mae**

DUCHESSES WHO HAVE MARRIED DUSTMEN: an article which an ungrateful editor returned to **James Cloyster**. **(NGW ptII ch2)**

DUCK, Donald: when **Vera Pym** attempted to utter 250 words in the time more customarily allocated to ten, she sounded like ... **(QUS ch18)**

DUFF, James Buchanan: as the surviving partner of **Duff & Trotter**, this Scottish-American enjoyed an annual income of about $200,000 but his manner generally bore a marked resemblance to something carved by **Epstein** on the morning after a New Year party, and even on a good day he looked like something out of *Revelation*. Once engaged to **Beatrice Chavender**, the match had been broken off owing to his stronger attachment to another, a **Paramount Ham**, and it was fifteen long years before circumstances changed sufficiently for the belated match to be put through. In his youth Jimmy had been a hammer-thrower of some repute, but after he allowed himself to put on weight his alimentary canal gave him a good deal of trouble. He was still capable of good business ideas, though, such as using **Joss Weatherby**'s portrait of Beatrice as an advertising poster. He terrified **Vera Pym** by appearing at the **Rose and Crown** in a soup-strainer moustache, which she quickly identified as false. **(QUS)**

DUFF AND TROTTER: London's leading provision merchants, which operated from an island site near Regent Street and specialised in **Paramount Ham**s. **(QUS ch1)**

DUKE OF MILAN (Ludovico il Moro Sforza, 1451-1508): was married in 1489. **(MLF-TLF)**

DUKES: ranked higher than **Earls**. **(LAG ch2)**

DUNLOP, T MORTIMER: an **American millionaire** of the first type, with purple face, red hands, bald head, wheezy voice and a penchant for **Dawns of Hope** which he persuaded his friend **Franklyn Bivatt** to try. **(Strand-JOW)**

DUNSANY, Edward John Moreton Drax Plunkett, 18th Baron (1878-1957): in a letter to William Townend dated 10 March, 1928 (see *Performing Flea*), Wodehouse wrote:

> I am re-reading Dunsany. I never get tired of his stories. I can always let them cool off for a month or two and then come back to them. He is the only writer I know who opens up an entirely new world to me. . . . He told me once that quite a lot of his stuff was written from [S H] Sime's pictures. They would hand him a Sime drawing of a wintry scene with a sinister-looking bird flying over it and he would brood on it for a while and come up with *The Bird of the Difficult Eye*.

It is a matter of some surprise that he did not use **Lady Underhill** as a model for this story when she was staring at **Jill Mariner** at the Savoy. **(JTR ch4)**

DUNSTERVILLE: a town in Canada from which emigrations were rare, but **Joe Rendal** and **Eddy Moore** set a fashion by going to New York, whither they were followed by **Mary Hill**. **(TMU-TFD)**

DUPLESSIS: the leader of a mob who operated on the Côte d'Azur in days gone by, one of whose members had been **Horace Appleby**. **(DBB ch13)**

DWORNITZCHEK, the Princess Heloise von und zu: was one of the few Wodehouse characters whom the reader was not only permitted, but actually encouraged, to dislike. While we are only *almost* certain that she was one of the few admitted mistresses in his fiction, we *know* she was a discreet murderess:

> "Why did you really leave home?"
> The smile suddenly faded out of his eyes. There was a short silence.
>
> . . .
>
> "I left because I have a constitutional dislike for watching murder done – especially slow, cold-blooded murder."
> "What do you mean?"
> "My father. He was alive then – just. She didn't actually succeed in killing him till about a year later."
> Jane stared at him. He appeared to be serious.

"Killing him?"

"Oh, I don't mean little-known Asiatic poisons. A resourceful woman with a sensitive subject to work on can make out quite well without the help of strychnine in the soup. Her method was just to make life hell for him."

Her life was one of frenetic and inevitably selfish activity, starting with a marriage to the wealthy **Spelvin**, partner of **Elmer Chinnery** in a fish-glue business. (Wealth did not spoil her; she was already too far gone for that, but neither did it improve her, and she once questioned a two-shilling cover charge in a night club with a vehemence which almost wrecked the establishment.) She then married **Franklin Vanringham**, the subject of her stepson **Joe Vanringham**'s outburst reproduced above. Two years after he died she married (and then divorced) the owner of the title which she was careful to preserve, while threatening her other stepson **Tubby** with a role as office-boy in the fish-glue business. The title and her fortune left her free to make a fool of herself with gigolos half her age, and the individual on whom she seemed to concentrate her attention appears to have been the equally selfish two-timer **Adrian Peake**. She didn't trust him, however, and announced that when they were married they would live in the country so she could keep an eye on him.

The book in which the Princess appears was published in 1937, and one is tempted to believe that there were one or more **Hollywood** models on which her character was based. It is so base a character, though, that we may assume that any individual who thought she was recognisable but misrepresented would have been sure to take legal action against author and publishers. The name Dwornitzchek may have been derived from the footman of the same name who appeared in *The Play's The Thing*, a play by Ferenc Molnar which Wodehouse had adapted in 1926. **(SUM)**

EALING WEST: was not the home of yet another of **Billie Bennett**'s fiancés, even though the one under discussion was imaginary. **(GOB ch13)**

EARLS: April June discovered enthusiastically that, though ranked lower than **Dukes**, ... were superior to Viscounts and their wives would be Countesses. The years immediately after the second world war were not good for them as a race, however, for thanks to income tax, land tax and all the other taxes, the boom days were over. **(LAG ch2; SPF ch4)**

EARL'S SECRET, The: in which the hero rescued the heroine from drowning. **(GOB ch16)**

EAST DULWICH PROGRESS CLUB: when **George Marlowe** found that preparation for his wife's lecture on *Some Tendencies of Modern Fiction* at the ... took priority over practice for the Ladies' Open he was rightly horrified. **(Strand-PAW)**

EASTHAMPTON (or EAST HAMPTON): a Long Island resort where **J B Duff** fell off a yacht and was returned to shore by **Joss Weatherby**. **(QUS ch9; SatEvePost-QUS ch9)**

EAST SIDE DELMONICO'S: the 14th Street eatery in New York where **Freddie Bowen** found a job, and discovered that the place also offered roulette, boxing and buck the tiger. **(Strand-JOW)**

EDDIE: with **Fred**[1] and **George**[2] he was a member of an amateur kidnapping gang in **Hollywood**. An expert in the art of pancake-preparation, provided the mixture did not get entangled with his beard, he claimed that they had to be chewed to be believed. He thought that in the scenario under discussion the part of **Public Enemy No 13** was right for **Lionel Barrymore** and that the part of the captain would be suitable for **Charles Butterworth**. **(LAG ch24; Pearson-LAG; ThisWeek-LAG)**

EDELWEISS: a flower growing in the Alps which it was forbidden to pick. **(WTT ch3)**

EDITH (d 1075): the wife of King Edward the Confessor, who searched for the body of **King Harold** after the **Battle of Hastings**. **(SUM ch21)**

EDWARDES, Joseph: a failure at eight stone four pounds. **(TMU-WDD)**

EDWIN: the male party in **James Cloyster**'s *Society Dialogues*, imitated in real life by **Sidney Price**. **(NGW ptII ch13)**

EDWIN: the brother of **Lady Underhill**, he gave out the opinion that she could talk the hind-leg off a donkey. **(JTR ch5)**

'EGG': was not a nickname by which **Blair Eggleston** wished to be known. **(HOW ch14)**

EGGLESTON, Blair: was small, slim and, if you ignore a little moustache resembling a smear of soot which anyway was shaved off in the course of his duties, passably good-looking. He had a job in the Drama department at the **BBC** as 'Noises Off', but thought more about his other life, as a writer of brilliant novels, which few read and fewer understood, though one critic noted that there were passages in *Worm i' the Root* and *Offal* which simply made you shiver, so sharp was their cynicism, so brutal the force with which they tore away the veils and disclosed Woman as she was.

Despite this reputation, when deprived of his fountain-pen Blair became timid with the sex, and though he had never yet found himself alone in an incense-scented studio with a scantily-clad princess reclining on a tiger-skin, he had mapped out his escape route and would have taken a chair as near to the door as possible and talk about the weather. His inexplicable engagement to the desirable **Jane Opal** was terminated after he had taken a job as valet to her father and, displaying unwarranted querulousness and self-pity, had failed to render the service which had been expected to cause heaps of blessings to rain down on the supposedly happy couple.

In a final twist of his fortune, however, he proposed again, this time to the redoubtable Honoria Glossop, as explained in *Volume 6*, and we have no reason to believe that the match failed to shine. **(HOW)**

EGGSHAW, Wibblesley: a client of **Sir Mallaby Marlowe**, who was being sued for £10,000, having written 23 letters (twelve in verse) to a girl, in 21 of which he had asked her to marry him. **(GOB ch8)**

EGGY: see **Mannering, Egremont**

ELAINE: was described as a 'wild unicorn'. **(TMU-SAG)**

ELECTRIC BOND AND SHARE: which **Soup Slattery** had bought at 169, **J Wellington Gedge** at 167. **(HOW ch1)**

ELIJAH, the prophet (fl c900BC): **Mr Bennett** once thought he had become ... **(MLF-CRH)**

ELLIS, Mrs: the cook at **Claines Hall**, who played bridge and displayed a natural aptitude for craps. She was considered by some to be the best cook in Sussex, though liable to find **Chibnall** weltering in his blood. **(QUS ch7,18)**

ELLISON, Tom: a close friend of **Dick Henley**, his declared rival for the love of **Dolly Burn**. He denied that he fell in love with every girl he met, such as **Ethel Something**, but agreed that a forthcoming cricket match would give the two friends an opportunity to determine in a gentlemanly manner the order of priority in approaching Dolly. **(TUW-TDH)**

ELOCUTION LESSON:

"How now, brown cow, do not frown beneath the bough."

(LAG ch14)

ELPHINSTONE, Hildebrand: the docile six-year-old son of **Mrs E**. **(TUW-BSA)**

ELPHINSTONE, Mrs: a former employer of **Eve Hendrie**, brother of **Peter Rayner** and mother of **Hildebrand**, she disapproved of Peter wooing Eve. **(TUW-BSA)**

ELSIE DINSMORE: **Mae West** wowed them in ... **(Pearson-LAG; ThisWeek-LAG)**

EMILY: see **Alphonso**

EMPIRE: **Freddie Rooke** had been arrested at the ... on Boat Race night in the days when it was expected of a chap, and it was visited on Boat Race night by **Tom Ellison** and **Dick Henley**. **Max Faucitt** was shocked when, returning after a spell in America, he found it had been turned from a music-hall into a theatre. **(JTR ch5; TAS ch12; TUW-TDH)**

EMPIRE STATE BUILDING, the: would have gone along with **Beulah Brinkmeyer** had she attached herself to its wrist like she did to **RH(TF)** and pulled. **(Pearson-LAG)**

EMPRESS OF STORMY EMOTION, the: see **Adela Shannon Cork**

ENCYCLOPAEDIA BRITANNICA: the source of **Henry Mills**'s wide range of knowledge. His current favourite was *BIS-CAL*, three earlier volumes having been completed, and Henry was not the sort of vapid wimp who would jump to *Volume 28* to see how it came out in the end. **(MLF-TLF)**

ENGINEERS' CLUB AT ROSLYN (LONG ISLAND), The: the scene of one of the rounds of **mental golf** played by **Sam Marlowe** whilst concealed in a cupboard at **Windles**. **(TMM ch16)**

ENGLAND: after Peace had come, there remained three questions for the country to deal with:

> How about Ireland? How about Labour? And what on earth are we to do with Archie?

It was regarded by **Billie Bennett** as a savage country, where you could not get ice, central heating, corn-on-the-cob or bathrooms. **(GOB ch9; Strand-MMH)**

ENGLISH ED: the name by which the **New York, London and Paris Insurance Company** allegedly knew **Blair Eggleston**. **(HOW ch13)**

'ENRY: his brother **Joe**'s wife's sister had a parrot, so he knew that parrots did not sting. **(JTR ch5)**

EPICTETUS (55-135): observed truly that

> "We know what awaiteth us around the corner, and the hand that counteth its chickens ere they be hatched oftimes graspeth but a lemon."

(Colliers-PAP)

EPIGRAMS:

> Mr Goble knocked the ash off his cigar. "The public don't want epigrams. The public don't like epigrams. I've been in the show business fifteen years, and I'm telling you! Epigrams give them a pain under the vest."

(JTR ch14)

EPSTEIN, (Sir Jacob, 1880-1959): Joss Weatherby came across **J B Duff** huddled in a chair, looking like an ... statue. **(QUS ch18)**

EPSTEIN: Reginald Sellers' agent, who agreed to handle **Beverley**'s *Child and Cat*. **(TMU-MUP)**

ERA: referred to unemployed actors and actresses as being 'at liberty'. **(JTR ch6)**

ERB: a proletariat spectator of **Bill**[1]'s antics. **(JTR ch5)**

ERICKSON, Cuthbert: starred in *Why Men Go Wrong*, one of the films shown at the **Bijou Dream**. **(Grand-COL)**

ERNIE: kicked **Beatrice Bracken** on the ankle whilst at **Waterloo Station**. **(HOW ch2)**

ESCHENBACH, Lord of: one of few successful assassins appearing in Wodehouse, the victim in his joint enterprise with the **Lord of Tegerfelden** being the **Emperor of Austria**. **(WTT ch15)**

ESCOFFIER (1845-1935): a French cook and author whom Providence had evidently used as its model when it bestowed on **Horace Appleby** a bride who not only could cook like an ... but also was blessed with a quick brain. **(DBB ch11)**

ESQUIRE: **Mike Cardinal**'s copy of ... was borrowed by **Augustus Robb** on **Stanwood Cobbold**'s behalf. **(SPF ch2)**

ETHELBERTINA: was **Sidney Price**'s 'slavey'. **(NGW ptII ch20)**

ETHICS: a new edition was published of **Aristotle**'s ..., prepared by the **Macrae**s on Mount Parnassus. **(NGW ptII ch3)**

ETON BOATING SONG: selected by **RH(JC)** for rendering in **April June**'s living-room. **(LAG ch21)**

EVANS, Chick: talk about his lofting shots, raised in conversation by **George Marlowe**, was heard absent-mindedly by **Grace Pemberton**. **(PicRev-PAW)**

EVANS, Llewellyn ('Basher'): a member of the **Appleby** gang, he was an expert at opening safes and colossal in size, being both impressively tall and bulging in every muscle. Following an accident in the Fulham Road, in which he collided with a sports model, he was out of action for a week (but the sports model had come off worse). During the planning period for the **Bond Bank** job, he got religion and retired to his Brixton home. **(DBB ch1,7,8)**

EVENING NEWS: its reporter said that **Joe Vanringham** was one of the few dramatists who counted. **(SatEvePost-SUM; Pearson-SUM)**

EVERSLEIGH, Eva: a cousin of **Julian**, she was considered to be the most beautiful person Nature ever created, for Nature had bestowed big, blue eyes, a retroussé nose and a rather wide mouth on a petite, dark frame. Her eyes reminded **James Cloyster** of Arcadia, **Helen of Troy** and the happy valleys of the early Greeks. Her personality, though, was more complex, her main hobbies seemingly being to promise the last two waltzes to a man and then let him down, and to become engaged. Although her commitment to James Cloyster was broken off, she may have actually fulfilled her obligation towards her second fiancé Julian. **(NGW ptII ch15*ff*)**

EVERSLEIGH, Julian: the victim of a couple of footpads in London, he was rescued by **James Cloyster**, with whom he carried on an on-and-off friendship. After a spell at Oxford, where he was a contemporary of **Malim**, he lived in a single room in Rupert Court, and received the princely sum of ten pounds for a four-act tragedy about the abuse of sloe gin. He loved his cousin **Eva**, a feeling which was complicated by her relationship with **James Cloyster**. The critic might argue that it was his own fault, as it was he who suggested to Cloyster the use of the pseudonyms which had delayed his marriage to his first love. But as matters sorted themselves out, he took responsibility for handling the advertising of a firm of linoleum manufacturers for a huge salary and accompanying Eva to a fancy dress ball. **(NGW)**

EVERYBODY WANTS A KEY TO MY CELLAR: the sort of tune which the man at the piano at a silent movie would play when a Spoken Title (or Cut-Back Sub-Caption) appeared on the screen. **(GOB ch4; TMM ch4)**

EVILEYE FLEAGLE OF BROOKLYN: would have described the look which **Adela Cork** directed at her brother-in-law as a "full whammy". **(TOR ch7)**

EXCELSIOR: a bunch of drunks dashed round the Public Amusement Gardens at **St Rocque** waving **Butch Carpenter**'s trousers like a banner with the strange device ... **(FRL ch4)**

EXCELSIOR BOARDING HOUSE: a popular Southampton waterfront establishment owned by **Mrs Pickett**, which had become famous in every corner of the world. **(TUW-DAE)**

EXPLANATIONS: the zero on the roulette-board of life. **(TMU-RIE)**

EXPLORERS: as a class they have weak eyes, caused by staring at the sunrise on the lower Zambesi. **(PLP-GCS)**

EXPLORERS CLUB: expected to receive a commissioned portrait of **Col Francis Pashley-Drake**. **(PLP-GCS)**

FACELESS FIEND: Drexdale Drew only had the unpleasantness with a ... because he imprudently let forth a long, low whistle of astonishment. **(QUS ch18)**

FAIR EXCHANGES: see page 94

FAIR EXCHANGES

"Go and get me a whisky and soda."

"Will the doctor approve?"

"He won't know," said Miss Bond.

(DBB ch2)

". . . I have bad news for you about your father."

"My father? He died ten years ago."

"You have your facts twisted," said Horace, correcting him. "He is not dead, but dangerously ill, . . ."

(DBB ch3)

". . . Mike and I are going to be married."

"What!"

"Yes."

"But you told me you didn't like him."

"Just a slip of the tongue."

(DBB ch6)

"Won't you have another game?"

"What's the use? I should only beat you."

(DBB ch7)

"What I don't know about safe locks isn't worth knowing."

"And what you do know about them isn't worth knowing either," said Frank sourly.

(DBB ch9)

"One could scarcely allow the poor girl to suffocate."

"Why not?"

(DBB ch11)

"Are you an artist?"

"Sort of. Cartoons, mostly."

"Well, that's better than painting Russian princesses lying in the nude on tiger skins."

(TGI ch2)

"She is a miniature by Gainsborough. She is wearing a blue dress, so the late Gainsborough, hunting around for a title, called her The Girl in Blue."

"Very clever of him. Think like lightning, these artists."

(TGI ch4)

"Bill, can you lend me two hundred and three pounds, six shillings and fourpence?"

. . .

"Odd sum," he said.

"It's for the repairs people."

"Won't they wait?"

"They've been waiting two years."

"Then they ought to have got the knack of it by now."

(TGI ch3)

"It ought to mean someone's left you a legacy."

"It ought, oughtn't it. But I can't think who."

"Some old school crony from Cheltenham? Some girl who scored a goal at hockey because you passed to her at just the right moment."

"But what would she be doing, dying? She would be in her early twenties."

(TGI ch6)

"What an ass!"

"Miss Hunnicutt, you are speaking of the man you love."

(TGI ch11)

"So you need a wife."

"I do."

"Try me," said Barney.

(TGI ch14)

"Let us rise and slay the tyrant."

". . . There is nothing I should enjoy more than slaying the tyrant, only I have an idea that the tyrant would slay us."

(WTT ch12)

"I disapprove heartily. I don't like that gingerheaded pipsqueak."

"That's all right, mother dear. You don't have to."

(TGI ch14)

"Barker!" [Freddie Rooke's] voice had a ring of pain.

"Sir?"

"What's this?"

"Poached egg, sir."

Freddie averted his eyes with a silent shudder.

"It looks just like an old aunt of mine," he said.

(JTR ch1)

"I say!" he said. "Are you broke?"

Nelly laughed.

"Am I? If dollars were doughnuts, I wouldn't even have the hole in the middle."

(JTR ch6)

"They can't do this sort of thing to me!" he growled.

"Well, they are doing it to someone, aren't they," said Wally, "and if it's not you, who is it?"

(JTR ch16)

"Thought I'd look in and see how you were."

"That was very kind of you. The morning is my busy time, . . ."

(GOB ch1)

"I've been looking for you everywhere."

"It's funny you didn't find me, then, for that's where I've been. I was looking for you."

(TAS ch3)

"Webster," said Mr Bennett, "I'm a dying man!"

"Indeed, sir?"

"A dying man!" repeated Mr Bennett.

"Very good, sir. Which of your suits would you wish me to lay out?"

(GOB ch11)

"Well, you've taken a weight off my mind."

"A mind, I should imagine, scarcely constructed to bear great weights."

(GOB ch1)

"This is my daughter, Mr Peters."

"My daughter! I mean, your daughter! Are – are you sure?"

(GOB ch15)

"My face hurts," persisted Mr Bennett.

"You can't expect a face like that not to hurt," said Mr Mortimer.

(GOB ch17)

"I am sorry," said Mr Carlyle ponderously, "if my eyes are fishy. The fact has not been called to my attention before."

"I suppose you never had any sisters," said Sally. "They would have told you."

(TAS ch3)

"If you have anything to say to me, lower your voice."

"He can't," observed Miss Winch. "He's a tenor."

(TAS ch6)

"She is the woman who is leading California out of the swamp of alcohol."

"Good God!" I could tell by Eggy's voice that he was interested. "Is there a swamp of alcohol in these parts? What an amazing country America is. Talk about every modern convenience. Do you mean you can simply go there and *lap*?"

(LAG ch9)

"You know Egremeont's record?"

I had to think a bit.

"Well, one Boat Race night I saw him put away sixteen double whiskies and soda, but whether he has beaten that since or not –"

(LAG ch1)

". . . your face seems extraordinarily familiar, too."

"You've probably seen it in pix."

"No, I've never been there."

(LAG ch2)

"But how can you be behind with the rent? I only left here the Saturday before last and you weren't in the place then. You can't have been here more than a week."

"I've been here just a week. That's the week I'm behind with."

(TAS ch9)

"There's lots of good stuff in Eggy."

"Quite. And more going in every minute."

(LAG ch4)

"Father's a pretty hard egg, isn't he?"

"It is not for me to criticize your father," said Packy primly, "but I can tell you this – if he ever asks me to come down a lonely alley with him to see his stamp collection I shall refuse with considerable firmness."

(HOW ch2)

"Be very careful how you remove spots from clothing. I knew a man who was fired for removing a spot from his employer's clothing."

"What a shame! Said Jane. "Why?"

"It was a ten-spot," explained Packy.

(HOW ch2)

"Blair's novels haven't any plots."

"No? Why's that?"

"He thinks they're crude."

(HOW ch8)

"She accused me of making love to you behind her back."

"But you haven't made love to me."

"I know. Silly idea. . . . "

"I wish you would," she said.

(HOW ch18)

"There are a hundred ways of getting to know girls at a seaside resort."

"Such as – ?"

"Save her from drowning."

(FRL ch5)

"[Jo's] hoping to marry a millionaire."

"What!"

"Lots of them in those parts."

"Do you mean that she is deliberately going to try to marry for money?"

"I wouldn't put it like that. She's just going where the money is."

(FRL ch1)

"Would you have me sell myself for gold?"

"Certainly, and the more gold the better."

(FRL ch3)

" . . .this girl who calls herself Miss Trent."

"It's her name."

"It may be her name. That has nothing to do with it."

(FRL ch5)

"You told them you were expecting to sell a hundred thousand copies?"

"We always tell them we're expecting to sell a hundred thousand copies," said Russell Clutterbuck, letting him in on one of the secrets of the publishing trade.

(FRL ch8)

"May I kiss you?"

"No, you may not. Holy smoke, do you think I've time to stand around getting kissed by girls.?"

(FRL ch10)

"And Mr Chinnery has been asking for waffles again."

"Oh, dash his waffles. What the dickens are these waffles he's always whining about?"

"They appear to be an American breakfast food."

. . .

"Would my wife know how to make the damn things?"

"I have consulted Lady Abbott, Sir Buckstone, and she informs me that she can make a substance called fudge, but not waffles."

(SUM ch2)

"Is your sister there? . . . I mean the one who looks at you like a Duchess looking at a potato bug."

(FRL ch10)

"You won't marry me?"

"No."

"Then will you order me a medium dry Martini?"

(SUM ch4)

"Don't you always feel," [Jane] said, "that what you really want is just sardines?"

"I thought I had made it abundantly clear that I wanted you."

(SUM ch5)

"I say . . . are there mice on that boat?"

. . .

"I don't know. Why? Would you like some?"

(SUM ch6)

"You don't like the Princess?"

"I regard her as the sand in Civilisation's spinach."

(SUM ch11)

"I've brought you my sketches for the new posters of ye Ham Paramount. I don't know if they're any good."

"They aren't."

"You've not seen them yet."

"I don't have to."

(QUS ch2)

". . . I saved your life."

"Yes, and the way I'm feeling this morning, I'd like to sue you."

(QUS ch2)

". . . I'm sorry I called you a louse."

"You didn't."

"Well, I was just going to . . ."

(QUS ch13)

"Did you know," said Mike, "that a flea one-twelfth of an inch long, weighing one eighty-thousandth of an ounce, can broad jump thirteen inches?"

"No," said Terry.

"A fact, I believe. Watching your father brought it to my mind. He's very agile."

(SPF ch12)

"We're going to live at the castle," explained Clare.

"So that's all right," said Cosmo Blair. . . . "We shall both be with you."

(SPF ch18)

"You aren't thinking of strolling in on Aunt Adela?"

"I might."

"I wouldn't."

"She can't eat me."

"I don't know so much. She's not a vegetarian."

(TOR ch2)

"What was that about glue?"

"Igloo. It's a sort of gloo they have up in the Arctic circle."

(TOR ch4)

"He was an American, and oddly enough, his name was the same as mine."

"What, Cobbold?"

"Well, you didn't think I meant Teresa?"

(SPF ch4)

"They'll murder you."

"They won't. Because if they so much as start trying to, I'll jolly well murder them first."

(QUS ch18)

"You know sea water?"

"The stuff that props the ship up when you come over from New York?"

(NSE-HTU)

"Don't the police want you?"

"No, the police do not want me."

"How I sympathise with the police. . . . I know just how they feel."

(TOR ch7)

"I'm a bird in a gilded cage."

"Sir?"

"I'm a worm."

"You are getting me confused, sir. I understood you to say you were a bird."

"A worm, too. A miserable, down-trodden, Hey-you of a worm on whose horizon there is no ray of light. What are those things they have in Mexico?"

"Tamales, sir?"

"Peons. I'm just a peon . . ."

(TOR ch1)

The policeman with the kind face met his colleague in the basement.

"Say, you know those guys in the dressing-room," he said.

"Uh-huh," said the colleague.

"They overpowered me and got away."

"Divvies," said the colleague.

(Colliers-JOW)

"He keeps stopping work to tell risky stories."

"Dear, dear. Off colour?"

"Very. There was one about a strip-tease dancer and a performing flea . . ." He looked at Kay, and paused. "But it wouldn't interest you."

"I've heard it," said Kay.

(TOR ch11)

"Gee, I miss that kid. Yes, sir. I certainly would like to see Elmer again."

I took a swift look at the photograph.

"Why?" I said.

(Strand-BTG)

"I always thought you were bad, . . . but I never realized before that you were bad enough to make the audience shoot at you."

"Have they found out who did it, sir?" . . .

"Not yet. . . . But they think it must have been the local dramatic critic."

(Strand-BTG)

"By the way, touching the matter of browsing and sluicing. What do I feed him on?"

"Oh, anything. Bread-and-milk or fruit or soft-boiled egg or dog-biscuit or ants'-eggs. You know – anything you have yourself."

(Cosmo-DSQ)

"If you never get into trouble," said the policeman sententiously, "you'll never have to get out of it."

"Um," said Mr Buffin.

(TUW-MIS)

"No wasps round here."

"Yes."

"Not in the pavilion at Lord's. You can't get in unless you're a member."

(NSE-HTU)

"Father's slogan is 'Do it now', and he's a tycoon."

"I thought a tycoon was a sort of storm."

(NSE-HTU)

"This is Brookport," said Mr Mariner. "That's Haydock's grocery store there by the post office. He charges sixty cents a pound for bacon, and I can get the same bacon by walking into Patchogue for fifty-seven!"

"How far is Patchogue?" asked Jill, feeling that some comment was required of her.

"Four miles," said Mr Mariner.

(TLW ch7; Grand-JTR)

FAIRMILE, Sally: a Saturday's child, this blue-eyed orphan niece of the society go-getter **Mrs Howard Steptoe**, with whom the luckless girl served a long sentence as poor relation. She was tiny and graceful, like a Tanagra figurine, with eyes of a dark blue like the sky on a summer's night, an amazingly attractive speaking voice and a smile which some said should not be used without warning. Her engagement to **George Holbeton** was influenced by his crooner's voice, but she soon realised he had feet of clay, and was pleased when he released her from her obligations on finding her kissing **Joss Weatherby**. **(QUS)**

FALERNIAN: after a night in a **Hollywood** jug, following his long-overdue bender, **Smedley Cork** resembled a soiled and crumpled Roman Emperor who had sat up too late over the ... **(TOR ch8)**

FAMILY CURSE, the: see **Underhill, Lady**

FANE: did the *People and Things* column on *The Orb*. **(NGW ch24)**

FARADAY: one of six acquaintances of **Joe Vanringham** not known to **Jane Abbott**. **(SUM ch5)**

FATE: **Sam Marlowe** resented being its toy. **(GOB ch9)**

FAUCITT, Maxwell: the privileged oldest member of **Mrs Meecher**'s boarding-house. New York might one day produce an occasion when Mr Faucitt did not feel compelled to say a few words, but the wise money said don't count on it. When taken ill, a lack of a blackish colouring helped to diagnose an allergy to **Toto** rather than Spanish influenza. When his brother died he revisited Cirencester, where he used to live, and took over the business of **Laurette et Cie**. **(TAS ch1,5,8)**

FAUNTLEROY: a London murderer who killed a woman because she had thick ankles. **(TUW-DAE)**

FAUNTLEROY, Gladys ('Toots'): a chorus lady who showed no qualm in letting the sun go down on her wrath. Her friend **Lord Topham** had commented lightheartedly that her new hat made her look like a famous film star, tactlessly adding that he had in mind **Boris Karloff**. **(TOR ch15,18)**

FAUNTLEROY, Little Lord: RH(JC) was not in a mood to forgive a comparison when uttered by **Orlando Flower**. **(JTR ch2; LAG ch16)**

FAYE, Dame Flora: an actress who had once been engaged to **Willoughby Scrope**, had married **Charles Upshaw** and was the

Joss Weatherby imitating a jumping bean on falling in love with Sally Fairmile

mother of **Vera**. She was radiantly lovely, with a velvet voice, but her *Theatre Memories* (as told to **Reginald Tressilian**) were no substitute for her daughter's *Daffodil Days*. **(TGI ch2,5,10)**.

FEATHERSTONE, General Sir Frederick: the tall, stringy white-moustached trustee of **Bond's Bank** in his late sixties who, according to **Isabel Bond**, was a guffin and a footler, a view vindicated by the threat of jail which came to hang over this aged ex-warrior like a Sword of **D**. **(DBB ch5,14)**

FEATURES: a magazine printing **James Cloyster**'s work under the **Sidney Price** imprint. **(NGW ptII ch19)**

FELLOWES: **Terry Trent** took the name, in her capacity of personal maid to her sister **Jo**, but its use led Terry into the hands of the police when she was recognised by **Chester Todd** under the temporary name. **(FRL ch1,9,10)**

FEMININE PSYCHOLOGY:

> Packy . . . felt how unerring had been Mr Slattery's knowledge of feminine psychology when he had said that he guessed that if there was going to be a murder in the home she would rather it was the old man than her.

(HOW ch13)

FENNELL: the general manager of the **Moon Assurance Co**, who assumed **Sidney Price** would be leaving to pursue his art, after reading a contribution which Price had made to *The Strawberry Leaf*. **(NGW ptII ch19)**

FERDIE THE FLY: see **Ripley, Ferdinand**

FERGUSON, Robert: the late employer of **Roland Bean**, with whom he was locked in the office building. He was the type of man who was prepared to spend eight shillings, or three dollars 45 cents, on lunch, so the prospect of spending a night locked in an office did not appeal to his sensitive parts. His lack of knowledge of real chorus girls led him to invent the unfortunate **Marie Templeton**, and his allergic reaction to Roland Bean led him to meet again his former fiancée, now acting as secretary in the neighbouring ofice of his acquaintance, **Blaythwayt**. **(TMU-MMM; Cosmo-MMM)**

FERMAIN BAY: the Guernsey location where **Margaret Goodwin** met **James Orlebar Cloyster** at 7.30 am on 28th July, some 50 yards from the shore. **(NGW ptI ch1)**

FERMIN, Charles: was responsible with **Gresham** for the *On Your Way* column for the *Orb*. Once a famous quarter-miler, he had also been president of Oxford University Athletic Club. He was a tall, thin man who always gave the impression of being in a hurry, but offered **Cloyster** five weeks holiday work. **(NGW ptII ch3)**

FERRIS: **Lady Underhill**'s maid, whom she told to find a porter, what he should do, and how much tip to give him. **(TLW ch1; Grand-JTR)**

FERRIS, Charles ('Charlie'): from **Ashley**, Maine, he was one of those earnest, persevering dancers, the kind that have taken twelve correspondence lessons, and while on honeymoon with **Mary** remember the New York professional dancer they took the floor with the previous April.

> "Shake hands with my friend Mr Ferris," I said. "He wants to show you the latest steps. He does most of them on your feet."

He was granted the ironic nicknames 'the Boy Wonder' and 'the debonair Pride of Ashley' by **Miss Roxborough**. **(MLF-ATG)**

FERRIS, Mary: an old-fashioned newly-wed from **Rodney**, Maine (though originally from Illinois), she had big, brown eyes, a grey dress with white muslin sleeves, a simple hair-do and a black hat. She did not dance much, but when at **Geisenheimer's** she danced on ticket 36 instead of number 10, she brightened up and made you think of fresh milk, new-laid eggs and birds singing, getting the audience completely on her side. **(MLF-ATG)**

FERRYMAN, the: would not take **Baumgarten** across the lake during a storm, even for double the normal fee. **(WTT ch3)**

FESTIVAL OF THE SAINT, the: was celebrated on the 15th July at **St Rocque**, but it brought to the surface all that was most austere in **Kate Trent**. **(HOW ch1,4; FRL ch4)**

FIDO: the name given to **The Mixer** by **Peter**: a name which all dogs detest. See **Nigger**. **(MLF-BIS)**

FIELD, Charlie: wore velvet **Lord Fauntleroy** suits and long golden curls when **Wally Mason** and **Jill Mariner** knew him. **(JTR ch2)**

FIELDS, William Claude Dukenfield (1879-1946): **Jeff d'Escrignon** looked like ... after his encounter with **M Boissonade**'s door. **(FRL ch11)**

FIFI: the repulsive name of a cocotte with high heels and lots of ribbon and lace who would be likely to address the **Comte d'Escrignon** as 'Chéri'. **(FRL ch6)**

FIGARO, Le: the sort of newspaper which elderly gentlemen read while sitting in the Public Amusement Gardens at **St Rocque**. **(HOW ch5; FRL ch4)**

FIJI ISLANDS: one of the places where **Joe Vanringham** thought **Adrian Peake** might have reached. **(SUM ch21)**

FILIPINO BUTLER: in **Hollywood**, indicated a step up the social ladder. **(TOR ch1)**

FILIPINO FOOTMAN: at the **Brinkmeyer**s, actually an American actor, specialising in comedy and homely pathos, who broke the news to **RH(JC)** that **Chaffinch** was leaving for New York immediately. **(LAG ch18)**

FILLMORE NICHOLAS THEATRICAL ENTERPRISES LTD: a company whose managing director was **Fillmore Nicholas**, and which employed **Ginger Kemp** at $50 per week. **(TAS ch10)**

FILM FANCIES: invested its proprietor's money in a **Clark Gable** undervest which proved to be spurious. **(LAG ch15)**

FINCH, Sir Rupert: Appleby had buttled for him and his good lady at Norton Court near Bridgnorth in Shropshire, and contrary to the general belief it was he who got the treasure, in the form of the Finch pearls. **(DBB ch2)**

FINCHLEY, Lord: a non-singing character in *The Rose of America* played by an English character actor, **Wentworth Hill**, who specialised in London's 'knuts'. The part was first taken over by **Freddie Rooke**, but he was replaced in turn when the nature of the part was changed to that of a Scotchman. **(JTR ch14)**

FINN, Mickey: together with a glass of champagne was a friend indeed as far as **M Boissonade** was concerned. It was realised too late that **Alice Topping** should have been given one in her bedtime glass of milk. **Bill** (or **Jane**) **Shannon** had received a sample from a bartender on Third Avenue and thought hard about whether to suggest to **Phipps** that he slip it in **Adela Cork**'s bedtime Ovaltine, but in the end she found a more creative use for it. **(SPF ch16; TOR ch5,13; FRL ch11; Colliers-PTR)**

FIRESIDE CHAT: one of the best-known of the penny weeklies, its 500,000 readers received each week a story about life in the highest circles (such as, perhaps, those written by Joan Valentine in *Something Fresh*), a short story packed with heart interest, plus, amongst other material, *In the Consulting Room*, advice on matters of the heart offered by **Doctor Cupid**. **(TMU-WDD)**

FIRESIDE CHATTER: had a page entitled *A Little Bird in Society* conducted by **Mary Mayfair**. **(HOW ch2)**

FIRST GHOST: a reference to the **Rev Mr Hatton**, who was invited by **James Cloyster** to put a name to his third book, *When It Was Lurid (A Tale of God and Allah)*, a pot-boiler for which he received a 15% commission. **(NGW ptII ch12)**

FISH: when **Isobel Bond** was but a girl, a friend of this name came home on New Year's morning, mistook the coal scuttle for a mad dog and tried to shoot it with fire tongs. In all probability he was the late Major-General Miles ('Fishy') Fish, CBE, father of Ronnie, who featured both in *Volume 5* of this *Concordance* and, more extensively, in Galahad Threepwood's excellent *Reminiscences*. **(DBB ch10)**

FITZPATRICK, Otis: one of the many aliases of **Herbert Higgs**. **(Ellery-MBD)**

FIZZO: a brand of sparkling table water whose manufacture was controlled by **Butch Carpenter**. **(FRL ch1)**

FLANNERY AND MARTIN'S: a bookshop in Sloane Square. **(TGI ch5)**

FLAUBERT, Gustave (1821-1880): would have preferred the French term 'étourdit' when he wanted to say 'boneless', and would not have merely used the word 'genial' had he wished to describe accurately the demeanour of **Tubby Vanringham** on the houseboat *Mignonette*. He would have needed to find a good French equivalent of 'rollicking' in order to paint a full word-picture of **Augustus Robb**'s deportment after a go at the crème de menthe, and when referring to the speech of a newly-confident **Shorty** acting the tiger to **Adela Topping** he would have preferred "thundered" to "said". **(SUM ch18; SPF ch16,23; TGI ch6)**

FLETCHER, Harry: a press agent who suggested that **Mae Gleason** should go on stage when he visited the **Hotel Cosmopolitan** for a manicure. After arranging for her to be in the chorus of *She's All*

Right, and supervising her transition from black hair to blond, he met his come-uppance with **Lancelot Purvis**'s uppercut. **(Grand-COL)**

FLETCHERIZE: what a raffish mongrel was trying to do to a Sealyham which was a stranger to it, in a **Roville** dogfight. **(TAS ch2)**

FLIP-FLAP: a fitting climax to an evening at **Luna Park**. **(TMU-WDD)**

FLOCHE, M: a clarinet player in a hotel orchestra, who applied to **M Boissonade** for a permit to carry a pistol and was refused without explanation. **(FRL ch6)**

FLORADORA: **Mrs Meecher** was in the first production of ... **(TAS ch5)**

FLORES, Carmen: the tempestuous but late Mexican film star who had once been the owner of the **Carmen Flores Place**, now owned by **Adela Shannon Cork**. Before being killed in a plane crash, she had recorded details of her past in a diary, and the stars and studio bosses who featured in it were prepared to bid against each other for the rights. **(TOR ch1)**

FLORIZEL OF BOHEMIA, Prince: from Shakespeare's *A Winter's Tale*, ended his days in Rupert Street on a tobacconist's divan. **(NGW ptII ch 4)**

FLOSSIE: see **Ralph**

FLOWER GARDEN, The: a dancing studio on Broadway where **Sally Nicholas** and **Mabel Hobson** were each engaged as instructresses. **(TAS ch2,15,16)**

FLOWER, Harold: a messenger at the **Planet Insurance Company**, who referred to **George Balmer** as a "tuppenny millionaire" on having his request for a "loan" of a pound turned down, later adding the epithet "a blanky little gor-blimey vegetable". **(TMU-TTM)**

FLOWER, Orlando: a small-time child film actor with red hair and spotty spots. He was probably tougher than **Tommy Murphy** but his allergy to oranges reduced his ability to handle **Joey Cooley**. **(LAG ch16,20)**

FLOWER, Teddy: the first name given to the child film star of singular personal beauty, with the ability to sprint and throw oranges but not to engage in unarmed combat, who became better known to us as **Joey Cooley**. He was known for a time as the 'Idol of American Motherhood', and had co-starred with **Hazel June** in at least one movie. He enjoyed a normal range of juvenile pursuits, such as eating candy until his teeth demanded the attention of **B K Burwash**. Such was the confusing nature of the revelations concerning this fourteen-year-old's adventures in the fourth dimension, that we are forced to refer to his actions whilst assuming a second *persona* as **Reggie Havershot** as those of **TF(RH)**, and it was while so disguised that he was able to use his inherited strength and poke a considerable proportion of his enemies in the snoot. **(ThisWeek-LAG)**

FLÜELEN: a harbour some two miles from **Küssnacht Castle**. **(WTT ch14)**

FLUSH THE FOUR, to: to swank, to deceive the world. **(Ainslee-RIE)**

FLYING CLOUD: a 45' yacht with sleeping accommodation for four which **Packy Franklyn** chartered and took to **St Rocque**, where it was the scene of a dramatic meeting. **(HOW ch2,16)**

FLYNN, Errol Leslie Thomas (1908-1959): after partially recovering from imbibing a **Mickey Finn**, **Joe Davenport** might have been expecting to feel like someone who had annoyed ... **(TOR ch14)**

FOCH, General Ferdinand (1851-1929): was described as a bird at changing preconceived plans to suit the exigencies of the moment. **(TMM ch2)**

FOLLOW THE GIRL: had run a long time at the **Regal Theatre** after coming from New York, with a book by **Wally Mason** and music by **George Bevan**. See *Volume 5*. **(JTR ch5)**

FOLSOM, Mrs: a guest at the rural doghouse run by **Sir Buckstone Abbott**, who suffered from large teeth and entertained herself with croquet and bridge. **(SUM ch1,16,25)**

FOOTPATHS OF FATE: following a misunderstanding between the hero and heroine, the hero kidnapped her little brother, returned him to the bosom of his family and received his due reward. Something similar, with a Peke rather than a brother in the starring role, was proposed by **Webster** for **Sam Marlowe**'s consideration. **(GOB ch16)**

FORD, Henry (1863-1947): the sort of brother one would wish one's wife to have. **(SUM ch10)**

FORD'S COFFEE HOUSE: an alternative eating-house in Glasshouse Street. **(NGW ptII ch6)**

FOREVER AMBER: the explanation of the noise in the projection room. **(TOR ch16)**

FORTESCUE, Mr Frank: the name which **Frank** was using this season. **(DBB ch11)**

FORT KNOX: a burglarious entry into ... might have been attempted by **Phipps**. **(TOR ch8)**

FOSTER: one of five acquaintances of **Jane Abbott** not known to **Joe Vanringham**. **(SUM ch5)**

FOSTER, Gerald: a young, lean, well-built Englishman in his mid-20s, he was secretly engaged to **Sally Nicholas**. Whilst at school with **Ginger Kemp** he had been a wing three-quarter with a fairly decent swerve but an inability to give the reverse pass, and was considered (though not for that reason) a worm, a tick, a rotter. Not straight. In **Maxwell Faucitt**'s view the sort of man on whom any hint of success would have the worst possible effect, he proved the point on becoming a successful playright, by declining to stay faithful to his fiancée. So, as he strayed, she was betrayed; as he moved round the roster, he lost 'er. He married his leading lady, **Elsa Doland**, instead, but she was soon to regret her impetuosity. **(TAS)**

FOSTER-FRENCHES, the: **Lady Teresa Cobbold** was connected with the Sussex ..., not the Devonshire lot, through her mother. **(SPF ch14)**

FOTHERGILL, Billy: a model for **Gerald Foster**. **(TAS ch5)**

FOTHERGILL, Jimmy: an author fighting for a knighthood. **(TGI ch11)**

FOTHERINGAY-PHIPPS, Barmy: a stray visitor from *Volume 7* (in particular). **Reggie Havershot** recalled the occasion when his fellow-**Drone** made their mutual friend **Oofy Prosser** as "shirty as dammit" by asking for a loan of ten bob until the following Wednesday. Reggie also mentioned the occasion when Barmy, faced by a creditor (in the amount of £2 6s 11d) talked to him about Hurst Park with such good results that the creditor not only stood him a pint but lent him a further five bob. **(LAG ch16,20)**

FOTHERINGHAM, Lord: took the rap in *'Twas Once in May.* **(SUM ch19)**

FOURNIER, Henri-Alban (1886-1914): had lifelike pictures printed in *La Vie Parisienne.* **(SUM ch5)**

FRAMLINGHAME, Hugo Percy de Wynter: (pronounced 'Froom'); see **Carricksteed, sixth Earl of. (MLF-OTN; McClure-BRF)**

FRAMPTON, George G: a commercial employee of the **Hollywood** magazine *Screen Beautiful* who witnessed **JC(RH)** poking **Cosmo Booch** and **Dikran Marsupial** in their respective snoots. **(LAG ch12)**

FRANCE, Ambassador to: Mrs Gedge planned to have her husband appointed as the American ..., not a prospect which appealed to him. He realised that such a post involved a uniform of cocked hats and satin knickerbockers, and carried the threat of being continually kissed by Frenchmen. **(HOW ch1)**

FRANCIS: the janitor or lift-man at **Elizabeth Herrold**'s block of flats. **(MLF-BFL; Strand-BFL)**

FRANCIS, Mabel: was expected to win the **Love-r-ly Silver Cup** on Tuesdays, Thursdays and Saturdays. **(MLF-ATG)**

FRANK: an American gun-toting friend of **Smithy**, who joined the **Appleby gang** for the proposed raid on **Bond's Bank**. He boasted a 'B' picture face and generally flamboyant dress including bright suits, sharply pointed shoes and a guards' tie. Younger than Smithy, he was also more highly strung, and after taking over **Charlie Yost**'s contract on **Mike Bond**, he shot **Sergeant Potter** instead. **(DBB ch5,9,11,14)**

FRANKENSTEIN: was considered probably to be an Old Harrovian, and it was pointed out with surprise that he got married despite his looks. These comments, made by Joey Cooley and Eggy Mannering, disclose a rare misunderstanding of the role of fictional characters, for Mary Shelley's character had been the student who created the infamous monster, not the creature himself. **(LAG ch28)**

FRANKLIN: an upstate New York town near the Canadian border from which **Pearl Delahay (Gooch)** had escaped, leaving behind her husband **Brewster**, son **Elmer** and the Always Open Garage on Main Street. **(Strand-BTG)**

FRANKLIN ARGUS-GAZETTE: the newspaper in **Franklin** which offered the *Ask Dad* management all the space it wanted for a write-up of **Pearl Delahay**. **(Strand-BTG)**

FRANKLIN OPERA HOUSE: gave its audience plenty of elbow-room, having apparently been built by someone who had thought that only Ben Hur with a company of 200 (not counting camels, ancient Roman senators and elephants) would ever play in it. **(Strand-BTG; BurrMcK-MIS)**

FRANKLYN, Patrick B ('Packy'): educated at **Yale**, this wealthy All-American half-back made a considerable impression on **Jane Opal** in particular with his touch-downs against **Notre Dame** and **Harvard**, but she thought little of it for some years. A man who enjoyed the sense of adventure, he was briefly engaged to **Myrtle Blandish** and for an even briefer spell took up the profession of barber. When Jane Opal stood face-to-face across the laid wastes of her father's head, he was attracted to her more quickly than to any girl ever before, even though he was conscious of his engagement to the incomparably beautiful **Lady Beatrice Bracken**. After adopting the identity of his friend, the **Vicomte de Blissac**, he gained the approval of **Senator Opal** for his engagement to Jane first by a ruse, and then over a meal in which he swallowed the senator's words. **(HOW; USHOW ch2)**

FRED[1]: with **Eddie** and **George**[2], he was a bearded member of an amateur kidnapping gang in **Hollywood**, who apologised about the chloroform and had been an extra in *Lepers of Broadway*. He regarded **Public Enemy No 13** as a **Warner Baxter** role with the part of the captain suitable for **Joe Cawthorne**. **(LAG ch24)**

FRED[2]: the son of a caretaker in a big house in Kent, he was the barman at the East End pub where **Nigger** spent his puppyhood. **(MLF-HMV)**

FRED[3]: a barman at the Eighth Avenue saloon where **Nigger** was also reported as having spent his puppyhood, this Fred's father being a caretaker in a big house on Long Island. **(Red-HMV)**

FREDDIE: a man in a walrus moustache who played for Surrey in 1911, was a friend of **Lord Plumpton**, and had his hat knocked off by tin foil at **Lord's**. **(NSE-HTU)**

Packy Franklyn reconstructs Senator Opal's hairstyle

FRED²'S FATHER: the caretaker of a big house in Kent whose dog **Bob** was poisoned and was replaced by **Nigger**. **(MLF-HMV)**

FRED³'S FATHER: an American caretaker of a Long Island property whose dog, also named **Bob,** was poisoned and succeeded by one named **Nigger**. **(MTL-HMV)**

FRIARS': another of the resorts of the artist, author, actor or Bohemian to which **Archie Moffam** was introduced by his new American friends. **(IOA ch4)**

FRIDA: the Norwegian cook who worked for **Elizabeth Herrold**. **(Strand-BFL)**

FRIEDMANN, Samuel: for scenery, charged $3,711. **(JTR ch17)**

FRIESSHARDT: one of **Gessler**'s bodyguards, who kept watch over the cap with **Leuthold**. He was attacked by the mob with eggs, cabbages, cats and missiles of every sort, but managed to hit **Tell** on the head with a pike. **(WTT ch7,8)**

FRISBY, Miss: the negative and anaemic secretary to **Mrs Peagrim**, whose involved pothooks and twiddleys achieved a reference to an ambassador with a fever instead of the Diva he had started with. **(JTR ch10,19)**

FRITH STREET GANG, the: its leader was **Sid Marks**; its members included **Otto the Sausage**, **Rabbit Butler** and possibly **Porky Binns** and **Spider Buffin**. **(TUW-MIS; BurrMcK-MIS)**

FULLER & BENJAMIN: where **Rosie** bought her spring frock and spring suit. **(Strand-TSF; SatEvePost-TSP)**

FÜRST, Walter: red-haired, fierce-looking leader of the group which was elected to complain to **Gessler** about his policy on **taxes**. As father of **Hedwig Tell**, he also led the delegation which asked for her husband's assistance in resolving the matter. **(WTT ch1,4,5)**

FUZZY-WUZZY: an offering rendered by a young man at the ship's concert. **(GOB ch6)**

GABLE, William Clark (1901-1960): to invest in his what purported to be his vest proved to be unwise. During **Harold Steptoe**'s **Hollywood** career, ... had never been cast ahead of him. The main things which distinguished him from **Patrolman Morehouse** were that he, Gable, had a moustache, ten million dollars, and Lady Sylvia Ashley. **(LAG ch15; QUS ch8; TOR ch16)**

GABY: was lower down the social scale than a guffin. **(DBB ch5)**

GADARENE SWINE: were made famous by *Mark*, ch5, for their prowess at the short sprint. **(TGI ch2)**

GAIETY CHORUS: Bruce Carmyle had no objection to the ... in its proper place, which was on the other side of the footlights. **(TAS ch16)**

GAINSBOROUGH, Thomas (1727-1788): a Regency artist who painted *The Girl in Blue*, and her sister in green. **(TGI ch3)**

GALAHAD: presumably Sir ...; see **Parsifal**

GALATEA:

> The butler came slowly to life like a male Galatea.

(TOR ch5)

GANDINOT, M: the president of **Roville** mont-de-piété and the ugliest man in town, who liked to practise his English on his employee, **Ruth Warden. (TMU-RIE)**

GANS, Joe (1874-1910): as a lightweight, he was the medium of comparison for his potential successors. **(TAS ch13)**

GARBO, Greta (Greta Lovisa Gustafsson, 1905-1990): one of three ingredients which, when mixed together, would produce **Lady Beatrice Bracken.** Had **Miss Attwater**'s hair been done in a different way, it would have resembled that of ... If she was as good as they said, **Clara Svelte** might find herself out of a job. **(HOW ch2; SUM ch16; Aldin-GOW)**

GARDENER, a: to the **Brinkmeyers.** He looked Japanese, had a squint and a wart on his nose and was in reality a character-actor hoping for a part in a new Japanese film. His gardening skills were not honed as sharply as his ability to locate horned toads and frogs. **(LAG ch16)**

GARDENIA TEA SHOPPE, the: in High Street, **Loose Chippings.** Like all Tea Shoppes, it was hermetically sealed, no crevice in its walls permitting even a particle of fresh air to steal in and dilute its peculiar atmosphere. **(QUS ch13)**

GARDEN CITY: scene of one of the rounds of **mental golf** played by **Sam Marlowe** whilst concealed in a cupboard at **Windles.** **(TMM ch 17)**

GARDEN OF THE HESPERIDES: the name of the area where **Reggie Havershot** took a bungalow while in **Hollywood**. **(LAG ch3)**

GARDNER, Erle Stanley (1889-1970): could not have turned out sixteen books a year if he had been cross-examined by **Old Nick** the whole time, but he seemed eager to leave 10% of his earnings with a literary agent. **(TOR ch18; FRL ch6)**

GARIBALDI, Giuseppe (1807-1882): was not an Italian composer beginning with 'P'. **(SUM ch22)**

GASPARD THE MISER: would have paid commission at a rate of less than 10%. **(TOR ch8)**

GAVARNI, Mme: lived in a convenient spot in a side street, from where she gave dancing lessons to **Henry Mills**. **(MLF-TLF)**

GEDGE, J Wellington: a tubby little man from **Glendale**, California, who had been exiled to Europe for the two years he had been married to **Mrs G**. The prospect of being appointed **Ambassador to France** offered no balm to his homesickness. Once a wealthy man, he had lost every penny, or every cent, in the big crash of 1929 (apart from the $60,000 which he had invested in a necklace and given to his wife), and was still in that condition when held up in the street by **Soup Slattery**. He cleverly turned the tables and borrowed a mille from the disgruntled mugger, giving the lie to **Ambrose Opal**'s description of him as half-witted, although he was neatly misled into believing that he had nearly killed the **Viscomte de Blissac** in a drunken brawl. **(HOW)**

GEDGE, Julia: she was possessed of one of the more difficult life histories for the commentator to write about in a balanced, unemotional manner. First, a most unusual circumstance for a leading character, we were left in the dark until the last moment as to her Christian name. For, secondly, she had started life as **Julia**, the best **inside stand** with whom **Soup Slattery** ever worked, a revelation to which we became party only at the dénouement. Thirdly, in the four years since an epoch-making departure from that partnership, she had married twice: initially to the now deceased **Wilmot Brewster**, from whom she had inherited many millions, and then to her husband of two years **J Wellington Gedge**, who had responded to the shock by losing all his money. Fourthly, she had got into trouble with her English income tax, which had necessitated a prolonged visit to London to see her lawyer and implied that she had lived in England for at least long enough for the sharks of the Inland Revenue to be interested in her affairs. Fifthly, she planned to blackmail **Senator Opal** after receiving from him a misaddressed letter, thus reverting, one might conclude, to type. **(HOW)**

GEISENHEIMER'S: a New York club near Longacre Square or Times Square with an expensive, glittering restaurant, usually full, where **Henry** and **Minnie Mills** celebrated their first wedding anniversary, and where employed professional dancers including **Miss Roxborough** and **Mabel Francis** competed nightly for the **Love-r-ly Silver Cup**. **(JTR ch11; MLF-ATG,TLF; SatEvePost-TLF)**

GENERAL MOTORS: the impact of their investments in ... on their overall fortunes was something which neither **Soup Slattery** nor **J Wellington Gedge** wanted to talk about. **(HOW ch1)**

GENEVIEVE[1]: a notoriously beautiful, tall, blond friend of **Katie Bennett**, who was regularly pestered by musical comedy managers to go on stage. Though a cloak model at **Macy's**, she could have been mistaken for an English duchess. **(MLF-CRH)**

GENEVIEVE[2]: a friend of **Katie MacFarland**, who dined at **Mac's**. **(Red-ROM)**

GENEVIEVE[3]: **Young Kelly**'s sister, a strong woman in vaudeville. **(SUM ch14)**

GEORGE[1]: a fictional husband who agreed to give up **Skeffington's Sloe Gin**. **(NGW ptII ch6)**

GEORGE[2]: with **Eddie** and **Fred[1]**, a bearded member of an amateur kidnapping gang in **Hollywood**, who helped **RH(JC)** and **RH(TF)** to sausages and suggested that eggs might come before the pancakes. He dreamed up a scenario for a film regarded a superstitious **Public Enemy No 13**, which he saw as a **Bill Powell** role with the captain's part suitable for **Edward Everett Horton**. **(LAG ch24; Pearson-LAG; ThisWeek-LAG)**

GEORGE[3]: a cousin of **Aubrey Jerningham** who wrote society dialogue for *Piccadilly Weekly*. **(Throne-KHE)**

GERALD: the hero in **Bill Shannon**'s story for *Passion Magazine*. **(TOR ch13)**

GERMAN, an anonymous: a short stout man with a derby hat, who claimed to the police, in the *persona* of **Mike Burke**, that **Tim**

Burke had assaulted him, and insisted on pressing charges. The defence offered – that Tim was merely trying to teach him to dance an Irish jig – cut no ice. **(PallMall-MLB)**

GESSLER, Hermann: the unpopular Governor of Switzerland, who insisted on being addressed as "Your Excellency" and who, though always willing to receive delegations, tended to punish his visitors with doses of boiling oil rather than respond to their grievances. One of his favourite activities was to forbid whatever the people liked doing, such as dancing, singing, playing musical instruments, eating (other than bread and simple meats) and all sorts of games. When the list ran out he had erected an old hat on a pole and required his subjects to bow down before it. When **William Tell** refused, he ordered him, on pain of death, to shoot an apple off his son's head with a single arrow. When this was achieved, he decided to imprison him for life, but Tell outwitted him en route to his castle at **Küssnacht**. **(WTT)**

GIANTS: *v* **White Sox**. **(MLF-OTN)**

GIBBONS, Stanley: was also among those prepared to defer to **Desborough Topping**. **(SPF ch3)**

GIBBS, Mr: lost a packet of banknotes to a kleptomaniac dining companion. **(TGI ch12)**

GIDEON BIBLE: all that was needed to make the *Mignonette* a true home for **Sam Bulpitt**. **(SUM ch14)**

GILBERT, Sir William Schwenk (1836-1911): wrote of **Lord Lardy**, and Policeman Forth, who had been discovered in Rupert Street at the end of his long wanderings through Soho. **Wally Mason**'s attempt to restore the tradition created by ... and **Sullivan** to New York was seen by the local speciality artists as a detrimental step. His **Alphonso**'s approach to making a proposal contrasted with that of **Sam Marlowe's grandfather**, but was similar to that of Sam himself. **(NGW ptII ch4; JTR ch9; FRL ch4; GOB ch4))**

GILDED SINNERS: a film starring **Adela Cork** containing the line "After that I wash my hands of the matter and the law can take its course." **(TOR ch20)**

GIMBELS: its autumn sale was liable to attract shoplifters. **(TGI ch1)**

GINGERY STORIES: **Mae d'Arcy** had assumed from reading ... that she had to act like a vamp with a millionaire on a string when she was mad about the fellow to whom she was engaged. **(JTR ch11)**

GINSBERG, Lew: the advance man for the *Ask Dad* **Number Two Company**, who didn't know who **Pearl Delahay** was. **(Strand-BTG)**

GIRL AGAINST THE WORLD, A: starring **Gloria Gooch**, a film that had been seen by **Rebecca Abraham**. **(TAS ch14)**

GIRL FROM BRIGHTON, The: a show whose cast, including **Alice Weston, Walter Jelliffe, Clarice Weaver** and **Sidney Crane**, was going on tour to such places as Bristol and Hull. **(MLF-BTB)**

GIRL FROM BROADWAY, The: the similar show whose cast, also including **Alice Weston, Walter Jelliffe, Clarice Weaver** and **Sidney Crane**, would be touring cities including Syracuse and Buffalo. **(Century-BTB)**

GIRL FROM YONKERS, The: the sort of title expected by New York critics to be attached to a **Wally Mason** show. **(JTR ch4)**

GIRL IN BLUE, The: a miniature by **Gainsborough** of the **Scrope** great-great-grandmother, or an even more distant ancestor. **(TGI ch3)**

GIRL WHO WAITED, The: a play written by **Margaret Goodwin** which she offered for production under **James Orlebar Cloyster**'s name. It was quaint and whimsical, with a suggestion of pathos and made enormous profits when put on by the **Briggs Theatre** in London. **(NGW pt1 ch3; ptII ch25)**

GISSING, George Robert (1857-1903): **James Cloyster** was scared away from Bohemianism partly by reading ... **(NGW ptII ch9)**

GIUSEPPE'S: one of the 487 Italian restaurants in the neighbourhood which **George Mellon** and **Rosie** generally patronised. **(Strand-TSF)**

GLADYS: a smoker and gunslinger in **Alcala**, she was an uninvited visitor to **Rutherford Maxwell**'s room. **(TMU-TGP)**

GLASS AND GLACIER: the inn of the town in which **Fürst, Stauffacher** and **Arnold of Melchthal** lived. **(WTT ch4)**

GLEASON, May: the manicure girl at the **Hotel Cosmpolitan**, she shared an apartment with **Ellabelle Bagster** until she toured with the stage production of *Oh, Mabel*. She had beautiful dark hair, like a great rolling black wave, a soft brooding cloud, a moonless night, water under the stars. And no doubt like many other poetic descriptions which would have evaporated just as quickly when she allowed herself to be persuaded to have the whole lot dyed yellow. She came to New York from her home town in **Ostoria**, Ohio, via Jersey City, and toured with the show *She's All Right* through Detroit, Toronto, Cleveland, Buffalo, Washington and New York, before leaving to marry **Lancelot Purvis**. **(Grand-COL)**

GLENCOE ATHLETIC CLUB: of New York, its star was **Ted Brady**, who could run the 100 yards in evens. **(MLF-CRH)**

GLENDALE: the Californian spiritual home of **J Wellington Gedge**, complete with filling stations and hot dogs. **(HOW ch1)**

GLUTZ, Jacob: of **Medulla-Oblongata-Glutz**, a luncheon guest of **Adela Cork** who looked like a lobster and offered **Phipps** a job in **Hollywood** doing butler parts, with a morality clause to prevent him cracking safes. **(TOR ch4)**

GOBLE: the producer with **Cahn** of musical comedies such as *Coralie*. **(Strand-BTG)**

GOBLE & CAHN: the producers of *Coralie*. **(Strand-BTG)**

GOBLE & COHN: the alternative producers of *Coralie*. This is also the preferred spelling of the firm in *Jill the Reckless* (*The Little Warrior* in the US), and in the US book *Mostly Sally*, and although utilised in *The Adventures of Sally*, the UK equivalent of the latter, it shared the honour there with **Goble & Kohn**. Cutting through the confusion, it was a firm of New York theatrical agents who had an office on the fifth floor of the **Gotham Theatre** on W42nd St, with whom **Nelly Bryant** obtained work on her return to the US and whose premises **Jill Mariner** stormed, breaking all the conventions. They declined to be associated with **Gerald Foster** but stole his wife, **Elsa Doland** for a new part. **(JTR ch9,10; TAS ch 14; MOS ch1,14; Cosmo-FFD)**

GOBLE & KOHN: see **Goble & Cohn**

GOBLE, Isaac:. a personal description of this partner in **Goble and Cohn** (or **Kohn**) could only be unflattering. He was thickset, a fleshy man in his early thirties. He had smooth yellow hair, a clean-shaven face displaying to its best advantage his double chin and his unwholesome complexion, while his small green eyes were too close-set. **Wally Mason** warned **Jill Mariner** that he pawed, and other descriptive words which sprang to mind were: stinker, prowler, leerer, pest, worm. On top of those, he was fat, soft, flabby and greasy, had a withered heart and an eye like a codfish. On being inspected by him, Jill felt inadequately clad and after snubbing his inevitable advances she was duly sacked. He was, though, man enough to personally break the news to **Gerald Foster** that his firm was not proposing to stage his play. **(JTR ch10,15,18; TAS ch1)**

GOD'S GOOD MAN: a book which told the secrets of Society. **(NGW ptII ch13)**

GOLDWYN, Sam (Schmuel Gelbfisz, 1879-1974):

> By the beard of Sam Goldwyn, there are moments when I feel an almost overpowering urge to bean you with a bottle.

(TOR ch2)

GOOCH, Brewster: the husband of **Pearl**, brother of **Ellabelle** and father of **Elmer**, he ran the Always Open Garage half way along Main Street, **Franklin**, and did a little bootlegging on the side. He was a long, skinny, freckled individual with a lantern-shaped jaw, big feet and a poor record of accuracy with a gun. **(Strand-BTG)**

GOOCH, Ellabelle: an unreliable sister of **Brewster** who was suspected of preaching vegetarianism and possibly Christian Science all the time she was baby-sitting **Elmer**. **(Strand-BTG)**

GOOCH, Elmer: the three-year-son of **Brewster** and **Pearl**, who would have had to be smart not to be indoctrinated by the dangerous views of his Aunt **Ellabelle**. As it was he had a tendency to break out in pink spots and hiccup. **(Strand-BTG)**

GOOCH, Gloria: the star of *A Girl Against the World*. **(TAS ch14)**

GOOCH, Mabelle: starred in *Lepers of the Great White Way*. **(SatEvePost-TSP)**

GOOCH, Pearl: see **Delahay, Pearl**

GOOCH, Police Constable: held on to **Meggs**'s arm while listening to the explanation for his sudden desire for **Miss Pillenger**'s company. **(MLF-AST)**

GOOD STUFF IN THIS BOY: see page 124

GOOD STUFF IN THIS BOY
ABOUT A TON OF IT

My children, if you fail to shine or triumph in your special line; if, let us say, your hopes are bent on some day being President, and folks ignore your proper worth, and say you've not a chance on earth – Cheer up! For in these stirring days Fame may be won in many ways. Consider, when your spirits fall, the case of Washington McCall.

Yes, cast your eye on Washy, please! He looks just like a piece of cheese: he's not a brilliant sort of chap: he has a dull and vacant map: his eyes are blank, his face is red, his ears stick out beside his head.   In fact, to end these compliments, he would be dear at thirty cents. Yet Fame has welcomed to her hall this selfsame Washington McCall.

His mother (*née* Miss Cora Bates) is one who frequently orates upon the proper kind of food which every menu should include.   With eloquence the world she weans from chops and steaks and pork and beans.   Such horrid things she'd like to crush, and make us live on milk and mush.   But oh! the thing that makes her sigh is when she sees us eating pie.   (We heard her lecture last July upon "The Nation's Menace – Pie".)   Alas, the hit it made was small with Master Washington McCall.

For yesterday we took a trip to see the great Pie Championship, where men with bulging cheeks and eyes consume vast quantities of pies.   A fashionable West Side crowd beheld the champion, Spike O'Dowd, endeavour to defend his throne against an upstart, Blake's Unknown. He wasn't an Unknown at all.   He was young Washington McCall.

We freely own we'd give a leg if we could borrow, steal or beg the skill old Homer used to show. (He wrote the *Iliad*, you know.) Old Homer swung a wicked pen, but we are ordinary men, and cannot even start to dream of doing justice to our theme. The subject of that great repast is too magnificent and vast. We can't describe (or even try) the way those rivals wolfed their pie. Enough to say that, when for hours each had extended all his pow'rs, toward the quiet evenfall O'Dowd succumbed to young McCall.

The champion was a willing lad. He gave the public all he had. He was a genuine, fighting soul. He'd lots of speed and much control. No yellow streak did he evince. He tackled apple-pie and mince. This was the motto on his shield – "O'Dowds may burst. They never yield." His eyes began to start and roll. He eased his belt another hole. Poor fellow! With a single glance one saw that he had not a chance. A python would have had to crawl and own defeat from young McCall.

At last, long last, the finish came. His features overcast with shame, O'Dowd, who'd faltered once or twice, declined to eat another slice. He tottered off, and kindly men rallied round with oxygen. But Washy, Cora Bates's son, seemed disappointed it was done. He somehow made those present feel he'd barely started on his meal. We asked him "Aren't you feeling bad?" "Me!" said the lion-hearted lad. "Lead me" – he started for the street – "where I can get a bite to eat!" Oh, what a lesson does it teach to all of us, that splendid speech! How better can the curtain fall on Master Washington McCall!

(IOA ch21)

The Great Pie-Eating Contest, featuring Washington McCall and Spike O'Dowd

GOODWIN, Archie: in Nero Wolfe stories, he would easily have recovered a stolen miniature. **(TGI ch10)**

GOODWIN, Eugene Grandison, LL D: the late father of **Margaret**. **(NGW ptII ch26)**

GOODWIN, Margaret: the narrator of the first part of *Not George Washington*, who started and finished the book as the fiancée of **James Orlebar Cloyster**. She was a good swimmer and put to good use skills which she obtained whilst pursuing water sports such as [mussel-]stalking, [prawn-]hunting, [fish-]snaring and [mushroom-]trapping when she spied JOC out in a boat. Within minutes, and before breakfast on the day they met, he had been stalked, hunted, snared, trapped and introduced to her mother. Margaret wrote a play *The Girl Who Waited* some three years after becoming engaged to James, and he added his name to it before having it produced most successfully, in London. **(NGW)**

GOODWIN, Mrs: the mother of **Margaret**, a philosopher who found daily pleasure with **Ibsen**, Kant, **Maeterlinck**, **Schopenhauer** and others. She advised **James Cloyster** to wait before marrying her daughter. Came to London for the premiere of Margaret's play, *The Girl Who Waited*. **(NGW ptI ch1; ptII ch26)**

GOOSE AND GANDER: the only pub in **Walsingford Parva**, of which **John B Attwater** was the landlord. **(SUM ch7)**

GOOSE AND GANDER: the only pub in **Mellingham-in-the-Vale**, of which **Beefy Hibbs** was the landlord. **(TGI ch8)**

GORGON, the: of Greek mythology, one of whose less engaging characteristics was an ability to turn voyeurs and voyeuses to stone. **(TGI ch11)**

GORGONZOLA CHEESEHOUND: according to **Fred²**, **Nigger** was an example of one. **(MLF-HMV)**

GORKY, Maxim (Alexsei Maksimovitch Peshkov, 1868-1936): might have made a stab at the writing of gloom. **(JTR ch8)**

GOSSETT, James J: a stout, bald, middle-aged motion-picture man who bulged in practically every place where a man can bulge. His lunchdate at the **Hotel Cosmopolis** Grill with **Mrs J L T Smith** proved to be fraught with interest, but it was only his natural diffidence which might have prevented it from being highly profitable. **(IOA ch20)**

GOSSIP, Mr: called **Jill Mariner** "one of the most charming and attractive of Society belles" when writing about her engagement in the *Morning Mirror*. **(JTR ch1)**

GOTHAM THEATRE: the 42nd Street home of **Goble and Cohn**, near Times Square. **(JTR ch9)**

GRACIE'S HERO: so bad an example of a manuscript that it brought tears to the eyes of its author, **Lucas Undershaw**. **(Throne-KHE)**

GRANT, Cary (Archibald Alexander Leach, 1904-1986): if you can look at **Conky Biddle**, why bother with ...? **(NSE-HTU)**

GRANT, John: the pen-name of **Wally Mason**. **(JTR ch2)**

GRAY, Gwenda: a star authoress on the unspeakable **Mortimer Busby**'s list, who left for an American lecture tour to help keep the depression going in that happy country. **(SUM ch3)**

GREAT PIE-EATING CONTEST, The: featured **Spike O'Dowd** and **Washington McCall**. **(IOA ch22)**

GREEK STREET REGISTRY OFFICE, the: a place where neither **Augustus Robb** nor **Alice Punter** had waited. **(SPF ch16,23)**

GREEN, Hetty: **J B Duff** suggested to **Vera Pym** that before she knew where she was she would be a ..., one of the richest women around. **(QUS ch13)**

GREENWAY, Walter: did not like **Alf Joblin**'s boxing style, but was knocked senseless by **Tom Blake**. **(NGW ptII ch10)**

GRENOUILLIÈRE: a restaurant at Aumale where **Hermione Pegler** invited the **Trent** sisters to dinner, in order that **Boissonade** should be able to search their rooms. **(FRL ch6)**

GRESHAM: helped **Fermin** on the *On Your Way* column. **(NGW ptII ch3)**

GRIMM (Jacob Ludwig Carl, 1785-1863, and Wilhelm Carl, 1786-1859): **Kit Malim** was dimly familiar with their fairy tales. **(NGW ptII ch8)**

GROGAN, Police Constable: a genial giant who was a terror to the riotous element of the Southampton waterfront but nervous in the presence of death, as personified by **Captain Gunner**. **(TUW-DAE)**

GROOME STREET GANG, the: its members included **Otto the Sausage**, **Rabbit Butler** and possibly **Porky Binns** and **Spider Buffin**, and was led by **Bat Jarvis**. **(BurrMcK-MIS)**

GROOM'S: the Fleet Street rendezvous for members of staff of *The Orb*, where **Cloyster** was able to find them again. **(NGW ch24)**

GROSSMAN, Ike: a celebrated New York impresario with similar attributes to **Ike Schumann**, and a surname similar at least in part to the British dedicatee of the story in which he appeared. (See next entry.) **(Colliers-TAS pt5)**

GROSSMITH, George (1874-1935): the dedicatee of *The Adventures of Sally*. He had worked with Wodehouse on *The Beauty Prize*, *The Cabaret Girl*, *Kissing Time* and *Sally*, all at the Winter Garden Theatre, London, between 1919 and 1923, where they ran for between 213 and 430 performances.

GRUBBINESS: in London, the gauge of a lawyer's respectability. **(WHC-TMM)**

GRUNDY, Mrs: **Kate Trent**'s gaze, on seeing **Freddie Carpenter** in blue pyjamas in her sister **Terry**'s room, was that of one who might have been ...'s twin sister. **(FRL ch7)**

GRUSCZINSKY: beamed on **Annette Brougham** as her fourth tune sold and he announced two new editions in a week. **(TMU-MUP)**

GRUSCZINSKY & BUCHTERKIRCH: a well-known London firm of music publishers. **(TMU-MUP)**

GUARDS: **Derek Underhill** didn't even know if **Chris Selby** had been in the ... **(TLW ch1; Grand-JTR)**

GUATEMALA: a man dressed in the uniform of a general in the army of ... acted as a doorman at **Chris Selby**'s supposed New York address. **(JTR ch9)**

GUELPH: a Paris Restaurant where **Henry**[1] called the head waiter a fat-headed vampire. **(MLF-MOM)**

GUILDENSTERN'S STORES: of Madison Avenue, New York, an emporium under threat from shoplifters. **(TGI ch1)**

GUINEVERE: **Terry Cobbold** to **Mike Cardinal**'s **King Arthur**, but see King Arthur. **(SPF ch22)**

GUM-SHOE GERTIE: see **Carlisle, Gertrude**

GUNGA DIN: a recitation within **Chris Selby**'s repertoire, rendered at a ship's concert by a younger man. The **Brinkmeyer** chauffeur proposed to recite it to **RH(JC)**, but **Smedley Cork** did not recite it despite expectations. **(JTR ch6; GOB ch6; LAG ch19; TOR ch6)**

GUNNER, Captain John: the recently deceased 55-year-old resident of the **Excelsior Boarding House**, who had been found lying with tightly clenched hands, a leg twisted oddly under him and teeth gleaming through a grey beard in a horrible grin as a result of cobra venom poisoning. He had been a tough old sailor with 40 years at sea, which had given him a tongue sufficiently bitter to make him unpopular. His hobbies included playing draughts with another resident, **Muller**, and the harmonica, to the distaste of the local feline population. **(TUW-DAE)**

GUNTON-CRESSWELL, Mr: a queer old Tory of the old school who wore a beaver hat, lived in South Kensington and was an acquaintance both of the **Goodwin**s and the **Cloysters**. He only spoke to grumble and was scandalised by the personal appearance of **Peter Pan**. **(NGW pt1 ch1; ptII ch23)**

GUNTON-CRESSWELL, Mrs: introduced **James Cloyster** to **Eva Eversleigh** her niece, for whom she was socially ambitious. **(NGW ptII ch15,21)**

GUSTAVE: late of **Chez Jimmy**, the kindly inventor of the Gustave Special was the genius presiding over the American Bar, **Hotel des Etrangers**. **(HOW ch1)**

HAILEYBURY: where **Wally Mason** had been to school. **(JTR ch2)**

HAIRY AINUS: a feature at **Luna Park** confronted by which **Arthur Welsh** developed a new level of facetiousness. **(TMU-WDD)**

HALE, Beatrice Forbes-Robertson: an illustrative example of the reason why **Adelaide Brewster Moggs** declined to add to her burden by taking her husband's surname as well. **(VanFair-AAI)**

HALL, Minnie: see **Mills, Minnie**

HALLIDAY, Alice: **Rutherford Maxwell**'s fiancée, whose framed picture was on the mantelpiece in his room in **Alcala**. **(TMU-INA)**

HALLIDAY, Johnny: legal counsel for the **Onapoulous**es and a personal friend of **Jerry West**. See *Volume 5*. **(TGI ch2)**

HALLIDAY, Spencer: see **Norcross, Minna**

HAMILTON: would not allow **Fermin** to use **Cloyster** as holiday relief after the paragraphs he wrote concerning **Stickney**. (NGW ch24)

HAMLET:

> Few men in alpaca coats and striped flannel trousers had ever so closely resembled Hamlet as did Mr Gedge at this moment.

He inspired **Meggs** to ask whether it was nobler in the mind to suffer, or to take arms against a sea of troubles, and by opposing, end them. **Joe Vanringham**'s play had a similar theme, whereby guilty parties in the audience can recognise themselves. (HOW ch6; SUM ch5; MLF-AST; PLP-GCS; Strand-BTG)

HAMMERSTEIN, Oscar, II (1895-1960): see **Dollen**

HANGER HILL: scene of one of the rounds of **mental golf** played by **Sam Marlowe** whilst concealed in a cupboard at **Windles**. (GOB ch 17)

HAPPY BIRTHDAY: represented in shorthand by two squiggles and a streptococcus, was sung to **Shorty** at 7am on his 52nd birthday. (SPF ch1)

HAPPY DAYS ARE HERE AGAIN: crooned by **Sam Bulpitt** when he worked out the Big Idea. (SUM ch15)

HAROLD[1]: a cousin of **Percy**, a bluebottle eliminated by **Jean Priaulx**. (TMU-MWD)

HAROLD[2]: **Joe Rendal**'s proud-looking office-boy. (TMU-TFD)

HARTFORD: the astute and discerning citizens of ..., Connecticut, welcomed *The Rose of America* with such a reception that hardened principals stared at each other in a wild surmise. (JTR ch17)

HARVARD: an American football team which did not include a Berserk Senator in its ranks, but against which **Packy Franklyn** made a critical touchdown. (HOW ch2; USHOW ch2)

HARVEST, Geoffrey: *pediculus oleaceus* (var *Hollywoodensis*), once fleetingly engaged to **Terry Cobbold**, whose final disillusionment was compared to being skinned alive in front of an amused audience. **Mike Cardinal** regarded him as a heel, a worm, an oleaginous louse, but admitted that he was handsome in a certain ghastly, greasy, nausea-promoting way, for he had seen him in action on stage as a juvenile in musical comedy who looked noble and sang tenor. **(SPF ch17)**

HASTINGS, Battle of (1066): **Shorty**'s ancestors were tough nuts at the ..., but see also **Edith**. **(SPF ch23)**

HATTON, Rev John: a parson friend of **Malim**, with whom he had been at Trinity, Oxford. When not running boys' clubs at Carnation Hall in Lambeth, but nevertheless away from his rooms at 62 Harcourt Buildings, he could often be found at the **Barrel Club**. He was offered a role as **First Ghost** by **Cloyster** and repaid him by supplanting his fiction. **(NGW)**

HAVERSHOT, the Rt Hon the second Earl of: the late father of the **third Earl**, he had been a gallant soldier and good at polo, but his face had looked more like a gorilla than that of most gorillas. As a result, he was affectionately known to his circle of cronies as **Consul, the Almost Human**. **(LAG ch3)**

HAVERSHOT, the Rt Hon the third Earl of ('Reggie'): Reginald John Peter Swithin, who started at the bottom and worked his way unexpectedly to the title. Aged 28-and-a-bit, he was 6' 1" tall, with brown eyes, carroty hair, a moustache and a face like a gorilla. He obtained his Cambridge boxing blue, became a member of the **Drones Club**, and took up residence at **Biddleford Castle**, Norfolk. As head of the family, he was despatched to **Hollywood** to rescue his cousin, **Egremont Mannering** from an undesirable entanglement, only to find himself mixed up in more ways than one.

Such was the confusing nature of the revelations concerning this peer's adventures in the fourth dimension, that we are forced to refer to his actions whilst assuming a second *persona*, that of **Joey Cooley** or **Teddy Flower**, as those of **RH(JC)** or **RH(TF)**, and it was while so disguised that he provided the interview with **Pomona Wycherley** that changed a number of lives.

His insistence that he loved the devious actress, **April** (or **Hazel**) **June**, was looked on with scorn by all who knew her, including his one-time fiancée **Ann Bannister**, and although he appeared to hold out no hope that reason would win out, he saw stars of a different kind and gave up the chase, falling back into Ann's arms more or less on cue. **(LAG; Pearson-LAG; ThisWeek-LAG)**

HAY, Ian Beith (Major-General John Hay Beith, 1876-1952): a meridian of longitude and a successful playwright of substance. **(SPF ch10)**

HAYDOCK'S GROCERY STORE: at **Brookport**, sold bacon at 60c a pound, compared to the 57c for which it could be obtained at **Patchogue. (TLW ch7; Grand-JTR)**

HAYS, Mr: was invited to perform the unveiling of **Mr Brinkmeyer**'s statue. **(LAG ch12)**

HEAD CLERK: J Rufus Bennett's, who was late bringing **Billie Bennett**'s money to the *Atlantic*, and as a result Swedes swam, dollars disappeared, **Sam Marlowe** spluttered and Billie benefited. **(GOB ch3)**

***HEART OF DELILAH BROWN, The*:** the second offering from **Aubrey Jerningham** in which, after judicious editing, a suicide was turned into a wedding. **(Throne-KHE)**

HEBBLETHWAITE, Mr: Editor of the ***Ladies' Sphere*** and **George Mellon**'s boss, who selected him ahead of twenty-six other applicants, and was proved right when George prevented his wife from visiting Hebblethwaite in the office. When **Rosie H** called to see the Editor without an appointment to obtain a copy of *Ten Delicious Moments from the Chafing-Dish*, she was correctly directed to the publishing department by George. **(Strand-TSF)**

HEBBLETHWAITE, Rosie: the disgruntled wife of an Editor. **(Strand-TSF)**

HELEN: Peter's mother, who spoiled him from birth. **(MLF-BIS)**

HELEN OF TROY (c13th cent BC): **Archie Moffam** would have been immune from her charms even if he had had to extract a fly from her eyes. **Vera Upshaw** was in her class as far as looks were concerned. See also **Cleopatra. (NGW ptII ch15; IOA ch12; TOR ch13; TGI ch5)**

HENDERSON: the father of **Marion**, who befriended **Jean Priaulx**, disliked **Lloyd George**, rescued **Polly** and lived in Eaton Square. **(TMU-MWD)**

HENDERSON, J D'Arcy: of *The Firs*. He sent a pug in a hamper as a present to **Sylvia Reynolds** for which he was called a blackguard by her father. **(TUW-WPS)**

HENDERSON, Marion: the owner of **Polly** and the object of two wooers' attentions. **(TMU-MWD)**

HENDERSON, Miss: **Marion**'s aunt, who had been present at a soirée in Eaton Square. **(TMU-MWD)**

HENDRIE, Eve: the proud paid companion to **Mrs Rastall-Retford** who, as part of her duties, had to share her spartan diet. She was a fragile, fairy-like, ethereal being who could play the piano and avoid revoking while playing bridge by concealing her offending ace in a cheese sandwich. Whilst governess to **Hildebrand Elphinstone** she had met **Peter Rayner** and after telling herself that she resented his advances, she came to realise that they were genuinely offered. **(TUW-BSA)**

HENLEY, Dick: a friend of **Tom Ellison** and **Dora Thingummy**, who was in love with **Dolly Burn**. **(TUW-TDH)**

HENNESSEY, Tough Tom: the cop that always got his man. **(TOR ch16)**

HENRY[1]: an old waiter who had served at **Mac's** since its foundation, after ten years at the **Guelph** or the **Aureata**. Known by **Katie MacFarland** as 'Uncle Bill', he had four young assistants to help him, but he didn't need much help when it came to stopping Katie from gassing herself. **(MLF-MOM; Red-ROM)**

HENRY[2]: the little, bald, bespectacled, nervous husband of **Jane**, who engaged in a minor rebellion after years of having the family purse-strings controlled by his wife. **(MLF-RUP)**

HENRY[3]: see **'Enry**

HENRY, O (William Sydney Porter, 1862-1910): **Jimmy Valentine**'s literary father. **(DBB ch12)**

HENS: whilst their aroma does not resemble that of **Chanel Number Five**, at least it stops short of smelling like an escape of sewer gas. **(FRL ch1)**

HENSON, Leslie (1891-1957): a goldfish in the **Brinkmeyer** pond made faces like ... when **RH(JC)** ate the derelict sausage to which it assumed entitlement. **(LAG ch12)**

HERBERT: the gardener at **George Tanner**'s school, carrying 200 lb of solid flesh, which was peppered in the behind from 20 yards with shotgun pellets by **Sir Godfrey Tanner**. **(Strand-COI)**

HERMITAGE: a picturesque summer hotel in the green heart of the mountains, owned by **Daniel Brewster**. It advertised unrivalled scenery, superb cuisine and the personal eye of the proprietor, although the latter was not always forthcoming. **(IOA ch12)**

HERROLD, Elizabeth: a young writer from Illinois, or from a small Canadian town, with a rich aunt who had seen her through college. By one version of the story she was used to the thud of returned manuscripts, and thus especially disappointed when the one magazine which took her stories expired. She acquired the stray **Joseph** as a good luck charm, and on his disappearance agreed a cat-sharing arrangement with his new hotelier, **James Boyd**, before going one small step further and agreeing to marry him. **(MLF-BFL; Strand-BFL; Red-BCL)**

HERROLD, Jack: **Elizabeth**'s brother, one of the secretaries to a restless old millionaire who had gone off to the Azores in a yacht. **(Strand-BFL)**

HESSELTYNE, Daphne: the secretary to **J B Duff**, known to **Joss Weatherby** as 'Lollipop'. **(QUS ch2)**

HETTY: a **Trent hen** who hid her eggs so that they went bad, but didn't cackle while doing so. **(FRL ch1)**

HIBBS, Beefy: the landlord, **Goose and Gander**, **Mellingham-in-the-Vale**. **(TGI ch11)**

HIBBS, Marlene: niece of the landlord at the **Goose and Gander**, she accepted bicycle lessons from **Chippendale**, using **Simms**'s mount as a steed. **(TGI ch8,11)**

HICK'S THEATRE: Shaftesbury Avenue, built on the site of the **Maison Suisse**. It was here that PGW obtained a staff role as additional lyric writer for Seymour Hicks' show *The Beauty of Bath* at two pounds a week in 1906. It was renamed the Globe some time later. **(NGW ptII ch6)**

HIGGINS: gave his name to a duck-pond at **Loose Chippings** where there was open country and no opportunity for eavesdropping. **(QUS ch6)**

HIGGS, Herbert: an elegant individual with several aliases who had a carnation in his buttonhole, a lighted cigarette in his mouth, the blame for a $15,000 jewel robbery at the Pierce and a conviction for one at the Claridge when he had been caught by **Mr McGee**. **(Ellery-MBD)**

HIGNETT, Adeline: widow of the late Horace, she was a world-famous writer on Theosophy, having been responsible for such masterpieces as *The Spreading Light, What of the Morrow* and others. She embarked on a lecture tour in the USA to promote her views, and dragged along her son **Eustace**, whom she was reluctant to let out of her sight, or to allow to speak to a woman under 50, in case he fell in love. That might have resulted in her having to leave **Windles**, which she held in trust for Eustace but adored. Having prevented Eustace's marriage to **Billie Bennett** by taking the shrewd precaution of pinching his trousers, she was powerless to stop either his shipboard romance with **Jane Hubbard** or his decision to rent Windles out for the summer in her absence. **(GOB ch1,17)**

HIGNETT, Eustace: the son of **Adeline** and the late Horace, he was a cousin of **Sam Marlowe**, with whom he had been at school (where he had kept Sam amused by such tricks as breaking gas – or glass – globes with a slipper) and Trinity, Oxford. He was a fragile young man with a pale, intellectual face, dark hair which fell in a sweep over his forehead, and gave the general impression, which proved founded, of a man who wrote *vers libre*. He was prevented from marrying **Billie Bennett** by shortages in the trousers department, but after being provided by **Jane Hubbard** with a medicine principally used in Africa for bull-calves with the staggers realised that she was his true life's mate. He was also the owner, *de jure* if not *de facto* of **Windles**, one of Hampshire's stateliest mansions, an impressive display of mumps and a sprained ankle, the last two of which necessitated Jane's close attention.. **(GOB; TMM ch15; WHC-TMM; Pan-TMM)**

HIGNETT, Horace: the late husband of **Adeline** and father of **Eustace**. **(GOB ch1)**

HILBURY: one of four places of similar names, with stations and trains critical to the construction of the plot of *Murder at Bilbury Manor*. **(SUM ch16)**

HILL, Mary: left **Dunsterville** to work as stenographer for her former admirer, **Joe Rendal**, after her predecessor had been found to confide too closely in **Eddy Moore**. New York changed her, as it does everyone, and soon after being shown the flaws in Eddy, she and Joe were sealing their future together. **(TMU-TFD)**

HILL, Wentworth: a former Oxford alumnus who, on being sent down for aggravated disorderliness, took away nothing but the Oxford manner. This was not to everyone's liking, and as a straight actor in *Rose of America*, Wentworth fell foul of the impresario, **Ike Goble**. **(JTR ch14)**

HINCKEL: **Stanley Briggs's** secretary. **(NGW ch25)**

HIPPARCHUS OF RHODES (c190-120BC): sneered at the mention of **Marinus of Tyre**'s name. **(TOR ch17)**

HIS FORGOTTEN BRIDE: a member of its cast on a small town tour once took a fiver off **Reggie Havershot** in a game of Persian Monarchs at Newmarket, during Reggie's spell as a Cambridge undergraduate. **(LAG ch17)**

HISTORIC HEARTBREAKERS: the authoress of this work took advantage of **George Mellon**'s inexperience, and was able to see **Hebblethwaite** without an appointment by claiming to be his wife. **(Strand-TSF)**

HISTORY OF THE CAT IN ANCIENT EGYPT, The: by **Professor Snyder Wilberforce**, although it would have been a race to see if he could publish his version before **M Sartines**. **(LHJ-FKA)**

HITLER, Adolf (1889-1945):

> . . . I had tended [my moustache] in sickness and in health, raising it with unremitting care from a sort of half-baked or Hitler smudge to its present robust and dapper condition.

(LAG ch13)

HOBSON, Mabel: was possessed of the beautiful face, perfect figure and other compelling charms which invariably attracted the **Reginald Cracknell**s of the world, and was thus scheduled to receive star billing in *The Primrose Way*, the play which he was backing. **(TAS ch1,5,6,16)**

HODGER: of Middlesex County Cricket Club, edged a rising ball into the hands of a fieldsman dozing in what is technically termed "the gully". **(NSE-HTU)**

HOLBETON, Percy, first Baron: the co-founder of the noted West End food shrine **Duff & Trotter** and late father of **George**. Although generally considered to be of sound intellect, he so over-played his admiration for his business partner **J B Duff** as to make him trustee of his estate for his son when he died. **(QUS ch1,5)**

HOLBETON, George, second Baron: with the family name Trotter, George was a svelte and willowy young man with butter-coloured hair, a prominent Adam's apple and a penchant for singing *Trees* in a quivery tenor voice that sounded like a swooning mosquito. Such gifts tended to cloy, in **Sally Fairmile**'s case about two days after she promised to marry him.   His trustee was the irascible **J B Duff**, who controlled a pot of money on his behalf, but kept a close eye on it following George's breach of promise case whilst at Oxford. He was attacked by **Patricia** as he tried to steal the portrait of **Beatrice Chavender**, and that helped him decide that the sort of wife he wanted was not one who routed him out at midnight to go and get portraits and be bitten in the leg by dogs. **(QUS)**

HOLLAND HOUSE: the New York resting place of **Chris Selby** in earlier years, which had been pulled down. **(JTR ch7)**

HOLLYWOOD:

> "Bright city of sorrows, where fame deceives and temptation lurks, where souls are shrivelled in the furnace of desire, whose streets are bathed with the shamed tears of betrayed maidens.   . . .   Home of mean glories and spangled wretchedness, where the deathless fire burns for the outspread wings of the guileless moth and beauty is broken on sin's cruel wheel."

Once a combination of **Santa Claus** and **Good King Wenceslas**, it evolved into an unreformed **Scrooge**. It was never a monastery but a place where women were thrust upon you, to whom it was necessary to be civil. Furthermore, to a dog it was a noisome spot, where a canine with self-respect would never live. **(LAG ch1,12; SPF ch17; TOR ch1; Aldin-GOW)**

HOLLYWOOD REPORTER: would have considered a law suit against **Adela Cork** to be front page material. **(TOR ch20)**

HOLLYWOOD WRITERS' CLUB: its members included **George G Frampton**. **(LAG ch12)**

HOLMES, Sherlock: would have noticed that it was hot. He had a knack of making **Dr Watson** feel foolish by the simple expedient of disclosing his thought processes. He might have gone so far as

George Holbeton is surprised as his fiancée, Sally Fairmile, kisses Joss Weatherby

to say that the sudden reappearance of **Sam Bulpitt** presented several features of interest, but would neither have been able to tell from his demeanour that **Spink** had been sacked nor guessed what vultures were gnawing at **Phipps**'s bosom in similar circumstances. Nor would he have been able to put more quiet sinisterness into the "Ah!" which **Henry Rice** said to **Walter Jeliffe**. **(SUM ch19; SPF ch21; TOR ch5; DBB ch5,13; TMU-INA; Century-BTB)**

HOME FOR BRAVE AILING MOTHERS: alias, **Oily Carlisle**. **(HOW ch10)**

HOME MOMENTS: **Arthur Welsh**'s adviser on the concept of jealousy. **(TMU-WDD)**

HOME WHISPERS: its series of chats with young mothers particularly interested **John Peters**. **(GOB ch12)**

HOOTS, MON!: a hit show starring **Mr McAndrew**. **(JTR ch16)**

HOPE, Bob (Sir Leslie Townes Hope, 1903-):   **Bill** (or **Jane**) **Shannon** advised **Joe Davenport** to cut the … content of his wooing to a minimum. **(TOR ch13; Colliers-PTR)**

HOPKINS, Peggy: was better known to the public than **Babe**[1]. **(Grand-COL)**

HORACE, Cuthbert de la Hay ('Stinker'):   a memorable friend of **J L T Smith**. **(IOA ch20)**

HORNE, Helena: gave **Teddy Flower** a notebook one Christmas and suggested that he write beautiful thoughts in it, so he jotted down the names of potential snoot-pokees. **(This Week-LAG)**

HORROR STORIES: **Bill** (or **Jane**) **Shannon** had evolved an idea for a 'B' picture which, after she had been fired by **Superba-Llewellyn**, she was proposing to offer to … It was all about a sinister scientist who tried to turn the heroine into a lobster by injecting the juice of a covey of lobsters into her spinal column. **(TOR ch5; Colliers-PTR)**

HORTON, Edward Everett: see **George**[2]

HOTEL BELVOIR: with an artistic hairdresser and a gay manicurist. **(TMU-WDD)**

HÔTEL CERCLE DE LA MÉDITERRANÉE: a popular hotel in **Roville**. **(TMU-TTM)**

HOTEL COSMOPOLIS: was owned by **Daniel Brewster** to whom, after his daughter **Lucille**, it was the dearest thing in the world, and it received the paternal touch. It was supposed to be the best place in the world to stay whilst in New York, and although **Archie Moffam** did not immediately agree with that view, experience convinced him that it was indeed a good egg. It was the spot chosen for a celebration between **Freddie Rooke** and **Nelly Bryant**, and was where **Lancelot Purvis** and **May Gleason** worked together in the hair-dressing salon. **(JTR ch15; IOA; Grand-COL)**

HOTEL COSMOPOLIS DETECTIVE: a bullet-headed gentleman with a bowler hat, who accompanied **Mme Brudowska** to **Archie Moffam**'s room in search of **Peter**[2]. **(IOA ch8)**

HOTEL DELEHAY: employed **Mr McGee** as its house detective. **(Ellery-MBD)**

HOTEL DES ETRANGERS: an establishment, spelt Hôtel des Étrangers in later editions, which was not far from the Casino Municipale in **St Rocque**. It had a cocktail bar overseen by **Gustave** and all modern improvements including a first-class orchestra and cuisine, telephones in the bedrooms, and a garden for the convenience of guests wishing to commit suicide. **(HOW ch1)**

HOTEL GUELPH: one of the three best hotels in London, it was the one selected by **Sir Godfrey Tanner** to have rooms including a private sitting-room. The bed was good, the food admirable, the furniture tasteful and the bathroom luxurious. **(Strand-COI)**

HOTEL JULES PRIAULX: fashionable premises run by **Jules Priaulx** into which his nephew **Jean** was introduced as cashier. A place frequented by the rich of many nations, often with dromedaries, giraffes (which might drink a dozen best champagne a day to keep their coats good), young lions, alligators or fat cats. **(TMU-MWD)**

HOTEL MAGNIFICENT: at **Bingley-on-the-Sea** sported waiters of an incomparable bungling incompetence for the service of such guests as **Sam Marlowe**. **(GOB ch8)**

HOTEL MAGNIFIQUE: the **St Rocque** holiday home of the **Trent** sisters. **(FRL ch4)**

HOTEL MEURICE: Chut! **(TMU-MWD)**

HOTEL NORTHUMBERLAND: its basement included a barber-shop, but the barber-shop included no barbers. **(HOW ch2)**

HOTEL PRINCE DE GALLES: one of the good hotels in **Roville-sur-Mer**. **(FRL ch5)**

HOTEL STATLER: a Detroit hotel where **Sally Nicholas** expecetd to meet **Gerald Foster**. **(TAS ch6)**

HOTEL SPLENDIDE: the best of the hotels at **Roville-sur-Mer**, where **Terry Trent** was trying her luck. **(FRL ch5,6)**

HOTEL SUPERBA: the pride of the Brighton Esplanade, a thin wooden edifice grabbed by **Henry Rice** to save himself from falling. **(MLF-BTB)**

HOUNDSDITCH WEDNESDAY: the football team for which **Jones** played in goal behind a mixed assortment of Scotsmen, Irishmen and Northcountrymen, seeking to uphold the honour of the London club. It lost to **Manchester United** in the Cup Final. **(TMU-TGP)**

HOUSE OF LORDS, the: Shorty threatened to take **Augustus Robb** to ... after he had stolen the Spanish stamp. **(SPF ch23)**

HOW I PRESERVE MY YOUTH: an article by **Katie MacFarland**. **(MLF-MOM)**

HOW TO BOOKS DALE CARNEGIE DID NOT WRITE BUT SHOULD HAVE DONE:

- ... Come To Roville And Not Feel Like A Leper
- ... Lure The Best People Into Occasionally Throwing You A Kind Word
- ... Obtain An Introduction To A Dark Young Gentleman With Brown Eyes And A Scar On His Cheek Who Looks Like Gregory Peck

(FRL ch5)

HOW TO TELL THE TIME:

> The hands of the Dutch clock in the hall pointed to thirteen minutes past nine; those of the ormolu clock in the sitting-room to eleven minutes past ten; those of the carriage clock on the bookshelf to fourteen minutes to six. In other words, it was exactly eight: ...

(GOB ch1)

HOW TO OPEN A SAFE:

1   Get your dynamite
2   Crumble it up
3   Put it in a sack
4   Fill a can half full of water
5   Boil
6   Let the grease sink to the bottom
7   Drain off the water, leaving the soup
8   Put it in a bottle
9   Check whether the safe has a keester in it
10 If so, blow the door open
11 Knock off the pressure bolt
12 Wedge something into the top edge of the keester door
13 Push in something thicker
14 Plug in gauze
15 Wet the gauze with the soup and touch it off.

Warning: Readers are advised not to try to follow this formula at home. **(HOW ch11)**

HOYLAKE: scene of one of the rounds of **mental golf** played by **Sam Marlowe** whilst concealed in a cupboard at **Windles**. **(GOB ch17)**

HUBBARD, Jane: a thoroughly wholesome, strapping, manly girl, a splendid specimen of bronzed womanhood, whose whole appearance screamed of the great wild spaces. Her strong chin and an eye used to looking leopards squarely in the face and causing them to withdraw abashed into the undergrowth prevented one from imagining her flirting lightly at a garden-party. On the other hand, one could see her restoring sweetness and light into the soul of a refractory mule. She suggested the old homestead, fried pancakes and pop coming home to dinner at Snake Bite, Mich, after the morning's ploughing, and her diction was that of one trained to call the cattle home in the teeth of a western hurricane. She liked her men to be dependent, and after suffering her first disappointment in love as an eleven-year-old (with a 47-year-old bald music-master who was afraid of cats), she scooped in the equally tentative **Eustace Hignett**. **(GOB)**

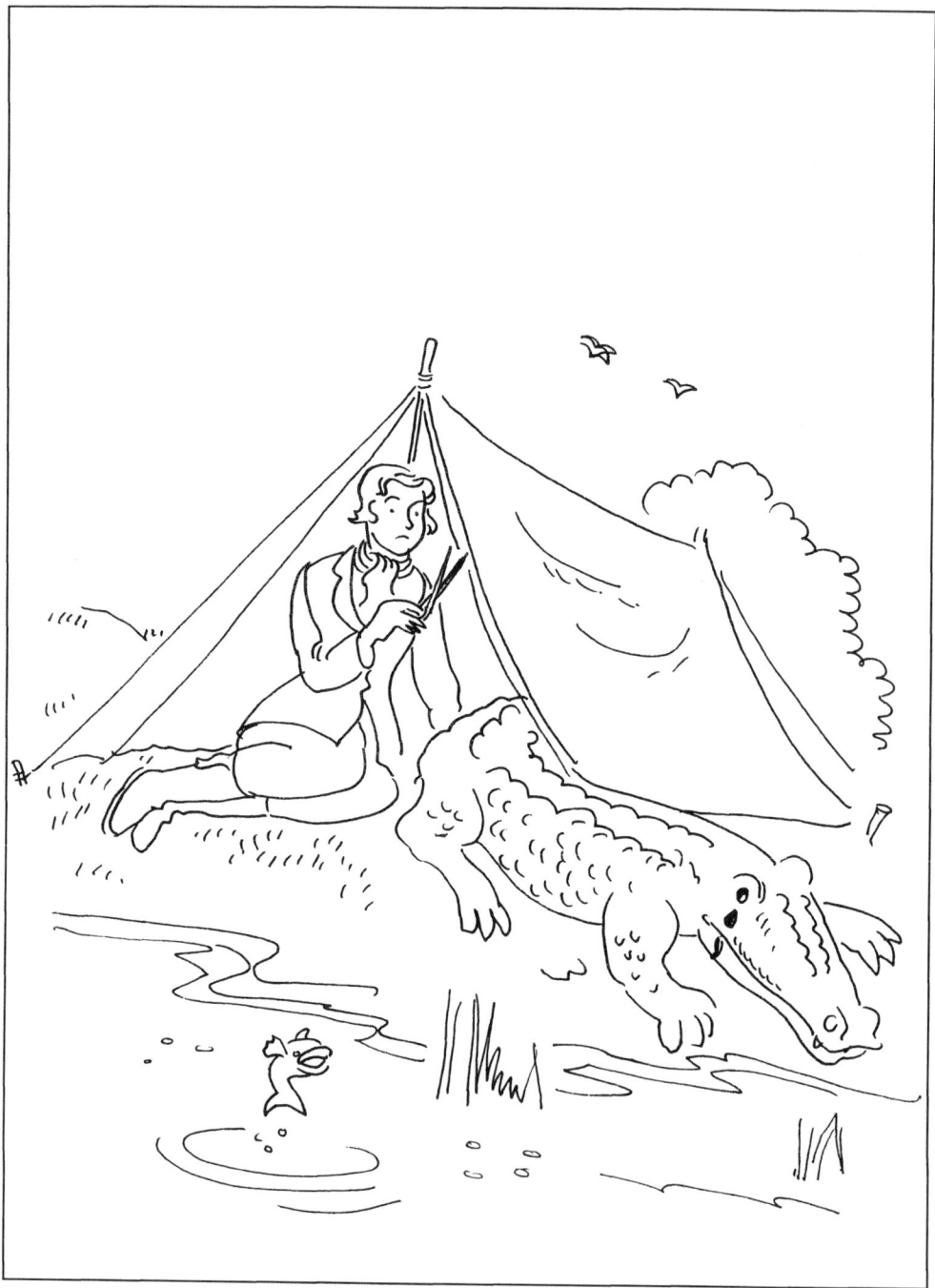

Jane Hubbard, getting rough with an alligator

HUDDLESTONE, Marcia the author of *Percy's Promise* (**Popgood and Grooly**, 1869), a three-volume novel, the second part of which **Terry Cobbold** perused at 1am on D-Day. **(SPF ch15)**

HUDSON, Henry: might have done a limited amount towards putting New York on the baseball map. **(Cosmo-FAL)**

HUNN, Conrad: **Friesshardt**'s pike fell on his toe at a time when he was not wearing thick boots. **(WTT ch8)**

HUNNICUTT, Jane: of trim and clean-cut appearance, she looked like the outdoor sort of girl who would dive perfectly from a high board or drive a golf ball 200 yards down the middle. She had soft, brown hair, a firm, rounded chin, eyes which were brown with golden lights and an attractive nose and lips. Educated at Cheltenham Girls' College, Jane had become an air hostess and a great admirer of **Jerry West**'s cartoons, an admiration which she later extended to the man himself. The turmoil created by an inheritance of $1.2 million from **Mr Donahue** was calmed by the belated attention given to the deceased's affairs by the United States Federal sharks in the form of claims for income tax, surtax, capital gains tax, death duties and the rest. **(TGI)**

HUSKISSON, Spectatia: from Snake Bite, Michigan, had read about Greenwich Village, and modelled herself on its reading-matter, going about in a kimono and bobbed hair. Nothing could hide the underlying impression that she was tall, blonde and substantial, with an appearance suggesting the old homestead and fried pancakes. Although to **Bill Brewster** (who called her 'Pootles' but not 'Tootles') she was Love's Young Dream and could hold on to the top note as a storming-party, spent but victorious, would hold the summit of a hard-won redoubt, the song she chose to illustrate her talent, *Mother's Knee*, sent her scurrying back to her roots. **(IOA ch23)**

HYACINTH:

> "Your poor mother," said Sir Mallaby, "wanted to call you Hyacinth, Sam. You may not know it, but in the nineties when you were born children were frequently called Hyacinth. Well, I saved you from that."

(GOB ch8)

HYACINTH: a novelette familiar to **Sidney Chibnall**, in which situations similar to that described by **Joss Weatherby** occurred. **(QUS ch7)**

HYMACK, Wilson: the composer and lyrist of *Mother's Knee*, who had met **Archie Moffam** in the neighbourhood of Armentières during the war (though there is no evidence to suggest that it was his friends in that town which inspired his song-writing). He had a distinctly artistic look, with bow-tie, trousers bagged at the knee and hair fallen about the ears in luxuriant disarray. **(IOA ch23)**

I: the narrator of *Mike's Little Brother*, the smallest of all possible reporters on the staff of the *Manhattan Daily Chronicle*, responsible for news from the Windle Street police station. Assumed wrongly that **Tim Burke** would have been a pale, slightly-built boy with curly hair and blue eyes. **(PallMall-MLB)**

IBEX, S S: a steamship which carried **Cloyster** from Guernsey to Southampton. **(NGW ptII ch1)**

IBSEN, Henrik (1828-1906):   *The Rose of America* was not ... **(NGW pt1, ch1; JTR ch14)**

IDEAL AFTER-DINNER SPEECH: in the opinion of many:

> "I'm sure you don't want a speech. Very good of you to drink our health. Thank you."

(TAS ch1)

ILLUSTRATED COUNTRY GENTLEMAN'S GAZETTE: **Adrian Peake** sat on an upturned copy of the ... in a cupboard in **Sir Buckstone Abbott**'s study, wearing nothing but sacking, and waiting for the delivery of more orthodox gents' wear. **(SUM ch24)**

I NEVER KNEW THAT!:

> "Did you know that when a cat's tail gets wet, it lengthens?"

(FRL ch3)

> He knew that French seashore resorts were lax and licentious, but he had not supposed them to be as lax and licentious as this.

(FRL ch7)

INSIDE STAND, the: the important role played in the planning of a burglary at a mansion or country house by such practitioners as **Julia**. Such was the critical importance of the role that it gave its name to the dramatised version of *Hot Water*. **(HOW ch1)**

ISLAND OF GIRLS, The: the chorus of the show at the **Melody Theatre** included **Peggy Norton**. **(TMU-TGP)**

ISSAWASSI RIVER: a Central African flower, where **Jane Hubbard** met an alligator within tent, and jabbed it in the eye with nail-scissors. **(GOB ch17)**

'ISTORY OF THE CAT IN ANCIENT EGYPT, The: see *History of the Cat in Ancient Egypt, The*

IVY: the parlourmaid at **Mallow Hall**, with an attractive face, trim figure, quantities of butter-coloured hair and a police escort. **(DBB ch2)**

IZZY: a sallow, hawk-faced man with a furtive eye who promised **Lois Denham** a sunburst after landing the hat-check privilege at the St Aurea. **(JTR ch11)**

JACK[1]: the terrier belonging to **Dick**, the groom at **Peter's father**'s house. He offered **Nigger** a bit of ratting whenever he cared to drop in, adding as a further inducement that he also had a bone or two put away. **(MLF-BIS)**

JACK[2]: the Boston bull-terrier of the **George Sipperley** whom **Jill Mariner** did not want. **(JTR ch9)**

JACK THE RIPPER (fl c1888): was regarded as genial compared to **J B Duff**. **(QUS ch1)**

JACKSON: one of three possible names, beginning with 'T', of the suppliers of honey to **Russell Clutterbuck** at what he thought was too damn high a price. **(FRL ch10)**

JACOB: the one at the National Sporting Club was known to **Freddie Bowen**. **(Strand-JOW)**

JACOB: the one in the Bible worked seven years for the girl, found she was the wrong one, and started all over again. **(Strand-JOW)**

JACQUERIE: the toffee-nosed **Lady Beatrice Bracken** resembled a ... princess among the rogues and peasant slaves. **(HOW ch2)**

JAMES[1]: a footman to the **Stableford** family, always liable to bring cold toast to the tea table. **(HOW ch2)**

JAMES[2]: like **John[1]**, a spaniel dogging **Lady Abbott** as she left Walsingford Hall looking like a stately galleon leaving port accompanied by a couple of skiffs, the two dogs not being slow to suspect a red plot when they saw a man sitting on a roof. **(SUM ch14)**

JAMES B FLAHERTY AGENCY: when you employed the ... (slogan: 'Service') of Seventh Avenue and 44th St, New York City, you got something, and **Mrs Wellington Gedge** got **Kate Putnam. (HOW ch13)**

JAMES, Henry (1843-1916): like **Marie Corelli**, and **Mr Prosser**, he might have had the courage to clip small boys over the ear or fling loaves of bread at bank clerks. **(TMU-POM)**

JAMES, Jesse [Woodson] (1847-1882): Wally Mason used his name to refer to **Goble** when he tried to skin **Otis Pilkington**. Head waiters at posh restaurants on Fifth Avenue, such as the **Aureata**, took on his character when seeking to deprive hard-working waiters of a fair share of the tips. **Isabel Rackstraw**[2] was wont to describe the umpire in baseball matches as a reincarnation of the late ... . **Jane Shannon** referred to her literary agent as her personal ... . **(JTR ch18; FRL ch8; Red-ROM; Colliers-PAP; Colliers-PTR)**

JANE[1]: called **PC Plimmer** to deal with two cases of petty theft by her cook **Ellen Brown**, only to discover that the more serious offence had been no more than a domestic reprisal. **(MLF-RUP)**

JANE[2]: a stumpy, flat-footed fictional girl with glasses, indigestion, big hands and an enormous waist. **(NGW ptII ch7)**

JANE[3]: **Jill Mariner**'s parlour-maid who, misunderstanding her mistress's silence, concluded that she had no heart. **(JTR ch6)**

JANE[4]: **Pearl Delahay** was chosen from the chorus of the *Ask Dad* company to play this part, and feed a comic line to **Walter Catfield. (Strand-BTG)**

JARVIS, Bat: leader of the **Groome Street Gang**, he emanated from Missouri and to **Spider Mullins**' dismay, he was in court to hear the trials of **Otto the Sausage** and **Rabbit Butler**. See *Volume 7* for the more comprehensive review of the assistance this genial crook offered to Psmith. **(BurrMcK-MIS)**

JARVIS, Inspector: of Scotland Yard, was advised by **Wetherall** to pick up **Benyon. (MLF-OTN)**

JC(RH): see **Cooley, Joey**

JEALOUSY: the hydra of calamities, the sevenfold death, as exhibited by **Arthur Welsh** to **Maud Peters**, although if kept within proper bounds it could be a compliment, the gin in the ginger-beer of emotion. **(TMU-WDD)**

JEANNE: the maid-of-all-work to **Mr Warden**. **(TMU-RIE)**

JEFFERSON, Thomas (1773-1826): twice President of the United States, he held certain truths to be self-evident: that all men were created equal; that they were endowed by their creator with certain inalienable rights; and that among those rights were life, liberty and the pursuit of happiness, but theatrical agents' office-boys did not agree. **(JTR ch10)**

JEFFSON, Colin: a ghostly individual linked to **Sandy McHoots**. **(TGI ch5)**

JELLIFFE, Walter: the fat and friendly comedian and star of *The Girl from Brighton*, who saw through the various disguises of **Henry Rice** and ran a sweepstake on the identity of the suspect he was following. **(MLF-BTB)**

JENKINS: a London resident known, to **Jill Mariner**'s surprise, to **Freddie Rooke**. **(JTR ch6)**

JENKINS: another of three possible names, beginning with 'T', of the suppliers of honey to **Russell Clutterbuck** at what he thought was too damn high a price. **(FRL ch10)**

JENKINS, Herbert (1876-1923): the author and publisher, who was mentioned in the preface of **GOB**. **(GOB-Preface)**

JENKINSON, Mrs: the *On Your Way*'s Mrs Malaprop. **(NGW ptII ch5)**

JERNINGHAM, Aubrey: his unsolicited contributions to *Piccadilly Weekly* all had to be rewritten by **Tudway**, including *The Vengeance of Jasper Murgatroyd*, *The Heart of Delilah Brown*, *The Ordeal of Percy Pilkington* and *Tales for the Tots*. Those from his brother **Samuel**, sister-in-law, Samuel's wife, cousin **George**[3] and aunt **Rachel** were progressively worse. **(Throne-KHE)**

JERNINGHAM, Rachel: an aunt of **Aubrey**. Describing **Tudway** as heartless and breaking down into tears were acts sufficient to earn her an offer of marriage which she accepted. **(Throne-KHE)**

JERNINGHAM, Samuel: a worse writer even than **Aubrey**. **(Throne-KHE)**

JERNINGHAM, Mrs Samuel: submitted military stories to **Tudway** for publication. **(Throne-KHE)**

JERSEY CITY:

> Wherever civilisation reigned, and in Jersey City, one question alone was on every lip: . . . Who would win?

(Colliers-PAP)

JESSOP, Mrs: the sister of **Claude Potter**, she had been married to her superintendent for many happy years. **(DBB ch7)**

JESSOP, Superintendent: of either the **Wellingford** or **Wallingford** constabularies, he was the brother-in-law of **Claude Potter**, who was apt to cause resentment by calling him a 'country copper', but if the truth were told the Superintendent was no **Sherlock Holmes**. When advised by Potter to visit **Bond's Bank**, he found the **Appleby gang** pretending to be bank auditors and was upset shortly afterwards to find that a burglary had taken place there after all. **(DBB ch7,11,12; USDBB ch7)**

JEVONS: after buttling for **Sir Godfrey Tanner** for 15 years, he succumbed to an impulse and popped a piece of ice down his master's back, thereafter resigning without delay. After retiring with a small pension to 193 Adelaide Street, Fulham Road, London, he was recalled to Sir Godfrey's service shortly after Sir Godfrey, too, had succumbed to temptation. **(Strand-COI)**

JEZEBEL: the biblical name (from *2 Kings*, ch9) which **Stanwood** proposed to use to address **Eileen Stoker** when he next wrote to her. She was the Biblical creature who reminded **Lord Plumpton** of **Clarissa Binstead**. **(SPF ch21; NSE-HTU)**

JIM: the fiancé of the **narrator** of BTG, who managed the *Ask Dad Number Two Company* while it was on the road. **(Strand-BTG)**

JIMMY[1]: a balcony waiter at **Geisenheimer's**, proud of the red plush on the tables. **(MLF-ATG)**

JIMMY[2]: a friend of **Katie MacFarland**, who brought a girl in to eat at **Mac's**. **(MLF-MOM)**

JIMMY[3]: lost his hat at **Lord's** to the mystery catapulter. **(NSE-HTU)**

JOAN OF ARC (St Jeanne d'Arc, c1412-1431): was wont to act promptly and, when ordering her army to advance, to have a look of stern determination. She did *not* hide in cupboards when she heard unexpected voices. **(DBB ch2,5; TGI ch12)**

JOB: one of the girls in the ensemble of *The Rose of America* would have been in her element looking in on ... hob-nobbing with Bildad the Shuhite and other friends. **(JTR ch16)**

JOBLIN, Alf: a Lambeth Boys' Club recruit who caught **Walter Greenway** with a random blow on the mark, before being stopped by **Tom Blake**. His appearance was not considered likely to impress editors as much as would be required from one of **James Cloyster**'s ghosts. **(NGW ptII ch10,13)**

JOE[1]: an old dog down the street at the grocer's shop. **(MLF-HMV)**

JOE[2]: brother of '**Enry**, who was also familiar with parrots. **(JTR ch5)**

JOE THE LASCAR: from his underground cellar at Limehouse, might he have been a white slaver pretending to be a lawyer, writing to **Jane Hunnicutt** that she was about to hear something to her advantage merely as a ruse? **(TGI ch6)**

JOEY COOLEY FAITHFUL FAN CLUB, the: had a branch in Michigan. **(LAG ch11)**

JOHN[1]: see **James[2]**

JOHN[2]: the chauffeur to **Peter's father**, who ran over **Nigger** while driving with **Peter** in the car. **(MLF-BIS)**

JOHN[3]: a servant at the **Reynolds** home who rightly suspected that the nineteen hampers which had suddenly arrived contained dogs. **(TUW-WPS)**

JOHN, poor: the subject of a music hall comic song rendered with great gusto by **Freddie Rooke** and **Jill Mariner** and referred to by **Terry Trent**. **(JTR ch1; FRL ch12)**

JOHN-JOHN: the Peke belonging to **Maureen O'Sullivan** which lodged with the Wodehouses in 1931, it was joined with them and **Miss Winks** as dedicator to her of *Hot Water*. In *Performing Flea* PGW describes her thus:

> Winks is in great form, and has got quite reconciled to having Johnnie, Maureen O'Sullivan's Peke, as a guest. We are putting Johnnie up while Maureen is in Ireland. Sex female in

spite of the name, and age about a year. Very rowdy towards Winks, who disapproves rather. Johnnie is the only ugly Peke I have ever seen. She was run over by a car some months ago and has lost an eye. She looks like one of your tougher sailors.

JOHNSON, Doctor Samuel (1709-1784): laid down a maxim that a man can write at any time if he sets himself to do it earnestly. **(NGW ch24)**

JOHNSON, Jack (John Arthur, 1878-1946): Freddie Bowen said he would fight ... if Johnson had eaten as much as the **Bearcat** had been doing. He was also featured on **Aubrey Devine**'s list of the seven most prominent men in the United States. **(Strand-JOW; VanFair-AAI)**

JOHNSTON OFFICE: of censorship, would never have passed the dialogue which would have appeared if the walls of the **Carmen Flores Place** could have spoken. **(TOR ch4)**

JOHNSTOWN:

The red-haired young man looked as a native of Johnstown might have looked on being requested to stop that city's celebrated flood.

(TAS ch2)

JONATHAN: see **David**

JONES[1]: a professional footballer, né **Clarence Tresillian**, he was a fine goalkeeper who blackmailed **Daniel Rackstraw** into parting with his daughter's hand. **(TMU-TGP)**

JONES[2]: the third of three possible names, each beginning with 'T', of the suppliers of honey to **Russell Clutterbuck** at what he thought was too damn high a price. **(FRL ch10)**

JONES: an author who had been fixed up solid for three years with *Blank's Magazine* by **Henderson Banks**. **(Strand-PAW)**

JONES, Alexander: a twelve-year-old who with **Rupert Atkinson** dared **Thomas Billing** to eat bread. **(Strand-COI)**

JONES, Jnr: the howler manufacturer in the *On Your Way* column. **(NGW ptII ch5)**

JONES, Miss: the name adopted by **Jill Willard** when taking dictation from **Smithy**. **(DBB ch11)**

JORKINS: was served by the wiles of **Sam Bulpitt** and the innocent assistance of a policeman. **(SUM ch14)**

JOSEPH: a comely black cat who, despite finding himself in reduced circumstances, nevertheless managed to retain a *tournure*. He demonstrated what a good trencherman he could be with the aid of **Elizabeth Herrold**'s milk and sardines, before leaving her for successively **James Boyd** (who renamed him **Reginald**) and **Paul Briggs**. **(MLF-BFL)**

JOSHUA: Joe Blossom thought that **Sally Preston** was nothing more or less than a ... **(TMU-STW)**

JOVE:

> Out of the welter of his thoughts, springing fully armed like Minerva from the brow of Jove, there had emerged a scheme
>
> . . .

(SUM ch15)

JUKES: one of six acquaintances of **Joe Vanringham** not known to **Jane Abbott**. **(SUM ch5)**

JULES[1]: the great Parisian chef at **Mac's** restaurant, Soho or on Seventh Avenue. **(MLF-MOM; Red-ROM)**

JULES[2]: the boots, ostler, day porter, night-clerk and lift attendant at the **Hotel Normandie**, **Roville-sur-Mer**, who shared the captivity of **Ginger Kemp** and **Sally Nicholas** in a lift cage, and gazed tearfully at the keys on his desk like **Moses** glancing at the Promised Land from the summit of Mount Pisgah. **(TAS ch2)**

JULIA: see **Gedge, Julia**

JULIET: undoubtedly would have edged into her balcony scene with **Romeo** with a few remarks on the pleasantness of the morning. **(GOB ch4)**

JUNE, April: though the loveliest girl **Reggie Havershot** had seen in his life, one must bear in mind his relatively sheltered existence, and fall in with the general opinion that, however decorative, she was a manipulative and clever actress in real life as well as on stage. Thus did her apparent sweet, wistful gentleness, her large blue eyes, her perfectly modelled chassis, her soft smile, her dimpled cheek, her sensitivity to bloodsports, her propensity towards teetotalism and smoke-free zones, and her liking for books, flowers and the kitchen all count for nought, when compared to the fury of an actress whose press interview had been hijacked. This brought to the forefront the side of her personality which more accurately resembled the truth: vain, affected, as hard as nails, utterly selfish, a pill, a cat, and had she been poked in the snoot by **JC(RH)** we can say with confidence that she would have deserved it. **(LAG)**

JUNE, Hazel: the name by which a character with personal attributes very similar to those of **April June** made her appearance in the original, novella, version of *Laughing Gas* but by some reports was exposed to the avenging spirit of both **JC(RH)** and **JC(TF)**. **(Pearson-LAG; ThisWeek-LAG)**

JUPITER: being whiskered to the eyebrow, he outsmarted **Joe Vanringham**. **(SUM ch17)**

KAHN, MORRIS & BROWN: the Wall Street brokers and the fortunate employers of **Augustus Bartlett**. **(TAS ch1)**

KAISER WILHELM II (1859-1941): kept **Archie Moffam** busy for five years. **(Strand-MMH)**

KANKAKEE INTELLIGENCER: its statement in a five-line review that a book is readable has been known to presage an Event, ie an occasion when the public's purse empties in droves to secure copies of a novel such as *Parted Ways*. **(PicRev-PAW)**

KARLOFF, Boris (William Henry Pratt, 1887-1969): see **Fauntleroy, Gladys**

KAUFMAN, George Simon (1889-1961): a successful American playwright of some substance, particularly vertically. **(USSPF ch10)**

KEATING, Mrs: though but a police constable's wife, she could still visit theatres to watch plays. **(TUW-MIS)**

KEATING, Police Constable: this conscientious man weighed in at almost 14 stone, which did not stop him arresting either **Spider Buffin** or **Porky Binns**. However, he was only saved from the damage of a joint assault by **Otto the Sausage** and **Rabbit Butler** by the unexpected intervention of the uncomprehending Buffin. **(TUW-MIS)**

KEATS, John (1795-1821): would have said that the word 'Imitation' was like a knell, and He was known to have been occasionally in need of a drink, specifically a beakerful of the warm south, full of

Hazel June, no longer wistful and gentle

the true, the blushful Hippocrene. **(GOB ch6; QUS ch11; TOR ch2; Colliers-PTR)**

KEELEY CURE INSTITUTE: the activities of the **Temple of the New Dawn** resembled a cross between the ... and a revival meeting. **J Wellington Gedge** speculated on whether the **Chateau Blissac** had become one of its satellites. **(LAG ch28; HOW ch1)**

KELLY: a small score against this member of the underworld was being settled with a sandbag when **P C Keating**, until then a distant spectator of the affair, arrested his assailant, **Spider Buffin**. **(TUW-MIS)**

KELLY, Officer: like **P C Keating**, he was a conscientious man who weighed in at almost 14 stone, which did not stop him arresting either **Spider Buffin** or **Porky Binns**. Similarly, the gallant officer was only saved from the prospective damage of a joint assault by **Otto the Sausage** and **Rabbit Butler** by the unexpected intervention of the uncomprehending Buffin. **(BurrMcK-MIS)**

KELLY, DUBINSKY, WIX, WEEMS & BESSINGER: a New York law firm of which **Henry Weems** was the junior partner. **(FRL ch1)**

KEMP, Lancelot 'Ginger': a sturdy, thick-set young orphan with an amiable freckled face and the reddest hair you would hope to see. The cousin of **Bruce Carmyle**, he had been at school with **Gerald Foster**. He was a Cambridge graduate with rugger and boxing blues, and had had an England trial at scrum-half. He tended to make a hash of all things, not merely those which were edible, and thus lost jobs first in his uncle's office, then as a schoolmaster, then with **Scrymgeour**, and finally in the theatre, but he eventually found his niche when owning and running a dog-breeding business. Having made clear within minutes of seeing her that **Sally Nicholas** was the prettiest girl he had ever seen, she eventually realised that he was indeed the right man for her, and a happy ending was assured. **(TAS)**

KEMPTON PARK: was not a meeting for which **Spink** would be likely to know any winners. **(SPF ch5)**

KENTISH TIMES: a good source of information about the 3.30 at Kempton Park. **(SPF ch21)**

KERR, Jean: her snake got all the lines. **(TGI ch1)**

KEY OF THE STREET, The: a magazine printing **James Cloyster**'s work under the **Sidney Price** imprint. **(NGW ptII ch19)**

KHAN, Jenghiz, or Genghis, or Genghiz (c1162-1227): one of few men who might have remained tranquil and composed if one of the ladies of his acquaintance had said "So!" at him. But would he have been so equable, though, towards the publishers who could not spell his name? **(SUM ch25; USSUM ch25; SUM (Penguin) ch25)**

KHAYYAM, Omar (c1048-1123): impresario **Ike Goble** preferred the unorthodox appellation, Omar *Of* Khayyam. But whichever way you cut it, he swung an alluring eyeball. **(JTR ch14; HOW ch14)**

KIDD, Captain William (1645-1701): his legendary skills paled into insignificance compared to those of **Jones**. **Chris Selby** was his direct lineal descendant. **(JTR ch13; TMU-TGP)**

KING ARTHUR (fl c6th cent): would have grovelled before **Queen Guinevere** for cake and cocoa if he had been locked in an office building with **Roland Bean** all night. Contrary to rumour, his Round Table of Knights included at least one who was not a model of physical strength and beauty, but they were all likely to have extracted flies from ladies' eyes. **Mike Cardinal** was compared to him.

> Chibnall relaxed. He had been looking like King Arthur interviewing Guinevere in the monastery. He now looked merely like a butler who has had a weight taken off his mind.

(IOA ch13; HOW ch8; QUS ch13; SPF ch22; TMU-MMM, SAG)

KING CHARLES I (1600-1649): supported by a **Rayner**. **(TUW-BSA)**

KING CHARLES II (1630-1685): see **de Querouaille, Louise**

KING COPHETUA: if **Derek Underhill** still wanted **Jill Mariner** after her money had been lost, she would come as did the beggar-maid to ... But Underhill did not realise that he would have to play that role when he travelled to New York to try to regain her affection. **Ruth Warden** resisted any idea of playing beggar-maid to the King. **(JTR ch6,20; TMU-RIE)**

KING ETHELRED THE UNREADY (c968-1016): the approximate name of the King who was in office when **Mellingham Hall** was first erected. **(TGI ch4)**

KING GEORGE V (1865-1936): was introduced to the **Giants** and **White Sox** baseball teams before the match. **(MLF-OTN)**

KING-HALL, B W: the dedicatee of *The Indiscretions of Archie*, who had been a friend of PGW since 1903.

KING-HALL, Ella: the dedicatee of *Not George Washington*.

KING HAROLD (1022-1066): see **Edith**

KING HENRY VIII (1491-1547): a seasoned performer like ... who, once he had started marrying couldn't stop so just carried on marrying everything in sight, would have taken the receipt of a letter from a young lady, announcing she would marry him, in his stride. And he was one of few men you can think of who might have remained tranquil and composed if one of the ladies of his acquaintance had said "So!" at him. **(SUM ch25; TOR ch21; FRL ch9)**

KING LEAR: was renowned for looking at **Cordelia**. **(SUM ch2)**

KING LOUIS XI (1423-1483): **George Marlowe** had written a historical novel of life at his Court which he had never had the gall to offer to a publisher. **(Strand-PAW)**

KING OF ALDEBARAN: was probably the idlest man in the entire world, for he sat on his throne doing nothing from morning to night. He launched his own revolt against such inactivity, however, going out to see the world for himself, and on his return changed things in the kingdom for ever. **(Sunday-IDK)**

KING OF DENMARK: would have got on well with **Jerry Moore**. **(TMU-BAC)**

KING'S HEAD: **Wellingford** or **Wallingford** pub which acted as a base for **Ferdie the Fly, Smithy** and **Frank. (DBB ch5; USDBB ch5)**

KING SOLOMON (c1015-977BC): since once he had started marrying he couldn't stop and just carried on marrying everything in sight, he would have taken in his stride the prospect of a further simultaneous betrothal. See also **Queen of Sheba. (TOR ch6; TOR ch21; TGI ch6)**

KING WENCESLAS, Good (c903-935): one of the constituent parts of the early **Hollywood**. **(TOR ch1; Colliers-PTR)**

KING WILLIAM THE CONQUEROR (1027-1087): had his bag carried down the gangway by the **First Earl of Datchet**. **Sam Bulpitt** did not deny that he had raised Old Harry back in his reign. **(SUM ch16; Strand-JOW)**

KIPLING, [Joseph] Rudyard (1865-1936): put words such as "peace, be still" into his soldiers' mouths. His work *If* was about a man like **Reginald Chippendale** and he also wrote the popular *Gunga Din*. He wrote a mouthful when he pointed out that "A woman is only a woman, but a good cigar is a smoke". It was quite possible that, with his reputation, he might have had a story accepted if submitted under his correct name which would have been rejected as inadequate if he had used a pseudonym. His story *The Mark of the Beast* is suggested by **Elliott Oakes** as possibly holding the key to the mystery surrounding **Captain Gunner**'s death. **(NGW ptII ch11; TOR ch6; TGI ch11,13; PLP-GCS; Pearson-EDO)**

KITCHENER, Thomas: a large, grave, self-effacing young man who by sheer application had become second gardener at the Hall by the age of only 25. He was a neighbour of **Jane Williams** and was hit on the back of the neck by a lump of mud projected by the bored **Sally Preston**. This experience seems to have awoken some sleeping emotions in Thomas, for he started conversing with **Mr Williams**, giving presents of vegetables and puppies to Sally, and bunches of fives to her other fiancés. **(TMU-STW)**

KLEIN, Patrolman: one of the policemen who attended the **Hotel Delehay** in support of **Sergeant O'Toole**. **(Ellery-MBD)**

KNICKERBOCKER ICE COMPANY:

> "When it came to the point, you thought it over and your dogs went Knickerbocker Ice Company on you."

'Dogs' in this quotation were **Gordon Carlisle**'s feet, and it was **Gertie Medway** who thought they had gone cold. **(USHOW ch11)**

KNIGHT, Winfield: we feel we should dislike intensely this actor who thought he had a beautiful profile, and did have pride in his skinny arms and his French accent, and a passion for golf, for he had been an undue influence in the life of **Peggy Norton**. But instead, he comes over as a rather sad, colourless individual, whose initial glamour fades quite easily, and we envisage instead a member of the acting profession whose career will rapidly fade to nothing, with a personal life destined to follow the downward trend. Our residual hope is that Peggy will have the sense and the ability to escape from his influence while there is still time. **(TMU-INA)**

KNOCK THREE TIMES: a popular song of the 1970s which included the line "Knock three times on the ceiling if you want me". It is to be hoped that the composers paid the Wodehouse estate a royalty for the theme, as expressed in the last paragraph of **TMU-MUP**, a story published in 1910:

> Suddenly [Annette Brougham] got up. In one corner of the room was a long pole used for raising and lowering the window-sash. She took it, and for a moment stood irresolute. Then with a quick movement, she lifted it and stabbed three times at the ceiling.

KÜSSNACHT: **William Tell** was sentenced to durance vile in the dungeons of the Castle of ..., two miles from **Flüelen**, on which no ray of sunlight or moonlight ever fell. But he never arrived. **(WTT ch13,14)**

KUTE-KUT KLOTHES: each of the suits made by this company were guaranteed for a year. **(SatEvePost-TSP)**

KYRKE, Joseph: knew a man at Oxford whose cousin had been introduced to **Popjoy**'s brother at a garden-party. After being sent down in relation to an occurrence not wholly unconnected with 'orgies in the Quad', he presumed upon the contact to apply to Popjoy for a job. He was invited to lunch, but fell asleep whilst receiving some good advice. **(Throne-KHE)**

LADIES, I BEG YOU: one of **Smedley Cork**'s failed investments. **(TOR ch21)**

LADIES' SPHERE: a journal edited by **Mr Hebblethwaite**, at whose offices beautiful and refined women were popping in and out all day like rabbits. **(Strand-TSF)**

LADS' CLUB: where **Chibnall** conducted morning exercises and evening boxing to create biceps strengthened to a steely hardness. **(QUS ch13)**

LADY MACBETH: **Beatrice Chavender**, when armed to the teeth with a knife, and **Beulah Brinkmeyer** looked like ... at her worst.

Gertie Carlisle was as brusque as she was when giving orders. (LAG ch16; HOW ch17; FRL ch7; QUS ch12)

LADY MARY'S MISTAKE: a short story by the real **Sidney Price** which appeared on page 324 of *Strawberry Leaf*. (NGW ch22)

LAERTIUS, Diogenes (fl 2nd cent): a volume of his helped **Mrs Goodwin** while away the time spent by her daughter and **James Cloyster** in mushroom-hunting before breakfast. (NGW ptI ch2)

LAMARR, Hedy (Hedwig Eva Maria Kiesler, 1913-2000): see **Cleopatra**

LAMBS' CLUB: yet another of the New York resorts of the artist, author, actor or Bohemian to which **Archie Moffam** was introduced by his new American friends. Members held that **Walter Jelliffe**'s cigars brought him within the scope of *Sullivan's Law* prohibiting the carrying of concealed weapons. (IOA ch4; Century-BTB)

LANDSEER, Sir Edwin Henry (1802-1873): would have enjoyed painting **Elmer Chinnery** in his startled image, like a stag at bay in horn-rimmed spectacles. (SUM ch10)

LANE, Godfrey: sang a patriotic song. (NGW ptII ch8)

LANGTRY, Lillie (Emilie Charlotte La Breton, 1853-1929): see **Cleopatra**

LARDY, Lord: commented on how strange were the customs of France. (FRL ch4)

LAURETTE ET CIE: a Regent Street dress salon inherited by the old trouper **Max Faucitt** on the death of his brother, which proved a valuable refuge for the vulnerable **Sally Nicholas**. (TAS ch11)

LAZLO: painted a portrait of **Lady Beatrice Bracken**. (HOW ch2)

LEACH: the cashier at the **Moon Assurance Co**, who was responsible for maintaining the attendance book. (NGW ptII ch19)

LEGREE, Simon: the slave-owner in H B Stowe's *Uncle Tom's Cabin*, who beat Uncle Tom to death, was closer in temperament and belief to Tom than was **Daniel Brewster** to **Archie Moffam** (although Daniel became matier after the deal relating to **Salvatore's mother**'s shop), but even he was well-mannered compared to **M Boissonade**. **Adela Cork** was thought to resemble some aspects of his personality, although she did not have his charm of manner. **(IOA ch4; TOR ch7; FRL ch6; Cosmo-SCH)**

LEICESTER THEATRE: was rented for a season by **Sir Chester Portwood. (JTR ch2)**

LELY, Sir Peter (Pieter van der Faes, 1618-1680): an example of an artist who not only might have enjoyed painting **Beatrice Chavender** but may have made an even better job of it than **Joss Weatherby. (QUS ch1)**

LENO, Dan (George Galvin, 1860-1904): a pantomime and music hall star favoured by **Charlie Cookson. (NGW ptII ch17)**

LESTRADE, Inspector: Jill Willard's name for **Sergeant Potter,** when she learned that he had visited the bank the previous night. **(DBB ch13)**

LETONDU, M: a colleague of **Old Nick** in the third bureau of the **Ministry of Dons and Legs** until the latter's departure, he appeared to be off his head, an idea given some credibility when he told Nick that he planned to murder his boss, **M de la Hourmerie** and then succeeded in catching him a glancing blow with a hatchet. **(FRL ch2,6)**

LEUTHOLD: one of **Gessler**'s bodyguards, who had short-lived success with his pike. **(WTT ch7)**

LEWIN, Miss: a songstress at the **Briggs Theatre. (NGW ptII ch25)**

LEWIS, Sadie: the shop assistant at **Fuller & Benjamin** whose tiredness earned the sympathy of **Rosie,** but almost led her into the misleading idea that her man was not interested. **(Strand-TSF)**

LEWIS, [Harry] Sinclair (1885-1951): he seemed eager to leave 10% of his earnings with a literary agent. **(TOR ch18)**

LIBERTY BONDS: Bartlett's suggested security for investment by the *nouvelle riche*. **(TAS ch1)**

LIFE: is asking for ham instead of scrambled eggs. **(QUS ch1)**

LILLIE, Beatrice (Lady Peel, 1898-1989): Smedley Cork did not do his imitation of her while out on a toot with **Joe Davenport.** **(TOR ch6)**

LIMAX MAXIMUS: the garden slug, the only exception to the tenet that New York theatrical managers are the lowest form of the order of intelligence known to science. **(JTR ch10)**

LINNET, the song of the:

> Tolic-gow-gow, tolic-joey-fair, tolic-hickey-gee, tolic-equay-quake, tuc-tuc-whizzie, tuc-tuc-joey, equay-equay-a-weet, tuc-tuc-wheet.

(SUM ch16)

LISS, Hon Adelaide: stayed at the **Hôtel Cercle de la Méditerranée**. **(TMU-MMT)**

LITTLE CHURCH ROUND THE CORNER, the: a Protestant Episcopal Church of the Transfiguration, a little bit of heaven dumped down on 29th Street in the middle of New York, with a little fountain playing in front of it (and now with a plaque commemorating P G Wodehouse on one wall). The news of her son's proposed marriage there caused **Adeline Hignett** to take steps, and they were not those leading to the entrance. **Henry Mills** married **Minnie Hill** there. **(GOB ch1; SatEvePost-TLF)**

LITTLE GEM SARDINES: were illustrated in magazines by **Reginald Sellers** **(TMU-MUP)**

LITTLE-SUDBURY-IN-THE-WOLD: where the policeman who arrested **Jill Mariner** had spent his novitiate. **(JTR ch5)**

LIVERPOOL:

> Wherever civilisation reigned, and in portions of Liverpool, one question alone was on every lip: . . . Who would win?

(TMU-TGP)

LIVINGSTONE, Dr David (1813-1873): failed to reach Walsingford in '66 only because the water ran out. **(SUM ch17)**

LIZ: a small baby on a **Blake** cargo-boat. **(NGW ptII ch14)**.

LIZARD, green a: **Veek**'s chosen fancy dress for the **Festival of the Saint**, which was planned on broad impressionistic lines, the bright green scales and long crimson beak suggesting, however, more a species of parrot. **(HOW ch3)**

LLEWELLYN, Ivor: caused men to throw the *Saturday Evening Post* at him, presumably in bound volumes. On the brighter side, his was the easily recognizable voice on a radio quiz on station WJZ which enabled **Joe Davenport** to win a jackpot which included countless cans of soup. **(TOR ch2)**

LLOYD GEORGE, David (1863-1945): referred to the House of Lords as blithering backwoodsmen and asinine anachronisms, presumably before he joined their ranks. There is no evidence as to whether this explains why he was disliked by **Henderson**. His was one of the names given by a male guest in Room 618 of the **Hotel Cosmopolis** following a sing-song and a raid. **(IOA ch19; TMU-MWD,TGP)**

LLOYD, Harold (1893-1971): appeared in a new picture to which **Brewster Gooch** wished to accompany **Pearl**. **(Strand-BTG)**

LLOYD'S: would issue insurance policies on such matters as incurring injury from an attack with intent to kill. **(DBB ch6)**

LO: the poor Indian who, having thrown away a pearl, suddenly found out what an ass he had been and expressed the kind of remorse later to be shown by **Adrian Peake**. **(SUM ch18)**

LOCHINVAR (or YOUNG LOCHINVAR): according to **Sam Marlowe** he drove his lady love up and down Piccadilly in a motor car, whilst wearing a helmet. **(GOB ch17)**

LONDON AND COUNTRY HOUSE TALES: an article by **James Cloyster**, which saw publication through the medium of **Sidney Price**. **(NGW ptII ch13)**

LONDON GOSSIP: one of its critics was preparing to write damning words about *Tried by Fire*, when he was. **(JTR ch2)**

LONGFELLOW, Henry Wadsworth (1807-1882): might as well have written:

> I flung a cat into the air
> It fell to earth
> On Uncle's hair

although this would have represented a modest helping of poetic licence, for **Alexander** actually landed right in the middle of **Jean Priaulx**'s face. **(TMU-MWD)**

LONGWOOD, John: an old gentleman in Pittsburgh who discussed his stock market proposals with **Joe Rendal**. **(TMU-TFD)**

LOOSE CHIPPINGS: a Sussex market town, (pop 4,916) with a pub, the **Rose and Crown**, and **Claines Hall**. **(QUS ch1)**

LORD CHIEF BUTLER, the: of Aldebaran, found himself unable to take the **King of Aldebaran** his usual pot of tea, plate of hot buttered toast and little cakes with chocolate on them, for the King could not be found. **(Sunday-IDK)**

LORD CHIEF FOOTMAN, the: of Aldebaran, generally knocked on the doors of tenants' cottages on the **King**'s behalf. **(Sunday-IDK)**

LORD CHIEF HUNTSMAN, the: of Aldebaran, went shooting for the **King**. **(Sunday-IDK)**

LORD CHIEF ROADMENDER, the: of Aldebaran, broke all the stones that the **King** might need. **(Sunday-IDK)**

LORD CHIEF TRAMP, the: of Aldebaran, would have been prepared to have taken the **King**'s walk for him if he had been warned. **(Sunday-IDK)**

LORD CHIEF WOODMAN, the: of Aldebaran, always chopped the wood for the **King**. **(Sunday-IDK)**

LORD HIGH EXECUTIONER: a kindly-looking old gentleman with white hair and a black robe, tastefully decorated with death's heads. **(WTT ch1)**

LORD PERCY: a traveller who ordered lamb so indistinctly that he was served ham. **(TMU-BAC)**

LORD'S CRICKET GROUND: **Lady Beatrice Bracken** always attracted attention during the luncheon interval of the Eton *v* Harrow match. Though popular with **Lord Plumpton**, the spot was less so with the soulless **Conky Biddle** and **Clarissa Binstead**. **(HOW ch2; PLP-HTU)**

LOS ANGELES CHRONICLE: in a scene reminiscent of PGW's own off-the-record disclosures to the *Los Angeles Times* in 1931, it was to **Pomona Wycherly** of this august journal that **RH(JC)** most notoriously revealed the change in his fortunes. **(LAG ch21)**

LOS ANGELES EXAMINER: **Smedley Cork** threatened to write to the ... about **Adela**'s theft of the **Carmen Flores** diary. **(TOR ch8)**

LOS ANGELES TRIBUNE: strangely, it was to **Amanda Wycherly** of the *Chronicle*'s closest rival that **RH(JC)** and **RH(TF)** <u>first</u> spoke out. **(Pearson-LAG; ThisWeek-LAG)**

LOST PATROL, The: an example of a film which proved the theory that if the story line was strong enough a film did not need a love interest. **(LAG ch24)**

LOT: the gentleman with a saline wife, whose statuesque posture was imitated by **Hermione Pegler** after she learnt of **Freddie Carpenter**'s engagement to **Terry Trent**. **(FRL ch9; TGI ch6)**

LOTTIE: the Afro-American lady who answered the front-door bell at **Henry Rice**'s boarding house. **(Century-BTB)**

LOUIS, Joe (Joseph Louis Barrow, 1914-1981): like **Joss Weatherby** and unlike **George Holbeton**, he would have stood his ground and investigated further the phenomenon of a densely moustached stranger galloping up shouting "Hey!" **(QUS ch10)**

LOUVRE: the Parisian art gallery, full to the brim of fat cherubs in seventeenth-century pictures who hover winged but naked above happy lovers. **(QUS ch20)**

LOVE-R-LY SILVER CUP: a trophy offered each evening to the best pair of dancers at **Geisenheimer's**, but invariably won by one of the professionals. **(MLF-ATG)**

LOVERS' WELL: the first tale submitted to *Piccadilly Weekly* by **Samuel Jerningham**. **(Throne-KHE)**

LOY, Myrna (Myrna Williams, 1905-1993): according to the boys in London, **Miss Attwater** resembled ... **(SUM ch16)**

LUCAS, Lew: the lightweight champion who had knocked **Bugs Butler** out in the third. **(TAS ch13,14)**

LUNA PARK: the site of **Skipper Shute**'s attempted seduction of **Maud Peters** and his subsequent come-uppance. **(TMU-WDD)**

LUSITANIA: its A deck was liable to vibrate rather. **(Strand-PAW)**

LYLY, John (c1554-1606): neatly put in his *Euphues*, "A burned child dreadeth the fire", which may have inspired later articles on the subject of *Reformed Criminals*. **(TOR ch4)**

MABEL: the receptionist at **Scrope, Ashby and Pemberton** who was blessed with an hour-glass figure, a good deal of golden hair, the ability to speak conversational French but a regrettable lack of skill in listening between the lines to office-boys such as **Perce**. **(TGI ch3,4,7)**

McANDREW: an actor who had had a hit with *Hoots, Mon!* before taking over the lead male role in *The Rose of America*. **(JTR ch16)**

McASTOR: where **George Mellon** planned to dine with **Rosie** on his birthday, but didn't. **(Strand-TSF)**

MACBETH: after two minutes' conversation with **Otis Pilkington**, **Wally Mason** was in a position to understand how ... would have felt chatting with Banquo, and **Eustace Hignett** once gazed upon a half-smoked cigar as he might have done at that individual's ghost. **Phipps'** reaction on seeing **Bill** (or **Jane**) **Shannon** had a similar quality. The spiritual shock which Macbeth experienced when witnessing the approach of the forest (which PGW insists is that of Dunsinane, but **Shakespeare** suggested was that of Birnam Wood moving towards Dunsinane) resembled that of a nervous person when confronted with an unexpected outbreak of face fungus on a stranger moving towards them. **(JTR ch17; GOB ch6; QUS ch10; TOR ch1; PLP-GCS; Colliers-PTR)**

McCALL, Cora Bates: an eminent lecturer on *Rational Eating*, this big, bullying woman practised what she preached, consuming for breakfast a slice of Health Bread and nut butter. But her skilful rhetoric, by which she converted **Blake's Unknown**, led to a welcome family revolution. **(IOA ch21)**

McCALL, Lindsay: the unfortunate husband of the food-crank **Cora**, he was a hunted-looking little man, the natural peculiarities of his face being accentuated by a pair of semi-circular glasses, looking like half-moons with the horns turned up. He chose to express his personality in dramatic fashion, by bringing the entire contents of an unwelcome breakfast table crashing to the floor, and declaring his intention to settle a dispute which he never had with **Dan Brewster** over adjacent plots of land in Westchester. **(IOA ch21)**

McCALL, Washington: see page 124 to read the eulogistic report of this long-suffering youth's successful rebellion against the constraints of the table. His suffering had left him, as a sixteen-year-old, long and thin, all legs and knuckles, his long neck, pale red hair and sandy eyelashes combining to make him look like a half-grown, half-starved hound, but one sniff of a *poulet en casserole* and there was no stopping him. **(IOA ch21)**

MacFADDEN, Clarence: was wishful to dance, but his feet wasn't gaited that way, so he sought a professor and asked him his price, and said he was willing to pay. The professor looked down with alarm at his feet, and marked their enormous expanse, and he tacked on a five to his regular price for teaching MacFadden to dance. Had this individual been a creation of the Master instead of a reference culled from the experiences of a wider world, he would have been a rarity, a human Clarence who was not the Earl of Emsworth. **(MLF-TLF)**

MacFARLAND, Andy: the adopted son of a restaurateur, who grew from a freckled little nipper with as much silent obstinacy as a mule into an Oxford (or Newhaven) undergraduate who had to quit college when his father had a stroke so that he could run the business. He threw **Katie** out as cashier when she went on stage, and would not even let her back to dance, but became reconciled with her when she tried to commit suicide. **(MLF-MOM; Red-ROM)**

MacFARLAND, Katie: characters in Wodehouse who got on with the job of trying to commit suicide were rare indeed, and Katy, the adopted daughter of the same restaurateur, was perhaps the chief example. If a thing were worth doing, she probably thought, 'twas well 'twere done quickly, so she did not merely think about the possibility in an off-hand way. Her natural father had been a dead friend of **Mr MacFarland**, and she had been sixteen when **Andy** went to Oxford (or Newhaven). A pretty girl, she was cashier at **Mac's** for some time, but her enthusiasm for dancing took her on to the stage, and she brought considerable fashionable business to the restaurant. Her life changed dramatically for the worse when she broke an ankle in rehearsal for a new dance, which left her with a permanent limp, and a temporary depression, from which she sought to make the ultimate climb. **(MLF-MOM; Red-ROM)**

MacFARLAND, Mr: the founder some fifteen years earlier of the Soho restaurant which bore his name. He was a widower who adopted both a son, **Andy**, and a daughter, **Katie**, but he suffered a stroke during Andy's second year at Oxford (or Newhaven) which left him bed-ridden and eventually killed him. **(MLF-MOM; Red-ROM)**

MacFARLAND'S: see **Mac's**

McGEE (or MacGEE), John: the house detective at the **Hotel Delehay** who never forgot a face and revelled in the nickname 'Old Eagle Eye'. He was a man of few words on topics other than motion pictures, on which his knowledge was encyclopaedic, and failed even to describe the highspots of his career to his wife. Although getting on in years he had brawny arms, good footwork and sufficient nous to outwit **Herbert Higgs** on two occasions. It is a matter of considerable surprise that the alternative spelling of his name appears in a French translation of the story in *Ellery Queen Mystère-Magazine*, for it never appeared in an English language book collection until it was included in *Plum Stones* (*Galahad Books*, 1993). **(Ellery-MBD)**

McGEE, Mrs: the long-suffering wife of the detective, who never heard any details of his cases. **(Ellery-MBD)**

McGINNIS, Patrolman: one of the policemen who attended the **Hotel Delehay** in support of **Sergeant O'Toole**. **(Ellery-MBD)**

McGUFFY, Aloysius (or Aloyius) St X: a stout, smooth-faced, white-jacketed ministering angel in his early fifties, who could be found behind the smaller of the two bars at **Barribault's Hotel**, he was the inventor of the **McGuffy Special**, than which there is no whicher. **(SPF ch5; SPF (Penguin) ch5)**

McGUFFY SPECIAL: enough said. **(SPF ch5)**

MACHIAVELLI, Niccolò (1469-1527): **Mervyn Spink**, stripped of his mask, revealed himself as a modern ... **(SPF ch10)**

McHOOTS, Sandy: his book *My Life on the Links* (as told to **Colin Jeffson**) was an inadequate substitute for *Daffodil Days*. **(TGI ch5)**

MacPHERSON: once paid £10 to **Gordon Carlisle** as agent for the **Home For Brave Ailing Mothers**. **(HOW ch10)**

MACRAE, David Ossian: of St Gabriel's, Cambridge, where he was held in awe and respect by such former pupils as **James Orlebar Cloyster**, for whom he wrote a letter of introduction to **Charles Fermin**. He was Scotch, and after marrying the senior historian of Newnham College, prepared an edition of **Aristotle**'s *Ethics* whilst on honeymoon. **(NGW ptII ch3)**

MACRAE, Mrs: a senior historian at Newnham College, who assisted her husband's literary composition whilst on honeymoon. **(NGW ptII ch3)**

MACRAE, Pericles Æschylus: the infant son of classical parents. **(NGW ptII ch3)**

MAC'S: a restaurant in Soho, or on Seventh Avenue, which started with three advantages (**Andy MacFarland**, the proprietor; **Jules**, the chef; and **Henry**[1], the head waiter), and acquired its fourth, and most significant, when its cashier forsook her post for a stage career. **(MLF-MOM; Red-ROM)**

MacSPORRAN: a philanthropist willing to share with anyone his inevitable profits from the distillation of gold from sea-water. **(NSE-HTU)**

McWHUSTLE OF McWHUSTLE, the: the name of the character played by **McAndrew**, replacing **Lord Finchley** in a later draft of *The Rose of America*. **(JTR ch17)**

MACEY'S: employed **Genevieve** as a cloak model. **(MLF-CRH)**

MADAME GARNIER'S: a confectioner at **St Peter's Port**, Guernsey. **(NGW ptI ch2)**

MADISON SQUARE GARDEN: Nigger asked **Jack** about prizes and ribbons he might have won at competitions held there. **(TMU-TGP; Red-BIS)**

MADISON THEATRE: a New York playhouse to which **Peggy Norton** returned after a tour in Chicago. **(TMU-INA)**

MAE: see **West, Mae**

MAETERLINCK, Count Maurice (1862-1949): would have called **Archie Moffam**'s scheme to have **Spectatia Huskisson** sing *Mother's Knee* a lallapaloosa. His work was described as the asparagus at **Mrs Goodwin**'s philosophical banquet. **(NGW pt1 ch1; IOA ch23)**

MAGEE, Red Dan: he had lived across the way in Skibbereen from the **Burke** brothers, **Mike** and **Tim**, before coming to visit New York, and finding a hotel at Wistaria. **(PallMall-MLB)**

MAGNOLIA HALL: a draughty cavern on W93rd St where many musical comedies were born. **(Strand-BTG)**

MAHAFFEY, Lulabelle: a gardener at her place was Mexican and could translate a diary written in Spanish. **(TOR ch7)**

MAINPRICE: one of the two principals in the firm **Mainprice and Bassett**, he was disappointed to find that **Grace Pemberton** only proposed to buy twenty copies of *Parted Ways* instead of the hoped-for hundred. **(Strand-PAW)**

MAINPRICE AND BASSETT: judiciously restricted the first edition of *Parted Ways* to 500 copies. **(Strand-PAW)**

MAISON SUISSE: on the corner of Rupert Street and Shaftesbury Avenue, it was the restaurant where **James Orlebar Cloyster** generally dined out before it was pulled down to make way for the **Hicks Theatre. (NGW ptII ch6)**

MALIM, Kit: bred in the gutter, this pretty, good-natured creature, née Blake, had been connected with the minor stage before marrying, and now worked in a Tottenham Court Road fried fish shop. **(NGW ptII ch6,7,9)**

MALIM, Mr: obtained a double-first at Oxford, where a fellow-student was **Julian Eversleigh**, before joining the Foreign Office and becoming secretary to Sir George Grant. He married **Kit**, with whom he could often be seen at **Pepolo's. (NGW ptII ch6)**

MALLORY, Sir Thomas (*fl* 15th century): an incorrect spelling selected by each of the magazine publishers: see **Malory, Sir Thomas. (Pearson-SAG; Colliers-SAG)**

MALLOW HALL: had been the Elizabethan home of the **Armitage** family for four centuries before entering into the possession of the **Bond** dynasty. It was located near **Wellingford** or **Wallingford**, in the Vale of Evesham, Worcestershire. **(DBB ch2)**

MALONE: was turned down by **Rice. (MLF-BTB)**

MALONE, Kate: an old acquaintance of the **Burke** brothers and **Red Magee**, she had been married for eight months to **Larry O'Brien**. **(PallMall-MLB)**

MALORY, Sir Thomas (*fl* 15th century): did not write about the weaker Knights of the Round Table. **(TMU-SAG)**

MALTED MILK BETTE DAVIS: Bill Shannon sought to console herself with a ... when given the brusheroo in **Hollywood**. **(TOR ch3)**

MANCHESTER UNITED: might have won the Cup, but were unworthy to be given the job of defending **Billy Meredith**'s ball. **(TMU-TGP)**

MANCHESTER WEEKLY FOOTBALL BOOT: reported the views of **Jacob Dodson. (TMU-TGP)**

MANDELBAUM, Mr: wanted to give **Katie MacFarland** a solo piece in *The Rose Girl*. **(MLF-MOM)**

MANGOES: **Jane Hubbard** knew how to make a nourishing soup from ... **(GOB ch7)**

MANHATTAN DAILY CHRONICLE, The: the narrator of *Mike's Little Brother* was the smallest of all its reporters, being specifically responsible for news from the Windle Street police station. **(PallMall-MLB)**

MANNERING, Lady Clara: née Swithin, she was the daughter of the **first Earl of Havershot**, mother of **Egremont**, about whom she constantly fretted, and aunt of the present earl. **(LAG ch1,3)**

MANNERING, Egremont ('Eggy'): the first cousin of the Earl regnant, the tall, slender Eggy of the butter-colour hair was generally recognised as the most outstanding souse in the W1 postal district of London. He escaped to **Hollywood** from a recuperative round-the-world cruise on which he had been sent following complaints about the shaky hands and the spiders on the back of his neck. During his short spell in the film capital he became engaged first to **Ann Bannister** and then to **Mabel Prescott**, and took a short-term post as elocution teacher of **RH(JC)**. **(LAG)**

MANNISTER, General: a middle-aged man with a face like a horse, a drooping grey moustache, a grey bowler hat flattened at the crown, who brought his nephew **Lord Seacliff** to New York and left him in the charge of **Archie Moffam**. **(IOA ch7)**

MANRESA ROAD: a Chelsea thoroughfare in which a Bohemian was thought to live at number 93a, the house owned by **Mrs Driver**. **James Cloyster** took a dingy, dark, commonplace second floor back, overlooking a sea of back yards, with a cat's club (social, musical and pugilistic) outside the window. It had furniture seemingly from George III's reign and, Cloyster suspected, had last been dusted in the reign of William and Mary. **(NGW ptII ch1)**

MARC ANTONY (c83-30BC): compared to **Brutus**, was no orator. **(TAS ch1)**

MARCUS AURELIUS (121-80 BC): Margaret Goodwin preferred to go for a walk on the sand than read his works. Being whiskered to the eyebrow, he outsmarted **Joe Vanringham** in his artistic endeavours, but would have had a hard time persuading **Smedley Cork** that nothing happens to a man which he is not fitted by nature to bear. See also **Parsifal** and **Moffam, Archie**. (**NGW ptI ch3; IOA ch3; SUM ch17; TOR ch11**)

MARDI GRAS: made **Coney Island** the greatest thing on earth. (**MLF-CRH**)

MARGATE: was too bracing for **Sam Marlowe** to have gone there when in a grey and dark mood. (**GOB ch8**)

MARIANA: had he had the measure of the expression, **Charlie Yost** would probably have been murmuring "He cometh not", like ... at the moated grange while waiting for **Horace Appleby** in Valley Fields. **Billie Bennett** was said to have had her demeanour at the rail of the *Atlantic* as she awaited the arrival of a messenger with a bundle of money, but **Smedley Cork** reached a stage of anxiety when he could have given her six bisques and still beaten her. (**TMM ch2; TOR ch10; DBB ch4**)

MARIE: a Pekingese belonging to **Mrs J L T Smith** which had biting comments on her husband's loss of memory. (**IOA ch20**)

MARINER, Mr Elmer: of **Brookport**, Long Island, he was a dreamy, parsimonious uncle of **Jill M**, being her late father's brother. Elmer was a corn farmer with a clean-shaven though wrinkled face and a shambling gait, tight where money was concerned for he put all his into Brookport real estate. When he realised that **Jill Mariner** only had $20 in the world, and he was down a week's breakfasts, lunches and dinners, he was appalled. The situation reminded him of the occasion when he had given a waiter $10 instead of $1, only to discover the disaster too late to permit retrieval. (**JTR ch7; TLW ch7**)

MARINER, Mrs Elmer: of **Brookport**, Long Island, was an equally dreamy, parsimonious aunt of **Jill M** with a perpetual cold. (**JTR ch7**)

MARINER, Jill: an American girl who had not lived in America since she was eight or nine. She had grown up in Worcestershire as a neighbour of **Freddie Rooke** and **Wally Mason** but after being orphaned she had been left in the charge of her uncle, the well-meaning but misguided **Major Selby**. Jill was a thoroughbred with a small, active body, a resolute chin, pale gold hair, small, even teeth, and a vivid, magnetic personality. Underlying her intense talent for living, however, was a major weakness, a too-ready impulse to believe others to be as honest and disinterested as herself and this showed up in her engagement to and treatment by the self-centred, ambitious **Sir Derek Underhill, MP**. She demonstrated in the resulting crises that she could cope admirably with matters involving integrity and judgment, and these skills were to gain for her not only a sense of objective discrimination but a loving fiancé in the shape of the ever-patient Wally. **(JTR)**

MARINER, Tibby: a gloomy boy aged eight who resembled his father, **Elmer**, but in addition was often naughty at breakfast or lunch. **(JTR ch7; TLW ch7)**

MARINUS OF TYRE (fl 2nd cent AD): was not universally liked, so much so that the *Pan* paperback editor referred to him as 'Marinus of Type'. **(TOR ch17; TOR (Pan) ch17)**

MARION HUNTER: a **Hollywood** bookshop and taxi-stand. **(TOR ch3)**

MARIUS, Gaius (155-86BC): after receiving an uppercut from **Howard Steptoe**, his wife's **Alsatian** resembled ... amongst the ruins of Carthage. **(QUS ch19)**

MARK DELAMERE, GENTLEMAN: a novelette familiar to **Sidney Chibnall**, in which situations similar to that described by **Joss Weatherby** occurred. **(QUS ch7)**

MARK OF THE BEAST, The: by **Kipling**, offered possible clues to the solution of a mysterious death. **(Pearson-EDO)**

MARKS, Sid: the youthful leader of the **Frith Street Gang** whom **Spider Buffin** always sought to avoid. **(TUW-MIS)**

MARLOWE, George: a young author who, on becoming engaged to **Grace Pemberton**, had been delighted to find that not only was she not an author but she had no wish to become one. He had a knack of writing and earned sufficient to indulge his passion for golf. After their marriage, strains appeared in their relationship as she forsook her golf for writing, but when George offered her some of his unpublished manuscripts to fulfil her contracts, the tension eased. **(Strand-PAW)**

MARLOWE, Grace: see **Pemberton, Grace**

MARLOWE, Sir Mallaby: of Bruton St, Mayfair, and Ridgway's Inn, London EC4, Sir Mallaby was an eminent London lawyer, the brother of **Adeline Hignett**, and father of **Samuel**. A dapper little man with a round, cheerful face, healthy complexion and bright eye, he boasted a golf handicap of twelve. **(GOB ch1,8,12)**

MARLOWE, Sam: the son of **Sir Mallaby** and cousin of **Eustace Hignett**, with whom he had been at school and Trinity, Oxford. Sam was 25 years old, 6' tall, had a 40" chest, weighed 13 stone and looked fitter than most. He had reached the semi-final of the US Amateur golf championship, and enjoyed in addition cricket, football, hunting, shooting, swimming and Swedish wrestling. A warm supporter of the courtship methods of **W S Gilbert**'s *Alphonso*, he did not need a year to make up his mind that **Billie Bennett** had been set aside since the beginning of time to be his bride, even though their engagement had several attempts before it was seriously established. **(GOB; TMM ch1)**

MARLOWE, Mr: **Sam**'s grandfather, who approached a forthcoming proposal in a roundabout way after eighteen months of respectful aloofness. **(GOB ch4)**

MARLOWE, THORPE, PRESCOTT, WINSLOW & APPLEBY: an old-established firm of solicitors in Ridgway's Inn, near Fleet Street, London EC4, whose only survivng member was **Sir Mallaby Marlowe**, son of the firm's founder. **(GOB ch8)**

MARS: **Appleby** could put on a face of stone, the voice of a sergeant-major, and an eye like ... to threaten and command. **(DBB ch7)**

MARSHALL PLAN: the loan of $100 by the almost penniless American, **Bill** (or **Jane**) **Shannon**, to the wealthy English peer, **Lord Topham**, to enable him to back **Betty Hutton** at the Santa Anita racecourse came under the head of the ... **(USTOR ch19; Colliers-PTR)**

MARSHMORETON, Earl of: the father of **Maud**, née Marsh, who married **George Bevan**; for more details about him see *Volume 5*. **(TLW ch4; Grand-JTR))**

MARSUPIAL, Dikran: an ace **Hollywood** film director, friend of **Cosmo Booch** and victim of **JC(RH)**. He was one who had worked with **Adela Cork**, and suffered **(LAG ch12; TOR ch6)**

MARTYN, Algy: like his friend **Ronny Devereux**, he could recognise a tick at sight, even when disguised as a baronet and an MP. **(JTR ch1,8)**

MARTYN, Miss: **Algy**'s sister and friend of **Jill Mariner**, she swore that all the girls she knew would cut **Underhill** after his dastardly behaviour. **(JTR ch8)**

MARVELLOUS MURPHY THE SMALLER: an unpleasant youth, snub-nosed and spotty. **(TAS ch1)**

MARVELLOUS MURPHYS, the: an equilibristic act newly resident at **Mrs Meecher**'s establishment, who were promptly enslaved by the charm of **Sally Nicholas**. **(TAS ch1)**

MARX, Groucho (Julius Henry, 1890-1977): **Kay Shannon** did not want to feel, when with the man she loved, that she had been wrecked on an island with ... **(TOR ch11)**

MARX, Karl: **Joss Weatherby** claimed that, when he told him that social distinctions ought to be abolished, Marx had replied that there might be a book in it. **(QUS ch9)**

MARY¹: **Mike Cardinal** realised dimly how ... must have felt about her lamb as he gambolled round **Terry Cobbold** and gave a genial "Boo" in her ear. **(SPF ch7)**

MARY²: a servant who brought the news to **Colonel Reynolds** that after the death of **Tommy** nineteen hampers had arrived for his daughter **Sylvia**, all of which proved to contain pugs. **(TUW-WPS)**

MARYLEBONE CRICKET CLUB, the: employed stern-faced men to eject spectators who used catapults to pepper members with tin-foil. **(NSE-HTU)**

MARYLEBONE CRICKET CLUB PRESIDENT, the: presided over the trial of **Clarissa Binstead**, but was worried about a possible international incident. **(NSE-HTU)**

MASON, Wallace ('Wally'): a successful and likeable librettist of light musicals in New York and London, sometimes under the pseudonym of **John Grant**. He was a friend of **George Bevan**, with whom he wrote *Follow the Girl*. His work was regarded as 'brainless trash and jingly tunes' by **Otis Pilkington**, but the effort he put into the revision of the hopeless *Rose of America* gave him the last laugh. During his Worcestershire childhood, Wally had not been a favourite of **Jill Mariner**, **Freddie Rooke** and others, but his excessively forthright conception of fun and games concealed a boyhood ideal (with Jill the target) which time converted into a subconscious single-mindedness of purpose. By his mid-twenties he had become a man of substance, with rough, wavy hair and a humorous mouth, the whole conveying the attractive ugliness of a large, loose, shaggy dog which breaks things in drawing-rooms. When he met Jill again at the premier of *Tried by Fire* she did not recognise him, but as he crept back into her life she appreciated his many previously hidden qualities, and welcomed him gladly as her removal man when the time came. **(JTR)**

MASTER, The Mixer's: ran an East End pub, and sold **The Mixer** for half a crown. **(MLF-HMV)**

MATTHEWSON, Mr: of the **New York Giants**, preserved his skill despite advanced years. **(Red-ROM)**

MAUD: **Tennyson**'s ... would have loved **Monk's Crofton**. **(TAS ch12)**

MAUFRINGNEUSE ET VALERIE-MOBERANNE (or VALÉRIE-MOBERANNE), Nicolas Jules St Xavier Auguste, M le Marquis de ('Old Nick'): he occupied the position of *employé attaché à l'expedition du troisième bureau* (ie clerk) at the **Ministry of Dons and Legs** (which is pronounced 'lay' and is short for Legacies), an appointment of unprecedented modesty which he contrived to make so much more inconspicuous by his infrequent attendance that he was eventually invited to make the inconspicuousness permanent. His first marriage to the rich but Bohemian **Loretta Ann Potter** had ended in divorce after the appearance of **Jefferson, Comte d'Escrignon**, and he had also completed a second marriage to **Hermione**, now **Pegler**. Old Nick was a handsome man with distinguished looks who liked to appear well-dressed, but in poverty had to accept such positions as head waiter at the **Mazarin** in New York, where he met and married his third wife, a cook. **(FRL; USFRL eg ch2)**

MAUGHAM, William Somerset (1874-1965): he seemed eager to leave 10% of his earnings with a literary agent. **(TOR ch18)**

MAUNDRELL: an old actor with a long beard who always wore a steeple hat and long coats. He said the business which had been arranged for the valet in *The Girl Who Waited* reminded him of a story about Leopold Lewis. **(NGW ptII ch8,26)**

MAURETANIA: a Cunard Liner with four funnels in which **Ginger Kemp** went from England to New York, and in which **Sally Nicholas**, unbeknown to Ginger, played the return date. **(TAS ch11)**

MAWSON: found a small china warrior of delicate workmanship on **Brewster**'s behalf. **(IOA ch2)**

MAXWELL, Rutherford: an English younger son employed in New York by the **New Asiatic Bank** and living in **Alcala**. He had nice eyes, a popular shape of nose and lovely hair. He left his fiancée **Alice Halliday** behind in Worcestershire as he sought to make a go of writing stories, but kept her picture on his shelf. Inspired by **Peggy Norton**, he wrote a most successful play, but Peggy resisted his personal advances and warned him that the magic and glamour of the theatrical world would fade, and we expect him to have long since returned to reclaim his Alice. **(TMU-INA)**.

MAYER, Louis B: a name assigned to the police by **Adela Cork** when they preferred to gossip about the movie business rather than investigate her burglary. The original model, a founder of **MGM**, lived from 1885 to 1957. **(TOR ch16)**

MAYFAIR MARY: in conducting the '*A Little Bird in Society*' page for *Fireside Chatter*, she wrote complimentary things in a foreign tongue about **Beatrice Bracken**'s appearance at the Spanish Embassy. **(HOW ch2)**

MAYFAIR MEN: Sidney Chibnall did not believe in them, unlike his fiancée, **Vera Pym**. **(QUS ch10)**

MAYFAIR, The: announced that it would be publishing *A Story in Dialogue* by **Sidney Price**. **(NGW ptII ch19)**

MAYFAIR GAZETTE, The: the publication edited by **Theodore Popjoy**. **(Throne-KHE)**

MAZARIN: the best place in town for a publisher to take a client's husband for lunch, before knocking the cost off against income tax under the heading of entertainment. **(FRL ch12)**

MEADOWES: the man acting for **Lord Peebles**, who took his lordship the daily bromoseltzer and anchovy on hot toast. **(SPF ch1)**

MEDULLA-OBLONGATA-GLUTZ: the **Hollywood** studio headed by **Jacob Glutz**, which was expected to offer big money for **Carmen Flores**' diary. It felt that **Patrolman Bill Morehouse**'s acting career wasn't right for whimsical comedy, but later accepted both him and **Sergeant Ward** for extra work. **(TOR ch7)**

MEDWAY, Gertie: **Julia Gedge**'s trim, personable, young maid whose discovery of **Senator Opal**'s half-smoked cigar in her mistress's room brought to life the story she had been reading about **Janice Devereux**. Her real identity became apparent as she proved to **Oily Carlisle** that her skill in wielding a large, hard, thick, solid vase had not declined in a year. **(HOW ch1,10,11,17; USHOW ch11)**

MEECHER, Mrs: a warm-hearted boarding-house proprietress with two brothers, one living in Portland, Oregon. **Sally Nicholas**, despite her new wealth, reflected that home was where the heart was, and returned to the bosom of ..., even though there were more prunes on the menu than the gourmet, if not the dietician, would consider judicious. Once a member of the theatrical profession, she had been in the original production of *Floradora*, although, like every other actress making the claim, she had not been in the original sextette. **(TAS ch1,5,8)**

MEEK STREET REGISTRY OFFICE: where **Alice Punter** waited in vain for **Augustus Robb**, while he was becoming increasingly nervous at **Beak Street**. **(SPF ch16,23)**

MEGGS, Mr: those who studied the matter apparently concluded that the tendency to commit suicide was greatest among those who had passed their fifty-fifth birthday, and that the rate was twice as great for unoccupied males as for occupied. Mr Meggs thus qualified with, so to speak, both barrels, as he was 56 and for the last 20 years had been indulging his natural taste for idleness with the practised hand of one who inherited a substantial legacy. He worked occasionally on the odd paragraph of proposed books on either *British Butterflies* or a *History of the Civil War*, but he was as indecisive as the creatures about which he wrote or the subject of his writings, flitting from indigestion cure to indigestion cure, and sipping at each one. Although he determined on **suicide** as the solution to his problems, he couldn't make up his mind as to when and how, and wouldn't you believe it, he was prevented from carrying out his plan by the intervention of a woman, his secretary (in giving whose name he was also indecisive) **Jane Pillinger** or **Jane Pillenger**. **(MLF-AST; McClure-AST)**

MEIER OF SARNEN: a neighbour of **Klaus von der Flue** who kept a flock of sheep. **(WTT ch2)**

MELLINGHAM HALL: the home of **Crispin Scrope**, who had to take in lodgers to try to make ends meet. It was miles from anywhere, about the size of Buckingham Palace and forever in need of repair. Telephone: Mellingham 631. It may have been the same place that was let to Grayce Llewellyn for a season (see *Volume 7*). **(TGI ch1)**

MELLINGHAM HALT: where trains to London stopped on request. **(TGI ch14)**

MELLINGHAM-IN-THE-VALE: a small English village boasting a post office and just one pub, the **Goose and Gander**. **(TGI ch8)**

MELLON, George: a sort of office boy at the *Ladies' Sphere*, he had faced severe competition before being awarded the post. He planned to obtain an increase in salary and then get married to the delightful **Rosie** which, after a short delay, he was in a position to do. **(Strand-TSF)**

MELODY THEATRE: a New York playhouse which featured *The Island of Girls*, with **Peggy Norton**. **(TMU-INA)**

MEMOIRS: those of **Adela Shannon Cork** were being written by her sister, **Bill** (or **Jane**) **Shannon**. **(TOR ch1; Colliers-PTR)**

MENDELSSOHN (Felix Mendelssohn-Bartholdy, 1809-1847): **Bill Shannon**'s humming of his *Wedding March* did not appeal to **Kay Shannon**. **(TOR ch6)**

MENJOU, Adolph: see **Lionel Barrymore**

MENTAL GOLF: a game played by **Sam Marlowe** whilst constrained in a cupboard at **Windles**. He completed the courses at Hoylake, St Andrews, Westward Ho, Hanger Hill, Mid-Surrey, Walton Heath, Sandwich, Garden City, the Engineers Club at Roslyn (Long Island) and the first fifteen holes at Muirfield. **(GOB ch17; TMM ch16)**

MEN WHO HAVE MISSED THEIR OWN WEDDINGS: for the publication of which which **Cloyster** received fifteen shillings. (PGW had an article of the same name published by *Tit-Bits* on November 24, 1900, and had received the same fee.) **(NGW ptII ch2)**

MERCER, Sidney: a New York bank paying-cashier, who threw up his job and the need for paper cuff-fasteners to join the chorus of a musical comedy. His passion for dancing left him ignorant on all other subjects, and his eventual position as a professional dancer was made secure by his faultless evening dress, his gleaming shoes of perfect patent leather, his lissom form, his

MEN WHO HAVE MISSED THEIR OWN WEDDINGS.

At Ipswich recently a marriage was about to take place when it was discovered that the bridegroom was not present. Nobody had seen or heard anything of him, and the greatest confusion reigned until, some twenty minutes after the hour appointed for the service, his brother appeared on a bicycle with the news that the missing gentleman was too busy to come, but would present himself at church on the following day.

When the wedding-party reassembled at the time mentioned the bridegroom was present, but this time the bride had absented herself. A search was instituted, and she was found at her home, arrayed in wedding-dress, but evidently determined to pay her *fiancé* back in his own coin. She yielded, however, at last, and this eccentric pair were successfully united.

Most men are apt to be nervous on the last evening of their bachelor life, and a man living in a town near Bristol was no exception. So agitated, indeed, was he that he had to take a powerful opiate before he could get to sleep. The draught proved instantly successful, and he was soon asleep. But, unfortunately, in his nervousness he had mixed so strong a dose that, when the appointed hour arrived, he was still in a deep stupor. Nor did he awake until late in the following afternoon, when he found everybody in the greatest consternation, thinking that he was in a cataleptic trance, from which he would never awake. Luckily for all concerned the drug left no bad effects, and the marriage was celebrated at the earliest possible moment.

A ludicrous case occurred recently where both bride and bridegroom missed the wedding. On the wedding-morning the bridegroom received a letter from the bride informing him that she had changed her mind and had married a more favored rival at a registry-office that morning. Curiously enough, the bridegroom had himself sent a letter the night before, begging her to release him from his engagement, as he was certain that they could never be really happy together.

Cases of either the man or the woman saying "No" when the marriage service requires them to say "Yes," though rare, have been known to happen. Several years ago a man lost his intended wife in this way owing to his irritable temper. On the marriage-day he had been the victim of a number of small accidents, and, thinking himself alone, he had indulged in some strong language, which the lady happened to overhear, and, thinking that life with a man of such bad temper would be most unpleasant, caused a unique sensation by saying "No" instead of "Yes," and walking out of the church. Nor could all the arguments of the bridegroom induce her to relent.

One of Wodehouse's earliest published articles: in Tit-Bits, *24th November, 1900* sleek, light hair, his chinless face and his spotless collar. **(MLF-TLF; SatEvePost-TLF)**

MEREDITH: the painted rubber ball he used when a boy was owned by **Jacob Dodson** until he offered it in a wager on a rematch between **Manchester United** and **Houndsditch Wednesday**. **(TMU-TGP)**

MERLIN: would, if asked, have provided a magic prescription against dragon-bites. **(TMU-SAG)**

MERRIDEW: one of five acquaintances of **Jane Abbott** not known to **Joe Vanringham**. **(SUM ch5)**

MERRIDEW, Miss: a sales assistant at **Fuller & Benjamin** who was sympathetic to **Rosie**'s plight after Rosie bought a spring frock and a spring suit that she didn't really want and didn't buy the ones she did want. After cheering Rosie up, she sang *Poor Butterfly* to herself. **(Strand-TSF)**

MERRY WIDOW, The: one of **Prosser**'s favourite shows. **Mrs Peagrim** forecast that *The Rose of America* would be another ..., and that **Otis Pilkington** would make thousands of dollars from it. **(JTR ch18; TMU-POM)**

MESHACH: needed to mop his forehead when leaving the fiery furnace. **(TOR ch19)**

MGM: were involved in a Darkest Africa movie, and it was thought possible that it was one of their gorillas who had escaped and started a campaign of poking people in the snoot. **(LAG ch18)**

MIASMA: an infection floating in the air, a deadly exhalation, otherwise known as **Roland Bean**. **(TMU-MMM)**

MICHAEL, Mr: a musical critic, who was a member of the **Barrel Club** and had once written an operetta which ran about two nights at the Court. **(NGW ptII ch8)**

MICHELANGELO (Michelagnolio di Lodovico Buonrotti, 1475-1564): like **Soup Slattery** centuries later, he refused to be satisfied with just one branch of Art. **(HOW ch1)**

MICHIGAN: a tune played by the band at **Geisenheimer's**. **(MLF-ATG)**

MICHIGAN MOTHERS: a press stunt involving 500 or 600 ... would have involved them all kissing a reluctant **Joey Cooley** had **Beulah Brinkmeyer** not been poked in the snoot. **(LAG ch10)**

MIDAS: Joe Davenport regarded **Smedley Cork** as a ... . **(Colliers-PTR)**

MIDGLEY, J B: **Eustace Hignett** scowled at the notice on the stateroom wall, informing him that the name of his steward was ... **(GOB ch2)**

MIDIAN, the troops of: **Johnny Miller** reminded **Freddie Rooke** of ..., also of a tiger at the Zoo at feeding time. **(JTR ch14)**

MID-SURREY: scene of one of the rounds of **mental golf** played by **Sam Marlowe** whilst concealed in a cupboard at **Windles**. **(GOB ch 17)**

MIGNONETTE: a houseboat on the Thames at **Walsingford Hall**, briefly the headquarters of the regrettable **Adrian Peake**, until he relinquished the property to **Sam Bulpitt**. It had once been snowy white, but the passage of time had converted it to a repellent gray, giving it the dishevelled, dissipated appearance of a houseboat which has been out with the boys. **(SUM ch2)**

MIKE: Young **Kelly**'s brother, an all-in wrestler. **(SUM ch14)**

MIKE ROMANOFF'S: first stop on **Smedley Cork**'s toot with **Joe Davenport**. **(TOR ch6)**

MILBURY: one of four places of similar names, with stations and trains critical to the construction of the plot of *Murder at Bilbury Manor*. **(SUM ch16)**

MILICZ (or MILITSCH) (d1374): the most influential among the divines in Moravia and Bohemia who, in a certain sense, paved the way for the reforming activities of Huss. Wow! **(MLF-TLF)**

MILLBOURNE: a village adjacent to **Millbourne Bay** with red-roofed houses, than which there was no sleepier spot in the whole of Hampshire. The description is evidently that of Emsworth, the story having been written when the author lived there. **(TMU-STW)**

MILLBOURNE BAY: a hole, according to **Sally Preston**, and not merely one of eighteen in a round of golf. It could be found in Hampshire and just across the water could be found the dreamy town of **Millbourne**. **(TMU-STW)**

MILLER, Johnson ('Johnny'): a little man with snow-white hair and the india-rubber physique of a juvenile acrobat, he was the producer of the new musical *Rose of America*. Johnny was something of a rarity in the theatrical world, for he not only knew his job, but was on the level. What he told you to your face was not revised behind your back. One of the beneficiaries of this policy was **Nelly Bryant**. **(JTR ch9,11)**

MILLICENT: the diminutive under-housemaid at **Walsingford Hall**, who served dinner on a tray to a nude **Sam Bulpitt**. **(SUM ch23)**

MILLIKEN, Miss: an elderly and respectable stenographer to **Sir Mallaby Marlowe**. **(GOB ch8)**

***MILLIONAIRES WHO HAVE NEVER SMOKED*:** **Roland Bean** was a walking edition of ... and other works. **(TMU-MMM)**

MILLS, Dick: once engaged to **Kay Shannon**, he was found to be a butterfly. **(TOR ch11)**

MILLS, Henry Wallace: pursued learning with the dispassionate relentlessness of a stoat pursuing a rabbit. He was a cashier at a New York bank, who had for many years been a steady bachelor, but after being promoted to a position which gave him the right to take his annual vaction in July or August, he reacted with unexpected liveliness. Thirty-four years old when he went on vacation to **Ye Bonnie Briar-Bush Farm** he felt a youngish 21 a week and a bit after his return, when he married **Minnie Hill**. **(MLF-TLF; SatEvePost-TLF)**

MILLS, Minnie: née Hill (or even Hall, when her maiden name was first reported), she was 26 when she married **Henry**, after knowing him for just two weeks or so. She had once been a professional instructress at a dance hall and although touched by Henry's attempt to take secret dancing lessons, the version of the Jelly Roll which he inadvertantly demonstrated led her to jump to the wrong conclusions. **(MLF-TLF)**

MILNER, Tommy: his absence made **Sidney Price** contemplate taking a girl out to tea at "The Cabin". **(NGW ptII ch17)**

MILTON, Heloise: the generic name of the official adviser to certain readers of a New York evening paper, on the resignation of the most recent incumbent of which the job was given to **Elizabeth Herrold**. **(MLF-BFL)**

MILVERY, Colonel: the head of a family of Hampshire landowners long settled around **Milbourne Bay**, on the edge of the New Forest, and the man who promoted a youthful **Tom Kitchener** to second gardener. **(TMU-STW)**

MILWAUKEE: one of the richest men in ... had eye-glasses, a thin nose and a penchant for transatlantic liners. **(JTR ch7)**

MIMI: the repulsive name of a cocotte with high heels and lots of ribbon and lace, who would be likely to address the **Comte d'Escrignon** as 'Chéri'. **(FRL ch6)**

MIND HOW YOU GO: **Milly Trevor** and **Mr Salzburg** had been involved in the production of this piece. **(JTR ch11)**

MINERVA: see **Jove**

MINISTRY OF DONS AND LEGS: if, as we were told, the last word was to be pronounced 'lay', we might legitimately wonder why the expressions *'ministère'*, *'de'* and *'et'* were not used. In any event, it represented that part of the French civil service in which **Old Nick** occasionally worked, alongside Messieurs **de la Hourmerie, Letondu, Ovide** and **Soupe**. **(FRL ch2)**

MINNESOTA: a gentleman beaned his father-in-law with a meat-axe in ... **(IOA ch5)**

MIRAMAR HOTEL: one of the good hotels in **Roville-sur-Mer**. **(FRL ch5)**

MIRROR: the extent of **Superintendent Jessop**'s reading. **(DBB ch7)**

MISS WINKS: a Wodehouse Peke who was joined with the author and others as the dedicator of *Hot Water* to **Maureen O'Sullivan.**

MISUNDERSTOOD: the history of the novel which started life as the serialisation in *Captain* of *Psmith Journalist* took another turn with this short story. The description in chapter 18 of the enmity between the New York street gangs, and the events at Shamrock Hall which regenerated local rivalry, was imitated in the *Burr McIntosh Monthly* version of this story, although not in the British *Nash* reading. It might have been expected that the incident would have been omitted from the American edition of *The Prince and Betty* (see *Volume 7*), the consolidation of *Psmith Journalist* and the British *The Prince and Betty*, which was published relatively soon after *Misunderstood*, but it did make a truncated appearance in chapter 21. **(Nash-MIS; BurrMcK-MIS)**

MIX, Tom: a neighbour of the **Brinkmeyer**s in Benedict Canyon, evidently close to where the Wodehouses lived in 1931 (Benedict Canyon Drive). **(Pearson-LAG; ThisWeek-LAG)**

MIXER, The: see **Nigger**

The Mixer greeting Fred

MOCAMBO: where **Smedley Cork** rather unbent to **Joe Davenport**. (TOR ch6)

MOFFAM, an ancestral: in the Middle Ages ... had had a spasm of energy and set out on a pilgrimage to Jerusalem dressed as a wandering friar, only to be set upon as he was leaving by his favourite hound, who mistook him for a scurvy knave, bit him in the fleshy part of the leg, and caused his stroll to be postponed indefinitely. (IOA ch7)

MOFFAM, Archie: a long, thin, string-beaned Englishman who was sent by his elder brother **Rupert** to find work in the United States, following a period of education at Eton, Oxford (with **Lord Seacliff**) and the bankruptcy court, and a worthwhile contribution to his country's efforts during the first world war. In soul, looks, manners, amiability and breeding he was 100% man, and by his contemporaries he was regarded as a sportsman, a good egg, one of the lads; in fact, All Right. He was considerate towards his fellow men (and women), as exemplified by the assistance given to the **Sausage Chappie** and **Vera Silverton**.

This view of Archie was not shared by his father-in-law, **Daniel Brewster**, who objected to him on two counts, both concerning his own two ewe lambs. Ewe lamb number one was his daughter **Lucille**, and Daniel disliked the way Archie had married her without as much as a by-your-leave. Ewe lamb number two was the **Hotel Cosmopolis**, and Archie had made hurtful remarks about its qualities in Daniel's hearing. Archie did not help matters in the popularity stakes by invariably beating his father-in-law at golf, although whether the margin was 10 and 8, or 9 down, seems to have been disputed. Daniel, concentrating on these points, and mixing in the undoubted facts that Archie was unemployed and had no private means, could not go along with the accepted view that the boy combined the more admirable characteristics of **Apollo**, **Sir Galahad** and **Marcus Aurelius**.

Archie did try to remedy the position by seeking work: modelling a vivid lemon-coloured two-piece bathing suit for his artist friend **James B Wheeler**, becoming a hotel manager, and generally making himself useful. He tried to please his father-in-law by bidding for **Pongo**'s identical twin, to help his brother-in-law **Bill Brewster** with his successive romantic entanglements, to reconcile **Looney Biddle** with his girl-friend, and to develop his own career by buying **Salvatore's Mother**'s shop. And all the time, he never ceased to wonder at his good fortune in tying the knot with the wonderful Lucille. **(IOA; Cosmo-DFB)**

MOFFAM, Lucille: née **Brewster**, she was the popular daughter of **Daniel**, and dearer to him even than his hotel. She had an animated face set in a cloud of dark hair, and in the eyes of her husband **Archie Moffam**, whom she met while staying with the **Van Tuyl**s, was so perfect that he felt compelled to take the marriage certificate from his pocket from time to time to verify the miracle of his good fortune. She jealously disapproved of **Vera Silverton** and her flies, and disapproved in a different way of her brother **Bill**'s romantic entanglements, for example, running around after a female with crimson hair, goggling with eyes popping out of the head like a bulldog waiting for a bone. As we left her, she was expecting her first baby, whom we confidently expect, when past the poached egg and baby-talk phase, to follow in his father's footsteps and become a thoroughly good thing. **(IOA)**

MOFFAM, Rupert: the head of the family of which **Archie** was so distinguished a member. **(Strand-MMH)**

MOFFAT, Ginger: a friend of **Appleby** who had recently escaped from Dartmoor. **(DBB ch2)**

MOGGS, Adelaide Brewster: on marrying **Aubrey Devine** she declined to add to her collection of names. An early leading exponent of on the subject of Woman's Rights, she spoke of *The Future of Woman* on any available public stage. **(VanFair-AAI)**

MOJAVE DESERT:

> "I went back to get a handkerchief, and there he was, if you please, under the dressing-table, with his fanny sticking up like a mesa in the Mojave desert."

(TOR ch5)

MOLOTOV (Skriabin Vyacheslav Mikhalovich, 1890-1986): because **Kay Shannon** had a habit of saying "No . . . No . . . No . . ." to **Joe Davenport**'s proposals, he thought she might as well be ... **(TOR ch2)**

MONA LISA: shared the copyright on weary eyelids with **Mike Bond**. **(DBB ch13)**

MONK'S CROFTON: Bruce Carmyle's home at Much Middlefold, Salop, to which both **Sally** and **Fillmore Nicholas** were invited.

It was large, low and square with a tower, an upper porch with battlements and woods full of rabbits. **(TAS ch12)**

MONROE, Jimmy: brought about a darkest hour for a number of his acquaintances by recommending an investment in **Amalgamated Dyes**, and one's view of **Chris Selby, Jill Mariner**'s uncle, was coloured by his related experience. **(JTR ch1,6)**

MONS, Battle of: a battle which **Jane Abbott** was exhorted to remember by **Joe Vanringham** because of the recognised military tactic of carrying a retreat. **(USSUM ch19)**

MONTE CRISTO, Count of: if he had applied to live in the stone apartment house at 18 E57th Street, New York, which **Chris Selby** used as a postal address, the authorities would probably have looked upon him a little doubtfully at first and hinted at the desirability of a month's rent in advance. **(JTR ch9)**

MONTGOMERY WARD: partners in misfortune **Soup Slattery** and **J Wellington Gedge** had each invested in this stock at 112. **(HOW ch1)**

MONTHLY SONGSTER: **Theodore Popjoy** had won first prize in a competition run by this paper, thereby starting his journalistic career. It should be remembered that PGW's first paid contribution to the literary world was a prize-winning submission to *The Public School Magazine*. **(Throne-KHE)**

MOON ASSURANCE COMPANY, the: offered a small bonus to employees each quarter if they had not been late. **(NGW ptII ch19)**

MOON, Elmer M: a tall, thin man in a hurry, with a name like the refrain of a vaudeville song hit, an automatic and a dictatorial manner. His object in life was to steal bonds, and if to do so successfully he had to tie up intrusive Englishmen and escape down drainpipes, that was alright by him. **(IOA ch5)**

MOORE, Eddy: a **Dunsterville** exile who placed **Mary Hill** in employment with **Joe Rendal** for a sinister purpose. He was a good-looking, tall, slim man with dark eyes and a ready flow of speech who had once said that he was prepared to die for Mary. But such talk proved to have been cheap, and instead, he asked her to die, professionally, for him by breaking an employer's confidence. **(TMU-TFD)**

MOORE, Jerry: a simple, big, quiet, rather handsome man, with blue eyes and straw-coloured hair, whose mild deafness in one ear was sufficient to protect his romance with **Jane Tuxton** from destruction by his friend **Gentleman Bailey**. Residence: a house outside Reigate inherited from his father. **(TMU-BAC)**

MOREHOUSE, Patrolman Bill: appeared to be hewn from the living rock. He had a wife with a bundle of nerves, a Boston Terrier named **Buster** and an ambition to be a movie star. **(TOR ch16)**

MORIARTY, Professor: **Horace Appleby** described himself as the poor man's ... **(DBB ch13)**

MORNING MIRROR: carried a report, written by **Mr Gossip**, about **Jill Mariner**'s engagement to **Derek Underhill**. **(JTR ch1)**

MORNING POST: reported **Joe Vanrigham**'s play as 'trenchant satire'. **(SUM ch3)**

MORNING SEARCHLIGHT: also carried a report about **Jill Mariner**'s engagement to **Derek Underhill**, their version being written by **Mr Whoknows**. **(Grand-JTR)**

MORNING'S AT SEVEN: an early publication by **Vera Upshaw**, described by **Homer Pyle** as 'charming, delightful and dainty', and by the reviews as helping 'to pass an idle hour', and 'not unreadable'. **(TGI ch5)**

MORRIS & BROWN: an alternative name for the Wall Street brokers who were the fortunate employers of **Augustus Bartlett**. **(Colliers-TAS pt1)**

MORRISON, Bobby: **Wally Mason** was not, and never had been. **(JTR ch2)**

MORRISON, Rupert: a novelist friend of **Bill Bates** who got more than he bargained for when he borrowed Bates's flat at the Albany and his home in Pittsburgh in order to finish a story. **(TMU-MUP; Cosmo-MUP)**

MORTIMER, Bream: tall and thin with spats, small, bright eyes and a sharply curving nose, he looked more like a parrot than most parrots did. A nasty sneak, he told **Adeline Hignett** that her son **Eustace** was planning to marry that morning, for he had been in love with the intended for at least ten years, and he later became engaged to her, **Wilhelmina Bennett**, on at least two occasions. **(GOB)**

MORTIMER, Henry: an eminent American lawyer and occasionally bosom friend of **J Rufus Bennett**, he was the small, thin, pale, semi-bald, bespectacled father of the psittacine **Bream**. (**GOB ch1**)

MORTLAKE Augustus: was a tall man in his late 30s, inclined to stoutness, and a trustee of **Bond's Bank**. Like his co-trustee, **General Featherstone**, he was not well respected by **Isabel Bond**, being referred to as a **gaby** and a footler, and also like his co-trustee, he was under a threat of confinement from which not even a family relationship to the Chief Constable or membership of the cricket team could have saved him. But did he <u>have</u> to have arranged a contract on **Mike Bond**? (**DBB ch5**)

MOSEBY, Arthur: a long-dead former juvenile in theatrical roles who had been a friend of **Max Faucitt**. (**TAS ch5**)

MOSES (c1250BC): on the summit of Pisgah he might have worn the look which appeared on **Jules²**'s face while gazing on the lift keys from the locked interior of that lift, the one on **Eugene Warden**'s face when he shook **George Vince** by the hand, or the one **Tubby Vanringham** wore under the large cedar. (**TAS ch2; SUM ch16; TMU-MWD**)

MOSQUITOES: none could ever be found in the neighbourhood of **Ye Bonnie Briar-Bush Farm**, despite appearances to the contrary. (**MLF-TLF**)

MOTHER'S KNEE: a devastatingly popular ballad boosting mother, not knocking short skirts, which went through the world like a pestilence, selling three million copies in the USA alone, with additional sales in the Bolsheviks, Borneo and Scotland. Two full verses and a refrain can be found in the text. (**IOA ch23**)

MOTION PICTURE MAGNATES' ANNUAL GOLF TOURNAMENT: at which **Theodore Brinkmeyer** once won a cup. (**LAG ch15**)

MOUQUIN'S: **Ted Brady** suggested the wedding breakfast be held at ... (**MLF-CRH**)

MR PAUL SNYDER'S DETECTIVE AGENCY: of New Oxford Street, grew in half a dozen, or possibly a dozen, years from a single room to a suite with eight assistants, which had recently been augmented by the self-opinionated **Oakes**. (**TUW-DAE; Pearson-EDO**)

MULLER, Captain: the German room-mate of **Captain Gunner** at the **Excelsior Boarding House** until the murder of the latter. He was a big, silent man who, after receiving a crate of bananas from a friend in Java which contained a live cobra, had used only natural ingredients and a live medium to effect the demise of his colleague. **(TUW-DAE)**

MÜLLER, John: of Schaffhausen, brought news of the death of the **Emperor of Austria**. **(WTT ch15)**

MULLINS, Cyclone: was beaten in 15 rounds by **Bugs Butler** and in five by **K-Leg Binns**. **(TAS ch13)**

MULTIPLE STEEL: an investment worth looking at, according to **Augustus Bartlett**, for in his view it would be up to 150 before the following Saturday. **(TAS ch1)**

MURAT, Joachim (1767-1815): there must surely have been moments during **Napoleon Bonaparte**'s retreat from Moscow when ... got off a good thing, or **Ney** said something worth having about the weather. **(TLW ch2; Grand-JTR)**

MURCHISON, Jane: a tall, toothy girl considered by **Archie Moffam** as a nuisance. He was unimpressed that she had been a friend of his wife **Lucille** since the age of eight:

> "If her parents had any proper feeling," said Archie, "they would have drowned her long before that."

(IOA ch21)

MURDER AT BILBURY MANOR: a whodunnit of the abstruse type, which proved too deep for **Tubby Vanringham**. **(SUM ch16)**

MURDER AT MURSLOW GRANGE: **Desborough Topping** recalled how in that book the butlers wanted watching. **(SPF ch19)**

MURDOCH, Mr: a glazier who came to the bookshop on Mondays, Wednesdays and Fridays to play draughts with **Mr Bennett**. **(MLF-CRH)**

MURGATROYD, Jasper: originally written as the villain of *The Vengeance of Jasper Murgatroyd*, his part was so rewritten by the editor of *Piccadilly Weekly* that he appeared as the story's hero, a rare occurrence for even a second-hand Wodehouse character named Jasper. **(Throne-KHE)**

MURPHY, Old Jack: owned a duck farm back in Ireland, but had fallen downstairs in the dark and died from his injuries. **(PallMall-MLB)**

MURPHY, Tommy: a now-forsaken Idol of American Motherhood with considerable muscular development. **(LAG ch18)**

MUSCATEL: bumped or bored at **Newmarket** and his relegation from first place had enabled **Brotherly Love** to be declared the winner. **(TGI ch14)**

MUTINY ON THE BOUNTY: the scuttling scene in ... was to be duplicated in **George**'s scenario. **(LAG ch24)**

MY HEART AND I: a number to be rendered in Act One of *Rose of America* by the leading lady and the male chorus. **(JTR ch14)**

MY HONOLULU QUEEN: sung by **Clarice Weaver** with a chorus of Japanese girls and Bulgarian Officers. **(MLF-BTB)**

MY LIFE ON THE LINKS: a recommended alternative to *Daffodil days.* **(TGI ch5)**

MY LIFE WITH ROD AND GUN: a book by **Francis Pashley-Drake** which offered clues about wapitis, moose, zebus, mountain goats and other things he used to shoot. **(Playboy-GCS)**

MY LITTLE GREY HOME IN THE WEST: was rendered at a ship's concert by the sister of a young man. **(GOB ch6)**

MY SPORTING MEMORIES: the book by **Sir Buckstone Abbott**, available at 15s, on which he incurred unexpected liabilities by arranging for it to be privately printed after it had been rejected by about ten publishers. **(SUM ch1,10)**

MYRTLE: a girl with adenoids who worked at the **Goose and Gander, Walsingford Parva. (SUM ch16)**

MYRTLE TAKES A TURKISH BATH: a swell show. **(TAS ch16)**

NAMES WHICH ARE NOT THAT OF THE SAUSAGE CHAPPIE:

Barrington	Debenham	Montgomery	Skillington
Carrington	Dennison	Sanderson	Wilberforce
Cunningham	Hepplethwaite	Skeffington	

(IOA ch20)

NAPOLEON: see **Bonaparte, Napoleon**

NARRATOR[1], the: of *The Man Who Disliked Cats*, a patron of the **Café Britannique** who had listened to the tale of **Jean Priaulx**. (TMU-MWD)

NARRATOR[2], the: of *Sir Agravaine*, who, while staying at the **Duke of Weatherstonehope**'s castle, had found an old black-letter manuscript on which he had based his tale. (TMU-SAG)

NARRATOR[3], the: of *Back to the Garage*, was a member of the chorus of *Ask Dad* and engaged to **Jim**. (Strand-BTG)

NARRATOR[4], the: of *Cupid and the Paint Brush*, was a man with the initials RA who thought it was an omen that he would have a painting picked by the **Royal Academy**, and was eventually successful with his proposal to **Marjorie Somerville**. (Windsor-CPB)

NATCHEZ: Adela Cork's unnamed **poodle** resembled the young lady from ..., who confided to her audience that "When Ah itches, Ah scratches". (TOR ch16)

NATIONAL CITY BANK: Soup Slattery was willing to bust the ... in return for services rendered by **Packy Franklyn**. (HOW ch6)

NATIONAL GEOGRAPHIC MAGAZINE: **Freddie Rooke** tried to read it to pass the time after being sacked, and **Reggie Havershot**, **Teddy Flower** and **Joey Cooley** all idly turned the pages of copies left in the joint waiting-room of their respective dentists, **I J Zizzbaum**, **B K Burwash** and **B K Burwash** again. (JTR ch17; LAG ch1)

NATIONAL PROVINCIAL BANK: see **Barclay's Bank**

NAZIMOVA, Alla (1879-1945): never threw paper-knives at cats. (TAS ch6)

NEBUCHADNEZZAR [II] (d562BC):

> The grass by the milestone having yielded no treasure, [Sam Bulpitt] was now crawling along the edge of the road with the air of Nebuchadnezzar in search of better pasture.

(SUM ch19)

NELSON, Horatio, Viscount (1758-1805): one has the Nelson touch or one doesn't. (DBB ch5)

NERO, Emperor (37-68): his smooth, bulbous face offered maximum scope to **Joe Vanringham**'s pencil. (SUM ch17)

NERVINO: a patent medicine advertised in person by **Chris Selby** at New York social events. **(JTR ch12)**

NETHER WALLOP: the name of an English village comparable in rumminess to Snake Bite, Michigan. **(IOA ch23)**

NEW ASIATIC BANK: its New York City branch was robbed of $100,000 by **John Benyon**. **(MLF-OTN)**

NEWMARKET: where as a youth **Crispin Scrope** had lost more money than at any other racecourse. **(TGI ch4)**

NEWPORT: Otis Pilkington claimed that the inhabitants of ..., Rhode Island, had liked the original version of *The Rose of America*. **(JTR ch17)**

NEWS OF THE WORLD: was full of stories about gangsters, **Mayfair Men** and hideouts. **(QUS ch10)**

NEW YORK: in a telegram to be sent by a millionaire, 'New York' is one word, thereby helping to look after the pennies. **(SPF ch4)**

NEW YORK CHRONICLE: a paper for whom **Waterall** was the London correspondent. **(MLF-OTN)**

NEW YORKER: a weekly which carried an advertisement for **Mellingham Hall**, describing it as an English country house where they took paying guests. **(TGI ch1)**

NEW YORK GIANTS: their victory against their Pittsburgh rivals earned $500 for **Archie Moffam**. **(IOA ch14; Red-ROM)**

NEW YORK HERALD: its continental edition was taken by **Oily Carlisle** in St Rocque. **(HOW ch1)**

NEW YORK HERALD-TRIBUNE (or HERALD TRIBUNE): a daily paper which announced the engagement of **Freddie Carpenter** to **Terry Trent** shortly after Freddie had been accepted by **Mavis Todd**. **Archie Brice**, a friend of **Jeff d'Escrignon** in its Paris office, knew **J Russell Clutterbuck**. **(FRL ch3,8; USFRL ch3,8)**

NEW YORK, LONDON AND PARIS INSURANCE COMPANY, the: the supposed employer of **Packy Franklyn**, who was on hand to keep an eye on **Mrs Gedge**'s jewels. **(HOW ch13)**

NEY Marshal Michel (1769-1815): there must surely have been moments during **Napoleon Bonaparte**'s retreat from Moscow when **Murat** got off a good thing, or ... said something worth having about the weather. **(TLW ch2; Grand-JTR)**

NIAGARA FALLS: George Holbeton would prefer others to go over them in a barrel. **(QUS ch1)**

NICHOLAS, Ezekiel: Sally and **Fillmore Nicholas**'s father, who left money for Sally at age 21 and Fillmore at age 25, in the trust of their **Uncle Donald. (TAS ch2)**

NICHOLAS, Fillmore: was not improved by inheriting wealth and, in the eyes of his democratic sister **Sally**, was insufferably pompous. Once an impecunious young man who had made a tweed suit last longer than might be thought possible, he fulfilled the promise of an extraordinarily beautiful seven-year-old by sporting immaculate evening dress and white waistcoat. Having been expelled from Harvard he turned to the theatre, taking over *The Primrose Way*, setting up **Fillmore Nicholas Theatrical Enterprises Limited**, making **Elsa Doland** a star, putting on a review that flopped and lost not only his money but Sally's too, and marrying **Gladys Winch. (TAS)**

NICHOLAS, Sally: the orphaned sister of **Fillmore**, she inherited $25,000 on her 21st birthday, lent most of it to Fillmore for investment in *The Primrose Way* and the rest to **Ginger Kemp** for his dog business. She was a trim wisp of a girl with tiny hands and feet, a friendly smile, a transient dimple on the curve of her chin, bright hazel eyes and a mass of soft, brown hair. Though generally of sweet temper and generous spirit her *persona* nevertheless concealed cyclonic possibilities. She was engaged, though secretly, to **Gerald Foster**, but evidently did not realise that he would regard it as such a secret that he felt free to marry elsewhere. She also resignedly accepted the attentions of **Bruce Carmyle**, only to find that he could not accept her intermittent job as ballroom dancing instructor at **The Flower Garden** on Broadway. Third time appears to have been lucky for Sally as she eventually realised that it was Ginger whom she wanted after all. **(TAS)**

NICHOLSONs: family with whom **Archie** and **Lucille** go to lunch. **(IOA ch17)**

NIGGER: unique in Wodehouse fiction as a canine narrator of two stories, he rendered his autobiography under the pen-name '**The Mixer**'. A politically incorrect animal of extremely mixed pedigree, he had a bulldog kind of face, the imprint of his poodle grandfather, and substantial quantities of terrier. He had been born in an East End pub, or an Eighth Avenue saloon. These genes combined to produce an ugly but friendly animal with a long tail sticking straight up, wiry hair, brown eyes, a white chest standing out from an otherwise jet-black body and a good deep voice. (One description, to the contrary, ascribes to him a pure white coat with one black eye.) His favourite dish was cold ham, though he was partial also to liver. His philosophy concerning rats was that if they looked like rats they were there to chase, even if in reality they proved to be **Totos**. His social nature caused him to try to help the **Shy Man** overcome his diffidence by introducing him to **Fred**[2], and his innate loyalty led him to save **Peter** from the Red Indians. Peter rechristened him **Fido** to his everlasting dismay. **(MLF-HMV,BIS; Strand-HMV; Red-HMV)**

NIGHTINGALE, Florence (1820-1910): could be austere when imitated by **Jane Hunnicutt**. **(TGI ch12)**

NIJINSKY, Vaslav (1890-1950):

The Ritz grillroom did a Nijinsky leap before Jeff's eyes.

(FRL ch8)

NOAH: the early days of the Flood must have affected him as an English summer would have an American. **(GOB ch10)**

NORCROSS, Minna: the quietly dressed woman in dark glasses who dropped her bag for **Mr McGee** to pick up whilst at the **Hotel Delehay**. She was a noted film star, having appeared, *inter alia*, in *Painted Sinners* and *As a Man Sows*, and having already enjoyed the regulation industry minimum three husbands: **George Delacourt** (divorced), **Cyril Westmacott** (divorced) and **Spencer Halliday** (not expected to last). **(Ellery-MBD)**

NORMANDIE: a cheap hotel near the station at **Roville-sur-Mer**, where the cooking was all right. **(TAS ch2)**

NORTH ATLANTIC: see **Dollen**

NORTH-WEST MOUNTED POLICE: had their pride. **(SUM ch14)**

NORTON, Peggy: Wodehouse did not often write explicitly about relationships outside marriage, but the amazing Peggy was one such, having been set up as **Winfield Knight**'s mistress in an apartment in **Alcala**. Because of this, and probably also because she knew of **Rutherford Maxwell**'s underlying love for **Alice**

197

Halliday and the rural 'hayseed' lifestyle in Worcestershire to which he was looking forward, she refused to marry him, even though they had grown very close. To Rutherford, she was bright and vivacious, a small, trim girl with a small, well-shaped face, delicately tip-tilted nose, determined chin, grey eyes and wide good-humoured mouth, who had provided all the details needed to convert his play from a journeyman effort to one which would attract the star, who just happened to be the same Winfield Knight. To Peggy, Rutherford was a friend whom she visited each evening, and would willingly have spent the night with on her return from Chicago had he not received a letter from Alice that same evening. Since her specific competition was restricted, as far as we can tell, to the **Princess von und zu Dwornitzchek**, we can say quite definitively that Peggy is our favourite liberal-minded girl in Wodehouse. **(TMU-INA)**

NORTON-SMITH: a paying guest at **Mellingham Hall** who had a fund of good stories of life in the Far East, and a car, in which he drove **Barney Clayborne** to Salisbury to see the cathedral. **(TGI ch8)**

NOSE THING, a: was not the same as jewellery from an unnamed suitor. **(SUM ch24)**

NOTRE-DAME: an American football team which did not include a Berserk Senator in its ranks. **Stanwood Cobbold**'s place kick had enabled his University to beat them 7–6 in the last half-minute. **(HOW ch2; SPF ch18)**

NUPPIE: a lad on the *Ashlade*. **(NGW ptII ch14)**

NURONIA, S S: one of the slowest Cunard liners, which brought **Adeline Hignett** back to the UK. **(GOB ch17)**

NURSE: a nurse. **(MLF-BIS)**

OAKES: a New York dweller for several years, yet he was not known to **Nelly Bryant**. **(JTR ch6)**

OAKES, Elliot(t): the most recent employee of **Mr Paul Snyder's Detective Agency**, he was an inexperienced young man, possibly American, who nevertheless planned to revolutionise the agency's methods. In looks he was lean, with evident nervous energy, dark eyes and a thin-lipped mouth that concealed his headstrong and conceited personality, which he exhibited both in his true name

and that of his alias, **James Burton**. (TUW-DAE; Pearson-
EDO; Ellery-DAE)

OAKLEY, Annie (Phoebe Anne Oakley Moses, 1860-1926):

"Half these folks with big houses take in paying guests nowadays. They have to or they don't eat."

"So I can just walk in and ask for a reservation."

"If you've got what it takes. Don't think that, because you're my brother, you can come in on an Annie Oakley. You pay as you enter. Can you ante up?"

(USSUM ch8)

OBITER DICTA: see page 200

O'BRIEN, Larry: married **Kate Malone**. (PallMall-MLB)

O'BRIEN, Philadelphia Jack: **Joe Vanringham** did something to him, but just what was never revealed. (SUM ch19)

OCTAVE: an enormous gendarme with a penchant for pie, who was betrothed to the cook at the **Château Blissac** and startled **Wellington Gedge** whilst he was in possession of a guilty secret. **(HOW ch12,14)**

ODDY, Jane: flirted on the open beach with the baritone of a troupe of pierrots. **(TMU-WDD)**

ODDY'S: **Mac's** resembled ... when it was fairly packed. **Freddie Rooke** met **Nelly Bryant** there at a party given by 'young' **Threepwood**. (JTR ch6; MLF-MOM)

O'DOWD, Spike: the dethroned pie-eating champion of the West Side, whose defeat by **Washington McCall** at the Clover Leaf Social and Outing Club was described so vividly by the reporter for the *New York Chronicle* (see page 124). **(IOA ch21)**

OFFAL: a book by **Blair Eggleston**, which contained passages that made you shiver, so stark was its cynicism, so brutal the force with which it tore away the veils and revealed Woman for what she was. **(HOW ch14)**

O'GRADY, Genevieve: she was employed by the Mammoth Store at the weekly salary of five dollars fifty cents, and obtained her fifteen minutes of fame by flinging herself off the side of a ferry-boat into the Hudson River, and being rescued by **Adelaide Brewster Moggs**'s husband. **(VanFair-AAI)**

OBITER DICTA

It would seem to be an inexorable law of Nature that no man shall shine at both ends. If he has a high forehead and a thirst for wisdom his fox-trotting (if any) shall be as the staggerings of the drunken; while, if he is a good dancer, he is nearly always petrified from the ears upward.

(MLF-TLF)

Musical comedy is the Irish stew of the drama. Anything may be put into it, with the certainty that it will improve the general effect.

(MLF-BTB)

Except for a little small change in the possession of the Messrs Rockefeller and Vincent Astor, Reggie [van Tuyl] had all the money in the world . . .

(IOA ch14)

Not only her mother but both her aunts had warned her never to go into bars. What went on in such places she had yet to learn, but she had formed a vague picture of something resembling Saturday night in the Casbah or one of the orgies which got Babylon such a bad name.

(DBB ch2)

What [Jill Willard] did not know of the methods of the criminal classes could have been written on a bloodstain.

(DBB ch3)

Life can never be unmixedly carefree for cat burglars.

(DBB ch4)

"It is very comforting to reflect, Ferdie, that nowadays with the security regulations so laxly observed by the prison authorities you can always leave if the place doesn't suit you."

(DBB ch4)

"I know you started to learn to play bridge this morning, Reggie, but what time this morning?"

(DBB ch5)

These Welshmen, he was thinking bitterly, you couldn't trust one of them. Take your eyes off them for half a second and the next thing you knew they had sneaked round the corner and found salvation.

(DBB ch7)

"I can't see why the fact that a man is large should deter a gunman from letting him have it. Makes him easier to hit."

(DBB ch13)

Paradoxically, she helped herself because she could not help herself.

(TGI ch1)

. . . but *fiat justitia, ruat coelum*, as the fellow said . . .

(TGI ch2)

"I nearly married for love when I was young and foolish, but I came out of the ether in time . . ."

(TGI ch5)

"A girl is either an attractive young prune or she is not an attractive young prune. If she is an attractive young prune, why not say so?"

(TGI ch10)

The Agee woman told us for three quarters of an hour how she came to write her beastly book, when a simple apology was all that was required, . . .

(TGI ch11)

The cupboard in the corner of the room, which had hitherto not spoken, suddenly sneezed.

(TGI ch11)

If one of the Three Musketeers had asked the other two Musketeers to push Cardinal Richelieu into the Seine, the other two Musketeers would have sprung to the task with their hair in a braid.

(TGI ch13)

Half the misery in life . . . is caused by horses that come in second; . . .

(TGI ch13)

In the income tax bracket in which [Barney Clayborne] belonged a hundred pounds or its equivalent in dollars was something which fell into the category of small change.

(TGI ch14)

Tell's first idea was that one of the larger mountains in the neighbourhood had fallen on top of him.

(WTT ch8)

(When a man repeats what he says three times, you can see that he is not in a good temper.)

(WTT ch10)

"It is excellent, as an English poet will say in a few hundred years, to have a giant's strength, but it is tyrannous to use it like a giant."

(WTT ch11)

A successful play gives you money and a name automatically. What the ordinary writer makes in a year the successful dramatist receives, without labour, in a fortnight.

(NGW ptI ch3)

"[Advertisements] are the life-essence of every newspaper, every periodical and every book."

(NGW ptII ch4)

Was I not . . . solving an addition sum in infantile poultry before their mother, the feathered denizen of the farmyard, had lured them from their shell?

(NGW ptII ch5)

[Lady Underhill] supposed the Almighty had had some wise purpose in creating Freddie, but it had always been inscrutable to her.

(JTR ch1)

There are men who fear repartee in a wife more keenly than a sword.

(JTR ch4)

Marriage had always appalled him, but there was this to be said for it, that married people had daughters.

(JTR ch6)

. . . Jane Hubbard had insisted on the front row. She always had a front-row seat at witch dances in Africa, and the thing had become a habit.

(GOB ch6)

Life was like one of those shots at squash which seem so simple till you go to knock the cover off the ball, when the ball sort of edges away from you and you miss it. Life, Freddie began to perceive, was apt to have a nasty back-spin on it.

(JTR ch14)

"I've seen worse shows than this turned into hits. All it wants is a new book and lyrics and a different score."

(JTR ch11)

Any line that is cut out of any actor's part is the only good line he has.

(JTR ch14)

"If one is expecting to be treated fairly," said the Duchess with a prolonged yawn, "one should not go into the show-business."

(JTR ch16)

Into each life some rain must fall. Quite a shower was falling now into young Mr Pilkington's.

(JTR ch18)

He looked more like a parrot than most parrots do. It gave strangers a momentary shock of surprise when they saw Bream Mortimer in restaurants, eating roast beef. They had the feeling that he would have preferred sunflower seeds.

(GOB ch1)

"I can't stand brave men," said Jane, "it makes them so independent."

(GOB ch4)

A White Star steward, waking you up at six-thirty, to tell you that your bath is ready, when you wanted to sleep on till twelve, is the nearest human approach to the nightingale.

(GOB ch7)

At the idea that any such mundane pursuit as practising putting could appeal to his broken spirit now, Sam uttered a bitter laugh. It was as if Dante had recommended some lost soul in the *Inferno* to occupy his mind by knitting jumpers.

(GOB ch8)

On the five occasions during recent years on which men had entered her tent with the object of murdering her, Jane Hubbard had shot without making enquiries.

(GOB ch11)

[Sam] was finding Widgery stiff reading. He had just got to the bit about *Raptu Haeredis*, which – as of course you know – is a writ for taking away an heir holding in socage.

(GOB ch12)

Billie knew all. And, terrible thought the fact is as an indictment of the male sex, when a woman knows all, there is invariably trouble ahead for some man.

(GOB ch15)

"If he says he's Samuel Marlowe," assented Mr Bennett grudgingly, "I suppose he is. I can't imagine anybody saying he was Samuel Marlowe if he didn't know it could be proved against him."

(GOB ch17)

. . . he could balance himself with one hand on an inverted ginger-ale bottle while revolving a barrel on the soles of his feet. There is good in all of us.

(TAS ch1)

It seems to be one of Nature's laws that the most attractive girls should have the least attractive brothers.

(TAS ch1)

All through her stay in Roville, [Sally] had found in dealing with the native population that actions spoke louder than words. If she wanted anything in a restaurant or a shop, she pointed; and, when she wished the lift to stop, she prodded the man in charge. It was a system worth a dozen French conversation books.

(TAS ch2)

"That's a good boy, Jakie," [Mr Abrahams] said.

He felt in his waistcoat pocket, found a dime, put it back again, and bent forward and patted master Abrahams on the head.

(TAS ch14)

For years everybody had been telling Eggy that it's hopeless for him to attempt to drink up all the alcoholic liquor in England, but he keeps on trying.

(LAG ch1)

"I can't imagine anyone more capable of worrying a family than Eggy. Just suppose if Job had had him as well as boils!"

(LAG ch4)

If I had been the Naval Treaty in a safe-deposit box at the Admiralty, I couldn't have been more securely tucked away.

(LAG ch8)

The purity of his enunciation surprised me a bit, for he looked Japanese and I should have expected something that sounded more like a buffalo pulling its foot out of a swamp.

(LAG ch16)

"Breakfast! So that was it? The moment I got back into this body of mine, I thought you must have been doing something to it since I had it last. It seemed fuller. It had kind of lost that hollow feeling."

(LAG ch27)

His face, which in repose resembled a slab of granite with suspicious eyes, was softened now by a genial smile. He had not actually parked his gun in the cloakroom, but he had the air of a man who has done so.

(HOW ch1)

He remained silent, pensively rubbing the scorched patch on his cheek where her eyes had rested.

(HOW ch2)

Although Mr Gedge's statement that the Vicomte de Blissac was never sober had been an exaggeration – for he was frequently sober, sometimes for hours at a time ...

(HOW ch3)

There are few things which call for so nice an exhibition of tact as the kissing of a girl in the presence of her fiancé.

(HOW ch8)

The world is full of men who ought never to shave their upper lip, and Blair Eggleston was one of them.

(HOW ch8)

"I left a burglar on the window-sill, and he's gone," said the Senator, rather in the manner of a householder complaining of the loss of a bottle of milk.

(HOW ch11)

Never again, he told himself, would he trust Confidence Trick men. They weren't honest.

(HOW ch17)

Everybody liked Bill Shannon, even in Hollywood, where nobody likes anybody.

(TOR ch1)

... it was only the fact of his teeth having snapped together with his tongue in between them that had prevented his heart leaping out of his mouth.

(HOW ch17)

The generosity of the late Albert Cork, combined with her personal and private fortune, the outcome of years of pulling down a huge salary in the days before there was any income tax to speak of, had left Adela with enough jewellery to equip half the blondes in Hollywood . . .

(TOR ch4)

"I trust," concluded Adela, her hand on the door handle,"that I am a broad-minded woman, but I am not going to share my bedroom with the butler."

(TOR ch5)

Every man has his price, and five thousand dollars was about Phipps'.

(TOR ch8)

Nothing, in his opinion, could actually convert his employer into an oil painting, but the blue suit and the heliotrope shirt might help to some small extent.

(SPF ch2)

"Ice, of course, would be better," said Stanwood, "but you look so silly ordering a bucket of ice and sticking your head in it."

(SPF ch5)

It is a very unintelligent butler who, expecting to see in a Blue Room a Stanwood Cobbold with a face like a hippopotamus and finding himself confronted by one with a face like a Greek god, does not suspect that there is funny business afoot.

(SPF ch11)

"We were saying such nice things about you, Mr Robb," said Terry. She knew she was being kittenish, but there are moments when a girl must not spare the kitten.

(SPF ch14)

"Ah," said Mike, as a thunder of large feet approached along the corridor, "here if I mistake not, Watson, is our client now."

(SPF ch22)

". . . the last bee, finding nobody left to sting, had winged its way back to the hive."

(FRL ch1)

In the rank undergrowth of M de La Hourmerie's prejudices there was no more luxuriant weed than his abhorrence of Old Nick's charming smile.

(FRL ch2)

"The Civil Service of France has its traditions, and one of them is that the *personnel* shall perform their duties with a certain languor. We expect it. In a way we like it."

(FRL ch2)

"She plays the violin, and he plays second fiddle."

(FRL ch4)

Everyone has some pet aversion – some dislike slugs, some cockroaches; George disliked women writers.

(Strand-PAW)

You cannot subject a bag containing half a million francs to even a dull-eyed scrutiny for long without forming the impression that there is something inside it.

(FRL ch9)

. . . a son . . . who . . . though handicapped by being a Frenchman, did not louse things up by talking French all the time.

(FRL ch10)

And though Tubby knew little or nothing of conditions at the bottom of fish-glue businesses, instinct told him that he would not like them.

(SUM ch1)

It is always disconcerting for a man of regular habits to find his wife unexpectedly presenting him with a bouncing brother-in-law.

(SUM ch2)

For, like so many substantial citizens of his native country, he had married young and kept on marrying, springing from blonde to blonde like the chamois of the Alps leaping from crag to crag.

(SUM ch2)

Even the most gifted of plasterers does not pay super-tax.

(SUM ch10)

She seemed so young, so frail to go up against one who even on his good mornings resembled something out of the Book of Revelation.

(QUS ch1)

In a really civilised society crooners would be shot on sight.

(QUS ch5)

[Lord Holbeton's dressing-gown] was of a pattern so loud and vivid that it seemed absurd to suppose it could encase an honest man.

(QUS ch10)

He clasped her in his arms, and went into his routine. Practice makes perfect. It was some time before he spoke again.

(QUS ch16)

There was an instant when it seemed as if Mrs Chavender would strike him with the Pekinese.

(QUS ch19)

She . . . dropped towards him and he gathered her in his arms. For a novice he did it uncommonly well.

(Escapade-RTR)

It isn't easy for a man to register a great deal of emotion in a dark theatre when he's only got a bald head to do it with, but Mr Pottinger was making a darned good try.

(Strand-BTG)

One leisured son-in-law struck him as sufficient. He was not bitten by a craze for becoming a collector.

(Strand-JOW)

It was hard to believe that this curious little being could be the father of a girl who did not look really repulsive even in a photograph in a new York Sunday paper.

(Strand-JOW)

As a colonial governor, he had had just had that taste of power and authority which is enough for the sensible man: more might have spoiled him for the simpler pleasures of life; less would have left him restless and unsatisfactory.

(Strand-COI)

OH, MABEL: the original title of a show which had just as little success after being renamed *She's All Right*. (Grand-COL)

"OH, YEAH": a good speech, according to **Howard Steptoe**. (QUS ch8)

OKLAHOMA: **Smedley Cork** might ask how much an angel would have made if he or she had invested in ... (TOR ch21)

OLD HUMMUMS: a suitable place for breakfast after a night out. (NGW ptII ch7)

OLD MAN RIVER: was sung in close harmony in a Parisian bar by **Russell Clutterbuck** and an American barman in the not so early hours of the morning. It was also a favourite of **Joss Weatherby**, familiar to **Sally Fairmile** and within the repertoire on the accordion of **Lancelot Bingley**. (QUS ch15; FRL ch10; PLP-GCS)

OLD MASTER, the: a soubriquet applied to **Jane Shannon**. (Colliers-PTR)

OLD NICK: see **Maufringneuse et Valerie-Moberanne, Nicolas Jules St Xavier Auguste, M le Marquis de**

OLD RELIABLE, the: a soubriquet applied to **Wilhelmina Shannon**. (TOR ch2,7,8)

OLD RELIABLE, The: one of PGW's more obvious examples of self-plagiarism, this book is *Spring Fever* rewritten and reset in the USA. Virtually all the characters and incidents are recognisable, including the butler with a past, the discovered valuable, the tricks by which the crook obtained it and even the advice he gave to the young buzzer to get on and kiss the reluctant heroine.

OLD ROYALTY: the old London theatre where **Max Faucitt** had played. (TAS ch5)

OLD SURESHOT: a nickname given to **Brewster Gooch** after his antics with a gun. (Strand-BTG)

OLIVER TWIST: had been a part of **Crispin Scrope**'s childhood reading. (TGI ch3)

OLYMPIC, R M S: **Sally Nicholas** sent a momentous cable from ... It was the vessel by which the **Birdseys** reached England. (TAS ch4; MLF-OTN)

OMAR THE TENT-MAKER: might have made **Basher Evans**'s costume or even **Theodore Brinkmeyer**'s tweed suit. **(LAG ch19; DBB ch1)**

ONAPOULOS, Emil: bore cross-examination in court. **(TGI ch2)**

ONAPOULOS AND ONAPOULOS v LINCOLNSHIRE AND EASTERN COUNTIES GLASS BOTTLING COMPANY: a law suit heard in front of a jury which included **Jerry West** and **Jane Hunnicutt**. **(TGI ch2)**

O'NEILL, Timothy ('Pieface'): the resident hotel detective at the **Cosmopolis**, New York, who deposed that **Miss Pauline Preston** was a lady with theories about direct action and that she had hit him with a brick, an iron casing and the Singer building. **(IOA ch19)**

ONE IN AUTHORITY: savaged **James Boyd**'s play, rent and tore it, jumped on it with large feet, poured cold water on it, chopped it in little bits and disembowelled it. He, or she, was considered a miserable incompetent by **Elizabeth Herrold**, but his, or her, opinion was endorsed by his colleagues in similar positions on other papers. **(MLF-BFL)**

ON YOUR WAY: a daily column appearing in the *Orb* which was the principal responsibility of **Charles Fermin**. (Its characteristics precisely match those of the *By The Way* column on the *Globe* with which PGW had so long an association.) **(NGW ptII ch3)**

OPAL, Senator Ambrose: a rabid, but non-practising, Dry, whose carelessness with his correspondence was to cost him dear. His physical appearance was a cross between the plain and the bizarre, for moving north on a man of merely medium height from a rather more than medium girth one encountered two piercing and penetrating eyes, a pair of jet-black eyebrows, a massive forehead and a jungle of snow-white hair. His bellow would have stopped the Scotch Express or even the Empire State Express, though we are not told if it was powerful enough to have stopped both at the same time. His inadvertent appointment of **Blair Eggleston** as his valet preceded his approval of the engagement (much to her surprise) of his daughter **Jane** to the imposter, **Packy Franklyn**. His character seems to match the popular perception of a politician, and the only matter we can find to report in his favour was that he flung oatmeal at Eggleston when he brought it to him for breakfast. **(HOW; USHOW ch2)**

OPAL, Jane: the daughter and sole redeeming feature of the **Senator**. To be acquainted with him would increase the pleasure of discovering how *nice* Jane was: she had a nice round face; nice black hair; a nice little figure; nice dark eyes; a nice voice; a nice little forehead; and nice little legs. It was her girlish desire to marry an intellectual, spiritual man with a great, unspoiled soul, but after becoming secretly engaged to **Blair Eggleston** she realised that in the maelstrom of life a wet fish was not much of a catch. Casting her mind back to the time when American football was a passion, and one particular exponent the idol of her girlish dreams, she chose to ignore her engagement when the idol was kissing her, for she was a macedoine of everything feminine that the idol, **Packy Franklyn**, admired. **(HOW)**

O'RAFFERTY SPECIAL: was a good brand of whisky which could be obtained from Bilby's in Oxford Street. **(TAS ch15)**

ORB*:** with offices on the Strand, this was the fictional equivalent of the *Globe* for which PGW worked, and featured the ***On Your Way column, all the work for which had to be undertaken between 9 am and 11 am. **(NGW ptII ch3)**

***ORDEAL OF PERCY PILKINGTON, The*:** the third story of **Aubrey Jerningham**. **(Throne-KHE)**

***ORIENTAL BELLE, The*:** a new musical comedy, the name being the same as that of a horse. **(NGW ptII ch20)**

OSTORIA: the home town in Ohio of both **Lancelot Purvis** and **May Gleason**. **(Grand-COL)**

O'SULLIVAN, Maureen (1911-1998): dedicatee of *Hot Water*.

OTHELLO: his wooing of Desdemona was like **Jane Hubbard**'s of **Eustace Hignett**, but he later set a standard for being perplexed in the extreme. **Blair Eggleston** resembled him whilst watching **Packy Franklyn** kiss **Jane Opal** at the express instruction of her father. He would not have been content with a mere "I say!" if he had been in the same circumstances as **George Holbeton** coming across **Joss Weatherby** and **Sally Fairmile**. Where he won the heart of **Desdemona** by speaking of most disastrous chances, of moving incidents by flood and field, of hairbreadth escapes in the imminent deadly breech, **Algy Wynbrace** produced similar results by letting his Desdemona relate her autobiography. **(GOB ch17; HOW ch8; FRL ch9; DBB ch12; LHJ-FKA)**

O'TOOLE, Sergeant: led the police contingent called to the **Hotel Delehay** to arrest **Herbert Higgs**. **(Ellery-MBD)**

OTTO THE OX: a likely name for a sinister character empowered to expel non-conformist American gangsters from their fraternities. **(DBB ch1)**

OTTO THE SAUSAGE: a member of the **Frith Street Gang** when arrested whilst assaulting **P C Keating**, and of the **Groome Street Gang** when doing the same to **Officer Kelly**. **(TUW-MIS; BurrMcK-MIS)**

OTWAY, Thomas (1616-1693): in his *Orphan* he wrote a number of sound things about Woman:

> "Who was't betrayed the Capitol? A woman. Who lost Marc Antony the world? A woman. Who was the cause of a long ten years' war and laid at last old Troy in ashes? Woman! Destructive, damnable, deceitful woman!."

It is a matter of record that **Eustace Hignett** approved these sentiments whole-heartedly. **(GOB ch2)**

O U A C: Oxford University Athletics Club. **(NGW pt II ch3)**

OUIDA, Marie Louise de la Ramée (1839-1908): **Kit Malim** was, surprisingly, acquainted with three of ...'s novels. **(NGW ptII ch8)**

OULED NAIL: a dancer with a distinctive muscular style, the equivalent action in the magazine serialisation being performed by a nautch dancer. **(TOR ch9; Colliers-PTR)**

OUR CITY: a statue in Longacre Square, New York, which featured a woman in grecian robes holding aloft a shield. **(TMU-TFD)**

OUR FIVE HORSE SPECIAL: in the **Punter** Stakes, had **Shorty** at shorter odds than **Mervyn Spink**. **(SPF ch4)**

OUSELEY v OUSELEY, FIGG, MOUNTJOY, MOSEBY-SMITH AND OTHERS: a *cause célèbre* in the Divorce and Admiralty division and a case of outstanding interest to legal and other minds. **(GOB ch9)**

OVER THE RAINBOW: a song which fell within the repertoire on the accordion of **Lancelot Bingley**. **(PLP-GCS)**

OVIDE, M: an underling in **M de la Hourmerie**'s office. **(FRL ch2)**

OWENS, Jesse (James Cleveland, 1913-1980): on hearing the dinner gong, **Sir Buckstone Abbott** resembled ... more than he did a baronet. **(SUM ch23)**

PACKARD: the **Steptoe** car which was having something done to it. **(QUS ch1)**

PAGLIACCI: Sir Buckstone Abbott knew better than did his wife that he filled all the known requirements of a crossword clue. **(SUM ch22)**

PALE HANDS I LOVED BESIDE THE SHALIMAR: a duet between **J Wellington Gedge** and **Soup Slattery** in Chicago, Slattery taking bass. **(HOW ch1)**

PALISADES PARK: Genevieve met **Ted Brady** on the ferry on the way to ..., and introduced him to **Katie Bennett**. **(MLF-CRH)**

PALM BEACH: where **Joss Weatherby** had painted **Beatrice Chavender**'s portrait. **(QUS ch2)**

PANGLOSS, Dr: Jill Mariner candidly likened her uncle to ... **(JTR ch6)**

PARAGUAY: to have started a revolution in ... in 1900 would only have cost $25,000. **(TAS ch1)**

PARAMOUNT HAMS: the collective ewe-lamb of **J B Duff**, which regrettably did not always live up to their reputation. **(QUS ch1)**

PARIS IN SPRINGTIME: when drawn by an artist of the ultra-modern school, consisted of a picture of a sardine can, two empty beer bottles, a bunch of carrots and a dead cat. **(PLP-GCS)**

PARKER: supervised **Lady Beatrice Bracken**'s luggage at **Waterloo Station**. **(HOW ch2)**

PARKER, Ellen: the wife of **Horace** and cook-housekeeper to **Freddie Rooke**. **(TLW ch1; Grand-JTR)**

PARKER, Herbert: an English valet to **Daniel Brewster**, whose shirts he borrowed on the sly and lost his job as a result. He took his revenge by arranging the theft and auction of **Pongo** and ensuring that potential competitive bidders were aware of the sale. **(IOA ch1,2,9)**

PARKER, Horace: the valet to **Freddie Rooke**, a discerning judge of his employer's port wine and Havanas. He also accurately judged the relative merits of **Jill Mariner** and **Derek Underhill**, approving of the first with an unerring eye and disliking the second. For the English version of his name, see **Barker**, although the name Parker stuck to him even in **JTR, ch18** where the reader can find the incident of his valet sending Freddie into the West End without spats, an omission not discovered until he was halfway up Piccadilly. **(TLW ch1,18; JTR ch18; Grand-JTR)**

PARKER, Jane: the violinist wife of **Chester Todd**. **(FRL ch4)**

PARKER, Mrs: the mother of **Horace**, to whom **Ellen** had taken straight away, and vice versa. **(TLW ch2)**.

PARROT: after asking **Lancelot Bingley** several times who he was, and ignoring the detailed response, it changed tack and invited him to have a nut. **(PLP-GCS)**

PARSIFAL: a syndicate of **Galahad**, **Marcus Aurelius** and ... might have been prepared to employ **Roland Bean** for longer than did **Robert Ferguson**. **(TMU-MMM)**

PARSONS, Albert: second in line for the treatment from **Thomas Kitchener**, he proved to be made of sterner stuff than **Ted Pringle**. Even so, when this ex-practised warrior with a travelling circus was knocked down, he concluded that no girl was worth the trouble, and that he would stay with the cows he knew. **(TMU-STW)**

PARSONS, Louella: gave **Joey Cooley** a notebook one Christmas and suggested that he write beautiful thoughts in it, so he jotted down the names of potential snoot-pokees. If informed of **Smedley Cork**'s arrest, she would have used her imagination to dramatise the report. **(LAG ch18; TOR ch7)**

PARTED WAYS: a story written by PGW for the magazine market in 1914, it was rewritten in 1930 for *Cosmopolitan* with the title *Best Seller*. After further amendment, it was converted into a Mulliner story and included in *Mulliner Nights*, again as *Best Seller*. See *Volume 2*.

PARTED WAYS: also the title of the book written by **Grace Marlowe** which was featured in the above. It was a story of her own romance, even including the quarrel she and her husband **George** had had within two days of their engagement. **(Strand-PAW)**

PARTRIDGE:

> "What did he say then?"
>
> "Something about losing something, it seemed to me."
>
> "I thought I caught the word *perdu*."
>
> "But that means a partridge, doesn't it? I'm sure I've seen it on the menus."
>
> "Would he talk about partridges at a time like this?"
>
> "He might. The French are extraordinary people."

(TAS ch2)

PASHLEY-DRAKE, Col Francis: Gladys Wetherby's uncle, who had been made trustee by her mother, and forbidden to disgorge until she married a man of whom he approved. Formerly a big game hunter, and author of *My Life with Rod and Gun*, he now owned a house at Bittleton in Sussex. He was short and stout, his body in keeping with the three chins nestling beneath his face, and although publicly known to be opposed to smoking, his private tendencies left him open to blackmail. He spoke Swahili, Cape Dutch, and of the merits of **Mrs Potter**'s cooking. (PLP-GCS)

PASSION MAGAZINE: for which **Bill Shannon** once wrote a story in which the hero grabbed his girl by the back hair and dragged her round the room with clenched teeth. (His, of course.) (TOR ch13)

PAT: **Jill Mariner**'s family dog from years ago, an Irish terrier with a characteristic look of grave melancholy. (JTR ch12)

PATCHOGUE: a small town on the New York State road four miles from **Brookport** and near to **Sally** and **Ginger Kemp**'s apartment. **Sam Bulpitt** was chased halfway there from **Bellport** by a millionaire with a pitchfork. Its grocery store sold its bacon at a bargain price. (TLW ch7; TAS ch18; SUM ch14; Grand-JTR)

PATRICIA: the peke belonging to **Beatrice Chavender**, who knew what she needed when she needed it, and explained her views in a voice reminiscent of a coloratura soprano. A slight disorder of her digestive tract due to a surfeit of cheese had led to a visit to the vet, following which she was apt to head for the lawn:

> Patricia pottered out, and for some minutes roamed the dewy lawn, sniffing at this blade of grass and that like a connoisseur savouring rival vintages of brandy. Presently she found some excellent stuff, and became absorbed in it.

(QUS ch10,11)

PAUL REVERE'S RIDE: **Robert Ferguson** wondered whether every girl who had recited ... at a church sociable without being lynched had been seized with the prospect of stardom on the Broadway stage. **(Cosmo-MMM)**

PAUNCEFORD-SMITH, Boko: of the East Surreys; anecdotes about such as he were **Col Tanner**'s staple fair. **(SUM ch25)**

PEACE, Charles: Ferdie thought **Appleby**'s brain ranked alongside that of ... **(DBB ch5)**

PEAGRIM, Olive: the relict of **Waddesleigh P**, she was the aunt of **Otis Pilkington** and employed **Miss Frisby** as secretary. At her home in Newport, Rhode Island, the world premier of the original version of *The Rose of America* had been staged in aid of Armenian orphans. **(JTR ch10,11,18)**

PEAGRIM, Waddesleigh: late husband of **Olive**, to whom he had bequeathed millions from the fortune made in smoked hams. **(JTR ch11)**

PEAKE, Adrian: slender of build and fragile of appearance, with wistful eyes, he was regarded by women as delicate, the result being that they told him to lie quietly while they bathed his forehead with eau-de-Cologne. One has the impression that he was the sort of man who would have looked good, dressed in ruffles, in an insipid period drama made for television. Ruffles certainly played a part with those in his immediate surroundings. It certainly ruffled Adrian himself to discover that not only had his younger fiancée, **Jane Abbott** no money but that she had withheld this critical information from him. A girl of sensibility, Jane, who having heard shortly after breakfast the man she loved called a **twerp** and a gigolo, was ruffled on hearing him described a few hours later as a kickworthy heel. And his elder fiancée, **Princess von und zu Dwornitzchek**, a woman of mature years but immature attitudes, was ruffled to learn of the cocktails he had given and the girls he had met in her absence. In view of Adrian's evident position as lap-dog of the latter, the question forms in one's mind as to whether his name should not have been spelt **Peke**. The pairing of him with the Princess certainly gives the book in which they appear a bite which is rarely seen in other volumes. **(SUM)**

PEARL STREET: a notorious New York thoroughfare whose changes in direction, unusual for the city, had become synonymous with the standard by which a person's crookedness was to be judged. **(PSJ ch9; TMU-TFD)**

PEARL STREET, first Earl of: if the USA had a peerage, **Eddy Moore** would be the ... **(TMU-TFD)**

PEARSON'S MAGAZINE: supplied a taking line in rejection forms to **James Cloyster**. **(NGW ptII ch2)**

PECK, Gregory (b1916): in looks, **Conky Biddle** began where ... left off. **(NSE-HTU)**

PEEBLES, Lord: in **Miss Sharples'** novel, woke at eleven o'clock and called for **Meadowes**. **(SPF ch1)**

PEERLESS MARKSMAN OF THE SIERRAS: the nickname given to **Brewster Gooch** after his antics with a gun. **(Strand-BTG)**

PEGLER, Hermione: presently the wife of Winthrop (misspelled 'Wintrop' on occasion) of Park Avenue, New York and Newport. He was the latest in a long run of husbands who had included **Old Nick** and **L J Quackenbush** and possible an earlier gentleman named Vokes. Hermione was, as one might surmise from the name, hard as nails and severe but handsome, the whole being topped by a head of elaborately waved hair and plucked iron-grey eyebrows. **(FRL ch1,4,5)**

PEKE, an unnamed: living at 1005 Benedict Canyon Drive, which had a secret known to **Stiffy**. Though he stood no nonsense from postmen, tradesmen and the like, he was not really the terror he appeared on the surface. **(Aldin-GOW)**

PEKE, the master of the unnamed: tied a black bandage over his eyes before retiring to bed, and on the occasion when he forgot to remove it, the sight so scared the **Peke** that it shot under the bed and stayed there. **(Aldin-GOW)**

PEMBERTON, Grace: the maiden name of **Grace Marlowe**, she was a magnificent golfer who had finished in the first six in the previous year's Ladies' Open. She drove divinely, putted to perfection and the image of her getting out of casual water reminded the viewer of a beautiful picture painted by a great master. After absorbing the conversation of **Henderson Banks**, she reneged on her promise to her husband that she did not wish to write, not only writing but insisting on reading twenty-four chapters of the book to him at one sitting. Called *Parted Ways*, it was expected to sell about half a dozen copies, with Grace paying the publishing costs, but it was an extraordinary success, selling 100,000 copies in hard-back alone. When the inspiration dried up, she relied on George to extract her from the mire when she went in too deep. **(Strand-PAW)**

PEN AND INK CLUB: where **Archie Moffam** met **James Wheeler**, and stepped on the bottom rung of the ladder of work. A literary pal of **Reggie Havershot**'s was a member. **Homer Pyle,** a writer of occasional poetry, attended one of its conferences **(IOA ch4; LAG ch1; TGI ch1)**

PENSION DURAND, le: St Rocque, Brittany, where the **Comte d'Escrignon** and his regrettable father maintained a modest holiday home. **(FRL ch4)**

PEOPLE:

> "People's people generally want people to marry people people don't want to marry," said Eustace, clothing in words a profound truth which from the earliest days of civilisation has deeply affected the youth of every country.

(GOB ch17)

PEPOLO'S: a restaurant with two entrances, one to the ground floor and one to a basement brasserie. **(NGW ptII ch6)**

PERCY[1]: a beastly great whacking brute of a dog which **Vera Silverton** insisted on bringing to rehearsals where it got kicked. It had a tilted nose and rheumatism, the latter, but not the former, being substantially cured by **Archie Moffam**'s remedy. **(IOA ch13)**

PERCY[2]: a bluebottle, cousin of the late **Harold[1]**, who put his longevity down to the beneficial properties of the mutton cutlets at the **Café Britannique**. **(TMU-MWD)**

PERCY[3]: the office boy at **Scrope, Ashby and Pemberton**, whose hearing was not as it should have been. **(TGI ch7)**

PERCY[4]: a pekinese pup sold to **Cracknell** by **Ginger Kemp** for $500. **(TAS ch16)**

PERCY[5]: Prudence Whittaker passed on in disdainful silence when **Tubby Vanringham** asked if she had a message for ... **(SUM ch1)**

PERCY[6]: a man with whom **Joe Vanringham** went three rounds in Walsingford High Street, and who confided that he loved **Clara**. (**SUM ch20**)

PERCY'S PROMISE: by **Marcia Huddlestone** (**Popgood and Grooly**, 1869), a three-volume work. (**SPF ch15**)

PERDU: French for 'lost', but not for 'partridge' as understood by **Sally Nicholas**. (In fact, the word she would have seen on restaurant menus is *'perdrix'*.) (**TAS ch2**)

PERELLI'S: a gaming joint down in Santa Monica, the proprietor of which spoke out of the side of his mouth while skinning his clientele. (**TOR ch3,18**)

PERFECTO PRUNE CORPORATION: **Ann Bannister** told their head office that **Joey Cooley** attributed his successful recovery from tooth extraction to the fact that he ate their product at every meal. (**LAG ch10**)

PERI: in the poem *The Veiled Prophet of Khorassan, Part IV* by Thomas Moore (1780-1852), one stood disconsolate at the gate of Eden, and that was how **Freddie Rooke** felt on his return to the **Gotham Theatre**. **Augustus Robb** felt like a horn-rimmed-spectacled ... excluded from Paradise when he heard of the revisions to **Stanwood Cobbold**'s plans. (**JTR ch20; SPF ch8**)

PERKINS, Police Constable: patrolled the Ludgate Circus area. (**NGW ptII ch8**)

PERKINS, Norah: a good-looking girl resembling **Angelina**, she became **Sid Price**'s fiancée. (**NGW ptII ch13**)

PERKINS AND BLISSETT: a firm represented by Romeo, a supplier of bad eggs. (**MLF-RUP**)

PERKINS'S PREMIER PAIN PREVENTER: strongly recommended by the sword-swallower at Barnum and Bailey's, but tried in vain by **Mr Meggs**. (**MLF-AST**)

PERSEUS: **Peter Rayner** declined to leave his Andromeda chained to the rocks for ... (**TUW-BSA**)

PERSONALITY THAT WINS, The: at just two dollars, it might have been the very thing for **Bill Brewster**. (**IOA ch17**)

PETER[1]: a small, spoiled, well-dressed boy who changed **Nigger**'s name to **Fido**. Despite a track record of tiring of individual dogs,

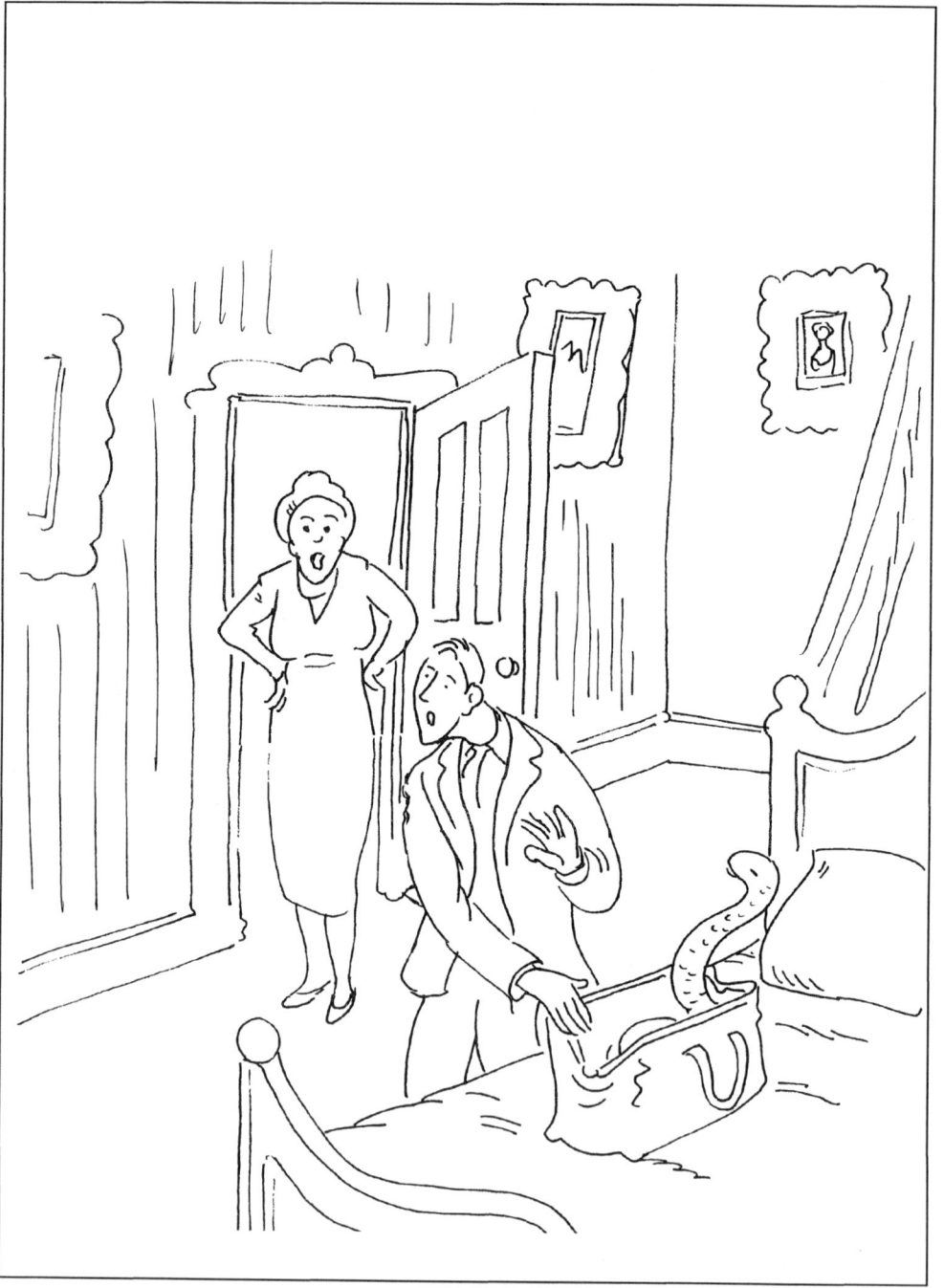

Peter and Madame Brudowska

he stuck by Fido, and Fido stuck by him, even when confronted by imaginary brigands. **(MLF-BIS)**

PETER²: a snake, or serpent, bought for **Mme Brudowska** by her publicity agent, **Roscoe Sherriff** as a publicity stunt, little realising how attached to the bright and merry chap she would become.

> "He doesn't bite, I suppose, or sting or what-not?"

> "He may what-not occasionally. It depends on the weather."

He was fed on bread and milk, or fruit, or soft-boiled egg, or dog-biscuit, or ants' eggs, and was best described as long and green with about 300 ribs, a distensible gullet and gastrosentrous vertebrae. **(IOA ch7)**

PETER PAN: Eva Eversleigh went to the ball as ..., scandalising old **Mr Gunton-Cresswell** in the process. **(NGW ch23)**

PETER¹'S FATHER: was thought to be possessed of all the money in the world. **(MLF-BIS)**

PETERS, Horace: the brother of **Maud**, claimed by her to have introduced a shadowy Lothario into the home. **(TMU-WDD)**

PETERS, John (or Jno): Sir Mallaby Marlowe's blameless clerk, proud owner of a sausage and a revolver. Though the cast in one eye gave him a sinister and truculent look, he had a heart of gold and in **Sam Marlowe**'s youth used to take him to the zoo. He was reported unfairly to have tried to shoot **Miss Milliken**. A traveller, he was sent to the United States to deliver papers in connection with case of *The People v Schultz and Bowen*. **(GOB ch8,12,15; WHC-TMM)**

PETERS, Maud: the manicurist fiancée of **Arthur Welsh**, who consulted **Dr Cupid** of *Fireside Chat* with disastrous results. **(TMU-WDD)**

PETIT ST ROCQUEOIS (or ROCQUOIS), Le: the sort of newspaper which elderly gentlemen read while sitting in the Public Amusement Gardens at **St Rocque**. **(FRL ch4; USFRL ch4)**

PHARAOH: according to **Augustus Robb**, he hardened his heart to **Mike Cardinal** when all the frogs came along. **(SPF ch17)**

PHILADELPHIA: a city whose censors would have insisted on a great many feet being removed from **Vera Upshaw**'s kiss. **(TGI ch15)**

PHILBRICK, Albert: an incidental 39-year-old unfortunate of Acacia Grove, Fulham, who, unwise enough to stray into Chelsea, paid promptly for his temerity with a broken rib, caused through falling into an excavation in the King's Road. **(QUS ch19)**

PHILIPPE: the bartender at the **Hotel Splendide, Roville-sur-Mer**, once of **Chez Jimmy**, in Paris. **(FRL ch5)**

PHILIPSON'S MAL-DE-MER-O: the seasickness remedy preferred by **Mrs Gedge**. **(HOW ch1)**

PHILMORE, Brewster: the cousin of **Otis Pilkington**, married to a film-star. **(JTR ch14)**

PHIPPS, James: the English butler to **Adela Cork**, a tall, decorous, dignified gentleman who provided **Smedley Cork**'s daily dose of yoghurt in place of the traditional cocktail. He had started his professional career as a hall boy in Worcestershire, and worked up to enter the employment of an American gentleman as butler, during the course of his duties visiting country houses and learning to blow safes. His criminal past in New York was known to **Bill** (or **Jane**) **Shannon**, for she had been a member of the jury which sent him down and although she kept mum, he was fired by Adela Cork for invading her bedroom searching for spiders, mice and diaries. His penchant for the diary led him to double-cross Bill and outwit Smedley twice; the latter not being an unduly onerous feat, but his activities earned for him the complimentary (to his ears) description of a 'sneaking, chiselling, two-timing, horn-swoggling highbinder'. **(TOR; Colliers-PTR)**

PICCADILLY THEATRE: where *White Roses* was staged for its somewhat short London run. **(TMU-POM)**

***PICCADILLY WEEKLY, The*:** a journal edited by **Alexander Tudway** which came to consist mainly of his adaptations of drafts submitted by the **Jerningham** family. Wodehouse was later to make a contribution, entitled *Butlers and the Buttled*, to the first issue of a short-lived weekly magazine named *Piccadilly* in 1929. **(Throne-KHE)**

PICKETT, Mrs: it would be most unfair to describe the owner of the **Excelsior Boarding House**, who was a tall, gaunt, old woman, as P G Wodehouse's Miss Marple, but she nevertheless achieved a magical exposé of a murderer in similar style. **(TUW-DAE)**

PICKFORD, Mary (Gladys Marie Smith, 1893-1979): was able to earn millions a year from the movies. **(TLW ch14)**

PICKLED LOVERS: whose plot included a girl becoming engaged to a chap to reform him, but him going and reforming himself. **(LAG ch28)**

PICKLES: a girl in the chorus of *Oh, Mabel*, who received a terrible call-down from the stage director. **(Grand-COL)**

PILGRIM, the: dwelt on the Delectable Mountains, but the tired traveller must never be tempted to forget the Slough of Despond. **(TLW ch7)**

PILGRIM'S PROGRESS, The: a book by John Bunyan (1628-1688) read by **Sally Fairmile** as a child. **(QUS ch3)**

PILKINGTON, Otis: the untalented librettist of the original version of the new musical *Rose of America*, as well as its financial backer and first producer. He was as equally and unutterably incompetent in each of these roles despite being the nephew of **Olive Peagrim** as he had been in his romantic attachments, but struck undeserved fortune when coming up against the supremely straight and honest **Jill Mariner**. **(JTR ch10,17,18)**

PILLENGER, Jane: a private secretary and typist who had worked for an Indiana novelist before joining **Mr Meggs**, she was a wary spinster with a deep-rooted suspicion of men. Her six years of work at five pounds a week had done nothing to dissuade her from the assumption that he was after her body, and a smile mistaken for flirtation added to a chaste goodbye kiss on the forehead led to erroneous conclusions with momentous results, and it seems that she was never to receive the legacy he proposed of £500. **(MLF-AST)**

PILLINGER, Jane: a private secretary and typist with a very similar background to **Jane Pillenger**, whose labours on behalf of **Mr Meggs** were rewarded by a weekly salary of $40, and a proposed legacy of $5,000. **(McClure-AST)**

PINKERTON'S: the famous American detective agency where **Mr McGee** and **Elliot Oakes** had each received their initial training. **(Pearson-EDO; Ellery-MBD)**

PINK LADY, The: brought together **Sir Buckstone** and **Lady Abbott**. **(SUM ch10)**

PINKY-BOODLES:

> "I hope he didn't hurt you much. You're the third person he's bitten today." She kissed the animal in a loving and congratulatory way on the nose. "Not counting waiters at the hotel, of course," she added. **(GOB ch2)**

PINNER, Lady: of the **Wellingford** (or **Wallingford**) **Women's Association**. **(DBB ch2; USDBB ch2)**

PIPPA PASSES: the poem by **Browning** which inspired an outlook on life which could be shattered by capricious and unforeseen misfortune. **(SPF ch10)**

PIRBRIGHT, Gloria: a chagrined lesser light of the lionhunting society set in **Hollywood**, whom **Adela Cork** dexterously relieved of her finest catch to date, **Lord Topham**. **(TOR ch4)**

PITTSBURGH: where **April June** claimed they ate her and no doubt some of her detractors wished they had. **(LAG ch4)**

PITTSBURGH PIRATES: a team which was after revenge against the **New York Giants**. **(IOA ch14)**

PLANET INSURANCE COMPANY: employed **George Balmer**, **Harold Flower** and a platoon of ear-biters. **(TMU-TTM)**

PLASTERER: the American term for writ-server, a vocation practised by **Sam Bulpitt** which generated recollections to be spoken of with pride:

> One time I slapped a plaster on Young Kelly, the middle-weight challenger, in his own home. He was having supper with his brother Mike, the all-in wrestler, his cousin Cyril, who killed rats with his teeth, and his sister Genevieve, who was a strong woman in vaudeville.

> . . . the time I handed the papers to that snake charmer. Sixteen snakes of all sizes, and he sicked 'em all on to me.

(SUM ch14)

PLAYERS': yet another of the resorts of the artist, author, actor or Bohemian to which **Archie Moffam** was introduced by his new American friends, it was the scene of the appointment between **Rutherford Maxwell** and **Winfield Knight**. **(IOA ch4; TMU-INA)**

PLAZA: the hotel where the newly-affluent **Ginger Kemp** stayed whilst in New York. **(TAS ch16)**

PLIMMER, Police Constable Edward: a red-faced copper with big feet and a broken nose, who was known as 'Eddie' to his friends and found Romance in bowery Battersea. **(MLF-RUP; Ainslee-RUP)**

PLIMSOLL, Horace: the bespectacled **Havershot** family lawyer. **(LAG ch1)**

PLINY THE ELDER (Gaius Plinius Secundus, 23-79):   pointed out that a man who let himself get above himself was simply asking for it. **(TGI ch9)**

PLUMPTON, Rt Hon Lord: **Everard Biddle**, Baron Plumpton, looked like a mass murderer, except that his face lacked the genial expression expected of that race.   He was on the committee of the **Marylebone Cricket Club,** and knew the batting average of every first-class cricketer back to the days when they used to play in top hats and whiskers, knowledge which he like to share with his nephew **Conky Biddle.** An unfortunate sequence of events which started when he was run over by **Clarissa Binstead**, continued when he was hit by missiles from her catapult and concluded when the **MCC President** declined to either have her skinned or give her 20 years solitary, led him, in his frustraton, to disinherit his nephew. **(NSE-HTU)**

POE, Edgar Allan (1809-1849): **Sam Marlowe**'s voice at the side of the road, from within an armoured helmet, was the sort which would have used in one of ...'s tales by a character who had been buried alive and was speaking from the family vault. **(GOB ch17)**

POETS' CLUB: a Bloomsbury establishment where **Gladys Wetherby** picked up new expletives. **(PLP-GCS)**

POLITICS:

> "I dislike the girl intensely, but I would not interfere in what would be your own private business.   No doubt there are plenty of sets in society where it matters very little what sort of woman a man marries.   But if you have a career, especially in politics, you know as well as I do that a suitable wife means everything."

(TLW ch5; Grand-JTR)

POLLEN: the butler at **Walsingford Hall**, who perhaps through an addiction to the Home Service on Sunday afternoons, was something of a bird expert and could give a cunning impression of the song of, for example, the linnet. His duties included arranging for a maid to sweep up broken glass, declining to replenish supplies of trousers and other clothes to undercover guests, and hitting **Adrian Peake** in the eye. **(SUM ch10,22,23,25)**

POLLY[1]: the caged parrot of the **Bodkin** family. **(HOW ch2)**

POLLY[2]: a lost parrot belonging to **Marion Henderson** which was found by **Jean Priaulx** and later told **Alexander** not to move or she would shoot. **(TMU-MWD)**

POLLY PARROT: with an ugly green tail and a Wellington nose, it wanted stuffing. **(TMU-BAC)**

POLLYANNA: **Wally Mason** joined ... in being glad, glad, glad. **(JTR ch16)**

POLO GROUNDS: a New York recreation ground where the **Giants** lost to the **Detroit Tigers.** **(Colliers-PAP)**

POLYANNA: having alternative spellings for one's name may be a sign of indecisiveness, but it was not the only reason that she did not have the sole rights to feeling three times glad. **(TGI ch8)**

POMEROY, Stinker: one of that versatile and uninhibited coterie of which **Reggie Havershot** and **Egremont Mannering** were leading spirits, each having been thrown kicking and screaming out of the **Café de l'Europe** after breaking 23 glasses. **(LAG ch3)**

PONGO: a nice piece of *objay dar* belonging to **Daniel Brewster** for which a matching partner was required if its true value were to emerge. It was a rummy-looking what-not, said to date back to the Ming dynasty, and died at **Archie Moffam**'s clumsy hands. **(IOA ch9)**

PONSFORD-YATES, Bertie: **Miss Bond** would probably have married him if he hadn't gone to Australia without stopping to pack. **(DBB ch5)**

PONT-ANDEMER, M le duc de: see **Carlisle, Oily**

PONTCHATRAIN (or PONTCHARTRAIN): the cigar-stand girl at the ... had informed the man who was playing the butler in *The Primrose Way* that the theatres at Toledo and Cleveland would be reopening the following day after the Spanish influenza outbreak. **(TAS ch7; Colliers-TAS pt5)**

PONTIFEX, Bishop: warned, on page 83 of the Oxford University Press 1839 edition of his *Collected Sermons*, that guilt and remorse would be the wages of sin. **(TGI ch9)**

PONTO¹: Margaret **Goodwin**'s dog. **(NGW ptI ch1)**

PONTO²: a faithful dog eulogised by a Duke. **(SPF ch14)**

POODLE: Adela Cork's ... had a sensitive skin and scratched like the young lady of **Natchez**. **(TOR ch16)**

POPGOOD AND GROOLY: the publishers of *Percy's Promise* by **Marcia Huddlestone**. **(SPF ch15)**

POPJOY, Theodore: the editor of *The Mayfair Gazette*, whose career in journalism had started by winning a prize in a competition run by *The Monthly Songster*. He was a good friend of **Tudway**, and tried to use Tudway's experience to illustrate why he was not able to offer **Joseph Kyrke** a job. **(Throne-KHE)**

POPP'S: a restaurant started in Pittsburgh by **Fillmore** and **Gladys Nicholas** as an outlet for Gladys's wonderful pork pies. **(TAS ch18)**

PORTLAND: the password, according to **Tom Ellison**. **(TUW-TDH)**

PORTWOOD, Sir Chester: an actor-manager of the tea-cup school of light comedy, he fell victim to the occupational delusion that he could, whenever he wanted, succeed equally in poetic drama. When he took the **Leicester Theatre** for a season, therefore, it was the Theatre rather than the Thames that he set on fire. **(JTR ch2)**

POST, Emily (1873-1960): though renowned for recommending rules of etiquette of the sort which **St Rocque** put to one side on the night of the **Festival of the Saint**, she would have been discouraged by the actions of **Howard Steptoe**, and she would have given **Joe Davenport** hell if he had beaned **Kay Shannon** with a bottle. **Joe Vanringham** wanted her approval of his wooing methods. **(SUM ch5; QUS ch1; TOR ch2; FRL ch4)**

POTHOS: by which the ancient Greeks meant a sudden, deplorable nostalgia for a regrettable past. **(HOW ch2)**

POTTER, Sergeant Claude: a young man with sleek, fair hair, a moustache and intelligent eyes who was educated at Oxford, trained at Hendon Police College and joined Scotland Yard. He travelled to **Wellingford** (or **Wallingford**) to see his brother-in-law, **Superintendent Jessop**, to whom he was superior and patronising even when it came to chess. He was smart enough to suspect a conspiracy surrounding the **Bond's Bank**'s affairs, but did not heed a warning from **Mike Bond** and was shot for his pains. **(DBB ch4,7,13,14; USDBB ch4)**

POTTER, Emily: the mother of **Loretta** and wife of **Jefferson**; res Ridgfield (or Ridgefield), Connecticut. **(FRL ch3; USFRL ch3)**

POTTER, Jefferson: the father of **Loretta** and husband of **Emily**; res Ridgfield (or Ridgefield), Connecticut. **(FRL ch3; USFRL ch3)**

POTTER, Loretta Ann: Bohemian painter daughter of **Jefferson** and **Emily Potter** of Rigdfield (or Ridgefield), Connecticut, who married **Old Nick** after knowing him for three weeks and helped him to produce the **Comte d'Escrignon**. **(FRL ch3; USFRL ch3)**

POTTER, Mrs: the cook to **Col Francis Pashley-Drake**, her former employer having conked out as a result of apoplexy, probably brought on by over-indulgence in her steak-and-kidney pies or her fried chicken, southern style. **(PLP-GCS; Playboy-GCS)**

POTTINGER: one of the producers of *Ask Dad* who liked to suggest gags for the comedian **Walter Catfield** to introduce into his part. **(Strand-BTG)**

POTTINGER AND ABELES: the producers of *Ask Dad*. **(Strand-BTG)**

POWELL, Bill: see **George**

POWER OF THE PRESS – 1: see page 229

POWER OF THE PRESS – 2: see page 230

POWICK, Rt Hon the Earl of: in whose service, and library, butler **Phipps** made a stimulating and memorable acquaintance with Lyly's *Euphues*. **(TOR ch4)**

PRESCOTT, Mabel: an eye-catching apostle of **Lora Luella Scott** and her **Temple of the New Dawn**, she caught the eye of **Eggy Mannering**. **(LAG ch9,28)**

POWER OF THE PRESS – 1
Headlines which might have been!

Crazed With Love He Slays Beautiful Blonde	**(MLF-AST)**
Spurned, He Stabs Her Thrice	**(MLF-AST)**
Spurned, He Stabs Her Twice	**(McClure-AST)**
Unrequited Passion Made This Man Murderer	**(MLF-AST)**
Plucky Actress Captures Burglar	**(IOA ch13)**
Stage Star and Midnight Marauder	**(IOA ch13)**
Footlight Favourite Foils Felon	**(IOA ch13)**
Tycoon in Coal Cellar	**(QUS ch20)**
Duff Dumped in Dust	**(QUS ch20)**

KIN OF ADELA SHANNON JAILED   **(TOR ch7)**
(with inset photograph of Adela Shannon)

DEVINE'S DASHING DEED   **(VanFair-AAI)**
DARINGLY DRAGS DAMSEL
FROM DIRE DESTRUCTION

DARE-DEVIL DEVINE   **(VanFair-AAI)**
DIVERTS DEATH
BY DROWNING

DEVINE DID IT   **(VanFair-AAI)**
Saw, Seized and Saved Suicidal
Shop-Girl

DEVINE SWALLOWS ALL   **(VanFair-AAI)**
OF THE HUDSON RIVER

POWER OF THE PRESS – 2
Headlines which were

REVELRY BY NIGHT
SPIRITED BATTLE ROYAL AT HOTEL
COSMOPOLIS
THE HOTEL DETECTIVE HAD A GOOD HEART
BUT PAULINE PACKED THE PUNCH

(IOA ch19)

STRANGE OCCURRENCE AT MALIBU
MYSTERY FIEND SMITES TWO
'POKED US IN SNOOT,' SAY VICTIMS

(LAG ch12)

MISS EILEEN STOKER
Universally Beloved Hollywood Star
Has arrived in England to take up her contract for
two pictures with the Beaumont Co. of London

(SPF ch1)

Reckless Speculator
Prominent Citizen's Gamble in Land!

(Colliers-PAP)

PRESCOTT, Mr: **Mabel**'s father, who had seen the light and given up drinking when he met a pink rabbit which asked him for a light. **(LAG ch9)**

PRESIDENT, the: presumably of the United States, was stated to have **Joey Cooley**'s confidence, even though there is no evidence that JC knew his identity. **(LAG ch10)**

PRESIDENTS WHO HAVE NEVER CHEWED: one of the books of which **Roland Bean** was a walking edition. **(Cosmo-MMM)**

PRESTON, Jane: see **Jane Williams**

PRESTON, Mr: the ex-butler father of **Sally**, who did not approve of moving-picture exhibitions, possibly because they might have disclosed what he saw in his previous career at Millbourne Hall. He was now letting lodgings in Ebury Street and rarely saw his sister **Jane**, who had married **Williams** and stayed at **Millbourne Bay**. **(TMU-STW)**

PRESTON, Pauline: with **Bobby St Clair** of the Frivolities and a few friends she was giving a feeling rendering of *There's A Place For Me in Heaven, For My Baby-Boy Is There* in room 618 at the **Hotel Cosmopolis** when she was informed by the hotel detective, **T 'Pieface' O'Neill**, that there was a place for them in the street, for a patrol-car was there. **(IOA ch19)**

PRESTON, Sally: the small, trim, pretty daughter of an austere ex-butler in Ebury St, London SW was the Bad Girl of the Family, banished to the remote Hampshire village of **Millbourne** to cure her predilection with the silver screen. London's loss was Millbourne's gain, and the starker emotions of the celluloid world of **Hollywood** were relentlessly unleashed on the innocent village after the winsome Sally became simultaneously engaged to four villagers, before selecting as her champion the emerging spirit, **Thomas Kitchener**. **(TMU-STW)**

PRIAULX, Jean: a Frenchman who was a dead shot with a napkin. As a young man in Paris he had intended to become an artist, but being dependent on his uncle **Jules Priaulx** had accepted a post as cashier at his hotel. Question-marks over his temperament led to his being sacked for throwing cats, following which he fell in love with **Marion Henderson** and, although he stayed with her family in London, he was eliminated from the running for her hand by the contents of a hat-box. His dislike of cats was complete when he accepted a position as secretary to **Paul Sartines**. **(TMU-MWD)**

PRIAULX, Jules: a hard task-master, the owner-manager of the hotel which bore his name, and the impatient uncle of **Jean**. **(TMU-MWD)**

PRICE, Sidney: an insurance clerk of the **Moon Assurance Co**, he was a member of the **Barrel Club** and lived at Hollyhocks, Belmont Park, Brixton, though for reasons best known to himself appears to have told the **Rev John Hatton** that he lived in Lambeth. An avid early film-goer, he had seen *Walls of Jericho* three times and *Visits of Elizabeth* but was also literate, having read works by Hall Caine and Guy Boothby and *Omar Khayyam*. It was his view that you couldn't be a Don What's-his-name on £60 pa. He became **Cloyster**'s sponsor for *Society Dialogues* until he felt confident enough to speak for himself. **(NGW)**

PRIMROSE WAY, The: by **Gerald Foster**, became a big hit when **Elsa Doland** replaced **Mabel Hobson** in the starring role of Ruth. **(TAS ch1)**

PRINCE, Timothy: a comedian at the **Briggs Theatre** who filled in between entrances. **(NGW ptII ch25)**

PRINCE OF WALES ROAD: as with the citizens of **Battersea Park Road**, its inhabitants specialised in Brain, not Crime, for they were authors, musicians, newspaper men, actors and artists. **(Strand-RUP)**

PRINCE'S: where **Freddie Rooke** introduced **Derek Underhill** to **Jill Mariner**. The skating rink, of course, not the restaurant. **(TLW ch1; Grand-JTR)**

PRINCETON: an American college football team which did not include a Berserk Senator in its ranks. **(HOW ch2)**

PRINGLE, Ted: a decent young man who sought to fascinate **Sally Preston** at close range, but after becoming one of her many engagements, he was the first victim of the vigorous **Thomas Kitchener**, losing the duel in two and a half minutes. **(TMU-STW)**

PROCTOR, Sam: see **Bearcat, Tennessee**

PRODDER AND WAY: published **James Cloyster**'s first novel, but displayed embarrassing coyness when the subject of a possible advance was raised. **(NGW ptII ch6)**

PROFESSOR POND'S PERFORMING POODLES: included one of **Nigger**'s grandfathers. **(MLF-HMV)**

PROFITT, Mr: another long, stringy paying guest at **Walsingford Hall**, whose penchant was for practising backhands against a wall, with bridge also on the menu. **(SUM ch1,23,25)**

PROMETHEUS: asking **Derek Underhill** if he was cross was like asking ..., when the vultures were tearing his liver, if he were piqued. **(JTR ch4)**

PROSSER, Mr: a literary gentleman operating under the pseudonym **Edith Butler**. He stayed at the **Dormans**' house at the same time as **Owen Bentley** and met him again in London, where he gave him both good and bad news about his financial prospects. Prosser was a large, black-bearded, shirt-sleeved individual with ferocious eyes, enormous eyebrows and an ego to match, and one can imagine him being played by James Robertson Justice in any biopic which might have been made of his life. **(TMU-POM)**

PROSSER, Oofy: the thought of **Barmy Fotheringay-Phipps** losing his shirt made him shirty. **(LAG ch16)**

PRYSKY, Yascha: gave a recital at the Queen's Hall, which **Packy Franklyn** was adjured not to miss. **(HOW ch2)**

PUBLIC ENEMY NO 13: a figment of **George**[2]'s imagination, a superstitious crook who sought to climb the charts and lose his unlucky tag by eliminating one or more of his superiors. **(LAG ch24)**

PUCCINI, Giacomo (Antonio Domenico Michele Secondo Maria, 1858-1924): an Italian composer who fulfilled some, but not all, of the requirements of the crossword clue in that his surname only boasted seven letters. **(SUM ch22)**

PUNCH: **James Cloyster** never cared for the cold, though neat, rejection slips from this august journal. An old illustration in the magazine showed two country visitors standing on the step of their railway carriage at a London terminus, with one saying to the other: "Don't speak! Just sniff! Doesn't it smell of the season?" It was also known to have carried pictures of **Derek Underhill**'s influential friends. **(NGW ptII ch2; TLW ch9,20; Grand-JTR)**

PUNEZ, M: in his fifties, he was the assistant to **Pierre Boissonade**, Commissaire de Police at **Roville-sur-Mer**, Picardy, who thought him both a fool and an imbecile. **(FRL ch6)**

PUNISHMENTS, Gessler's actual: the Governor of Switzerland, who was not a nice man, imposed as punishments:

- dipping a forefinger in boiling oil,
- requiring an apple to be shot off a boy's head with a crossbow arrow at 100 yards' range, and
- incarceration in the dungeons of **Küssnacht** Castle.

(WTT ch1,11,13)

PUNISHMENTS, Gessler's threatened: the unpopular leader also suggested that if certain subjects were identified they would be:

- bitten in the neck by wild elephants,
- stung on the soles of the feet by pink scorpions,
- tied up and teased by trained bluebottles,
- pecked on the nose by infuriated blackbirds.

(WTT ch6)

PUNTER, Alice: the cook at **Beevor Castle**, for whose plump and pleasing person plenty planned proposals, had relatives at Walham Green, London SW6 whom she visited. The principal tussle for her hand between **Shorty** and **Mervyn Spink** was overtaken by a reunion with the love whom she had lost many years earlier when she had attended **Meek Street Registry Office** while **Augustus Robb** was awaiting her presence at **Beak Street**. **(SPF ch3,23)**

PURBACH, George (1423-1461): quarrelled with **Regiomontanus**. **(TOR ch17)**

PURKIS: Mrs Steptoe's chauffeur. **(QUS ch1)**

PURPLE CHICKEN: an uninhibited Greenwich Village restaurant where **Joe Davenport** proposed again to **Kay Shannon**. **(TOR ch2)**

PURVIS, Lancelot: a conscientious barber at the **Hotel Cosmopolis** in New York, who fell for the manicure girl, **May Gleason**. His ambition was to save sufficient money to open a barber shop in his home town of **Ostoria**, preferably with May alongside, but before this could be achieved he had to take unexpectedly aggressive action to assert his rights against the parasitic **Harry Fletcher**. **(Grand-COL)**

PURVIS, Mabel: once the President of her school Debating Society, she arranged an old school reunion to which **Jane Abbott** was invited. **(SUM ch1)**

PURVIS, May: bore the married name of **May Gleason**. **(Grand-COL)**

PUTNAM, Kate Amelia: doubling as **Julia Gedge**'s social secretary and as the pride of the **James B Flaherty Detective Agency**, this thin, colourless featherweight with horn-rimmed spectacles and an air of quiet respectability had all the qualities of a Grade A gumboil, but could recognise deceptions at sight, whether perpetrated by **Oily Carlisle** or **Packy Franklyn**. But even she had not detected the true nature of her employer's past. **(HOW ch1,9,13,17)**

PYKE, Mrs Lucy: see **Maynard, Lucy**

PYLE, Homer: the brother of **Barney Clayborne**, Homer was an eminent corporate lawyer with a large, round face and horn-rimmed spectacles. He had read and admired **Vera Upshaw**'s *Morning's At Seven*. When, solely in the interest of security, he moved the **Girl in Blue**, he sought to inform its owner, but the message passed on was garbled and unintelligible. Homer then attended the **Pen And Ink Club** conference in **Brussels** and whilst there wooed Vera but, although he had not realised she was a gold-digger, he refrained from proposing, and the sight of her kissing **Jerry West** was eventually enough to dampen his love. **(TGI)**

PYLE, WISBEACH AND HOLLISTER: the firm of corporation lawyers of which **Homer Pyle** was a member. **(TGI ch15)**

PYM, Vera: the copper-haired barmaid at the **Rose and Crown, Loose Chippings**, who was engaged to marry **Sidney Chibnall**, the wristy butler at **Claines Manor**. Her long and enthusiastic study of detective fiction enabled her to identify unerringly the background and predatory pursuits of any casual visitor, and it explained her shocked horror when the heavily moustached food specialist **J B Duff** swam into her ken:

> She had a complex about moustaches. So many of the worst bounders in the crime fiction to which she was addicted had

affected them. The mysterious leper and the man with the missing toe were examples that leaped to her mind.

(QUS ch1,7,10)

PYRAMUS: the scene between ... and **Thisbe** was copied by **Sam Bulpitt** and **Prudence Whittaker**. (SUM ch23)

PYTHIAS: see **Damon**

QUACKENBUSH, L J: the mercurial **Hermione Pegler**, who seems to have considered the day wasted on which she had not divorced somebody, married Mr Q after the dissolution of her marriage to **Old Nick**. (FRL ch3)

QUEEN GUINEVERE: see **King Arthur**

QUEEN OF CONEY: Mary Ferris was as popular as the ... at Mardi Gras after winning the dancing competition at **Geisenheimer's**. (SatEvePost-ATG)

QUEEN OF SHEBA (fl 10th cent BC): felt that the half had not been told her, but when welcoming **King Solomon** she was as polite as **Adela Cork** receiving **Joe Davenport**. (TOR ch6; DBB ch2)

QUEEN OF THE HAREM:

I shall think twice before chucking up cig. smoking as long as "Queen of the Harem" don't go above tuppence-halfpenny per ten.

(NGW ptII ch17)

QUEEN VICTORIA (1819-1901): Bill Shannon mused that she could have been a model for **Phipps'** mother.

". . . art editors, like Queen Victoria, are not easily amused."

(TOR ch18; TGI ch6)

QUEEN'S BENCH DIVISION NO 3 COURT: where **Jerry West** and **Jane Hunnicutt** met whilst on jury duty. **(TGI ch2)**

QUEENSBERRY RULES, the: might never have been written as far as **Lancelot Purvis** and **Harry Fletcher** were concerned. **(Grand-COL)**

QUIBOLLE, M: the subject of a dossier under review by **Old Nick**, which he did not make readily available to his former boss, **M de la Hourmerie**. (FRL ch2, 6)

RA: according to **Joe Vanringham** at a certain time of the year, the inhabitants of **Walsingford** went in for weird rites and made human sacrifices to the sun god ... **(SUM ch19)**

RACKSTRAW, Daniel[1]: a multi-millionaire City man, who during his career had caused the ruin of the **Runnymede** family. He was a white-haired radical politician, father of the angel **Isabel[1]** and owner of the finest library of football literature in the country, not to mention the **Bloomer** boots. He welcomed the blackmailing **Jones** into his family as a prospective son-in-law and was even prepared to ring the Prime Minister to buy himself a title. **(TMU-TGP)**

RACKSTRAW, Daniel[2]: a **Tainted Millionaire** of New York, in the course of whose business career he had caused the ruin of the **van Puyster** family. He was the father of the angel **Isabel[2]** and owner of a fine collection of baseball memorabilia including the **Neal Ball** glove. He welcomed the blackmailing **Brown** into his family as a prospective son-in-law and business partner, to **Isabel[2]**'s considerable satisfaction. **(Colliers-PAP)**

RACKSTRAW, Isabel[1]: an angel who was presiding over a Billiken, Teddy-bear and Fancy Goods stall at a charity bazaar, where she met and won **Clarence Tresillian**. **(TMU-TGP)**

RACKSTRAW, Isabel[2]: another angel who presided over a Billiken, Teddy-bear and Fancy Goods stall at a charity bazaar, where she met and won **Clarence van Puysten**. **(Colliers-PAP)**

RAFT, George (1895-1980): Frank resembled the film star ... when regretting that **Charlie Yost** had not blown a hole in **Basher Evans**. **(DBB ch9)**

RAIKES & COURTENAY: the prospective employers of **Roland Bean** had bases in both Edinburgh and San Francisco. **(TMU-MMM; Cosmo-MMM)**

RAINSBY: living on the seventh floor at 18 E57th Street, New York, he was a Wall Street broker, short and with a speech impediment. **(JTR ch9)**

RALPH[1]: an office-boy at **Goble & Cohn** who had been the star pupil in the training-school where he had systematically learned rudeness. He was blessed with pink-rimmed eyes, a snub-nose, vermilion hair and ears and, by way of compensation, a collection of seven hundred and forty-three pimples. **(JTR ch10)**

RALPH²: presumably a brother of **Flossie**, the two representing the flower of English youth who had to be detached from the legs of a healthy young man at Waterloo Station and handed back to their parents. **(HOW ch2)**

RAPHAEL (Raffaello Sanzio, 1483-1520): a painter who, if asked to draw a pavement picture, might have looked as did **Shute** when told by **Arthur Welsh** to put 'em up. **(TMU-WDD)**

RASSENDYLL, Rudolf: Sir Anthony Hope Hawkins's adventurer in Ruritania, who spent part of his time in Rupert Street. **(NGW ptII ch4)**

RASTALL-RETFORD: the son of **Mrs** and a fellow-student of **Peter Rayner** at Cambridge, where he had once had half his moustache removed by a group of festive revellers. He was young, tall and nervous with gold-rimmed glasses, and so enjoyed solitude that he was a confirmed vanisher. **(TUW-BSA)**

RASTALL-RETFORD, Mrs: a massive woman with prominent forehead and half a dozen chins, she was sentenced by her doctor to a Spartan diet, at which her manner to her employees, such as **Eve Hendrie**, always irritable, deteriorated. The thought of her reaction on hearing that Eve, her bridge partner, had to revoke, caused Eve to use more of her brain cells at one go than she had ever been called on to do before. **(TUW-BSA)**

RATHBONE, Basil (1892-1967): the photo in **April June**'s living-room inscribed "All the best from Basil" presumably emanated from his hand. **(LAG ch21)**

RATTIGAN, Sir Terence Mervyn (1911-1977): a successful playwright of some substance, particularly vertically. **(SPF ch10)**

RAYNER: a member of this family of the Civil War period had been **King Charles I**'s right hand man, frequently eating despatches to prevent them falling into the hands of the enemy. **(TUW-BSA)**

RAYNER, Peter (or Billy): the brother of **Mrs Elphinstone**, he fell in love at first sight with his nephew's governess, **Eve Hendrie**, and then adopted as a friend Cambridge acquaintance, **Rastall-Retford**, to enable him to visit the family with which Eve had gone to stay. **(TUW-BSA; PicRev-DOH)**

RECENT EXCAVATIONS IN EGYPT: an article in the *National Geographic Magazine* which **Reggie Havershot** was perusing whilst awaiting the attentions of **I J Zizzbaum**, and which he thought showed poor taste on the part of the dentist in leaving it lying around in the waiting room. **(Pearson-LAG; This Week-LAG)**

RECTORS': the restaurant where **Peggy Norton** and **Rutherford Maxwell** had their reunion supper. **(TMU-INA)**

REDDY: the sparring partner for **Butler**; in reality **Ginger Kemp** in disguise. **(TAS ch13)**

REGAL THEATRE: where *Follow the Girl* had enjoyed a long run. See *Volume 5*. **(JTR ch5)**

REGAN, Andy: his love affairs undermined **Tim Burke** in his fight against his brother, **Mike**. **(PallMall-MLB)**

REGINALD: see **Joseph**

REGIOMONTANUS (Joh de Monteregio, 1436-1476): quarrelled with **Purbach**. **(TOR ch17)**

REJECTION FORMS: a collection of such slips can look very striking if properly displayed, the ones with a touch of colour being preferred by **James Cloyster**. **(NGW ptII ch2)**

RENDAL, Joe (or **Peter**): a **Dunsterville** exile who used to moon round **Mary Hill**, a silent, shambling youth, all hands, feet and shyness, who twisted his fingers and stared adoringly from afar. Removing himself to New York to recover from his passion, he became cheerful, flippant, extremely confident, successful and hard-working, with an office in the heart of the financial district; so much so that he thought nothing of subjecting Mary to a dictation test before employing her when she too arrived in New York. **(TMU-TFD; PicRev-TMD)**

RESTAWHILE SETTEE, the: **Reginald Sellers** illustrated, in return for payment, the supposed merits of ... **(TMU-MUP)**

RESTHARROW: see **Resthaven**

RESTHAVEN: trying to ascertain the name of **Horace Appleby**'s house in Croxley Road, Valley Fields, is fraught with unexpected problems. The house is mentioned in two separate sections of chapter 4 of *Do Butlers Burgle Banks*, namely sections 4.1 and 4.4, but the three editions of the text seen by the writer all offer different solutions. The publising firm, *Herbert Jenkins*, suggests Restharrow in 4.1 and Resthaven in 4.4, *Penguin* plumps more logically for Resthaven in both places, whilst the American *Simon and Schuster* prefers Restharrow each time. You pay your money, and you take your choice, but a knowledgeable bookmaker would surely make the Penguin version favourite. **(DBB ch4; DBB (Penguin) ch4; USDBB ch4)**

REUBEN S WATSON: a tug which won the race to rescue **Sam Marlowe**. **(GOB ch2)**

REVERE, Paul (1735-1818): when **Jane Pillinger** saw **Mr Meggs** smile, all that was maidenly and defensive in Miss Pillinger came to arms and ran in and out amongst her nerve centres like an intangible ... **(McClure-AST)**

REYNOLDS, Col: a holder of the VC and the father of **Sylvia**, he disliked most things and expressed his views about them in Hindustani. The catalogue of his distaste included suitors for his daughter's hand who were better shots than he was, dogs such as **Tommy** who dug up his best carnations, and multiple deliveries of live hampers to his home. **(TUW-WPS)**

REYNOLDS, Sir Joshua (1723-1792): an example of an artist who not only might have enjoyed painting **Beatrice Chavender** but may have made an even better job of it than did **Joss Weatherby**. **(QUS ch1)**

REYNOLDS, Sylvia: the unfortunate blue-eyed daughter of the irascible **Colonel**, who wanted to marry **Reginald Dallas**, but was granted her wish only after the unfortunate death of her other love, **Tommy**. **(TUW-WPS)**

RHEUMATISM: to ease the pains of ..., one recommendation is for a good, hot bath, the application of 10 to 20 grains of salicylate of soda three times a day in an ounce of water, and a rub with a good embrocation. If you are a bulldog, of course. **(IOA ch13)**

RH(JC): see **Havershot, Rt Hon the third Earl of**

RH(TF): see **Havershot, Rt Hon the third Earl of**

RICE, Henry Pifield: of Guildford (or Guilford) St, London WC1, or Fourth Avenue, New York, was an indifferent private detective, known variously to his colleagues at **Stafford's International Investigation Bureau** as 'that fathead', 'that blighter what's-his-name' and 'Here, you'. When disguised as a Scotch or German businessman with spectacles and a bushy beard, he resembled a motor car emerging from a haystack, and when impersonating an Anglo-Indian colonel, he looked like something between a youngish centenarian and an octogenarian who had seen a good deal of trouble. But there was good in him, and when he fell in love with **Alice Weston**, he did not give up his love when he was initially rejected. Instead he wormed his way into her profession, earning the soubriquet 'Bill the Bloodhound' and a job as professional theatrical mascot to **Walter Jelliffe** (**MLF-BTB; Strand-BTB; Century-BTB**)

RICHARDS, J B: of **Richards, Price and Gregory**, was a potential investor in **Bond's Bank** who turned the opportunity down flat. (**DBB ch2**)

RICHARDS, Miss: a waitress in the smoking-room of the Piccadilly Cabin, sporting fuzzy golden hair done low. (**NGW ptII ch20**)

RICHELIEU, Duc de, Cardinal Armand Jean Duplessis (1585-1642): was perhaps lucky not to have been pushed into the Seine. (**TGI ch13**)

RIGGS, Police Constable: Simmons threw his right boot at his head. (**GOB ch8**)

RIGOLETTO: was being sung by **Salvatore** as he signed on the dotted line. (**IOA ch16**)

RINGWOOD, Euphemia: the wife of **J Macklin R**, who accompanied him and their daughter **Marion** to the UK and took to **Algy Wynbrace**. (**LHJ-FKA**)

RINGWOOD, J Macklin: a New York millionaire who, with his wife and daughter, rented 8 Grosvenor Square for the season. He was a captain of finance, a friend of **Lord Wildersham** and the dedicatee of *America and its People*. (**LHJ-FKA**)

RINGWOOD, Marion: visited London with her parents and was initially enthusiastic about the prospects offered by a lifetime with **Algy Wynbrace**. However, her liking of cats such as **Alexander**, and her overall preference for the society of bright, alert, able, ambitious young men rather than human jellyfish, meant that the banns went up instead for her union with **Chester Bassett**. (**LHJ-FKA**)

RIPLEY, Ferdinand ('Ferdie the Fly'): the small, wizened, member of the **Appleby Gang** who was capable of climbing up the side of any house using nothing but his toes, fingers and personal magnetism. As home help to **Horace Appleby** he showed what a good egg he could fry, and by investing in the recovery of **Bond's Bank** he demonstrated what a good egg he was. (**DBB ch4,15**)

RITZ HOTEL: in London, was preferable to **Barribault**'s in **Terry Cobbold**'s opinion, for the latter harboured a **Stoker**-toting **Mike Cardinal**. **(SPF ch20)**

RITZ HOTEL: in Paris, bah! **(TMU-MWD)**

ROACH, Jack: a tall, stringy, apparently spineless waiter with sandy hair, weak, close-set eyes, red stubble and a hearing difficulty, who drooped like a flower and narrated the story about his friends **Gentleman Bailey** and **Jerry Moore**. **(TMU-BAC)**

ROBB, Augustus: a former London safe-breaker who was engaged by **Ellery Cobbold** to accompany **Stanwood** to London and keep him out of trouble. Ellery was inspired in his selection principally by a pair of solid-looking horn-rimmed spectacles which hid rather than accentuated his bald forehead, small eyes, extensive ears and pasty face. Despite his background, he was a snob, and thoroughly enjoyed his visit to **Beevor Castle**, all the more when he discovered that its cook was none other than his long-lost fiancée, who he thought had let him down at the registry office, only to discover that they had each waited at a different, though rhyming, location. He double-crossed his employer by reclaiming a rare unused Spanish stamp and claiming to have accidentally swallowed it after storing it on his tongue for safe-keeping. He couldn't have done so, of course, for its principal value arose from the fact that it still had the original gum, and if that was licked off the value would have been diminished substantially even if it had not been swallowed. **(SPF)**

ROBERT: the assistant to the **Lord High Executioner** of the Court of His Excellency the Governor of Switzerland, he dressed in a suit of armour and a black mask, and was burdened by cauldrons of boiling oil. **(WTT ch1)**

ROBERTS, Lord: cried out and jumped in the air if a cat were present. **(TMU-MWD)**

ROBERTSON: a dark-complexioned friend of **George Sipperley**, who wore a moustache and stayed with George in the fall. **(JTR ch9)**

ROBINSON, Edward G (Emanuel Goldenberg, 1893-1973): there was a rising demand in **Hollywood** for actors such as ..., with maps like **Howard Steptoe**. **(QUS ch8)**

ROBINSON, Matilda: was by no means the first person to have been conned into giving a cat a man's name, only to be presented with kittens. **(LHJ-FKA)**

ROCHE, Sir Boyle:

> I went downstairs and waited on the prompt side. Sir Boyle
> Roche's bird was sedentary compared to this elusive man.

(NGW ch25)

ROCHESTER: audiences at ... generally fall asleep, cloaking their deeper feelings. *Follow That Girl* died a horrendous death there, but went on to play two years in New York and one in London. **(JTR ch17; TLW ch17)**

ROCKEFELLER, John Davison (1839-1937): was generally possessed of small change, unlike **J Wellington Gedge**, so if called upon he would have been able to tip the butler. It almost became necessary to call him in as an angel to rescue *The Rose of America*. He featured on **Aubrey Devine**'s list of the seven most prominent men in the United States. **(JTR ch11; IOA ch14; HOW ch14; VanFair-AAI)**

ROCKMETTELLER, Mrs Balderstone: the original spelling of the name of the fat, rich owner of **Alexander**, whom she sold to **Bassett**. **(Strand-MWD)**

ROCKMETTLER, Mrs Balderstone: a later spelling. **(TMU-MWD)**

RODERICK THE RUNT: a veritable midget, at 5' 6", and flaccid muscles, pale eyes, snub nose, protruding upper teeth and receding chin completed his resemblance to a rabbit with a great deal on his mind. Yet he rose to volunteer to fight **Yvonne**'s dragon, for he had fallen in love with her at first sight, and was rewarded for his valour in a way he had never expected. **(Escapade-RTR)**

RODGERS, Richard (1902-1979): see **Dollen**

RODIN (François Auguste René, 1840-1917): Willoughby Scrope brooded like ...'s *Le Penseur*, for whom **James Phipps** would have been an ideal model. **(TOR ch1; TGI ch10)**

RODNEY: a small town in Maine from where both **Miss Roxborough** and **Charlie Ferris**'s wife came. **(MLF-ATG)**

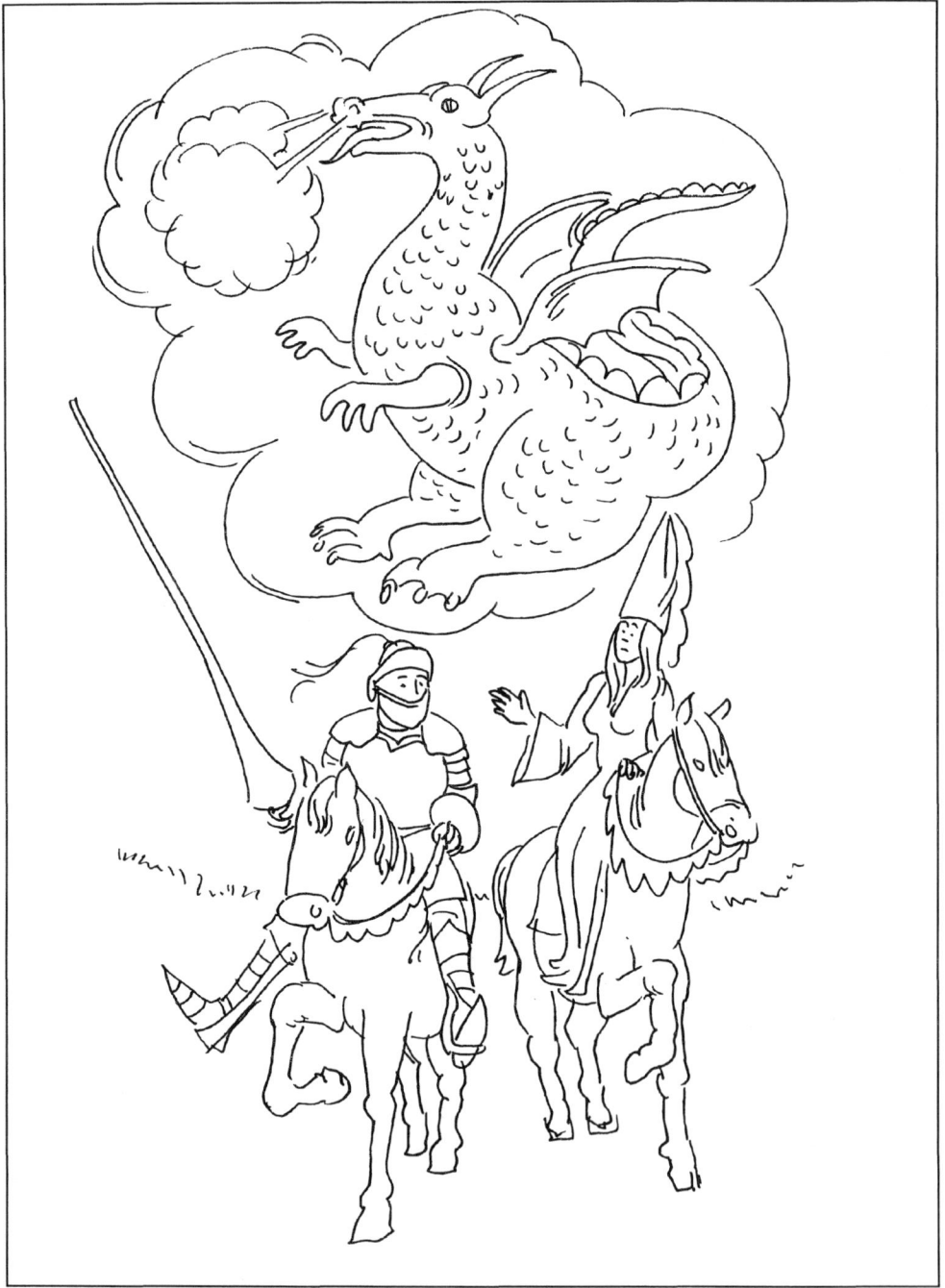

Yvonne describing the dragon to Roderick the Runt

A roller-skating race

ROGERS, Ginger (Virginia Katherine McMath, b1911): Miss **Attwood** had a touch of ... about her. **(SUM ch16)**

ROGET, Peter Mark (1779-1869): would have described **Joe Vanringham** as he walked to **Walsingford Hall** as glad, happy, elated, entranced, ecstatic and overjoyed, and **Bill** (or **Jane**) **Shannon** as surprised, astonished, perplexed, bewildered and at a loss when **Adela Cork** fired **Phipps**. **(SUM ch8; TOR ch5; Colliers-PTR)**

ROGOMMIER, a: Punez regarded **Boissonade** as ..., a term having the sense of 'drunkard' and not intended to be complimentary. **(FRL ch6)**

ROLLER-SKATING RACE, a: a challenge by **Rev John Hatton** to **Malim** to ... was modified to a race from Fleet Street (the Middle Temple Lane entrance) to Ludgate Circus and back, between the reverend gentleman on skates and a cab containing Malim and **James Orlebar Cloyster**. **(NGW pt II ch8)**

ROLLITT, Farmer: lent some land for use as a cricket pitch on the twin conditions that he himself could umpire and his son **Ted** could open the bowling. **(TUW-TDH)**

ROLLITT, Ted: bowled **Dick Henley** first ball. **(TUW-TDH)**

ROLLO: a stage hand at the **Leicester Theatre** who was given a coin by **Wally Mason** as he led **Jill Mariner** to safety after the fire. **(TLW ch3; Grand-JTR)**

ROLLS-ROYCE: the **Princess von und zu Dwornitzchek**'s preferred make of car. That belonging to the **Steptoe**s was needed for the day by **Beatrice Chavender**. **(SUM ch20; QUS ch1)**

ROMANO'S: Mac's resembled ... when it was fairly packed. **(MLF-MOM)**

ROMEO: see also **Juliet**. He may have fallen in love at first sight, but surely could not have made love to her while the stage manager was saying "Sh!" **(GOB ch4; QUS ch9; MLF-BTB)**

ROMEO AND JULIET: a play in which Gregory showed himself possessed of a swashing blow. **(SPF ch5)**

ROMEO AND JULIET, the first meeting between:

> ... the thought that, if he played his cards right, he too might one day be in a position to call this god-like man Uncle George, so electrified Freddie that he choked on his roast veal

and had to have his back slapped by a waiter. When his eyes had ceased to water, he turned them on Mavis with such a wealth of passion that she in her turn swallowed a mouthful the wrong way. The whole thing would have reminded a Shakespearian scholar of the first meeting between Romeo and Juliet.

(FRL ch7)

ROMERO, Caesar: Terry Cobbold said that Cobbolds had scruples about accepting gifts worth hundreds of pounds from young men who looked like ... (SPF ch13)

ROOKE, Freddie L: a bachelor who had been educated first at Winchester, where he had fagged for Derek Underhill, and then at Magdalen College, Oxford, where he had broken a wrist playing soccer in a friendly match. He spent the rest of his youth at the family home in Worcestershire as neighbour to, amongst others, Jill Mariner and Wally Mason. He started wearing an eyeglass when an adult, and was liable to be spatted when stepping out but although an expert squash player, he was not a member of the Drones Club. A well-meaning individual, Freddie showed poor judgment by retaining a loyalty towards Derek Underhill which went far beyond what was necessary, and he came within a whisker of being tarred with the same brush as that undesirable. He also proved to be a broken reed when it came to preventing 'Enry from hitting Bill and partly as a result he and Jill were arrested, but also as a result he met and fell in love with Nelly Bryant, to whom he became engaged. He acted in the role of real-life ambassador to Jill on behalf of Derek Underhill and on stage, as Lord Finchley, until he was sacked when the part was rewritten for a Scotchman. (JTR)

ROOSEVELT, President Theodore (1858-1919): Mr Bennett ceased to be ... one night while asleep. (MLF-CRH)

ROSARY, The: there may be two helpings of ... on a ship's concert agenda. (GOB ch4)

ROSE AND CROWN: a Loose Chippings pub where Vera Pym was barmaid-in-chief, and to which J B Duff planned to go to receive the swag. (QUS ch1)

ROSE GIRL, The: a play in which **Katie MacFarland** danced solo to critical acclaim both in London and on Broadway. **(MLF-MOM; Red-ROM)**

ROSE OF AMERICA, The: **Goble and Cohn**'s excursion into musical fantasy with book and lyrics by **Otis Pilkington** and music by **Roland Trevis**, redeemed from negation, as it were, by **Wally Mason**. **(JTR ch10)**

ROSENBLOOM, Maxie: there was a rising demand in **Hollywood** for actors such as ..., who had started as a champion box fighter with a map like **Howard Steptoe**. **(QUS ch8)**

ROSE-RED LIPS OF VIVETTE, The: a sex-novel by **Swaffham** which had incorrectly been forecast to be the hit novel of the season. **(Strand-PAW)**

ROSIE: a ticket seller at the local cinema and the fiancée of **George Mellon** who could be relied on to smile and beam. She wanted to buy a new spring frock (or, as the case may be, suit) for George's birthday. She always had a cheerful face except when under the mistaken impression that George did not like the frock (or suit) she had bought out of sympathy for the salesgirl. **(Strand-TSF; SatEvePost-TSP)**

ROSS, W K: of *The Elms*. Like **J D'Arcy Henderson** he sent a pug in a hamper as a present to **Sylvia Reynolds** for which he was called a blackguard by her father. **(TUW-WPS)**

RÖSSELMANN: a priest who fixed **Gessler** with a stern eye, and later brought news that the Governor was dead. **(WTT ch13,15)**

ROSSITERS: an American family, one member of whom was badly impersonated at the behest of **Mervyn Spink**. **(SPF ch4)**

ROTHSCHILDS: as a family could not afford to go strewing libraries all over the place. **(DBB ch10)**

ROUNDER: an expression taken from a 1915 film *The Rounders*, meant to describe a daring man-about-town. **Peggy Norton** told **Rutherford Maxwell** that he was getting "quite the rounder" when he threatened to buy her a whole hotel instead of merely supper, and **Sidney Mercer** was reported as saying to **Henry Mills** "Our little rounder. Always here.", when he took his wife to **Geisenheimer's** for the second time in as many months. Interestingly, the expression was also used by John Dickson Carr as late as 1941 when, in *The Case of the Constant Suicides*, his

character Alan Campbell was referred to as 'a rip or a rounder'.
(TMU-INA; SatEvePost-TLF)

ROVER¹: the **Mariner** spaniel, a great devotee of the garbage can, who was generally sick after the evening meal, although, to make a change, he occasionally performed at mid-day instead. **(TLW ch7; Grand-JTR)**

ROVER²: the fat, yellow **Tuxton** dog, booted to the far wall by **Jerry Moore**. **(TMU-BAC)**

ROVILLE-SUR-MER: known as the Jewel of Picardy, the Mecca of the Fashionable World; in reality a French fishing village with golden sand, blue sky and boules, which had evolved into a seaside resort with two casinos, half a dozen snow-white hotels on the Promenade des Anglais and a maniac, **Boissonade**, as its chief of police. **(TAS ch2; FRL ch4,5; TMU-RIE,TTM)**

ROXBOROUGH, Miss: an example of the relatively rare phenomenon in Wodehouse, a female narrator. She was a professional dancer at **Geisenheimer's**, and destined by the house rules to win the competition on Mondays, Wednesdays and Fridays assuming that she did not change tickets with genuine competitors. Originally from **Rodney**, she was still affected by the pull of the country on spring days, and left New York after two or three years to see whether a combination of Rodney and her husband, **Jack Tyson**, was what she really wanted. **(MLF-ATG; Strand-LSC)**

ROYAL ACADEMY: its President was to be asked to judge which was the better of two pictures, painted by **Marjorie Somerville** and her suitor. **(Windsor-CPB)**

ROYLOTT, Dr Grimesby: **Sir Arthur Conan Doyle**'s fictional character, who wore a yellow band with brownish speckles round his head, and gave **Lord Seacliff** ideas. **(Cosmo-DSQ)**

RULE'S: an English hostelry where **Max Faucitt** had passed pleasant hours. **(TAS ch5)**

RUNNYMEDE, Lady: née Trotter, this proud old aristocrat came from Chicago and was mother of **Clarence Tresillian**, **Lord Staines** and an unspecified number of daughters. Her income of £100,000 per annum, which was sufficient to permit a residence in Belgrave Square, was reduced by unfortunate investments to a mere $60,000, and economies had to be made. **(TMU-TGP)**

RUNNYMEDE, Lord: the silver-haired husband of his financial resource became in a state of collapse on learning of the family's financial problems. **(TMU-TGP)**

RUODI: a fisherman who helped hoist **William Tell** on to his shoulders. **(WTT ch9)**

RUPERT STREET RIFLE RANGE: John Peters was a client of this Soho club. **(GOB ch8)**

RURITANIAN NAVY, Admiral of the: an eight foot high, four foot wide functionary, meeting cars and taxis outside **Barribault's** Hotel. **(SPF ch20)**

RUTH: a leading part in *A Primrose Way* which had been scheduled to be played by **Mabel Hobson**, but was taken over by **Elsa Doland. (TAS ch1)**

RYLOTT, Dr Grimesby: the incorrect spelling of **Dr Roylott**, to be found in all the book editions, American and British, hardback or paperback. **(IOA ch8)**

ST ANDREWS: scene of one of the rounds of **mental golf** played by **Sam Marlowe** whilst concealed in a cupboard at **Windles**. **(GOB ch 17)**

ST ANTHONY: would only have matched **Packy Franklyn**'s stare on one of his best days. **(HOW ch3)**

ST CLAIR, Bobbie: was having a nice time with her friend **Pauline Preston**, helping to move the evening along, when they were interrupted by the hotel detective. **(IOA ch19)**

ST GEORGE: the look which a timid young man might have given ... when he set out to do battle with the dragon was similar to that which **Freddie Rooke** cast on **Derek Underhill** when discussing the prospect of meeting Derek's Lady mother. **(JTR ch1)**

ST GEORGE'S THEATRE: the home of **Charlie Cockburn**, who would probably be the director of **Cosmo Blair**'s next play. **(SPF ch10)**

ST MARTIN'S: the Guernsey town where **Margaret Goodwin** lived with her mother (real name St Martin). **(NGW ptI ch1)**

ST MIHIEL: where the **Sausage Chappie** played the Good Samaritan to **Archie Moffam** in the first world war by giving him his first bite to eat in eight hours. **(IOA ch18)**

ST PETER'S PORT: the capital of Guernsey, where **James Orlebar Cloyster** was staying during his visit to the island (Real name St Peter Port). **(NGW ptI ch1)**

ST ROCQUE: normally a staid and peaceful town in Brittany with a Public Amusement Gardens, eleven hotels, fifteen restaurants, two casinos and the **Château Blissac** close by, it was transformed during the celebration of its founder's day in July by a Costume Carnival and the **Festival of the Saint**. **(HOW; FRL ch4)**

ST STEPHEN'S GAZETTE: a major taker of **James Cloyster**'s serious verse. **(NGW ptII ch14)**

ST VITUS: Lady Abbott, in her theatrical days, had little in common with the ...-like modern chorus-girl. **(SUM ch10)**

SALTZBURG, Mr: the musical director of *The Rose of America*, a brisk, busy, little man with benevolent eyes and big spectacles. **(JTR ch11)**

SALVATORE: a dark, sinister-looking waiter in the grill-room at the **Hotel Cosmopolis**. He was nicknamed 'the Italian Whirlwind', and his mother owned a newspaper and tobacco shop on 7th Avenue. After he had been dismissed by **Daniel Brewster**, he sold his mother's shop to **Archie Moffam**. **(IOA ch9; Cosmo-MMH)**

SALVATORE'S MOTHER: owned a newspaper and tobacco shop in the middle of a site which **Daniel Brewster** wished to develop as a new hotel. **(IOA ch16)**

SANDOW **SYSTEM, the:** for fitness, did not involve carrying around parcels weighing between one and two tons. PGW himself wrote articles on such subjects as boxing for *Sandow's Magazine of Physical Culture*. **(NGW ptII ch12)**

SANDRINGHAM: Elmer Mariner's house in **Brookport**, whose administation was supported by a girl at $50 per month and by a man who received $20 for looking after the furnace and chopping wood. Apart from the Mariner family, it was also home to a spaniel and an intermittent cat. **(JTR ch7)**

SANDWICH: the scene of one of the rounds of **mental golf** played by **Sam Marlowe** whilst concealed in a cupboard at **Windles**. **(GOB ch 17)**

SANTA BARBARA WHIRLWIND: the nickname spontaneously generated for the first professional fight of **Jimmy Smith**. (Strand-JOW)

SANTA CLAUS: the old **Hollywood** was considered to have been rather like … in its generosity. (TOR ch1)

SAPPHIRA: acted a lie, to the disgust of **Augustus Robb**. (SPF ch16)

SARDI'S: where **Smedley Cork** might expect to lunch if he married **Jane Shannon**. (Colliers-PTR)

SARNEN, Meier of: see **Meier of Sarnen**

SARTINES, Paul: an acquaintance of **Jules Priaulx**, he employed Jules' nephew **Jean** as his secretary to assist in the preparation of his *'Istory of the Cat in Ancient Egypt*. (TMU-MWD)

SARTOR RESARTUS: the lightest reading of **Mrs Goodwin**. (NGW ptI ch1)

SATURDAY EVENING POST, The: it was when **Joe Davenport** threw a copy, richly-bound, at the studio boss's head that he was fired from **Superba-Llewellyn**, although in the original serialisation in *Colliers*, the journal was reduced to an anonymous dictionary. (TOR ch2; Colliers-PTR)

SAUSAGE CHAPPIE: see **Smith, John Lancelot Tracy**

SAVED FROM THE SCAFFOLD: a film brought to **Sam Marlowe**'s recollection when **Billie Bennett** broke their engagement. (GOB ch7)

SAVOY: where **Ferguson** celebrated the return of his fiancée, **Prosser** broke the news of his good fortune to **Owen Bentley**, and **Birdsey** proposed to dine after the baseball match. **Jerry West**, **Willoughby Scrope** and **Barney Clayborne** lunched together there. (TGI ch2,4; TMU-MMM,POM; MLF-OTN)

SAVOY GRILL: where **Joe Vanrigham** first proposed lunch to **Jane Abbott**. (SUM ch4)

SCARLET WOMAN OF BABYLON, the: a literary acquaintance of **Augustus Robb**. (SPF ch21)

SCHÄCHENTHAL, the wild ravine of: where **William Tell** spoke scornfully to **Gessler** about the **taxes** he levied on bread and sheep, and prophesied a bad end. (WTT ch3)

SCHENK, Nick: an acquaintance of **Adela Cork**. (TOR ch4)

SCHOENSTEIN, Lee: the master of ceremonies at the **Flower Garden**. (TAS ch16)

SCHOPENHAUER, Artur (1788-1860): had derogatory things to say about the female sex. **Bream Mortimer** thought his works might sooth his seasick state. A comparison could be drawn between the mood of **J Wellington Gedge** after drinking an excess of the milk of Paradise and ... after a bad night. But even one with as low an opinion of women as he would have whistled incredulously if he learnt how **Prudence Whittaker** had treated **Tubby Vanringham**. (NGW pt1 ch1; GOB ch5; HOW ch5; SUM ch1; DBB ch5)

SCHUMANN, Ike: a celebrated New York impresario, who stamped the Detroit production of **Gerald Foster**'s play *The Primrose Way* with his approval, but was wise enough to keep **Fillmore Nicholas**'s proposed revue out of his theatres. (TAS ch8,14)

SCHWARTZ: a stout saloon-keeper, who was **Bennett**'s draughts companion on Tuesdays, Thursdays and Saturdays. (MLF-CRH)

SCHWARTZ AND CARDINAL: purveyors of ham to the cinema-going public of **Hollywood**. (SPF ch23)

SCHWARTZ AND GUILDENSTERN: a New York fashion store. (JTR ch11)

SCHWERTFEGER: a Berlin statistician who claimed that of all the young men turned down by the girls they love (including those who have their engagements broken) 6.08% clench their hands and stare silently before them; 12.02% take the next train to the Rockies and shoot grizzly bears; while 11.07% sit down at their desks and become modern novelists. The remainder nip round the corner for a good stiff drink. (HOW ch16)

SCOTT, Sir Walter (1771-1832): wrote of ministering angels. (TMU-MWD)

SCREEN BEAUTIFUL: the ace **Hollywood** motion picture magazine, which employed **George G Frampton** to raise subscriptions and obtain advertisements. **Chaffinch** thought it could be persuaded to pay $2,000 for **Joey Cooley**'s tooth. (LAG ch12,15)

SCREEN SECRETS: journal read by **Lord Topham**. (TOR ch4)

SCREEN TOPICS: another journal read by **Lord Topham**. **(TOR ch4)**

SCROOGE: the sudden spasm of open-handedness displayed by **Adela Topping** resembled the Christmas Day activities of ..., whereas the modern **Hollywood** was more like the man before his vision. **(SPF ch4; TOR ch3)**

SCROPE, ASHBY AND PEMBERTON: a firm of Bedford Row solicitors whose premises, against all tradition, were bright, airy and tastefully furnished. **(TGI ch3)**

SCROPE, Crispin Lancelot Gawain: the brother of **Willoughby** and uncle of **Jerry West**, he obtained his latter two christian names courtesy of his mother who had been very fond of **Tennyson**. Crispin was an elderly man with thinning hair, watery blue eyes, a drooping moustache and debts of £203 6s 4d. Although he owned **Mellingham Hall**, such were his financial circumstances that he was forced to take in paying guests. He had been blessed with all the external qualities a man could require, for he was amiable, apparently intelligent, understanding, sober, honest and kind to animals, yet the whole was not greater than the sum of its parts. It was not even equal to the sum of its parts, for it was claimed that if men were dominoes, Crispin would be the double blank. In his younger days he had survived two breach-of-promise cases, but doesn't seem to have had much more luck until he scooped in **Barney Clayborne** as home help, and over a thousand pounds from his bookmaker, when the £100 bet at 100-8 which he had placed on **Brotherly Love** paid out even though the horse only finished second, after an objection against the winner had been sustained. **(TGI)**

SCROPE, Willoughby: the brother of **Crispin** and a successful London lawyer, of the firm **Scrope, Ashby and Pemberton**. He lived at 31 Chelsea Square, played golf to a handicap of 18, had once been engaged to **Flora Faye** and was in the highest income tax bracket. He trusted **Barney Clayborne** with his **Girl in Blue** despite being aware of her criminal tendencies, and then resorted to blaming her unfairly when the miniature disappeared. **(TGI)**

SCRUM-HALF: the half who works the scrum, being responsible for slinging the pill out to the fly-half, who in turn starts the three-quarters going. **(TAS ch2)**

SCRYMGEOUR: a dyspeptic who was at one time the employer of **Ginger Kemp**, until that spirited redhead forcibly prevented him from continuing to beat his spaniel **Billy**. He was a big bug at the Bar, with sufficient pomposity and self-confidence to believe that one day he would become Prime Minister. **(TAS ch2)**

SCULLERY-MAID: at **Windles**, was shocked at the way **Billie Bennett** sent a note to **Sam Marlowe** whilst engaged to **Bream Mortimer**. **(GOB ch15)**

SEACLIFF, Rt Hon the Lord: shock-headed, red-faced and a contemporary at Eton, Oxford and the bankruptcy court of **Archie Moffam**, Squiffy Seacliff was a nephew on his mother's side of **General Mannister**. Having suffered from shrapnel in his foot during the war, he had become a lad for the wassail bowl, happiest when indulging his natural instinct for looking on the jolly old stuff when it was red and a genius for lapping it up. Naturally, with such a background, the USA with Prohibition was, in theory, the place to go, although Squiffy did not seem to experience too many problems in obtaining supplies. So much so that his consumption, coupled with a horror of snakes, led him to throw away six cases of the sauce when he saw **Peter**[2]. Squiffy was never regarded as having a superfluous supply of brain, although he was rumoured to have been on the point of making a bright remark in 1913. **(IOA ch7)**

SEALYHAM: two examples of the species were attached to infants at **Waterloo Station**. The one at no 415 [Benedict Canyon Drive, Beverley Hills] rolled in a box of toffee. **(HOW ch2; Aldin-GOW)**

SECOND GHOST: Sidney Price. **(NGW ch13)**

SEE THE CONQUERING HERO COMES: the tune which **Captain Gunner** used to play on his harmonica whenever he saw **Captain Muller** approaching, thereby annoying the Captain and his **cat** so intensely that Capt Gunner's demise was inevitable. **(Pearson-EDO)**

SELBY, Major Christopher: the mildly dishonest uncle of **Jill Mariner** who had acted as her trustee and guardian, and lived at Ovington Square (incorrectly given as Ovingdon Square in, strangely, the UK edition), London.

"In a sense, my dear child I admit, it is Brompton Road, but it opens into Lennox Gardens, which makes it to all intents and purposes Sloane Street."

He had known **Derek Underhill**'s father at Simla, in India, but as the cheque with which he redeemed an IOU for a card debt had bounced, he was not in good standing with that family. The Major remained a fine, upstanding man of forty-nine, with firm chin, smiling mouth, closely-clipped moustache, bright blue eyes, fresh, and sanguine complexion though with an ominous thinning of the hair. He dressed well and looked after Jill when she was orphaned at fourteen, taking her to Lord's, Hurlingham and the Academy. He lost his money, and Jill's too, on **Amalgamated Dyes**, before going to New York and borrowing a flat on the 22nd floor of an apartment block on E41st Street. His latent goodness emerged when he prepared to sacrifice his life's happiness for Jill's sake in a transaction involving **Mrs Olive Peagrim**. **(JTR; TLW ch4; Grand-JTR)**

SELLERS, Reginald: an offensively patronising, would-be painter who concentrated his talents on the **Restawhile Settee**, **Little Gem Sardines** and the **Waukeesy Shoe**. **(TMU-MUP)**

SENIOR BUFFERS: a club whose membership list included the **fifth Earl of Shortlands**. **(SPF ch20)**

SENNETT, Mack (Michael Sinnott, 1880-1960): would be offered the chance to act as agent to **J L T Smith** if **Gossett** prevaricated. **(IOA ch20)**

SEPPI: a cowboy ancestor of Buffalo Bill, who fell before a blow by **Friesshardt**. **(WTT ch9)**

SERFS D'AVENIR, Les: a newly-formed organisation which had rashly and recently elected **Mrs Gunton-Cresswell** a member. **(NGW ch23)**

SERPENTS: reptiles of the saurian class *Ophidia*, characterised by an elongated cylindrical limbless scaly form, distinguished from lizards by the fact that the halves (rami) of the lower jaw are not solidly united at the chin, but movably connected by elastic ligament. So now you know. **(IOA ch7)**

SEVEN DIALS: **Augustus Robb** had a friend who looked after his tools and was a resident of ... **(SPF ch14)**

SEVENOAKS: an intermediate station on the line from **Beevor Castle** to London. **(SPF ch20)**

SEX PROBLEM IN MODERN FICTION: SHOULD THERE BE A CENSOR, THE: a newspaper discussion arranged by **Mainprice and Bassett** to support the publication of *The Rose-Red Lips of Vivette.* **(Strand-PAW)**

SHADRACH: needed to mop his forehead when leaving the fiery furnace. **(TOR ch19)**

SHAKESPEARE, William (1564-1616): an example of a gifted man who was notoriously unlucky in his love life. Although he had his sources for plots, he proposed the notion that there are more things on heaven and earth than are dreamed of in our philosophy, and was astute enough to realise that perilous stuff could weigh upon the heart, even though he did not fully acknowledge the inevitability of great emotional scenes commencing in a prosaic way. His description of someone as a 'fat and greasy citizen' in *As You Like It*, Act II, Scene I, could have fitted **Chris Selby** like a glove. His characters had been portrayed, with the assistance of hats and false hair, at ships' concerts. He did appreciate the tedium of a twice-told tale. Had he had cause to contemplate the extra inches by which **Russell Clutterbuck**'s waistline had expanded in just nine months, he might have asked himself "Upon what meat doth this our Clutterbuck feed that he is grown so great?" He maintained that on the morning after, the state of man suffers the nature of an insurrection. His *Collected Works* was a big hit on the Valparaiso steamer run. **(JTR ch6; GOB ch6; LAG ch7; HOW ch7; SUM ch5; TOR ch4,13; FRL preface, ch12; DBB ch9; TGI ch13; PLP-GCS; Strand-BTG; PallMall-MLB)**

SHALE, Bill: was knocked out by **Tom Blake.** **(NGW ptII ch10)**

SHALOTT, the Lady of: **Anthony Willard** felt as she must have done, knowing the curse had come upon her, whenever he was visited by his brother **Willie.** **(DBB ch9)**

SHAMROCK HALL: the Merlin St, New York, dance centre which was the scene of the disagreement between **Spider Buffin** and **Robert Sloan.** **(BurrMcK-MIS)**

SHANNON, Jane: in the original, magazine, version of *Phipps to the Rescue*, Jane was the name of the character more familiar to us as **Wilhelmina Shannon**, and her soubriquet was '**The Old Master**', not 'The Old Reliable'. In most of the entries in which Wilhelmina, or 'Bill' appears, the name 'Jane' can be found in brackets, but there are occasions when she did not share the limelight with her successor. (Colliers-PTR)

SHANNON, Kay: even in the opinion of close relatives such as **Wilhelmina Shannon** herself, Kay was considered to be an attractive young cheesemite, with highly proper ideas about a sense of responsibility as a necessary quality in a prospective husband. **Adela Cork** expected her to marry **Lord Topham**, a suggestion which was on neither of their agendas but he may have been a slight improvement on her first fiancé, **Dick Mills**. She took the view that when with the man she loved, a girl did not want to feel that she had been wrecked on a desert island with **Groucho Marx**. Thus she would not accept **Joe Davenport** until she was sure he was an *homme sérieux*, and she was not convinced of this until she saw him lying apparently dead, under the influence of a **Mickey Finn**. (TOR)

SHANNON, Wilhelmina ('Bill'): also known as **the Old Reliable**, she was breezy, hearty, genial, in her early 40s and built on generous lines. She had a rugged face with high cheekbones and a masterful chin, with large, humorous eyes of bright blue and a powerful contralto voice. She had always loved **Smedley Cork**, whom she had known for 25 years, watching him graduate from a wealthy man with one chin to a pauper with two chins, and her patience finally snapped when he threw away, almost literally, $50,000.

Bill had a good sense of humour, and was popular with practically everybody, one exception being the traffic cop whose rear wheel she chained to a hydrant, causing him to be brought up short and flung over his handlebars. She was the only living being who could exert a modicum of influence, when helped by a favourable wind, over her formidable and temperamental sister, the once famous **Adela Cork**, whose memoirs she was engaged in drafting. Bill developed the notion of setting up a literary agency with **Joe Davenport**, for which the capital of $50,000 was required, and managed to persuade Adela to provide it. (TOR)

SHARPLES, Miss: **Ellery Cobbold**'s efficient secretary, who was a mine of information on such topics as when an English peer might be expected to wake in the mornings. (SPF ch1)

SHAW, Artie: such was the extent of **John McGee**'s knowledge of the cinema that he knew how many times ... had been married, a statistic he may not even have known himself. **(Ellery-MBD)**

SHAW, George Bernard (1856-1950): provided his characters such as Admirable Bashville with useful phrases. **(DBB ch15)**

SHAW, Minnie: without whom there would have been no tale. **(TGI ch7)**

SHEARER, [Edith] Norma (1904-1993): one of three ingredients which, mixed together, would produce **Lady Beatrice Bracken**. **(HOW ch2)**

SHELLEY, Percy Bysshe (1792-1822): a volume of poetry by ..., with some of the passages marked in pencil, was part of **Sam Marlowe**'s grandfather's courtship process. **(GOB ch4)**

SHEPLEY, Mrs: the sort of paying guest at **Walsingford Hall** who wore spectacles, knitted socks and objected to pigeons cooing outside her window, although she did help to make up a bridge four. **(SUM ch1,2,16,25)**

SHEPPHERD, Audrey: the daughter of **Mr S**, and lovelight in **Owen Bentley**'s eye, whose regular use of the telephone led indirectly to wealth and perhaps even fame. **(TMU-POM)**

SHEPPHERD, Mr: the disapproving father of **Audrey**. **(TMU-POM)**

SHERRIFF, Roscoe: the press agent to, amongst others, **Mme Brudowska**, and a friend of **Archie Moffam** at the **Pen and Ink Club**. He was fond of his own voice, an Apostle of Energy, and had a persuasive manner in getting his friends to help him steal snakes. **(IOA ch7)**

SHERWOOD, Robert Emmet (1896-1955): a meridian of longitude and a successful playwright of substance. **(USSPF ch10)**

SHE'S ALL RIGHT: the final name of a piece which had started life as *Oh, Mabel* and which, even after a five city try-out tour, remained a frost when it opened in New York. **(Grand-COL)**

SHORTY: see **Shortlands, Claude Percival John Delamere, fifth Earl of**

SHORTLANDS, Gervase, fourth Earl of: died of apoplexy to be succeeded by his nephew. **(SPF ch9)**

SHORTLANDS, Claude Percival John Delamere, fifth Earl of: the nephew of the **fourth Earl**, resident at **Beevor Castle** with his three daughters, **Adela**, **Clare** and **Teresa** but not his son and heir, **Lord Beevor**, who lived in Kenya. His was a very old family, having come over with the Conqueror, and been devils of fellows amongst the Paynim. For all his earldom, he was kept on a very tight rein by the family financier, Clare, as far as an allocation of pocket-money went, two shillings and eightpence being a not untypical example of the sums which he freely had at his disposal. Shorty had been born on May 12th, fully equipped with the family susceptibility to high blood presure, and was 52-years-old, short, square and plebeian-looking, though smooth-faced. His despondent air was caused by an inability to think of a way of accumulating £200 quicker than his butler **Spink**, his rival for the hand of the cook, **Alice Punter**. The sum was the price of a pub, and a pub was the price of her consent. **(SPF)**

SHORT'S: an English hostelry where **Max Faucitt** passed pleasant hours. **(TAS ch5)**

SHRINERS' CONVENTIONS: memories of ... in San Francisco turned **J Wellington Gedge**'s blood to flame. **(HOW ch4,6)**

SHROPSHIRE, Dowager Duchess of: the 87-year-old grandmother of **Algy Wynbrace**, of **Drexdale Castle**, she retained keen faculties and a sterling instinct for business matters that made her known throughout her wide circle of tenants as 'the horse-leech'. **(LHJ-FKA)**

SHROPSHIRE ARGUS: an article in its pages referred to **Basher Evans**' skills as 'thoroughly expert'. **(DBB ch7)**

SHUBERT: **Joe Vanringham** was worried that, knowing the **Princess von und zu Dwornitzchek**'s proclivities, he might end up with a stepfather half a dozen years younger than himself who looked like a ... chorus boy. **(SUM ch5)**

SHUTE, Clarence 'Skipper': an American boxer who, having won his qualifying match in Britain against **Joesph Edwardes**, then did his celebrated, but inaudible, monologue on the halls. He finally lost his crown against the unfancied **Arthur Welsh** and in trying to recover it found himself up against a different set of Queensberry rules. **(TMU-WDD)**

SHYLOCK: **Jane Abbott** did not want her father to be a ... **(SUM ch2)**

SHY MAN, the: bought the ugly but loyal dog **Nigger** for half-a-crown, trained him not to bark when the house he was guarding was broken into, and sold him on to the caretaker of a house in Kent. **(MLF-HMV)**

SIDDONS, Mrs Sarah (1755-1831): with a stretch of imagination one could picture ... or even the mother of the Gracchi playing golf, but not **Adela Cork**. In her role as **Lady Macbeth**, she was imitated by **Kate Trent** on observing a pyjamaed **Freddie Carpenter**. **Beatrice Chavender** made entrances like Sarah in her more regal roles. **(QUS ch1; TOR ch4; FRL ch7)**

SIDNEY, Sir Philip (1554-1586): would have surprised the wounded soldier if, instead of offering him the cup of water, he had drained it with a careless "Cheerio!", but would have been no nippier than **RH(JC)** at handing him an ice cream. **Elizabeth Herrold** decided that, following Sidney's *credo*, she would concede the ownership of **Joseph** to **James Boyd** because his need was greater than hers. To have intercepted a phone call and given a hotel guest a haircut was the sort of altruistic act that he would have been proud of. **(JTR ch8; LAG ch11; HOW ch2; Strand-BFL)**

SIGSBEE'S SUPERFINE FEATHERWEIGHT: **Eustace Hignett** wore a self-satisfied smirk like that of a model for ... fine-mesh underwear. **(GOB ch7)**

SILBURY: one of four places of similar names, with stations and trains critical to the construction of the plot of *Murder at Bilbury Manor*. **(SUM ch16)**

SILVER KING: the winner, at 100-8, of the 3.30 at Kempton Park, providing **Mervyn Spink** with a considerable lead in the steaks stakes. **(SPF ch21)**

SILVERTON, Vera:

> "She used to be married to someone, and she divorced him. Then she was married to someone else, and he divorced her. And I'm certain her hair wasn't that colour two years ago, and I don't think a woman ought to make up like that, and her dress is all wrong for the country, and those pearls can't be genuine, and I hate the way she rolls her eyes about, and pink doesn't suit her a bit. I think she's an awful woman and I wish you wouldn't keep talking about her."

There is of course an alternative, man's-eye view of the sleazy but awfully pretty Vera, who had such a wonderful figure, but on balance it is likely that **Lucille Brewster**'s description will prove to be the more accurate. **(IOA ch12)**

SILVERTON, Vera,'s husband[1]:

> ". . . was a travelling man. I gave him a two-weeks' try-out, and then told him to go on travelling."

(IOA ch13)

SILVERTON, Vera,'s husband[2]:

> ". . . now *he* wasn't a gentleman in any sense of the word."

(IOA ch13)

SILVERTON, Vera,'s husband[3]:

> ". . . said '—' ."

(IOA ch13)

SIMILES: see page 263

SIMMONDS: a fellow-employee of **Henry Rice**'s at **Stafford's**. **(MLF-BTB)**

SIMMONS: the floor waiter at the **Hotel Cosmopolis** who reported seeing **Parker** in the same room as **Pongo**. **(IOA ch11)**

SIMMONS, 'Horseface': a man with a broken nose whom **Paul Snyder** had helped to convict on a charge of robbery with violence, and was now understood to have settled in the Southampton district. **(Pearson-EDO)**

SIMMONS, John: a meat salesman who, after having been upset by his young lady, had been accused of assaulting **P C Riggs** and using profane language. **(GOB ch8)**

SIMMS, Police Constable Ernest: cut an impressive figure of 200lb, well calculated to strike terror into the hearts of evildoers, provided they did not learn of such human failings as the trouble he had with his feet. **(TGI ch8,12)**

SIMMS, Mrs: P C **Ernest**'s mother, living in Hunstanton, Norfolk. **(TGI ch8)**

SIMMS, Mrs Willoughby: discussed the contents of a *Daily Mirror* with **Julia Gedge** whilst in a beauty-parlour. **(HOW ch12)**

SIMMS & WEINSTEIN: of Detroit, with whom **Ellery Cobbold** was able to agree the terms of a business deal. **(SPF ch1)**

SIMILES

"We've got about as much chance, if Jerry marries that girl, ... as a couple of helpless chocolate creams at a schoolgirls' picnic."

(TMU-BAC)

Horace stood transfixed, still clutching the wallet. It was swollen as if with elephantiasis, . . .

(DBB ch2)

[He] addressed her in a voice like a good sound burgundy made audible.

(DBB ch2)

. . . a gun . . . as liberally pitted with notches as a Swiss cheese.

(DBB ch2)

Parted lips and bulging eyes showed how keen was their interest, but no verbal comment emerged. Except for a difference in clothes, they might have been a couple of Trappist monks listening to a playlet of suspense on the radio.

(DBB ch13)

He was perspiring in a manner which would have reminded a traveller in France of the fountains of Versailles.

(TGI ch11)

He stared at Homer as a snail might have stared at another snail which had said something to shake it to its depths.

(TGI ch13)

. . . a girl Sheiks of Araby would dash into tents after like seals in pursuit of slices of fish; . . .

(TGI ch14)

It was the sort of kiss which in the days before Hollywood adopted the slogan of Anything Goes would never have been permitted on the silver screen.

(TGI ch15)

. . . she made him feel as if he had omitted to shave and, in addition to that, had swallowed some drug which had caused him to swell unpleasantly, particularly about the hands and feet.

(GOB ch1)

He looked like a man who would write *vers libre*, as indeed he did.

263

(GOB ch2)

. . . Bream's back looked like that of a man to whom the thought has occurred that, given a couple of fiddles and a piano, he would have made a good hired orchestra.

(GOB ch3)

"[Jane Hubbard] looks as you as if you were a giraffe or something and she would like to take a pot at you with a rifle."

(GOB ch4)

Mr Bennett peered at Sam with protruding eyes which gave him the appearance of a rather unusually stout prawn.

(GOB ch9)

She was in the mood which had caused spines in Somaliland to curl up like withered leaves.

(GOB ch17)

He had the same effect on the almost inextricably entwined belligerents [of the dogfight] as, in mediaeval legend, the Holy Grail, sliding down the sunbeam, used to have on battling knights.

(TAS ch2)

The chauffeur, a moody man, opened one half-closed eye and spat cautiously. It was the way Rockefeller would have spat when approaching the crisis of some delicate financial negotiation.

(TAS ch11)

Uncle Donald's walrus moustache heaved gently upon his laboured breath, like seaweed on a ground-swell.

(TAS ch15)

He looked like a high priest sicking the young chief of the tribe on to noble deeds.

(LAG ch1)

She looked like a vicar's daughter who plays hockey and ticks off the villagers when they want to marry their deceased wives' sisters.

(LAG ch9)

It was as if I had walked into a right swing while boxing with the village blacksmith.

(LAG ch12)

It was as if we had been a couple of the lads at the dear old school surprised by the head master while enjoying a quiet smoke in a corner of the cricket field.

(LAG ch12)

She looked as if she might be an important official on the staff of some well-known female convict establishment.

(Pearson-LAG)

Somebody was yelling hoarsely like a moose calling to its mate in the primeval forests of Canada.

(Pearson-LAG; ThisWeek-LAG)

Blair Eggleston was looking as like a younger English novelist who has just stopped a sandbag with the back of his head as any younger English novelist had ever looked since first younger English novelists began to write novels, . . .

(HOW ch2)

"And go and get your hair cut," screamed Beatrice. "You look like a chrysanthemum."

(HOW ch2)

His face had the vacant look of one doing mental arithmetic.

(Colliers-HOWpt3)

"You've been about as much good so far as a sick headache."

(HOW ch8)

"You'll feel like Noah trying to keep the tiger from chewing up the hippopotamus."

(FRL ch4)

"[She] looked like an elderly Gibson girl with something on her mind."

(FRL ch5)

He was aware that he was being insulted, but his attitude towards insults was much the same as that of Pooh-Bah in *The Mikado*.

(FRL ch6)

. . . [it was] when she did that quick pad-pad across a room and sank into a chair, that she reminded the spectator most forcibly of a leopardess in its cage.

(SUM ch13)

265

The look he cast at Freddie as he turned in the doorway could hardly have been more censorious if the latter had been a veiled adventuress diffusing a strange exotic scent whom he had discovered in the act of stealing secret treaties from the drawer of his desk in Whitehall.

(FRL ch7)

. . . with his round face, round eyes and round spectacles [he] looked like an owl which has been doing itself too well on the field-mice.

(FRL ch8)

. . . her manner had come to resemble that of a leopardess which has just been deprived of a T-bone steak.

(SUM ch13)

. . . advancing on him like a pink-faced puma . . .

(SUM ch15)

". . . looking a little like a rattlesnake, if one can imagine a rattlesnake stirring coffee, . . ."

(QUS ch1)

She was looking like a Roman Matron who has unexpectedly backed the winning chariot at the Circus Maximus.

(QUS ch1)

"Great," said Mr Duff and sat back feeling like somebody in one of his companion's favourite works of fiction who has been trapped by one-eyed Chinamen in a ruined mill.

(QUS ch13)

He looked like a cartoon of Capital in a labour paper . . .

(SPF ch1)

He frowned, as if he had found a snake in his lap.

(SPF ch1)

Mervyn Spink reeled. His clean-cut face twisted. If he had had a moustache he would have looked like a baffled baronet.

(SPF ch11)

Mike's left eye was closed, and a bruise had begun to spread over the side of his face, giving him the appearance of a man who has been stung by bees.

(SPF ch17)

If he had had his elbow on his knee and his chin in his hand, he might have been posing for Rodin's *penseur*.

(TOR ch1)

If in repose he had looked like a Roman Emperor, he now looked like a Roman Emperor talking over a prospective murder with his second vice-president in charge of assassinations.

(TOR ch1)

As [Smedley Cork] stood there waiting for zero hour, his substantial frame twitched and quivered and rippled, as if he had been an Ouled Nail dancer about to go into her muscle dance.

. . .

. . . [he] leaped like an Ouled Nail dancer who has trodden on a tin-tack.

(TOR ch9)

Girls are like monkeys when it comes to artfulness.

(MLF-MOM)

He looked like Shakespeare getting the idea for Hamlet.

(Strand-BTG)

". . . heaving gently . . . like a Welsh rarebit about to come to the height of its fever."

(TOR ch18)

The Rev Henry looked as disturbed as if he had suddenly detected Pelagianism in a member of his Sunday-school class.

(TUW-TDH)

There was the umpire with his hands raised, as if he were the Pope bestowing a blessing.

(TUW-TDH)

There is a type of man who makes love with a secrecy and sheepish reserve of a cowboy shooting up a Wild West saloon.

(TUW-TBS)

She looked up at me as if I had suggested that she should jump off the Brooklyn Bridge.

(SatEvePost-ATG)

SINGER'S MIDGET: **Willoughby Scrope** said that his brother **Crispin** wouldn't be able to push a ... into a brook. **(TGI ch13)**

SINGLE DAY MARRIAGES: for the publication of which which **Cloyster** received a guinea. (PGW had an article of the same name published by *Tit-Bits* on March 8, 1902, for which he had received the same fee.) **(NGW ptII ch2)**

SING-SING: **Phipps** had not found the experience of a spell in residence agreeable. **(TOR ch1)**

SINGULAR SCENES IN COURT: one of eleven articles by **James Orlebar Cloyster** which were rejected by three magazines in two weeks. **(NGW ptII ch2)**

SIPPERLEY, George H: lived on the fourth floor at 18 E57th Street, New York, had blond hair, was in the real-estate business and owned a Boston bull-dog. **(JTR ch9; Grand-JTR)**

SIR AGRAVAINE THE DOLOROUS: suffered his umpteenth successive defeat at jousting against **Sir Galahad**, but was better equipped with grey matter than most of his contemporary knights. He was a veritable midget, at 5' 4", and his flaccid muscles, pale eyes, snub nose, protruding upper teeth and receding chin made him stand out amongst them. Yet he rose to volunteer to fight **Yvonne**'s dragon, for he had fallen in love with her at first sight. **(TMU-SAG)**

SIR BALIN: the eye which had been closed during the tournament was the only one not on **Sir Agravaine** or **Roderick the Runt** when they rose. **(TMU-SAG; Escapade-RTR)**

SIR DAGONET: a jester, ignored by **Sir Agravaine**. **(TMU-SAG)**

SIR GALAHAD: known also as 'Battling', in which guise he out-jousted **Sir Agravaine** and his approach generally was more in **Billie Bennett**'s line than that of the less-than-dynamic **Eustace Hignett**. According to **Yvonne**, though, he was as a comic valentine when compared to **Roderick the Runt**. He, like the **Chevalier Bayard**, would have shaken hands warmly with **Soup Slattery** had he been present to hear Soup observe that "I never choked no woman yet, boy, and I don't aim to begin". **Joss Weatherby** was reminded of him when contemplating **J B Duff**'s sweet and lovely and touching and wonderful desire to have **Mrs Chavender**'s portrait fifteen years after they split up. See also

Cromwell, Oliver and **Moffam, Archie**. (IOA ch3; HOW ch11; GOB ch2; TMU-SAG; Escapade-RTR)

SIR GAWAIN: one of the middleweights at **Camelot**, who had strained a muscle at the last tournament. (TMU-SAG)

SIR KAY: not supported by **Sir Agravaine** in his argument with **Sir Percivale**. (TMU-SAG)

SIR LANCELOT: a popular favourite at **Camelot**, another example of a knight whose actions were more in **Billie Bennett**'s line than those of the less-than-dynamic **Eustace Hignett**. (GOB ch2; TMU-SAG)

SIR MALIBRAN OF DEVON: went from **Camelot** to protect **Earl Dorm of the Hills**' castle against a wild unicorn, and married **Elaine**. (TMU-SAG)

SIR PELLEAS: suffered from an ingrowing toe-nail. (TMU-SAG)

SIR PERCIVALE: did not believe that **Sir Gawain** lacked the necessary punch. (TMU-SAG)

SIR SAGRAMORE: went from **Camelot** to protect **Earl Dorm of the Hills**' castle against a giant with three heads, and won the beautiful **Yseult**. (TMU-SAG)

SKEFFINGTON'S POULTRY FARMER: an advertising weekly paper issued free to country customers. (NGW ptII ch4)

SKEFFINGTON'S SLOE GIN: paid **Julian Eversleigh** well for his advertising slogans. (NGW ptII ch4)

SKEGNESS: **Eggy Mannering** could not imagine anything more calculated than marrying an Oil to buck an average dame up like a week in ... (LAG ch28)

SKIPPER, the: of the *Reuben S Watson*, fished for dollar bills with a boathook. (GOB ch2)

SKIPPER'S DAUGHTER, the: was an intermediary in a deal by which **Sam Marlowe** returned to the *Atlantic* on board the *Reuben S Watson* for the sum of fifty dollars. (GOB ch2)

SKIPPY: an example of a film which proved the theory that if the story line was strong enough a film did not need a love interest. (LAG ch24)

SLATTERY, 'Soup': a tough-looking man whose tight suit suggested dubious morals. He was an expert safe-blower from the other

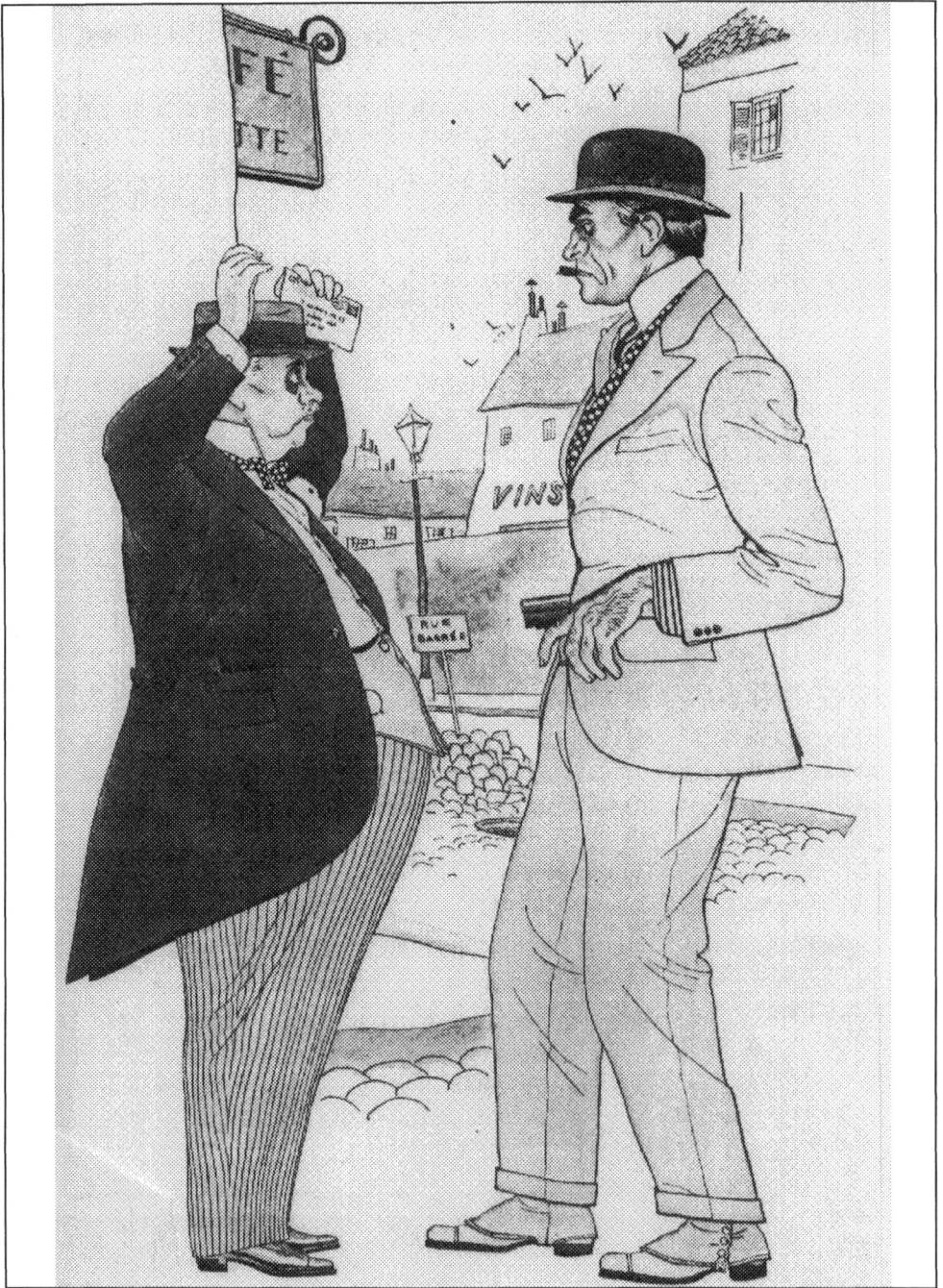

J Wellington Gedge responds to Soup Slattery's suggestion that he raise his hands

side, whose face resembled a slab of granite with suspicious eyes. He had a scar on his forearm courtesy of a quick-drawing householder at Des Moines, Iowa, and after being deserted by **Julia**, his **inside stand**, and caught in the Stock Market crash, had sought to augment his income with stick-up work. Soup disliked breaking into safes in rooms occupied by women in view of the sex's propensity to scream, and disliked equally being forced by householders on whom he had intruded to sit on windowsills for the night, for he was scared of heights. For the persistence he showed, and his general willingness to be of service, he was rewarded for his last job before retirement by a haul of two rings, a pendant and a sunburst (or as he put it himself, sun-boist). **(HOW)**

SLEEP WHILST I SING, LOVE: a lyric written by **James Cloyster** which became a catch-phrase used by comics opening their turns on the music-halls. **(NGW ptII ch14)**

SLINGSBY'S: the bookmaker with which **Crispin Scrope** had an account. **(TGI ch4)**

SLOAN, Robert ('Nigger'): when this member of the underworld, relaxing in the **Shamrock Hall**, received from **Spider Buffin** the opinion that his girl friend of eight days standing had two left feet, they entered into an animated conversation. The subsequent familiarity by Buffin, calling him 'Coon', when close friends were permitted no liberty more extreme than 'Nig', was answered by a bite in the cheek, to which Buffin had responded with an accurately-placed beer-mug. **(TUW-MIS; BurrMcK-MIS)**

SMITH[1]: a plug-ugly bulldog of sweet temper (as best illustrated by his friendship with **Pinky-Boodles**), who regarded his home, **Windles**, not in the light of a beat which it was his job to protect, but as a club, of which all stray burglars were members. **(GOB ch10)**

SMITH[2]: twelve of his short stories were sold to *Asterisk* by **Henderson Bates**. **(Strand-PAW)**

SMITH, Gunboat: an overhand swing of the quality of one by ... was **George Marlowe**'s reaction to time-wasting while he was in the middle of his novel. **(Strand-PAW)**

SMITH, Jimmy: the pseudonym given to **Freddie Brown** for his fight with the **Tennessee Bearcat**, selected to give the paying public at least an impression that he was **One-Round**'s brother. **(Strand-JOW)**

SMITH, John Lancelot Tracy: the 'Sausage Chappie' of **Archie Moffam**'s wartime anecdote lost his memory after being struck, and for some time wandered lonely as a tramp. He was short and thickset, and such was the state to which he had been reduced that he could have posed without rehearsal for a poster on *What the Well-Dressed Man Should Not Wear*. Pick of the day included a green scarf, an evening-dress coat, tweed trousers built for a larger man, a straw hat, brown shoes and no shirt. The scar from the corner of his mouth halfway across his cheek owed nothing to stage make-up.

He had met Archie outside **St Mihiel** during the war, and given him a piece of sausage at a time of considerable hunger, an example of generosity. When Archie recalled this kindness years later, he had him taken on as a waiter at the **Hotel Cosmopolis** and almost appointed him manager of the new hotel. As his life improved, so did his memory: first as to his place of birth, Springfield, Ohio; secondly as to his name; thirdly that he was a pal of **'Stinker' Horace**; fourthly that he was married; and fifthly that the correct way to deal with men whom he caught patting his newly recalled wife at luncheon parties was to throw a huckleberry pie at them. **(IOA ch20; Cosmo-SCH)**

SMITH, Montgomery: introduced **Frank** into the **Appleby Gang**. He had a long, mild face featuring clear, honest eyes, horn-rimmed spectacles, prominent ears (standing out from his head like the handles of a Greek vase) and a drooping moustache. He had served one sentence of eighteen months for a historical misdemeanour, but invested £25,000 towards the redemption of **Bond's Bank**. **(DBB ch5,9,10,15)**

SMITH, Mrs John Lancelot Tracy: had blue eyes, brown hair, a mole on her chin, a Pekingese dog named **Marie** under her chair and **Gossett** as a lunch companion. **(IOA ch20)**

SMITH, One-Round: despite having 47 successful contests under his belt, he pulled out of a match with the **Tennessee Bearcat** claiming a sprained foot. **(Strand-JOW)**

SMITH'S SUPREME DIGESTIVE PELLETS: were given a fair but disappointing trial by **Mr Meggs**. **(MLF-AST)**

SMITHY: see **Smith, Montgomery**

SMOKING: Jane Hunnicutt's aunt did not approve, for she claimed it caused dyspepsia, sleeplessness, headache, weak eyes, asthma, bronchitis, rheumatism, lumbago and sciatica, as well as bringing one out in red spots. **(TGI ch6)**

SNOGSON: see **Blogson**

SNOW QUEEN: a rather apt description of **Prudence Whittaker**. **(SatEvePost-SUM)**

SNYDER, Paul: owner of a detective agency bearing his name, he sent **Elliot(t) Oakes** to investigate the death of **Captain Gunner**. **(TUW-DAE)**

SO!:

> There are very few men capable of remaining composed and tranquil when a woman is saying "So!" at them, especially when a sweeping gesture accompanies the word. Napoleon could have done it, and Henry VIII, and probably Jenghiz Khan, but Sir Abbott was not of their number.

(SUM ch25)

SOCIALISM:

> "You're talking Socialism, Horace."
>
> "No, I'm not. I'm talking sense."

(JTR ch2)

SOCIAL SOLECISMS: committed by **George Balmer** in the space of a single moment:

1 he remained seated throughout an interview with a lady,

2 he failed to raise his fascinating Homburg hat,

3 he failed to raise his fascinating Homburg hat again at the end of the interview,

4 he gaped like a fool, and

5 he did not utter a single word to the lady in reply to her thanks.

(TMU-TTM)

SOCIETY DIALOGUES: pieces written by **James Cloyster** where the humour was thin, the satire cheap and the vulgarity appropriate to the readership. **(NGW ptII ch13)**

SOCIETY OF AUTHORS, The: for years waged a fruitless war with **Mortimer Busby**. **(SUM ch3)**

SOME RECOLLECTIONS OF THE SILENT SCREEN: the topic of **Adela Cork**'s address to a ladies' club in Pasadena. **(TOR ch4)**

SOME TENDENCIES OF MODERN FICTION: the subject of a lecture to be given by **Grace Marlowe** to the **East Dulwich Progress Club**. **(Strand-PAW)**

SOMERVILLE, Marjorie: instinctively knew when a proposal was imminent from **Narrator**[4], even though she made it clear she would prefer to paint than be married. Her painting was a landscape with a cow in one corner, which was rejected by the **Royal Academy**. **(Windsor-CPB)**

SOMETHING, Ethel: an old friend of **Tom Ellison** who collected autographs. **(TUW-TDH)**

SOTHEBY'S LTD: auctioneers of Bond Street, London, where **Willoughby Scrope** bought *The Girl in Blue*. A New Yorker in the same profession remarked that when he had been there, "this" kind of bidding had been commonplace. **(IOA ch10; TGI ch3)**

SOUP: see **Slattery, 'Soup'**

SOUPE, M: a colleague of **Old Nick** at the **Ministry of Dons and Legs**, who was in his 42nd year of service and no doubt looked forward to a retirement in which he would be able to spend more time on his hobby: collecting spiders and studying their habits. **(FRL ch2,5)**

SOUTHBOURNE, Countess of: stayed at the **Hôtel Cercle de la Méditerranée**. **(TMU-MMT)**

SOUTH PACIFIC: **Smedley Cork** might ask how much an angel would have made if he or she had invested in ... **(TOR ch21)**

SOUTHERN CALIFORNIA, University of: against which **Yale** is too smart to try to play football. **(HOW ch5)**

SOUTHERN GIRL, a: an ensemble member of the *Rose of America* production with, wait for it, a Southern accent. **(JTR ch11)**

SPAIN: the unused blue 1851 *dos reales* stamp from that country, identified by **Desborough Topping** in the mysterious stamp album, was an error of colour estimated to be worth a thousand pounds. **(SPF ch9)**

S P C A, the: would have been down hard on **Sellers** for savaging a cat. **Skipper Shute** said he did not want trouble from it. **(TMU-MUP,WDD)**

SPECKLED BAND, The: see *Adventure of the Speckled Band, The*

SPEEDWELL AUTO COMPANY: **Mae D'Arcy** was engaged to **Cuthbert**, a demonstrator for the ... **(JTR ch11)**

SPENCER, 'ERBERT (1820-1903): a real swell in writing, who didn't push out something every day. **(NGW ptII ch13)**

SPERRY, Harry: a telephone worker from Westport, Connecticut, who, while boring a hole in a brick wall, selected the precise spot where lay a concealed leaden water-pipe. **(TUW-BSA)**

SPILLANE, Mickey (Frank Morrison, b1918): knew neat ways of putting a man out of action. **(FRL ch11)**

SPINK, Mervyn: the miscast butler to the **fifth Earl of Shortlands** at **Beevor Castle**. Miscast for two reasons, one should add. Nature is a haphazard caster, and when called upon to provide an Earl and a butler, on this occasion she produced a square, short plebeian Earl who looked like a butler, and a tall, elegant, aristocratic butler who looked like an Earl. But miscast also because he let down the buttling fraternity by dishonestly seeking twice to convert other people's property to his own use: a valuable stamp belonging to a member of his employer's family, and a cook belonging to his employer. Neither was he averse to blackmail, a thing no true butler would have even considered. So against these faults, his ability to imitate Spencer Tracy and do tricks with bits of string should count for very little. **(SPF)**

SPINK, Mrs: the mother of the butler, living in East Dulwich. **(SPF ch11)**

SPIRIT OF FRIGIDAIRE: a rather apt description of **Prudence Whittaker.** **(SUM ch12)**

SPLENDIDE: the hotel where **Bruce Carlyle** proposed to dine with **Scrymgeour** in **Roville**, though the latter was actually in Paris. **(TAS ch2)**

SPORTING TIMES: **Freddie Rooke**'s regular daily reading. **(JTR ch4)**

STABLEFORD, the Countess of: a staunch audience for the lifetime of huntin', shootin' and fishin' anecdotes which flowed from the

Earl's ample store, and indeed she had an equally generous repertoire of parish gossip on her own account, supplied on the Dorset grapevine. **(HOW ch17)**

STABLEFORD, Rt Hon the Earl of: lived with his **Countess** in a state of mutual loquacity at **Worbles**, the family seat in Dorset. He was the father of **Lady Beatrice Bracken**, which might seem sufficient for most people, but it should be added for the record that most of Dorset was prepared to concede that his lordship was himself a tough baby. **(HOW ch2,17)**

STAFF: to **Adeline Hignett**, a gaunt Irish lady of advanced years. **(GOB ch1)**

STAFFORD'S INTERNATIONAL INVESTIGATION BUREAU: a self-explanatory business with branches at Strand, London, and New York, its employees including **Henry Pifield Rice** and an unspecified **Simmonds**. **(MLF-BTB; Century-BTB)**

STAINES, Lord: the elder son of **Runnymede**. **(TMU-TGP)**

STALIN Joseph (Iosif Vissarionovitch Dzhugashvili, 1879-1953): **Weasel** wished for …'s help in giving **Jane Abbott** a piece of his mind. **(SUM ch19)**

STANDARD OIL: one would not worry about … **(DBB ch2)**

STAR-SPANGLED BANNER, The: an anthem sung behind the scenes by the ensemble of *The Rose of America*, who actually knew the words. **(JTR ch16)**

STAUFFACHER, Werner: was not sure how his name should be pronounced, but was sure that he wanted to protest against the imposition of taxes, and became one of the delegation to discuss the subject with **Gessler**. **(WTT ch1,4)**

STEINBURG, Carl: a friend of **Lucille Moffam**, to whom she planned to write about **Spectatia Huskisson**. **(IOA ch23)**

STEPHANO'S: a restaurant where **Eddy Moore** and **Mary Hill** lunched. **(TMU-TFD)**

STEPPING STONES TO SUCCESS: another book of which **Roland Bean** was a walking edition. **(TMU-MMM)**

STEPTOE, Howard ('Mugsy' or 'Muggsy'): **Mabel**'s husband was an enormous mass of man with a squashed nose and ears like the handles of an old Greek vase, for he had once been the white hope of the boxing rings on the Pacific slope, and followed that with a brief career as an extra in **Hollywood**, on one occasion having three distinct lines. He now pined in a gilded cage, causing successive valets, engaged to take him in hand by strong-arm methods, to retire as broken men. **(QUS; SatEvePost-QUS ch7)**

STEPTOE, Mabel: a determined social aspirant from California, she commandeered **Claines Hall** as her battle HQ from which to conquer and subdue the County. A wiry little person with hard, blue eyes, she had the stuff in gobs, but rarely saw fit to unbelt. Poor relations such as **Sally Fairmile** were given a particularly hard row to hoe, though the equally impecunious **Beatrice Chavender** managed to live on the fat of her sister's land by successfully concealing the fact that she had lost the whole of her former fortune. **(QUS)**

STICK-IN-THE-MUD: American for bohunkus. **(USFRL ch4)**

STICKNEY: a butterscotch man who was ragged by **James Cloyster** in his column in the *Orb* when he received his peerage, and pulled £500 worth of advertising as a result. **(NGW ch24)**

STIFFY: a sort of bull-terrier with variations: its hind legs were pure black, its body white with a few black stripes. Once charming and unaffected in personality, with many good stories about a Peke and a Sealyham, it changed dramatically after being employed by the **Bigger and Better** studio. **(Aldin-GOW)**

STOGANBUHLER: **Jane Hunnicutt**'s American lawyer. **(TGI ch15)**

STOKER. Eileen: the large eyes, curving hips and lemon-coloured hair of this **Hollywood** starlet frequently appeared in daily papers, and one evocative picture led **Ellery Cobbold**, father of her erstwhile suitor **Stanwood**, to denounce her as a designing siren, not to be trusted for a moment. In fact, she was the one with money, and after trying a couple of marriages to husbands who lacked the stuff, she vowed she would only marry a third who stood possessed, to avoid the problems that otherwise arose. She came to the UK to make two pictures for the **Beaumont Co**, and whilst here put her future in the hands of **Mike Cardinal**'s agency for five years, at a commission rate of 10%. **(SPF)**

STOKES, Percy: one of the many aliases of **Herbert Higgs**. **(Ellery-MBD)**

STONE, Marcus: did 'pitchers' of guys in three-cornered hats and short pants. **(SUM ch10)**

STOTT, Sister Lora Luella: was trying to lead California out of its swamp of alcohol through the **Temple of the New Dawn**. **(LAG ch9)**

STOTTLEMEYER, Duane: a sleek, shiny, unsympathetic employee of **Guildenstern's Stores** who broke the news to **Homer Pyle** that charges would not be brought against his sister. He wrote occasional poetry, protest songs against capitalists, for smaller magazines. **(TGI ch1)**

STRACHEY, [Giles] Lytton (1880-1932): did not race through his *Life of Queen Victoria* like a Bowery bum charging into a saloon for a quick beer. **(TOR ch4)**

STRAWBERRY LEAF: a journal to which **Fennell** subscribed and **Sidney Price** contributed. **(NGW ch19,22)**

STUDD, Archie: one of **Algy Martyn**'s friends who knew **Jill Mariner**, thought she was a topper and felt strongly about **Underhill**'s breaking of the engagement. **(JTR ch8)**

STYLITES, St Simeon (387-459): took up a position on top of a pillar, and stayed there for thirty years. **(TMU-MMM)**

SUICIDE, methods of committing: the knife, the pistol, the rope, drowning, leaping to destruction from a great height, each of which had flaws in that they were either messy or painful. Poison, easy to take and quick to work, was the thing. But procrastination is the enemy of suicide:

> "I'll be hanged if I commit suicide," he yelled.

Katie MacFarland did go rather further than most in seeking an easy end to her spell of depression, selecting gas as the mechanism, but even that method had its flaws. **Genevieve O'Grady** flung herself off the side of a ferry-boat into the Hudson river but she, too, was rescued. **(MLF-AST,MOM; VanFair-AAI)**

SUICIDE CLAUSE: it was thought that the one in **Mike Bond**'s life assurance policy could undoubtedly have been avoided with a little ingenuity. **(USDBB ch6)**

SULLIVAN, Sir Arthur (1842-1900): Wally Mason's attempt to restore to New York the tradition created by **W S Gilbert** and ... was seen by the local speciality artists as a detrimental step. **(JTR ch9)**

SULLIVAN'S LAW: forbade the carrying of concealed weapons. **(Century-BTB)**

SUNDAY, Billy: was featured on **Aubrey Devine**'s list of the seven most prominent men in the United States. **(VanFair-AAI)**

SUPERBA-LLEWELLYN: only briefly the employer both of **Bill** (or **Jane**) **Shannon** and **Joe Davenport**. **(TOR ch1)**

SUSAN: a maid at **Windles**, she was engaged to the second assistant at Green's Grocery Stores in **Windlehurst**. **(GOB ch15)**

SVELTE, Clara ('Clarry'): with whom **Stiffy** was working at the **Bigger and Better**. Stiffy thought her a nice little thing, with whom he was content unless **Garbo** was as good as they said. **(Aldin-GOW)**

SVENSK!: is quite probably the expression used by natives of Sweden to express annoyance. **(GOB ch2)**

SWAFFHAM: author of a sex-novel entitled *The Rose-Red Lips of Vivette* which had been incorrectly expected by its publishers, **Mainprice and Bassett**, to become the hit novel of the season. **(Strand-PAW)**

SWEENEY, Officer: poured whisky down **Spider Buffin**'s throat after he had saved **Officer Kelly** from **Otto the Sausage** and **Rabbit Butler**. **(BurrMcK-MIS)**

SWEET ADELINE: hearing about the attributes of this young lady enabled **Phipps'** employer to locate him in juxtaposition to the safe. **(TOR ch10)**

SWENSON, Oscar: a 6' mass, made apparently of steel and india-rubber, this emotional man was perhaps the thriftiest soul who ever came out of Sweden, though something of a dressy swimmer. **(GOB ch2)**

SWISS, the: disagreed with **Hermann Gessler** on the subject of **taxes** for, being a thrifty people, they objected to taxes of any sort. **(WTT ch1)**

SWITHIN, Reginald John Peter: see **Havershot, the Right Hon the third Earl of**

SYRACUSE: the theatre audiences in this American city were always bad. **(TLW ch17)**

TAILOR, an anonymous: off-loaded a saffron coloured suit on to **Archie Moffam** for $70 after hiding him from his pursuers. **(IOA ch15)**

TAILORED WOMAN: a store which supplied form-fitting tweed dresses to dog-rescuers. **(TGI ch1)**

TAINTED MILLIONAIRES and TAINTED MILLIONS:

> [Rackstraw] was *the* Tainted Millionaire. The Tainted Millions of other Tainted Millionaires were as attar of roses compared with the Tainted Millions of Tainted Millionaire Rackstraw. He preferred his millions tainted. His attitude towards an untainted million was that of the sportsman to the sitting bird. These things are purely a matter of taste. Some people like Limburger cheese.

(Colliers-PAP)

TALES FOR THE TOTS: another piece submitted by **Aubrey Jerningham**. **(Throne-KHE)**

TANNER, George: the nephew of **Sir Godfrey**, from whom he had received finance for his venture running a private school for boys in Kent. A headmaster with a sense of humour, he employed **Herbert** as gardener, and on the roll were **Rupert Atkinson**, **Thomas Billing** and **Alexander Jones**. **(Strand-COI)**

TANNER, Lt Col Percival: had vivid memories of life at Poona in the days of the British Raj, and a long-suffering audience of fellow-guests on whom to inflict them. He was surprised to find **Adrian Peake** hiding in a cupboard in his bedroom, and beat the gong to enable others to share his emotion. **(SUM ch1,23,25)**

TANNER, P P: **Thomas Billing** was no ..., for P P was one of the finest footballers alive. **(McClure-COI)**

TANNER, Sir Godfrey, KCMG: was just a bachelor in chambers at the **Albany**, attended by his butler **Jevons,** until he sacked the latter after fifteen years' service for providing too much ice. After staying briefly at the **Hotel Guelph** in an attempt to overcome the shock, he then visited his nephew **George Tanner** at the Kent school he had helped him establish. He joined in cricket and some other species of ball-game not unrelated to football with the inmates, and made himself sufficiently popular for one, **Thomas Billing**, to take the blame for his marksmanship in an incident involving an airgun and the gardener, **Herbert**. **(Strand-COI; McClure-COI)**

TAVERN BILKERS: the first descriptive ballet seen in London, performed at Drury Lane in 17-something. **(MLF-TLF)**

TAXES: **Gessler** imposed on the people of Switzerland taxes on flocks of sheep, herds of cows, bread, biscuits (including mixed biscuits), jam, buns, lemonade and anything else he could think of. **(WTT ch1)**

TAYLOR, **Robert (Spangler Arlington Brugh, 1911-1969):** see **Blore, Eric**

TED[1]: see **Alfred**

TED[2]: a friend of **Katie MacFarland**, who brought a girl in to eat at **Mac's**. **(MLF-MOM)**

TEDDY: an actor who preferred to skip most of his speeches during rehearsal and was amongst the first with the news that the influenza ban on theatres was to be lifted. **(TAS ch6,7)**

TEGERFELDEN, **Lord of:** was one of few successful assassins appearing in Wodehouse, the victim in his joint enterprise with the **Lord of Eschenbach** being the **Emperor of Austria**. **(WTT ch15)**

TELEGRAPH: reported the death of **Reggie Voules**. **(DBB ch5)**

TELL, **Hedwig:** the daughter of **Walter Fürst** and wife of **William**, who believed that boys should stay at home and help mother wash up rather than go out shooting and hunting. **(WTT ch3,4,5)**

TELL, **Walter:** the elder son of **William** and **Hedwig** who told **Gessler** that his father was the best marksman in the country, and bravely stood still while the apple was shot from the top of his head. **(WTT ch3,5,10,11)**

TELL, **William (fl 14th cent):** elected in his absence as leader of the **Swiss** people in their battle with **Hermann Gssler**. He lived with his family in a picturesque chalet, had the courage of a lion, the sure-footedness of a wild goat, the agility of a squirrel and a beautiful beard. He invited the visiting delegation to send him a postcard when action was required and did not let them down. First he put an arrow through Gessler's hat, then he declined to bow before it, shot an apple of **Walter**'s head at 100 yards, steered Gessler's ship through the rocks during a storm and shot him while making his escape. **(WTT)**

TELL, William, Jnr (fl 14th cent): the younger son of **William** and **Hedwig**. **(WTT ch3)**

TEMPLE OF THE NEW DAWN, The: based in Culver City, it was the guiding light for **Sister Lora Luella Scott, Mabel Prescott,** assorted **Brinkmeyer**s and, after a certain initial reluctance, **Eggy Mannering. (LAG ch9,14)**

TEMPLETON, Marie: a fictitious elderly chorus-girl, with whom **Robert Ferguson** claimed to have a date, but whom his ex-fiancée knew to be burdened with two children, including one already in the profession, playing heavy parts on tour. **(TMU-MMM)**

TENNESSEE BEAR-CAT: **Ted Brady**'s companion at **Palisades Park**, who had a broken nose and a face like a good-natured bulldog. If allergic to hyphens, see **Bearcat, Tennessee (MLF-CRH)**

TENNYSON, Alfred Lord (1809-1892): had he met him, he would have probably described **Appleby** as a "gentleman of stateliest port", to reflect both his shape and his drinking habits. He realised that thoughts could be too deep for tears and was **Billy Bennett**'s favourite poet; she particularly appreciated his *Idylls of the King*. He wrote a celebrated scene relating King Arthur's interview with Guinevere in the convent but completely ignored the merits of **Sir Agravaine. (GOB ch3; HOW ch8; DBB ch3; TGI ch13; TMU-SAG)**

TERRY, Dame Ellen [Alice] (1847-1928): had nothing on **Gladys Winch** when it came to delivering the line: "Yes, madam". **(TAS ch10)**

TESTS OF SOBRIETY:

British Constitution

The Leith police dismisseth us

He sits under Sister Stott

A perfectly natural psychic phenomenon

(LAG ch14)

TETRAZZINI: could pick the last note of *Mother's Knee* off the roof and hold it until the janitor came round to lock up the building for the night. **(IOA ch23)**

TEXAS MILLIONAIRE: scarcely noticed when he rammed **Jerry West** in the back at **Barribault's hotel**. **(TGI ch6)**

TF(RH): see **Flower, Teddy**

THEATRE MEMORIES: by **Dame Flora Faye**. **(TGI ch5)**

THEOPHRASTUS (c372-286BC): said time was the most valuable thing a man could spend. **(NGW ptI ch2)**

THEOSOPHY: to prepare lectures on the subject required an equable frame of mind. **(GOB ch1)**

THERSITES: in Homer's *Iliad*, recklessly slandered his betters. **(TMU-TFD)**

THING IN THE CELLAR: it was only because **Drexdale Drew** imprudently let forth a long, low whistle of astonishment that he had the unpleasantness with a ... **(QUS ch18)**

THINGUMMY, Dora: a friend of **Dick Henley** who always sliced with her brassy. **(TUW-TDH)**

THIRD GHOST: Thomas Blake. **(NGW ch14)**

THISBE: see **Pyramus**

THOMAS¹: was an intermittent cat at **Elmer Mariner**'s home **Sandringham**, whose colour scheme, like a **Whistler** picture, was an arrangement in black and white. He had green eyes and a purr like a racing car, and was the energetic and popular secretary of the local cats' debating society. **(TLW ch7; Grand-JTR)**

THOMAS²: an accident-prone **Mallow Hall** cat. **(DBB ch5)**

THOMPSON: one of six acquaintances of **Joe Vanringham** not known to **Jane Abbott**. **(SUM ch5)**

THREE DEAD AT MIDWAYS COURT: a whodunnit which was the inspiration for **Phipps'** second career, in which the heavy turned out to be the butler, even though no one suspected him until the final chapter. **(TOR ch4)**

THREE MEN AND A MAID: the American title of the novel which became *The Girl on the Boat* **(GOB)** when published three months later in the UK. It lacks one sub-plot, as a result of which the development of the relationship between **Eustace Hignett** and

Jane Hubbard takes longer to narrate, and **Sir Mallaby Marlowe** never holds his dramatic dinner party. **(TMM)**

THREEPWOOD, 'young': the description given is palpably that of Freddie, but we are not specifically told that this is the case. We know that the young man in question was a friend of **Freddie Rooke**, lost £30 at piquet to **Chris Selby** and gave a lunch at **Oddy**'s at which **Nelly Bryant** was one of the guests. **(JTR ch1,6)**

TIBERIUS, Emperor (Tiberius Claudius Nero, 42BC-37AD): there was that about **Sally Nicholas**'s **Uncle Donald** which would have cast a sobering influence over the orgies of the Emperor at Capri. **(TAS ch4)**

TIERRA DEL FUEGO: one of the places where **Joe Vanringham** thought **Adrian Peake** might have reached. **(SUM ch21)**

TIMES, The: an advertisement in ... would have brought in dozens of offers of matrimony to **Crispin Scrope**, a member of a family generations of whom had, over the years, submitted letters to the Editor. It reported that **Joe Vanringham**'s play had got over. **(SUM ch3; TGI ch8,14)**

TINNEY, Frank: **Eustace Hignett** performed a hit imitation of him at a Trinity smoker. **(GOB ch1)**

TIT-BITS: **Sidney Price** preferred to spend a penny on a copy of ... than on liquorice. **(NGW ptII ch19)**

TIVOLI: another former music-hall haunt of **Max Faucitt** which no longer existed. **(TAS ch12)**

TODD, Chester: an amiable, rich, young man with little brain, he lived whole-heartedly for pleasure. He had been a nephew of **Hermione Pegler** even before her marriage to **Old Nick**, he was a friend of **Butch Carpenter**, married to the violinist **Jane Parker** and interested with his sister in the well-known table-water **Clear Spring**. **(FRL ch4,5,7)**

TODD, George ('Snake'): the uncle of **Chester** and **Mavis**. As an All-American half-back for three years, also known as 'Greasy' Todd and 'The Shimmering Spectre', he had been one of the great fixed stars in the football firmament, in 1930 achieving an 87-yard run which had ended in a touchdown. **(FRL ch7)**

TODD, Mavis: the niece of **Hermione Pegler**, she was a silent child with large eyes, a part owner of the controlling interest in the

Clear Spring table-water business and only too willing to miss a concert to go to the pictures with **Butch Carpenter**. **(FRL ch5)**

TOLSTOI, Count Leo Nikolayevich (1882-1945):

> . . . Freddie experienced the sort of abysmal soul-sadness which afflicts one of Tolstoi's Russian peasants when, after putting in a heavy day's work strangling his father, beating his wife, and dropping the baby into the city reservoir, he turns to the cupboard, only to find the vodka-bottle empty.

(JTR ch8)

TOMMY: an unfortunate pug, given to **Sylvia Reynolds** by **Reginald Dallas**, who came to a sticky end as a result of his compulsive attraction to carnations. **(TUW-WPS)**

TOOFER: a type of cheap cigar offered by **Freddie Rooke** to **Wally Mason**, which derived its name from the expression 'two for the price of one'. **(JTR ch8)**

TOOTS: see **Fauntleroy, Gladys**

TOPHAM, Rt Hon the Viscount: a long, lean, young golfer with the ability to break 100 shots for a round, who appeared to have giraffe blood in him. He was invited by **Adela Cork** to stay, on the assumption that he would marry **Kay Shannon**, but he was in love with the temperamental **Toots Fauntleroy**. He was wealthy, but unable to raise a bean because of the "sinister goings-on of this bally Labour Government". **(TOR ch4)**

TOPPING, Adela: the eldest daughter of **Shorty** and a hard woman, who made him drink a glass of malted milk each morning and refused to lend him the £200 he needed to buy a pub for **Alice Punter**. She was tall, handsome, some 15 years younger than her husband **Desborough** and built on the lines of **Queen Catherine of Russia**, with a similar force of character and imperiousness of outlook. **(SPF)**

TOPPING, Desborough: after having been at school with **Stanwood Cobbold**, he had married **Adela Cobbold** and become one of those Americans at the mention of whose name **Bradstreet** raised his hat with a deferential flourish. And since Desborough was a noted philatelist, **Stanley Gibbons** did the same. He was a slight, well-meaning man in his mid-40s who wore pince-nez and sympathized with Shorty's predicament but whose scope to assist was constrained by a joint bank account. **(SPF ch1,3,4,7,13,20)**

TORQUIL: couldn't decide whether or not to be psychoanalysed. **(DBB ch2)**

TOSTI, Sir Francesco Paolo (1846-1916): his *Good-bye* was played late into the night by **Henry Mortimer** on the gas-engine in the drawing-room at **Windles. (GOB ch10)**

TOTO[1]: a small, woolly quadruped with a persistent and penetrating yap who stained the fair name of the canine race by posing as a dog. **(TAS ch5)**

TOTO[2]: resembled a rat, and was mistaken for one by **Nigger. (MLF-BIS)**

TOTTIE: a young lady who worked on the cash-desk at a Mecca, and received regular bottles of scent from an admirer whom she favoured with kisses. **(NGW ptII ch13)**

TRAÜMEREI: a composer whose tunes were liable to stimulate dreams of ideal love, except in the case of **Jimmy Duff**, who used the opportunity offered by the band to explain to his fiancée how hams were cured. **(SUM ch17; QUS ch1)**

TRAVELLER, an anonymous: a stone-deaf confidant of **Jack Roach. (TMU-BAC)**

TRAVERS, Sir Courtenay: when he fell in love with the milkmaid he was dependent on his mother, the Countess, for everything. **(JTR ch2)**

TRAVIS, Walter J: imitating one of his shots, hitting at an invisible ball with a walking stick, occasionally helped to relieve **George Marlowe**'s frustrations during his golfless days. **(PicRev-PAW)**

TREACHER, Arthur: Bill Shannon told **Adela Cork** that **Phipps** out-Arthured Treacher. (Arthur Treacher was a noted actor, playing butler and similar roles, and had appeared as Jeeves in two films, ie *Step Lively, Jeeves* and *Thank You, Jeeves*.) **(TOR ch5)**

TREASURY PEOPLE:

> "I had to go over [to New York] and see my lawyer about my income tax. The Treasury people were making the most absurd claims."
>
> "Soaking the rich?"

"Trying to soak the rich."

"I hope they skinned you to the bone."

"No. As a matter of fact, I came out of it very well."

(SUM ch20)

TREES: the sort of song which, performed after dinner in a soft, quivery voice, was likely to attract **Sally Fairmile**. **(QUS ch1)**

TREFUSIS, Lady Blanche: in *Cupid or Mammon*, she sent a note to her humble lover informing him it could not be. **(GOB ch16)**

TRENT, Edgar: the late father of **Kate**, **Jo** and **Terry**, whose forte was intellect rather than beauty. He had been the author of a successful farce, ***Brother Masons***, on the $6,000 proceeds from the sale of the television rights to which the sisters took a holiday in France. **(FRL ch1)**

TRENT, Josephine ('Jo'): the younger sister of **Kate** and elder of **Terry**, who would have preferred ducks at the **Bensonburg** farm but was outvoted. She was strikingly pretty, to a greater degree even than Terry, and hoped to find a millionaire to marry during a holiday in France during which she and Terry proposed to take it in turns to be the 'rich' Miss Trent, with the other acting as her maid. Although she had won the toss which entitled her to the first month, it ended without conclusive results. **(FRL)**

TRENT, Kate: the eldest of the three sisters, who treated the others as problem children. It had been her idea to buy the chicken farm at Bensonburg, with bees as a sideline. She looked more like her father than did her sisters, and was always able to scare the daylights out of **Henry Weems**, whom she reminded of a childhood governess whose forceful personality had made a deep impression on his plastic mind. Kate decided to chaperone **Jo** and **Terry** on their French adventure, but was uncomfortable with such events as the **St Rocque festival**. **(FRL)**

TRENT, Teresa ('Terry'): agreed with **Jo** that their inheritance of $2,000 (or $3,000) should be spent on holiday at **St Rocque** or **Roville**, but her three-spot relegated her to the position of maid for the first month. Terry had the face of a **Botticelli** angel, blue eyes, teeth like pearls, a lovely mouth, beautiful arms, a perfect figure and a nose that turned up slightly to two small freckles at the end. Her romantic entanglements in France were suitably complex for a Wodehouse heroine, for after falling in love with

Jeff d'Escrignon, she decided to marry **Freddie Carpenter** when he was caught in her room in his pyjamas at a time when she didn't believe that Jeff had really gone to Paris on business. But readers must not overlook the prerogative of woman to change her mind more than once. **(FRL; USFRL ch1)**

TRESILLIAN, the Hon Clarence: a man with the appearance of a Greek God, who bought a Teddy-bear from **Isabel Rackstraw** at sixteen times face value, and ended the afternoon they first met with four Teddies, seven photo frames, five golliwogs, a billiken and a fiancée. When not at Oxford University, he lived with his parents, **Lord** and **Lady Runnymede**, in Belgrave Square. He was a member of the **Bachelors' Club** and after financial difficulties hit the family, he became a professional footballer masquerading under the name **Jones**. His prospective father-in-law called him a 'preposterous excrescence on the social cosmos' even before he caught the mumps, and then realised that that was exactly what he needed to help run his business. **(TMU-TGP)**

TRESILLIAN, Jnr: the young son of **Isabel** and **Clarence**, who looked questioningly at the **Meredith** ball. **(TMU-TGP)**

TRESSILLIAN, Reginald: was literally a ghost as far as **Flora Faye** was concerned. **(TGI ch5)**

TREVELYAN, Cecil: took the rap in *Hearts Astir*. **(SUM ch19)**

TREVELYAN, Cyril: **Bill Bates** preferred **Alan Beverley** to ... **(TMU-MUP)**

TREVIS, Angela: the fifteen-year-old frivolous and freckled sister of **Roland**, who was destined to walk down the aisle at St Thomas's with **Otis Pilkington** some five years after the New York first night of *The Rose of America*. **(JTR ch20)**

TREVIS, Roland: the composer of *The Rose of America*. **(JTR ch10)**

TREVOR, Milly: a popular member of the *Rose of America* cast, she was small, perky and capable, and sported golden hair, the round face of a wandering cherub and a lisp. **(JTR ch11,16)**

TRIED BY FIRE: such an unusual type of fare served up by **Wally Mason** that he disguised his responsibility under the name **John Grant**. This thought-provoking play opened at the **Leicester Theatre** but as it failed to entertain the **Underhill–Mariner** part of the **Rooke–Underhill–Mariner** party it may be assumed that the thoughts it provoked were unkind. It was a grievously heavy poetic drama, which the audience, though loath to do anybody an injustice, started to suspect had been written in blank verse. And the second act, fortuitously cancelled, was said to be worse than the first! **(JTR ch2)**

TRIMBLETT, Miss: **Billie Bennett**'s maid, who was walking out with **Webster**. **(GOB ch15)**

TRUE AS STEEL: in which the hero rescued the heroine from a burning building. **(GOB ch16)**

TRUE HEART NOVELETTE SERIES: more than half its output concerned courses of true love which did not run smooth. **(JTR ch2)**

TUDWAY, Alexander: the kind-hearted editor of *Piccadilly Weekly* who, because of the extra work he had absorbed in relation to contributions from the **Jerningham** family, had aged prematurely and now sported white hair, a wrinkled brow, a wild and haggard eye and a bowed and meagre form. He even went so far as to marry **Rachel**, when he realised that her literary offerings were just too bad to be edited. **(Throne-KHE)**

TURPIN, Dick (1706-1739): referees in Cup Finals tended to take on the character of ..., as did head waiters at posh restaurants in Paris, such as the **Guelph**, when seeking to deprive hard-working waiters of a fair share of the tips. **(TMU-TGP; MLF-MOM)**

TUXTON, Dick: a fat uncle of **Jane**'s. **(TMU-BAC)**

TUXTON, Jane: a brown, slim, wiry-looking young lady with eyes the colour of Scotch whisky and a preference for the new **Jerry Moore**. **(TMU-BAC)**

TUXTON, Jane's little brother: with his snub nose and a cheeky manner, deserved to be clipped on the side of his head for a remark about **Jerry Moore**'s nose. **(TMU-BAC)**

TUXTON, Pa: an old fellow with a beard, glasses, a parrot and a fat yellow dog. **(TMU-BAC)**

TUXTON, Ralph: the big brother of **Jane** who worked in a bank and dressed like Moses in all his glory. **(TMU-BAC)**

TWENTIETH CENTURY LIMITED: the train from New York to Chicago, on which **Reggie Havershot** proposed to travel. **(LAG ch1)**

TWERP: whether **Adrian Peake** was a ..., as **Tubby Vanringham** suggested, all turned on what one was. If it was someone who lived like a locust on what he could pick up, such as selling cars on commission, dabbling in gossip writing, making film tests, doing interior decorating or running bottle-party night clubs, all the while preferring to exist on a supply of free lunches, free dinners, free suppers and free cocktails with little sausages on sticks, then he was a twerp in good standing. **(SUM ch6)**

TWINGO, Old: a pal of **Lord Topham** in London, to whom he broke the news by transatlantic telephone that he had completed a round of golf in under a hundred. **(TOR ch4)**

TWIN-SIX COMPLEX: the make of car owned by **J Rufus Bennett** was not one which would decline to stall if the driver failed to give it 100% concentration and, as driven by **Billie Bennett** when thinking of the alternative qualities of **Bream Mortimer** and **Sam Marlowe**, it stalled. **(GOB ch17)**

TWISTLETON-TWISTLETON, Pongo: once told **Reggie Havershot** that faced by a creditor for £3 6s 11d he had worked him into a discussion on 'Spats: Should they have three buttons or four?', as a result of which Pongo had been stood a pint and lent half a crown until Wednesday. For more information on Pongo, see *Volumes 5, 6 and 7.* **(Pearson-LAG)**

TWO-GUN THOMAS: to be a successful gunman you have to be able to draw like a flash of lightning and make vital use of the first shot, as demonstrated in the movie to **John Peters**. **(GOB ch8, 13)**

TYSON, John ('Jack'): of **Rodney**, Maine, was a patient and loyal husband who waited two or three years for his wife to escape the lure of the city lights. **(MLF-ATG; Strand-LSC)**

TYSON, Mrs John: see **Roxborough, Miss**

UJI VILLAGE: where the chief apparently called for a hair-cut. **(TMU-WDD)**

ULRIC THE SMITH: was anxious about the tax on jam. **(WTT ch2,4,9)**

UMBRELLA CLUB: an idea formulated by **Old Nick** which would have enabled any club member to walk into a participating establishment when it was raining, borrow an umbrella and leave it at another place near the member's destination. **Freddie**

Carpenter declined to finance it, although it was reported in *Gracious Living Limited*, by Guy Bolton (1966, Herbert Jenkins Ltd), ch1, that a Josephine Peabody's nephew Robin had later tried, though unsuccessfully, to get such a club off the ground. **(FRL ch2,9)**

UNCLE DONALD: that of **Ginger Kemp** and **Bruce Carmyle** was a worthy man, highly respected in the National Liberal Club, the head of the family, but never a favourite of Ginger's. The way he employed his moustache during meals as a sort of zareba or earthwork against the assaults of soup was by itself enough to make him disliked, but when this was combined with his habit of summoning errant members of the family to dine at such a morgue of a restaurant as **Bleke's**, the sensitive spirit was liable to revolt. **(TAS ch4,9)**

UNCLE EDGAR: **Reggie van Tuyl**'s, who thought he was twins, even though one edition would have been enough. **(IOA ch26)**

UNCLE FRANCIS: **Gladys Wetherby**'s, see **Pashley-Drake, Col Francis**. **(PLP-GCS)**

UNCLE FRED: **Augustus Robb**'s, who gave his nephew peppermints as an inducement to stop reciting. **(SPF ch8)**

UNCLE GEORGE: one of the minor relatives of **Ginger Kemp** and **Bruce Carmyle**, he was puzzled by Bruce's attempts to win **Sally Nicholas**'s hand. **(TAS ch4,15)**

UNCLE GERVASE: **Shorty**'s, whose death from apoplexy enabled Shorty to succeed to the title. **(SPF ch9)**

UNCLE HENRY: **Owen Bentley**'s, who had ten other nephews, far more than he knew what to do with. **(TMU-POM)**

UNCLE REGGIE: **Reginald Chippendale**'s, who would have been pinched for street betting if his **Aunt Myrtle** hadn't soaked the copper. **(TGI ch13)**

UNCLE REGINALD: **Augustus Robb**'s, who was not master in the 'ome, presumably because the little woman had the fuller sock. **(SPF ch8)**

UNCLE ROBERT: **George Balmer**'s, with whom he lived as a paying guest, suggested that George should invest his inheritance in Consols. **(TMU-TTM)**

UNCLE RONALD: **Ginger Kemp**'s, who was actually a figment of **Sally Nicholas**'s imagination, for the name for which she had been searching was **Uncle Donald**. (Colliers-TAS pt6)

UNCLE SAM: **Barney Clayborne**'s, who took money from her for years. (TGI ch14)

UNCLE SIGSBEE, Looney Biddle's girl-friend's: had low, sneaky cracks made about him by **Looney**. (IOA ch14)

UNCLE TED: **Freddie Rooke**'s, a jovial, puffy-faced man who died of apoplexy. (JTR ch13)

UNCLE, Unnamed: that of **Sally** and **Fillmore Nicholas** was a grim 62-year-old who had presided over a hectic scene some three years before Sally inherited her money which had resulted in the brother and sister going together out into the world like a second Adam and Eve. (TAS ch1)

UNCLE WILLIAM: another minor relative of **Ginger Kemp** and **Bruce Carmyle**. (TAS ch4)

UNCLE WILLIE: **Jill Willard**'s late ..., whose funeral she attended, but who had been a twister. (DBB ch5)

UNCLE ZIP: alias 'the Hump-Curer', 'the Grouch Curer' or 'the Man Who Makes You Smile', was a proposed toy, like a Billiken, which would have features based on those of **Gandinot**, but the project was vetoed by **Ruth Warden**. (TMU-RIE; Ainslee-RIE)

UNDERHILL, Sir Derek, Bart, MP: in those far-off days when a baronetcy was a pass to a safe Parliamentary seat, the precious Derek was a pretty example of privilege in action, proving that even Winchester and New College have their disasters. A strikingly handsome, tall, well-built man of about thirty, he was dark and clean-shaven, with heavy eyebrows which gave him a forbidding appearance. His facial features – large, brown eyes, a long upper lip, a thin, firm mouth and the prominent family chin – made him look as though he never quite escaped from permanent misery, although his fortune in becoming engaged to **Jill Mariner**, who worshipped him, should have made him one of the happiest men in London. He nevertheless cynically discarded her in the supposed interests of his career. Many Eggs, Beans, Crumpets and other sound judges of character resented somewhat hotly the world's tendency to let down its Dereks lightly, but perhaps the tendency was more apparent than real, and even his most loyal friend, **Freddie Rooke**, finally saw through the veneer and cut him stone dead. **(JTR)**

UNDERHILL, Lady: the eagle-faced, widowed mother of **Derek** who had small, keen, black eyes, a long upper lip, a thin, firm mouth, a prominent nose and a jutting chin. As well as all the innate snobbery of her class. As a boy, Derek had been firmly under her control, and the sway of her aggressive personality endured through his manhood. Distant cousins quaked at her name, and she was known by her closer male relatives as 'The Family Curse'. **(JTR ch1; TLW ch1; Grand-JTR)**

UNDERSHAW, Lucas: the pseudonym of **Rachel Jerningham**, aunt of **Aubrey**, whose manuscript of *Gracie's Hero* was so bad that it became **Tudway**'s first outright rejection. **(Throne-KHE)**

UNDERSTATEMENT:

> . . . life's difficult enough as it is. You don't want to aggravate the general complexity of things by getting changed into a kid with knickerbockers and golden curls.

(LAG ch7)

UNFAIR EXCHANGES:

> "Have you no regard for her happiness?"
> "I am the best judge of what is best for her."

(GOB ch14)

> " . . . this animal came to us in a curious way. A messenger boy came, asking us to destroy him at once."
> "Why did the messenger boy want to be destroyed?" asked Chester Bennett.

(LHJ-FKA)

UNION LEAGUE CLUB: the proper place for a discussion about the iniquities and defects of the American Administration. **(QUS ch13)**

UNITED BEEF AND DAUGHTER: see **Consolidated Popcorn**

UNITT AND WICKES: for scenery, $2,120. **(JTR ch17)**

UNIVERSITY OF SOUTHERN CALIFORNIA AT LOS ANGELES: the campus of which lay in the valley beneath **Smedley Cork**. **(TOR ch1)**

UPSHAW, Charles: "Good Old Charlie" was a frequent shout of approbation of the husband of **Flora Faye** and father of **Vera**. He inherited the 'Upshaw's Dietbread' millions and spots, the latter from a surfeit of champagne, but was otherwise very handsome. **(TGI ch2)**

UPSHAW, Vera: a spectacular-looking product of the union between **Charles** and **Flora Faye**, although her lustrous eyes flashed in a disconcerting manner when she was displeased and her voice was harsh. She wrote whimsical essays published in slim volumes, such as *Morning's At Seven* and *Daffodil Days* and went to **Brussels** for the **Pen and Ink Club** conference. After having once been engaged to **Jerry West**, she turned her attention to the wealthier **Homer Pyle**, but when he held back from proposing she tried unsuccessfully to return to **Jerry**'s life. The impression she made did depend very much on the mood and thinking of the recipient, for while to **Barney Clayborne** she was a designing Delilah, a vampire, to the smitten but cautious Homer she was Ethereal, Refined, Graceful, Light, Dainty and Elfin. **(TGI ch2,3,5,14,15)**

VALENTINE, Jimmy: a character in a story by **O Henry** who claimed wrongly to have been able to open a safe just by feel. **(TOR ch10; DBB ch9,12)**

VALETORIUM: the right place to acquire a valet. **(QUS ch3)**

VANCOTT: a baker, who was **Julian Eversleigh**'s landlord, started work at 5 am and also wrote advertisements. **(NGW ptII ch4)**

VAN DER WATER, Virginia Terhune: an illustrative example of the reason why **Adelaide Brewster Moggs** declined to add to her burden by taking her husband's surname as well. **(VanFair-AAI)**

VAN DYKE, Mrs Stuyvesant: a character in *The Rose of America*, the wall of whose Long Island residence was being placed too far down the stage. Her character was changed during the rewrite to become that of the wife of a pickle manufacturer; the consequential name change remained undisclosed. **(JTR ch16,17)**

VAN PUYSTER, Clarence: a Greek God, who fell in love with **Isabel Rackstraw** but whose suit was rejected by his prospective father-in-law. Simultaneously, his home life changed, his father being reduced to relative penury and requesting Clarence to earn his living. This he chose to do as a pitcher for the **New York Giants**, using the pseudonym **Brown**, and the team's dependence on him was shown up when he developed mumps. When he received the opportunity to put pressure on Isabel's father to do the decent thing and approve their match he did not hesitate, and neither did **Rackstraw**, realising at once that Clarence was exactly what he needed to run his business. **(Colliers-PAP)**

VAN PUYSTER, Isabel: using her married name the former **Isabel Rackstraw**[2] was the mother of **Junior**. **(Colliers-PAP)**

VAN PUYSTER, Jnr: the son of **Isabel** and **Clarence**, he looked at the **Neal Ball** glove in a questioning manner. **(Colliers-PAP)**

VAN PUYSTER, Mrs: the wealthy wife of **Vansuyther** and mother of **Clarence**. **(Colliers-PAP)**

VAN PUYSTER, Vansuyther: lived near Washington Square with his wife and son **Clarence**. He was descended from an ancestor who came over in **Governor Stuyvesant**'s time in one of the 94 day boats and acquired a square mile or so of Manhattan for $10 and a quarter interest in a pedlar's outfit. He told Clarence that the family had been financially ruined by **Rackstraw**, and that the consequence of their income being reduced from $300,000 per annum to $50,000 was that Clarence would have to go out to work. **(Colliers-PAP)**

VANRINGHAM, Franklin: the late father of **Joe** and **Tubby**, he was a victim of the woman who subsequently became the **Princess von und zu Dwornitzchek**. **(SUM ch1,5)**

VANRINGHAM, Joseph J ('Joe'): the difference between Joe and his younger brother **Tubby** was the fundamental one that exists between a tough cat which has had to fend for itself among the alleys, and its softer kinsman who is the well-nourished pet in a good home. Joe's effervescence did not conceal the fact that he came up the hard way, having left the home in which the stepmother who hated him was slowly murdering his father, and he did not, unlike his brother, subscribe to the Princess's fan club. The fortune of $10 with which he left home accompanied him to careers on a tramp steamer, in the boxing ring and as a bouncer. He then obtained a job with a publishing firm and found that women such as **Gwenda Gray** were putty in his hands. He wrote *The Angel in the House*, a play which clearly featured his stepmother in the leading part and although it would have made him a fortune, she was astute enough to buy up the rights and close the piece down before too many of her acquaintances had

Tubby Vanringham holding a diplomatic towel

seen it. He fell in love on seeing **Jane Abbott**, and used all his guile, freshness and charm to convert her affections from the wholly unworthy **Adrian Peake**. **(SUM)**

VANRINGHAM, Theodore ('Tubby'): a stout young American paying guest at **Walsingford Hall**, he was a keen and natural bather who showed good judgment in regarding **Adrian Peake** as a **twerp**. After he had become engaged to **Prudence Whittaker**, the romance had fallen apart following an incident, although Tubby still wanted to crush her to him and cover her face with burning kisses. Tubby boasted a history of being sued by women he had loved and lost, and Prudence commenced an action in turn, but the pair were reconciled after Tubby nosily investigated a suspicious parcel she had received. **(SUM)**

VAN TUYL, Mrs: invited **Archie Moffam** to a house party in Miami (or Bar Harbour), from which he emerged with an unexpected, but very welcome, encumbrance. **(IOA ch1; Strand-MMH)**

VAN TUYL, Reggie: the son of the Florida hostess, who introduced **Archie Moffam** to fashionable 5th Avenue clubs. He went with Archie to the auction sale for **Pongo**, and later lost a $500 bet to Archie over the outcome of a baseball match. He was never at his strongest in the morning, but had a sensitive eye for clothes, having resigned from clubs because of excesses of members in their sartorial matters, and been mortified that on one occasion, thanks to a negligent valet, he had been sent into Fifth Avenue with only one spat on. Reggie was a sentimentalist, a bachelor who had shown no pretensions to romance until he became engaged to **Mabel Winchester**. **(IOA ch4,9,10,14,18,19; Strand-PWM)**

VAN WHAT-WAS-HIS-NAME, Toddy: had had $200,000 awarded against him for breach of promise, even though he was practically a pauper. **(FRL ch9)**

VARDON, Harry (1870-1937): **Gertie Carlisle** took the full ... swing when hitting people on the back of the head with vases, and used plenty of follow-through. Imitating one of his shots at an invisible ball with a walking stick occasionally relieved **George Marlowe**'s frustrations during his golfless days. **(HOW ch17; Strand-PAW)**

VARIETY: the journal which, next to **Toto**, **Mrs Meecher** loved best in the world. **Smedley Cork** threatened to write to its Editor about **Adela**'s theft of the **Carmen Flores** diary. A copy was always to be found at 9 **Daubeny Street**. **(JTR ch5; TAS ch8; TOR ch8)**

VEEK: see **Blissac, Vicomte de**

VENGEANCE OF JASPER MURGATROYD, The: the first proposed contribution by **Aubrey Jerningham** to *Piccadilly Weekly*, which had to be considerably altered to make it suitable for publication. **(Throne-KHE)**

VENUS: a fruity painting by **James Wheeler**'s fiancée, which **Archie Moffam** gave his wife for her birthday, although she was duly unimpressed. **(IOA ch25)**

VERE DE VERE: neither **Algy Wynbrace** in the presence of a cat, **Bill**[1] when barked at by a dog, nor **Sergeant Potter**'s manners had the repose which marked the caste of ... **(JTR ch5; DBB ch14; LHJ-FKA)**

VEUVE 51: one of the late **Sir Hugo Bond**'s favourite vintages. **(DBB ch5)**

VIE PARISIENNE, La: featured pictures of girls with a sort of how-shall-I-describe-it look. **(SUM ch5)**

VILLAGE CRICKET: compared to country house cricket, tended to be played on a pitch on which cows were apt to stroll before the innings started, with cover-point standing up to his neck in a furze-bush. **(TUW-TDH)**

VINCE, Dana: an honorary dog, in love with **Ruth Warden**, to whom he started proposing at their first meeting. Somewhat Psmithian in conversation, he claimed a crust of diffidence and an ability to draw caricatures. He won Ruth while she supposed him to be poor, although he was in fact the heir to **Vince's Stores**. **(Ainslee-RIE)**

VINCE, George: also an honorary dog, who changed his name from **Dana** when promoted to book publication. **(TMU-RIE)**

VINCE'S STORES: an important business owned by **George Vince**'s father whose speciality was children's toys, and on whose behalf George was in Europe seeking inspiration for new ideas. **(TMU-RIE)**

VIOLET[1]: a friend of **Katie MacFarland**, who ate at **Mac's**. **(MLF-MOM)**

VIOLET²: a fictional divine whose hair reached to her knees, eyes were like blue saucers and complexion was a pink poem. **(NGW ptII ch7)**

VIRGIL (Publius Vergilius Maro, 70-19BC): was always liable to smirk at inopportune moments. See also **Dante**. **(HOW ch9)**

VITAMIN B TONIC: Chippendale swigged his mother's ... to nerve himself to the task of hunting. **(TGI ch11)**

VITELLIUS, Aulus (15-69): a Roman emperor who enjoyed his lunch. **(TGI ch6)**

VIZIER, the: of Aldebaran, would never let the **King** pass a law for himself, always calling Parliament together and getting them to do it. **(Sunday-IDL)**

VOICE THAT BREATHED O'ER EDEN, The: **Reggie Havershot**'s desire to walk up the aisle with **April June** while the organ played ... was not merely tempered but shattered by a kick in the pants. **Mike Cardinal** assumed he would be there to hear it in **Terry Cobbold**'s company, and **Bill Shannon** wanted to be there with **Kay Shannon** and **Joe Davenport**. **(LAG ch22; SPF ch12; TOR ch11)**

VOKES, Buffy: anecdotes about such old friends from the Bengal Lancers were **Col Tanner**'s staple fare. **(SUM ch25)**

VOLSTEAD ACT: the existing prohibition legislation, which was as nothing compared to the proposed Opal law. **(HOW ch2)**

VOLTAIRE, (François Marie de Arouet, 1694-1778): the hedonism of ..., the author of *Candide*, was said by **Mrs Goodwin** to be the indictment of an honest bore. **(NGW ptI ch1; JTR ch6)**

VON DER FLUE, Klaus: a chimney-sweep who loved mixed biscuits and read a paper on *Governors – their drawbacks and how to get rid of them*. During the fight he was knocked head over heels by **Leuthold**. **(WTT ch2,4,9)**

VOULES, Reggie: had once been a very close friend of **Miss Bond**, nearly marrying her some forty years before his death from a heart attack at 70. His life had in fact been spent with the dumbest girl in Worcestershire. **(DBB ch5)**

WADDESLEY, Col: a shipboard acquaintance of the **Princess von und zu Dwornitzchek**, and a dinner guest, with his wife, at Berkeley Square. **(SUM ch13)**

WADDESLEY, Mrs: her marriage to the **Colonel** may have brought many good things, but it also brought her into contact with the untrustworthy **Princess von und zu Dwornitzchek**. (SUM ch13)

WAGNER, Hans: **Dodson**[2] owned the bat he had used as a boy. (Colliers-PAP)

WAILING LADY, the: the name given to the ghost of **Biddleford** Castle. (LAG ch9)

WAITING: the name of **Narrator**[4]'s picture to be submitted to the **Royal Academy**, supposed to represent a beautiful young lady dressed in a neat creation of white, standing on a rustic bridge with her back to a rather sweet thing in Turneresque sunsets. (Windsor-CPB)

WALLACE, Edgar (1875-1932): **Packy Franklyn** had read all the works of ... (HOW ch2)

WALLINGFORD: American for **Wellingford** (USDBB ch2 *et alia*)

WALLINGFORD RACES: see **Wellingford Races** (USDBB ch1)

WALLINGFORD WOMEN'S ASSOCIATION: see **Wellingford Women's Association**. (USDBB ch2)

WALPOLE STREET: where **James Cloyster** took a fairly large bed-sitting-room. (NGW ptII ch3)

WALSINGFORD HALL: the ancestral home overlooking the Thames in Berkshire of the **Abbott** line of baronets. It is perhaps not surprising that the present holder, **Sir Buckstone Abbott**, who was in the habit of taking a quick look every morning, liked it less each time. Built in the time of **Queen Elizabeth I**, it must originally have been a lovely place, for it was a big fire halfway through **Queen Victoria**'s reign which was the principal reason why **Sir Wellington Abbott** was enabled to rebuild it from the foundations up.

Whatever may be said about the Victorians, it is pretty generally accepted that few of them were to be trusted within reach of a trowel and a pile of bricks. Sir Wellington was as virulent an amateur architect as ever grew a whisker and having recovered from the heat of the fire and the chill of the wind he saw an opportunity to do a big job, regardless of expense, and so he created what came to be known locally as **Abbott's Folly**.

Walsingford Hall, now known as Chateau Impney, Droitwich

What sensitive oarsmen rounding the bend of the river could then see, therefore, before they caught the inevitable crab, was a vast edifice constructed of glazed red brick, in some respects resembling a French château, but on the whole having more the appearance of one of those model dwellings in which a certain number of working-class families were assured of a certain number of cubic feet of air. It had a huge leaden roof, tapering to a point and topped by a weather-vane, and from one side, like some unpleasant growth, there protruded a conservatory, whose only good point was that it deflected attention for a few seconds from the dome and minarets. But the houseboat at the foot of its meadows offered the only safe place in the locality to dive into deep water or swim in the nude.

[Authorities such as Norman Murphy, in *In Search of Blandings* point to Château Impney, near Droitwich, as the probable source of this monstrosity. Wodehouse spent several periods at the Château and would have had plenty of time to study the gory details.] **(SUM ch1,2)**

WALSINGFORD PARVA: the village closest to **Walsingford Hall**, with a Jubilee Watering Trough and the **Goose and Gander** pub within its city limits. **(SUM ch7)**

WALT: the plug-ugly guard who fell out with **Dickon** over love for a kitchen-maid. **(TMU-SAG)**

WALTON HEATH: a golf club where **Sir Mallaby Marlowe** played in a weekly foursome, and the scene of one of the rounds of **mental golf** played by **Sam Marlowe** whilst concealed in a cupboard at **Windles**. **(GOB ch12)**

WANTAGH, Lord: **Appleby** had buttled for him and his good lady, and contrary to the general belief it was Appleby who got the treasure, in the form of the Wantagh diamonds. **(DBB ch2)**

WAPSHOTT, P P: a name temporarily assigned to **J B Duff** by **Joss Weatherby**, together with responsibility for the pressed beef and pâté de foie gras department. **(QUS ch4)**

WARD, Sergeant: was a tough, formidable officer who appeared to be hewn from the living rock. He had a wife with a bundle of nerves, a Scottie and an ambition to be a movie star. **(TOR ch16)**

WARDEN, Eugene: a delightful, erratic, irresponsible man, as deadly as a Upas tree to his familiars. He drifted aimlessly though amiably through life, funded by a brother-in-law whose sole requirement was that he promised to stay out of England. He hoped his daughter **Ruth** would marry a rich, open-handed young man. **(TMU-RIE)**

WARDEN, Ruth: the daughter of **Eugene** and secretary-clerk to **M Gandinot** in **Roville**. She consistently disclaimed any belief in affinities. Possessed of grey eyes, she was dark, and had a shocking temper, but once she thought **George Vince** was poor she felt differently about him. **(TMU-RIE)**

WARNER BROTHERS: **John McGee** was reputed to know how many there were. **(Ellery-MBD)**

WASHBURN, Bryant: a film actor, one of whose efforts was watched by **Looney Biddle** and his girl-friend, but Looney concluded that he was a pill. **(IOA ch14)**

WASHINGTON: when it came to the theatre, it would take anything. **(TLW ch17)**

WASHINGTON, George (1732-1799): like **Jill Mariner**, he told the truth. **(JTR ch13)**

WASP OF FATE, The: London's first wasp, appearing on May 12th, landed on **Stanwood Cobbold**'s coat, thereby offering **Shorty**'s large, flat hand an opportunity to make an introduction. **(SPF ch5)**

WATERALL: a young, clean-shaven man with a cold, impassive face and a vulturine countenance, he reported the trial of **John Benyon** for the *New York Chronicle* and became their London correspondent. **(MLF-OTN)**

WATERLOO STATION: an austere cavern which at the beginning of the Holiday Rush sneered at glorious weather, remaining sombre in its customary gloom. **(HOW ch2)**

WATSON, Dr: the inferiority he felt when listening to **Sherlock Holmes** explain his methods was familiar to **Ferdie** on hearing **Appleby**. **(DBB ch5)**

Having become every bit as frequent a reference point for a particular type of individual as Jeeves, or Bertie Wooster, or Lord Emsworth, it was inevitable that Watson should also have attributed to him participation in conversations outside the actual experience provided by his creator.

"When I first got here, you know, it seemed to me the only thing to do was to round up a merry old detective and put the matter in his hands, like they do in stories. *You* know! Ring at the bell. 'And this, if I mistake not, Watson, is my client now.'"

(JTR ch13)

WATTS, A R K: once played for Sussex. **(NSE-HTU)**

WAUGH-BONNER, Everard: a long, stringy, deaf septuagenarian who had lived in the Malay States, and clock-golfed assiduously when not engaged in preparing his daily report on the mice in his bedroom. **(SUM ch1,2,17,23)**

WAUGH, Evelyn Arthur St John (1903-1966): Russell Clutterbuck was reminded of ... by **Jeff d'Escrignon**'s novel. **(FRL ch8)**

WAUKEESY SHOE, the: advertisements for ... were illustrated by **Reginald Sellers** **(TMU-MUP)**

WAVENEY, Lady Julia: the name found inside a book belonging to an elderly lady who looked like an aunt and disapproved of her **companion** gambling. **(TMU-TTM)**

WAVENEY, Lady Julia's companion: visited the casino against her employer's wishes, and asked **George Balmer** to place her stake on 8. The fact that he placed it on 3, thus converting a winning bet into a loser, was overlooked in the chaotic conditions which prevailed thereafter, matters only being restored to some semblance of peace after the two of them had agreed to marry and, as an afterthought, to exchange names. **(TMU-TTM)**

WEARING OF THE GREEN, The: a lugubrious song as a rule but, when rendered by English or American police officers wending their way home with theatre tickets for self and wife, one with all the joyousness of a march. **(TUW-MIS; BurrMcK-MIS)**

WEASEL: a small, sharp-nosed individual who looked like a pimply weasel and when he stared at the dishevelled **Bulpitt** every pimple seemed alive with curiosity. He verbally attacked **Jane Abbott** as she sat in her car with Bulpitt, and caused a scene with a man in a bowler hat and a woman in a cricket cap. **(SUM ch19)**

WEATHERBY, Jocelyn Parmalee (Joss): a young buzzer in the best Wodehouse tradition, who had been named Parmalee after a godfather and had his inheritance converted to his own use by his trustee lawyer. As an artist he at least temporarily sold his soul

Joss Weatherby extracts a custard apple from the display

to the commercial devil, being employed in the advertising department of **Duff and Trotter** preparing posters for **Paramount Ham**. He was a lean, cheerful, loose-limbed young man with a frsh attitude and the nerve of an army mule. He fell for **Sally Fairmile** at first sight and was inspired by her presence to throw **J B Duff** out of his own office. Having been sacked as a result, despite having saved the tyrant's life at **Easthampton**, he became valet to **Howard Steptoe** before returning to Paramount as Head of the Art Department. **(QUS)**

WEATHERSTONEHOPE, Duke of: had a name pronounced 'Wop' and an ancestral castle. **(TMU-SAG)**

WEAVER, Clarice: the leading lady of the *The Girl From Brighton* company sang badly even when the song was an inspirational one concerning 'the moon' and 'June'. She was an indifferent actress who was hard to please, never backward in showing it, and liable to go into hysterics and resign if interrupted while singing *My Honolulu Queen*. **(MLF-BTB)**

WEBSTER: a dictionary to which journalists had had to refer after their interviews with **Grace Marlowe**. **(Strand-PAW)**

WEBSTER 'ALL: the New York venue for a fête of artists, a sort of prototype for the **Festival of the Saint** at **St Rocque**. **(HOW ch3)**

WEBSTER, Montagu (or Montague): **J Rufus Bennett**'s dignified and intellectual-looking valet withdrew like a duke leaving a royal presence, not actually walking backwards, but giving every impression of doing so. He handed in his notice for being cursed and sworn at, but liked **Billie Bennett**, and knew well the lane where she had assignations, for he had escorted **Miss Trimble** there twice. It was the *Digit* paperback edition which cast doubt upon the correct spelling of his Christian name, trying both 'Montague' and 'Montagu' within twenty lines at the end of chapter 15. **(GOB ch10,15; GOB (Digit) ch15)**

WEEKLY ROOTER: a Detroit newspaper which interviewed **Jacob Dodson**[2] about the Tigers' prospects. **(Colliers-PAP)**

WEEKS: the butler to **Peter's father**, who was instructed to arrange **Fido**'s execution. **(MLF-BIS)**

WEEMS, Henry: a grave, solid, young man, the junior partner of the New York legal firm of **Kelly, Dubinsky, Wix, Weems and**

Bassinger, who was devoted to the interests of the **Trent** sisters, and especially to those of **Jo**, to whom he issued the invitation to call him 'Hen'. **(FRL ch1)**

WEILER, Jost: thought **Stauffacher** and **Tell** had each expressed themselves well.**(WTT ch4,9)**

WEINSTEIN: a red-haired Shriner in the Real Estate business who paid for a crack about the Californian climate with a sock from **J Wellington Gedge**. **(HOW ch6)**

WELLINGFORD: the nearest town to **Mallow Hall**, with the Bond library, 4 tea shoppes in the High Street, the Bond Hospital and a 12.20 express to Paddington. **(DBB ch2,4)**

WELLINGFORD RACES: **Horace Appleby**'s objective when he was mugged and rescued by **Ada Cootes**. **(DBB ch1)**

WELLINGFORD WOMEN'S ASSOCIATION: was planning to erect a statue in memory of **Sir Hugo Bond** in the town market square. **(DBB ch2)**

WELLINGTON, Arthur Wellesley, first Duke of (1769-1852): his adage "When in doubt, retire and dig yourself in" was interpreted by **Eustace Hignett** as advising that one should subside within one's bed and pull the sheets over one's head. After the Battle of Waterloo, he had probably been as pompous as **Shorty** after seeing off his daughter **Adela**. **(GOB ch17; SPF ch23)**

WELSH, Arthur: took his troubles to a heart specialist, but found that doctors could disagree. **(TMU-WDD)**

WENTWORTH: one of five acquaintances of **Jane Abbott** not known to **Joe Vanringham**. **(SUM ch5)**

WERNI: a huntsman hit by **Friesshardt**'s pike. **(WTT ch9)**

WERTHEIMER, Isadore: production manager at the **Bigger and Better Studio**, who addressed **Stiffy** as 'Mr Stiffy'. **(Aldin-GOW)**

WEST, Gerald Godfrey Francis ('Jerry'): a nephew of **Crispin Scrope** and the beneficiary of a trust created by his late father and run by **Willoughby S**, Jerry was a skilled cartoonist who occupied himself whilst on jury duty by sketching counsel and others in court. This devotion to his art brought him to **Jane Hunnicutt**, a fellow juror and genuine fan of his work, and he dated her while overlooking the fact that he was engaged to **Vera Upshaw**. He lived in a street off the King's Road when he was not practising his golf or playing in the US Amateur Championship, for which he qualified with a handicap of plus 2. **(TGI)**

WEST, Joseph ('Joe'): **Jerry**'s late father, who perhaps had sound reasons for not letting his son touch his capital until he reached thirty. Joe had been a total loss as a young man, having married a cinema usherette with a taste for drink when he was 22 and had become a widower two years later. He appeared to undergo some sort of conversion after that, marrying **Jerry**'s mother around the age of thirty and settling down to becoming a successful businessman, manufacturing chinaware up north. **(TGI ch2,10)**

WEST, Mae (1892-1980): the photo in **April June**'s living-room inscribed "Fondest love from Mae" had presumably been sent by her. She had wowed them in *Elsie Dinsmore* and was rumoured to be considering making *Alice in Wonderland* as her next picture. Had **Jane Abbott** been of the same build, she could not have been hoisted gently into the driver's seat of her car by **Joe Vanringham**. **(LAG ch21,24; SUM ch17; Pearson-LAG; This Week-LAG)**

WESTBROOK, Herbert: co-author of *Not George Washington*.

WESTERN UNION: in the days before multi-media information technology processors, companies such as the ... were the natural means by which singing birthday telegrams were sent to English peers by distant but sycophantic American relatives. **(SPF ch1)**

WESTINGHOUSE: **Vera Pym** won £100 by backing ... for the Ascot Gold Cup at 100-8. **(QUS ch13)**

WESTMACOTT, Cyril: see **Norcross, Minna**

WESTMINSTER KENNEL SHOW: into which there was no point in entering a mongrel. **(TGI ch5)**

WESTON, Alice: a small, quiet, rather pretty chorus girl in the show *The Girl from Broadway*, who played the part of a Japanese girl during the rendition of *My Honolulu Queen* and declined **Henry Rice**'s proposal because she was determined to marry into the profession. **(MLF-BTB)**

WESTON, Lord Frederick: stayed at the **Hôtel Cercle de la Méditerranée**. **(TMU-MMT)**

WESTON, Genevieve: married out of the theatrical profession, and rarely saw her commercial traveller husband for more than five minutes a year. **(MLF-BTB)**

WESTON, Jack: Eddy Moore asked **Mary Hill** to send him a copy of a letter which **Joe Rendal** would be writing to Jack the following Thursday. **(TMU-TFD)**

WEST POINT: another of the college football teams against which **Packy Franklyn** played for **Yale**. **(Colliers-HOWpt2)**

WESTWARD HO: the scene of one of the rounds of **mental golf** played by **Sam Marlowe** whilst concealed in a cupboard at **Windles**. **(GOB ch 17)**

WETHERBY, Gladys: the poetess niece of **Col Pashley-Drake**, who lived in Garbidge Mews, Fulham and was engaged to **Lancelot Bingley**. Her face and figure were those of the better type of pin-up girl, featuring starlike eyes the colour of the Mediterranean on a good day, a slender figure and a little freckle on the tip of her nose. Only two things told against her: an unfortunate tendency to be imperious, and her output of six sonnets, a ballade and half a pound of *vers libre*. **(PLP-GCS; Playboy-GCS)**

WETHERBY, Mrs: the late mother of **Gladys** and sister of **Francis Pashley-Drake**, whom she had made trustee of the money left to Gladys. **(PLP-GCS)**

WHALEN, Grover:

> "There must be a certain code in these matters. Either a man is Grover Whalen or he is not Grover Whalen. If he is not, he has no right to wear a moustache like that."

(QUS ch10)

*WHAT'LL I DO***:** the sort of tune to which **Sam Bulpitt** would think out his best coups. **(SUM ch15)**

WHEELER, James B: an artist friend of **Archie Moffam** whom he met at the **Pen-and-Ink Club**, and engaged as an artist's model for the August number of an unnamed magazine. He made his own hooch, which caused an explosion over, but not in, Archie's head. James was engaged to **Alice Wigmore**. **(IOA ch4,25)**

*WHEN IT WAS LURID***: James Cloyster**'s first novel, writing as the **Rev Mr Hatton**, which caused no less than a furore. **(NGW ptII ch20)**

WHEN THE HEART IS YOUNG: the title of a picture which by rights should have been called *Venus*. **(IOA ch25)**

WHERE DID YOU GET THAT HAT?: a catch-phrase invented by the **Swiss** which they would not drop in a hurry. **(WTT ch7)**

WHISKERS: a boon companion of **Shorty**, to whose ingrowing depression he added by becoming sick of a fever. **(SPF ch3)**

WHISTLER, Benny: was expected by some to beat **Battling Tuke**. **(TAS ch1)**

WHISTLER, Canon: said a lot about hell fire. **(TGI ch11)**

WHITE CITY: a night spent there by **Henry** should be a bygone left as a bygone! **(MLF-MOM)**

WHITE RABBIT, the: **Kate Trent**'s news, imparted to **Old Nick**, sent him scurrying off to tell **Jefferson d'Escrignon** rather like ... in *Alice in Wonderland*. But whether it scurried off to see the Duchess, or the Queen, seems to be uncertain. **(HOW ch16; USHOW ch16; FRL ch6)**

WHITE ROSES: a book by **Edith Butler**, dramatised for the stage by **Owen Bentley**, which was successful in New York (for two seasons), Chicago and had three companies on the road in the USA. It was less popular in London, coming off soon after opening at the **Piccadilly Theatre**. **(TMU-POM)**

WHITE SOX: came over to London to play the **Giants** at **Chelsea Football Ground**. **(MLF-OTN)**

WHITE STAR: a shipping line by which some of **Freddie Rooke**'s acquaintances swore. **(JTR ch6)**

WHITE THISTLE: what **Eggy** thought he was drinking (see also, **Black Ruin**). **(LAG ch9)**

WHITTAKER, Prudence: was secretary to **Sir Buckstone Abbott**, twice fiancée of **Tubby Vanringham** but the plaintiff in a law suit against him for breach of promise. She was tall, slender and elegant with a tiptilted, almost perky nose and a cold, crisp voice. Born in Kensington, Prudence had trained in business college and could not have been spoken to like a Dutch Uncle even if she had turned out to be both Dutch and male. She took a strong anti-American line on pronunciation, for example trying to insist on 'tomarto' rather than 'tomayto'. She found herself caught in Tubby's room at the Hall when he returned from a swim clothed only in embarrassment, which helped to break down the barriers which had been thrown up between the two, and she then played two leading cameo roles: first in capturing **Adrian Peake** after he had escaped from **Tanner**'s room, and secondly by grabbing **Princess von und zu Dwornitzchek** when she tried to assault her. Overall, she could best be described as a spunky young lady, who will probably manage to control the occasionally errant young Tubby as they address the challenges of life. **(SUM)**

WHOKNOWS, Mr: called **Jill Mariner** "one of the most charming and attractive of Society belles" when writing about her engagement in the *Morning Searchlight*. **(Grand-JTR)**

"WHY GIRLS GO WRONG": one of the questions to which, on paper, **Blair Eggleston** could probably have supplied the answer. **(Colliers-HOWpt9)**

WIDGEON, Joe: the partner of **Phil Brown** in the New York jazz-and-hocum team. **(JTR ch9)**

WIDGEON SEVEN: a two-seater beloved of **Imogen Abbott**. **(SUM ch1)**

WIDGERY: his best-seller on *Nisi Prius Evidence* was considered highly improving, and as interesting to **Sir Mallaby Marlowe** as some novels. **(GOB ch12)**

WIGAN: where **Max Faucitt**, **Arthur Moseby** and an impresario's bird opened and closed in two days. **(TAS ch5)**

WIGGINS v BLUEBODY: a test case which should be consulted by anybody interested in the application of the law to the problems caused by stray cats. **(MLF-BFL)**

WIGGLE-WOGGLE: a feature at **Luna Park** on which **Arthur Welsh** displayed light-hearted abandon. **(TMU-WDD)**

WIGMORE, Alice: the fiancée of **James B Wheeler**, who was tickled to death when she heard that her painting of *Venus* had been stolen. To the joy of the world, she gave up painting after being taught the infinitely less harmful sport of golf. **(IOA ch25)**

WILBERFORCE, Prof Snyder: was engaged in writing a great work, *The History of the Cat in Ancient Egypt*, on which he had so far spent just two of the twelve years he expected the project to take. He appointed **Algy Wynbrace** as his secretary to assist him with his researches. **(LHJ-FKA)**

WILBERFORCE v BAYLISS: a *cause célèbre* which in **Henry Mortimer**'s expert opinion established the legal precedent that every dog was entitled to one free bite. **(GOB ch10)**

WILBRAHAM'S HOTEL: a Cheltenham establishment from which **Owen Bentley** sent his manuscript of the play *White Roses*. **(TMU-POM)**

WILBURFLOSSES: the sort of people **Beatrice Chavender** would make **J B Duff** have dinner with after they were married. **(QUS ch18)**

WILDCAT WIX: whaled the tar out of **J B Duff** at the **American Legion Stadium** in Hollywood. **(QUS ch7)**

WILDERSHAM, Lady: on hearing that the **Ringwood**s were in town, she instructed her husband to send **Algy Wynbrace** round at once to meet **Marion Ringwood**. **(LHJ-FKA)**

WILDERSHAM, Lord: the uncle of **Algy Wynbrace**, whose title was pronounced 'Wing' to rhyme with 'Chiddingfold'. He wrote *America and its People*. **(LHJ-FKA)**

WILD ROSE, The: a new piece by **Gerald Foster** which was such a failure that its first-night audience were upset at wasting \$2.75 per head (including tax). **(TAS ch14)**

WILHELMINA (or JANE) SHANNON SPECIAL: mild, or liquid dynamite, depending on your point of view. **(TOR ch10)**

WILLARD, Anthony: the father of **Jill**, he enjoyed investing in strange commercial (or, more strictly, uncommercial) ventures, but their associated problems switched off his natural exuberance as with a tap. **(DBB ch5,9)**

WILLARD, Jill: the daughter of the impecunious west country squire, she trained as a nurse and after working for the **Finch**es while **Appleby** buttled there, she obtained a post with **Isabel Bond**. Being keen on mystery novels, she became suspicious when Appleby reappeared in her life, but such considerations did not prevent her from organising a break-in to the **Bond Bank**'s safe or from proposing to **Mike Bond** when he seemed to be reluctant to take the initiative. **(DBB)**

P. G. WODEHOUSE
REMSENBURG, LONG ISLAND

July 13.1958

Dear Mr Claghorn.

        Fancy you having got hold of a William
Tell Told Again! It was written over fifty years ago
at the time when I was game to write anything that would
help pay the rent. If I remember, they sent me the
pictures and gave me ten pounds for writing a story round
them!

        My books for boys - all published by A & C
Black, 4 Soho Square, London W - are:-

           The Pothunters
           Tales of St Austin's
           The Gold Bat
           The Head of Kay's
           The White Feather
           Mike
           Psmith In The City
           Psmith Journalist
           A Prefect's Uncle

but I don't think they are still in print.

        The White Hope, if I remember, was the
pulp magazine serial title of the book subsequently
published over here as Their Mutual Child and in England
as The Coming Of Bill. It's not one of the ones I'm
proud of.

        Yours sincerelu

P. G. Wodehouse

William Tell: *the reason why it was told again*

WILLARD, William: Anthony's brother and Jill's uncle, he had powers like those of **the Lady of Shalott**. **(DBB ch9)**

WILLIAMS, Bert: **Billie Bennett** could not distinguish between imitations of ... and those of **Frank Tinney**. **(GOB ch7)**

WILLIAMS, George Washington: a talented Ethiopian gentleman who performed the tap-drumming speciality at the **Flower Garden**. **(TAS ch16)**

WILLIAMS, Jane: the sister of **Mr Preston** who had been parlour-maid at the Old Rectory in Millbourne, and after marrying **Williams** had stayed there. **(TMU-STW)**

WILLIAMS, Mr: his cottage became a *salon* as a result of **Sally Preston**'s presence, but the extra bodily warmth in the front room did nothing for his chronic rheumatism. **(TMU-STW)**

WILLIAMSON: one of the many New York dwellers not known to **Nelly Bryant**. **(JTR ch6)**

WILLIAM TELL: **Kate Putnam**, acting out ..., shot a rabbit from the top of **Oily Carlisle**'s head. **(HOW ch17)**

WILLIE: a species of acolyte who, in the dim religious light of **Beale's Auction Rooms**, New York City, was adjured to turn the pedestal around slowly while the auctioneer, playing for time, recounted the adventure of a young lady named Lou. **(IOA ch10)**

WILLIE, Boston: **Franklyn Bivatt** was mistaken for the safe-blower of this name. **(Strand-JOW)**

WILLIE IN THE WILDERNESS: a story written and successfully dramatised by **Rutherford Maxwell**, with **Peggy Norton**'s help, to star **Winfield Knight**. **(TMU-INA)**

WILLOUGHBY: lived on the eighth floor at 18E57th Street, New York. **(JTR ch9)**

WILLOUGHBY, Ernest: his role for the Jockey Club might be vulnerable to an application from **P C Perkins**. **(NGW ptII ch8)**

WILLOUGHBYS: the misguided family who introduced **Adrian Peake** to **Jane Abbott**. **(SUM ch2)**

WILSON, Thomas Woodrow (1856-1924): one of the names given by a male guest in Room 618 of the **Hotel Cosmopolis** following a sing-song and a raid. He also featured on **Aubrey Devine**'s list of the seven most prominent men in the United States. **(IOA ch19; VanFair-AAI)**

WILSON'S: American monthly magazine which took a story from **Rutherford Maxwell**, entitled *Willie In The Wilderness*. **(TMU-INA)**

WIMPOLE, Dick: one of **Algy Martyn**'s friends who knew **Jill Mariner**, thought she was a topper and felt strongly about **Underhill**'s breaking of the engagement. **(JTR ch8)**

WINCH, Gladys: a square, wholesome, good-humoured actress with freckles, deep grey eyes and a serious face who first engaged herself to **Fillmore Nicholas** and then married him. She appeared in *The Primrose Way* with memorable lines such as "Did you ring, madam?", and accused **Mabel Hobson** of removing a prop. **(TAS)**

WINCH & CLUTTERBUCK: the publishing house in which **J Russell Clutterbuck** was a partner. **(FRL ch1)**

WINCHELL, Walter: **Smedley Cork** threatened to write to him about **Adela**'s theft of the **Carmen Flores** diary. **(TOR ch8)**

WINCHESTER: the public school where **Freddie Rooke** fagged for **Derek Underhill**. **(JTR ch1)**

WINCHESTER, Mabel: blessed with eyes like twin stars shining in a clear sky on a summer-night, teeth like pearls, hair a lovely brown like leaves in autumn. She sang in the chorus to help pay for the education of her little brother, and was all set to become **Bill Brewster**'s intended if he could ever pluck up courage to introduce her to his father. It scarcely needed the combination of crimson hair and the acumen of **Lucille Moffam** to discern that, beneath the phoney manner, she was a sly, creepy, slinky, feline vampire to whom **Reggie van Tuyl** was welcome. **(IOA ch17)**

WINDLEHURST: the town closest to **Windles**, with a pub and Green's Grocery Store. **(GOB ch15)**

WINDLES: the seat of the **Hignett** family for many years, it had shady walks, a silver lake, noble elms, lawns rivalling those of an Oxford college and old, grey stone walls. **Mrs Hignett** held it in trust for her son **Eustace** until he married. People, particularly Americans, unsuccessfully pestered her to let it, but Eustace obliged Messrs **Bennett** and **Mortimer** in his mother's absence. The name may have been taken from Windlesham, the country house belonging to Sir Arthur Conan Doyle, to which PGW had been a regular visitor for cricket weeks. **(GOB ch1,10)**

WINTER, Roland: a tall, thin nephew of **Mervyn Spink**, with a slight squint, funny-shaped mouth and red hair, who was due to play the junior **Rossiter** in *The Great Spanish Stamp Swindle*, a one-act play by his uncle, due to have its only performance at **Beevor Castle** on 13th May. The première was called off due to the indispositon of the leading performer, ie the fact that he was known to **Cosmo Blair**. **(SPF ch10)**

WINTERBOTHAM, James: of Pleasant Cottage, Rhodesia Terrace, Stockwell, was advised that **Stanley Briggs** had no opening for his daughter. **(NGW ch25)**

WISE MAN: in days of yore, anyone who was not a perfect bonehead could set up as one, and get away with it if he lived in a forest and grew a white beard. **(TMU-SAG)**

WISTARIA: where **Red Dan Magee** had a hotel. **(PallMall-MLB)**

WITCHING WAVES: where **Skipper Shute** had lost **Arthur Welsh**. **(TMU-WDD)**

WITHERS, Mrs: the cook at **Windles**. **(GOB ch15)**

WITHERSPOON: a grocer who, together with his wife and four children Alice, Bertram, Daisy and Percy, threatened to invade **Lady Batrice Bracken**'s compartment at **Waterloo Station** but quailed before the eye of **Packy Franklin**. **(HOW ch2)**

WODEHOUSE, Ethel (1885-1984): the dedicatee of *Jill the Reckless*. She was joined with the author and others as the dedicator of *Hot Water* to **Maureen O'Sullivan**.

WODEHOUSE, Leonora (1904-1944): was also one of dedicators of *Hot Water*.

WODGER, D C L: it remained a moot point as to whether he fielded at square leg or extra cover for Gloucestershire in 1904. **(NSE-HTU)**

WOLVES OF THE BOWERY: an American film which had been seen by **John Peters**. **(GOB ch8)**

WOODWARD, Mr: of Chelsea, preserved his skill despite advanced years. **(MLF-MOM)**

WORBLES: the Dorsetshire seat of the **Earl of Stableford**. **(HOW ch2)**

WORDSWORTH, William (1770-1850): when he saw a flower, he experienced thoughts too deep for words, but his heart leaped on beholding a rainbow in the sky. **(TOR ch9; DBB ch8)**

WORK! WORK! WORK!

> Oh, I think a man's crazy who's idle and lazy,
>> I pity the people who shirk.
> It's a pound to a shilling, you'll smile if you're willing
>> To work! work! work!
>
> If you don't see the beauty of doing your duty
>> Your happiness stops with a jerk
> So I counsel you, dunce, to start learning at once,
>> And work! work! work!

(Sunday-IDL)

WORLD WELL LOST, The: a novelette familiar to **Sidney Chibnall**, in which situations similar to that described by **Joss Weatherby** occurred. **(QUS ch7)**

WORM I' THE ROOT: a book by **Blair Eggleston** which seemed to express sentiments similar to those of *Offal*. **(HOW ch14)**

WORSHIPFUL DRY-SALTER COMPANY, The: **Derek Underhill** attended the semi-annual banquet of the ... in the City of London, acting as understudy for one of the speakers. **(JTR ch8)**

WOTHERSPOON: a friend of **Ralph Tuxton**. **(TMU-BAC)**

WOW! WOW!: the sort of title expected by New York critics to be attached to a **Wally Mason** show. **(JTR ch4)**

WUNCH: how the only Detroit critic to mention **Gladys Winch**'s performance in *The Primrose Way* spelt her surname. **(TAS ch8)**

WYCHERLY, Amanda: an elderly reporter of the *Los Angeles Tribune*, to whom **RH(JC)** and **RH(TF)** confessed all. **(Pearson-LAG; ThisWeek-LAG)**

WYCHERLY, Pomona: of the *Los Angeles Chronicle*, to whom **RH(JC)** also told the truth about his situation. **(LAG ch21)**

WYNBRACE, Hon Algernon: this 24-year-old Old Etonian with a pleasing countenance, amiable temperament and fondness for musical comedy amounting almost to an obsession, was inclined by nature to look on the negative side. He was encouraged by his family (**Lord** and **Lady Wildersham** and the **Dowager Duchess of Shropshire**) to make up to **Marion Ringwood** but his dislike for cats (let alone that for oysters) and his attempt to have Marion's pet **Alexander** consigned to the wastes of the **Cats' House at Battersea** was sufficient burden for his cause to be lost. **(LHJ-FKA)**

X-RAY EYES:

> There before her, looking more sinister than ever, stood the lunatic Peters; and there was an ominous bulge in his right coat-pocket which to her excited senses betrayed the presence of the revolver. What Jno Peters was, as a matter of fact, carrying in his right coat-pocket was a bag of mixed chocolates which he had purchased in Windlehurst. But Billie's eyes, though bright, had no X-ray quality. Her simple creed was that, if Jno Peters bulged at any point, that bulge must be caused by a pistol. She screamed, and backed against the wall. Her whole acquaintance with Jno Peters had been one constant backing against walls.

(GOB ch15)

YALE: the *alma mater* of **Packy Franklin**, for which he played football, despite **J Wellington Gedge**'s stated belief that they didn't play football there, only beanbags. But platoons of human mastodons were prepared to die for the college against Princeton. **(HOW ch2; FRL ch7)**

YALE REVIEW: carried convincing articles about the 'Reformed Criminal'. **(TOR ch4)**

YE BLUE BIRD: the sort of investment which **Sally Nicholas** tended to prefer as a home for her money, as compared to a theatrical performance. **(TAS ch6)**

YE BONNIE BRIAR-BUSH FARM: where **Henry Mills** first met **Minnie Hill**, a spot which featured a Lovers' Leap, a Grotto, a 5-hole golf course with goats among the hazards, and a silvery lake, but no **mosquitoes**. **(MLF-TLF)**

YE CORNER SHOPPE: like **Ye Blue Bird**, the sort of investment which **Sally Nicholas** was inclined to favour. **(TAS ch6)**

YEOVIL: the destination of the 4.21 from **Waterloo**. **(HOW ch2)**

YONKERS: what are they? **(MLF-CRH)**

YOST, Charlie: a Chicago gunman who had once been a member of the **Appleby Gang**, but had lost his position (and his share of the last job's earnings) for carrying a gun. A pleasant, soft-spoken individual with an inoffensive face and eyes hidden by large horn-rimmed spectacles, Charlie subscribed to homes for unwanted cats and dogs but claimed to feel nude without his gun, with which he gave pleasure to **Gussie Mortlake**. Until, that is, he was physically threatened by **Basher Evans**. **(DBB ch1,7,8)**

YOUNG, Brigham (1801-1877): since once he had started marrying he just kept on marrying everything in sight, he would have taken in his stride the prospect of a second simultaneous betrothal or the receipt of a letter from a young lady, announcing she would marry him. **(TOR ch21; FRL ch9; TGI ch6)**

YOUNG KELLY: a middle-weight challenger who was slapped with a writ by **Sam Bulpitt** in his own home, even though he was dining with **Cyril**, **Genevieve** and **Mike**. **(SUM ch14)**

YOUNG MAN, GET UP EARLY: yet another publication of which **Roland Bean** was a walking edition. **(TMU-MMM)**

YOUNGER NOVELISTS: their whole tone tended to be that of disillusioned, sardonic philanderers who had drunk the wine-cup of illicit love to its dregs but were always ready to fill up again and have another. **(HOW ch14)**

YSEULT: was described as a 'Giant with three heads'. **(TMU-SAG)**

YVONNE: a daughter of **Earl Dorm of the Hills**, the only plain or homely girl ever known to have visited **Camelot**. She suggested to **Sir Agravaine** and **Roderick the Runt** that they should fly from her castle, but they kept their feet firmly on the ground. **(TMU-SAG; Escapade-RTR)**

ZABRISKI, Patrolman: one of the policemen who attended the **Hotel Delehay** in support of **Sergeant O'Toole**. **(Ellery-MBD)**

ZAGORIN, Elmer B: the Night Club King, who refused to break into a fortune worth $50 million in order to pay a $40 bill for hair restorer, and defeated **Sam Bulpitt** by dying of a weak heart after being chased up and down the country. He left his fortune to Sam, saying he hadn't had so much fun in years. **(SUM ch14)**

ZANUCK, Mr [Darryl Francis] (b1902): a name not so laughingly assigned to the police by **Adela Cork** when they preferred to gossip about the movie business rather than investigate her burglary. **(TOR ch16)**

ZIEGFELD, Florenz (or Florenx) (1869-1932): one of very few who could have surpassed **Toots Fauntleroy** in the matter of vitriolic cables. **(TOR ch18; Colliers-PTR)**

ZINC SPELTERS: the entry in the *Classified Telephone Directory* under this heading suggested the possibility of a new career to **Joss Weatherby. (QUS ch20)**

ZIZZBAUM, I J: the strong, silent, gloomy dentist to whom **Reggie Havershot** took his aching wisdom tooth, and whose part in the history of travel in the fourth dimension may well be overlooked by posterity. He had the common sense to employ, however briefly, **Ann Bannister** as his doorkeeper. **(LAG ch4,5; Pearson-LAG; ThisWeek-LAG)**

ZOLA, Emile (1840-1902): **Priaulx** said there was no need to be so ...-esque, a reflection, presumably, of that author's skill in tackling questions of gloom. **(JTR ch8; TMU-MWD)**

A COMPREHENSIVE LIST OF DEDICATIONS IN BOOKS BY P G WODEHOUSE

With most texts reproduced

Title	US or UK	Year	Dedication
The Pothunters	UK	1902	Joan, Effie and Ernestine Bowes-Lyon
A Prefect's Uncle	UK	1903	W Townend
Tales of St Austin's	UK	1903	Ad Matrem
The Gold Bat	UK	1904	That Prince of Slackers, Herbert Westbrook
William Tell Told Again	UK	1904	Biddy O'Sullivan for a Christmas Present
The Head of Kay's	UK/US	1905/22	My Father
Love Among the Chickens	UK	1906	Sir Bargrave and Lady Deane
Love Among the Chickens	UK	1921	W Townend (Extensive text)
The White Feather	UK	1907	My Brother Dick
Not George Washington	UK	1907	Ella King-Hall
Mike	UK	1909	Alan Durand
A Gentleman of Leisure	UK (Alston Rivers edition)	1910	Herbert Westbrook, without whose never failing advice, help, and encouragement this book would have been finished in half the time.
A Gentleman of Leisure	UK (Herbert Jenkins)	1910	To Douglas Fairbanks who many years ago played 'Jimmy' in the dramatized version of this novel.
Psmith in the City	UK	1910	Leslie Havergal Bradshaw
The Prince and Betty	UK	1912	Ellaline Terriss from The Hermit
Uneasy Money	US	1917	My Wife, Bless Her
Piccadilly Jim	US	1918	To my step-daughter Lenora – conservatively speaking the most wonderful child on earth.
A Damsel in Distress	US	1919	Maud and Ivan Caryll
Indiscretions of Archie	UK/US	1921	B W King-Hall (Extensive text)
The Clicking of Cuthbert	UK	1922	John Henrie, Pat Rogie and Robert Robertson
The Adventures of Sally	UK	1922	George Grossmith (Extensive text)
Leave It To Psmith	UK/US	1923	My daughter Leonora, Queen of her species
Golf Without Tears	US	1924	John Henrie, Pat Rogie and R T B Denby (differs from Clicking of Cuthbert)

Ukridge/ *He Rather Enjoyed It*	UK/ US	1924/ 1925	Dedicated with esteem and gratitude to Old Bill Townend, My Friend from Boyhood's Days who first introduced me to Stanley Featherstonehaugh Ukridge
Bill the Conqueror	UK/US	1924/25	My Mother and Father
Carry On, Jeeves	UK/US	1925/27	Bernard Le Strange
Sam the Sudden	UK	1925	Edgar Wallace
The Heart of a Goof/ *Divots*	UK/ US	1926/ 1927	To my daughter Leonora without whose never-failing sympathy and encouragement this book would have been finished in half the time
Meet Mr Mulliner	UK/US	1927/28	The Earl of Oxford and Asquith
Money For Nothing	UK	1928	Ian Hay Beith
Summer Lightning	UK	1929	Denis Mackail, Author of *Greenery Street*, *The Flower Show* and other books I wish I had written
Very Good, Jeeves	UK	1930	E Phillips Oppenheim
If I Were You	UK	1931	Guy Bolton
Louder and Funnier	UK	1932	George Blake. A Splendid Fellow and Very Sound on Pekes. But he should guard against the tendency to claim that his Peke fights Alsatians. Mine is the only one that does this.
Hot Water	UK/US	1932	Maureen O'Sullivan with love from Ethel Leonora Miss Winks John-John and the Author
Right Ho Jeeves	UK	1934	Raymond Needham QC, with affection and admiration
Money in the Bank	Tauchnitz	1949	Bert Haskins, with deep affection from the author
Angel Cake	US	1952	To the onlie begetter of these insuing sonnets Mr G S K
Bertie Wooster Sees It Through	US	1954	Peter Schwed (Extensive text)
Stiff Upper Lip, Jeeves	US	1963	David Jasen
The Brinkmanship of Galahad Threepwood	US	1964	Scott Meredith, Prince of Literary Agents and best of friends
The Purloined Paperwight	US	1967	Peter Schwed, best of publishers
Pearls, Girls and Monty Bodkin	UK	1972	To Sheran with love
Bachelors Anonymous	US	1974	Peter Schwed, as always

THE EVOLUTION OF LAUGHING GAS

The evolution of *Laughing Gas* demonstrates how an experienced professional writer can expand a plot from the length required (30,000 words) for a novelette commissioned for the purpose of serialisation into a full-length novel.

It was written for *This Week*, a syndicated supplement which became part of the weekend edition of many daily papers, including for example *The Milwaukee Journal* and the *New York Herald Tribune*, and appeared in six instalments. (In England it was serialised in just three instalments in *Pearson's*, from August to October 1935.)

The novelette opens with Reggie Havershot, the third Earl of Havershot, asking a writer friend to comment on a narrative he has written about his recent adventures. The friend, asking whether this bilge is to be published, suggests that he rewrites it explaining the background, the characters involved, and the events leading up to the reported opening. Thus we learn Reggie is in Hollywood towards the end of a round-the-world cruise about a year after his engagement, to Ann Bannister, had been broken off in Cannes soon after they agreed to tie the knot.

Reggie fell in love with the actress Hazel June while Hollywood and was about to propose during an outdoor dinner party in Beverly Hills when he suffered an agonising toothache. When he eventually reached a dentist's waiting-room, the Idol of American Motherhood, Teddy Flower, was also sitting there, biding his time before being called to the presence for the removal of a tooth weakened by prolonged exposure to illicit chocolate creams and all-day suckers.

While awaiting the summons from their respective dentists, Reggie and Teddy indulged in idle banter, which took an acrimonious turn when Teddy expressed the view that Hazel June was a 'pill'. He obtained the sympathy of his audience far more readily when outlining the tyrannous regime of the Brinkmeyers, under which he laboured.

Eventually Teddy was led off and almost immediately Ann Bannister appeared, in the guise of dental assistant, to lead Reggie to his doom. She explained that her role was a temporary one pending an expected appointment as press agent to Hazel June, though Reggie's pleasure at seeing her again was somewhat reduced by her coincidental reference to her erstwhile boss as a 'pill'.

Whilst under the ether, Reggie Havershot and Teddy Flower swapped bodies, and Reggie awoke to find himself in Teddy's body, saddled with golden ringlets and a contract which required him to eat prunes at every meal. He was dragged home by the tyrant Beulah Brinkmeyer, and shortly afterwards was amused to hear that she had been chased by a stranger and knocked into the swimming-pool.

The stranger, of course, turned out to be Teddy Flower, in the Earl's body, and he had come to find Reggie in order to discuss what had occurred. He also asked for a notebook in which he kept the names of potential further victims for his avenging spirit and Reggie, unwisely and unthinkingly, gave it to him. Teddy Flower realised at once that Hazel June was top of his list, and as he left Reggie to find her he mentioned in passing that he advised Reggie to look out for Tommy Murphy, his predecessor in the Idol of American Motherhood stakes.

Reggie, his soul still in love with Hazel June, determined to warn her and left the Brinkmeyer home in secret. Running into Tommy Murphy, he unwisely asked him whether he wanted his autograph, but when Tommy advanced to attack him, Reggie cleverly turned on the garden sprinkler systems which even then were a feature of the Hollywood roadscape. While Tommy learned to cope with the prospect of a clean face, Reggie escaped into Hazel June's home.

Thinking himself to be alone, he reached for the decanter and the cigarettes, and had started to relax when he discovered the presence of Amanda Wycherley, a reporter who had come to interview Hazel June. Naturally showing considerable interest in his activities, she arranged a photograph and took down his comments, so that when Hazel entered the room it was already clear that her interview had been hijacked. After Amanda left with her scoop, it was left to Hazel to recoup what satisfaction she could from a prolonged assault on the physical embodiment in which the soul of Reggie Havershot resided, and that soul realised that perhaps she was not as divine as it had supposed after all.

Tommy Murphy was still waiting as Reggie painfully left the June residence, but any thoughts Tommy may have had of avenging himself had to be put in abeyance as Ann Bannister arrived and agreed to escort Reggie back to the Brinkmeyers'. That kindly action opened Reggie's eyes, and he realised that he still loved Ann.

As he was about to go into the house, Reggie was chloroformed and kidnapped by Eddie, Fred and George, three frustrated actors imposing their interpretation on to a publicity stunt which had been arranged by Ann for Hazel June, designed to show Hazel as the rescuing angel. But over-elaboration, as ever the curse of the stage, and the disclosure in the following day's newspaper that Teddy Flower drank and smoked, meant that the Idol's career had abruptly ended and once again no publicity was to be enjoyed by Hazel June.

Ann Bannister went off to arrange for Reggie to be returned home to his physical mother in Chillicothe, Ohio, and to pass the time Reggie wandered off down the lane, only to be hit by a motor-bike ridden by Teddy in his aristocratic form.

When they came to, the leading characters were once more themselves. Ann, returning, heard Reggie mutter "Hazel June" in an uncomplimentary way, sympathised with his bloodied head, called him "Darling" and agreed to marry him after all. Reggie agreed to restore Teddy to his mother and, to escape further questioning from the police in respect of his assaults on the Brinkmeyers, he left vowing to meet Ann very soon, in New York.

Once he had delivered his novelette manuscript, of which the above is a very brief synopsis, Plum was able to turn his attention to the creation of a full-length book. It needed to be at least double the length and a brief calculation suggests it reached about the 75,000 word level.

Broadly, the changes that were made can be divided into three types: the introduction of new sub-plots, the use of new characters and the lengthening of existing scenes and phrases as part of his normal polishing exercise. Wodehouse also made some cosmetic changes, so that Hazel June became April June, Teddy Flower became Joey Cooley and Amanda Wycherley was renamed Pomona.

The new characters and sub-plots were substantially integrated into the existing material, and the principal new character, Reggie Havershot's cousin Eggy Mannering, was given a leading part in many of the scenes. Thus the reason why Reggie went to Hollywood was converted into one of family responsibility: the family lawyer told him that as its head he should go and rescue Eggy from the clutches of a Hollywood girl to whom he had become engaged.

The predicament of Eggy, who himself had been sent on a round-the-world-trip by the family in an attempt to wean him off alcohol, and the attempts to reform him by Mabel Prescott of the Temple of the New Dawn, opened the way for some of the best nifties Wodehouse ever wrote about alcohol and its effects.

Ann Bannister's role was substantially enlarged, and in reality she became the heroine. Not only was she Eggy's fiancée at the start of the book, but she was also the minder in the Brinkmeyer household to Joey Cooley until she was sacked for smuggling pork pies to the hungry adolescent. The Brinkmeyers were given expanded parts, and the reader shown more reason to sympathise with the troubles of the hen-pecked Mr Brinkmeyer than the complaints of Joey Cooley would have suggested.

Joey Cooley, in his new corporate form, extended his snoot-poking activity along a wider horizon than the Brinkmeyers alone, and more play was given to the encounters between Reggie Havershot (in the body of Joey Cooley) and his contemporaries, Tommy Murphy and Orlando Flower. Another new character, Chaffinch, an opportunist budding actor who was the Brinkmeyers' butler, stole Joey Cooley's extracted molar on the pretence of acting as agent for its sale, and made himself a sizeable packet into the bargain. Note that this was one of few instances in Wodehouse where a criminal minor character was permitted to retain the spoils of his crime. Perhaps the very incidental nature of the theft meant that a second scene, to regularise the position, could not be justified.

When writing *Laughing Gas*, Plum was in his early 50s, and at the peak of his writing ability. The expansion of the plot to fulfil the required number of words proved to be of little difficulty, though he did say to William Townend in a letter included in *Performing Flea*:

> I'm sorry you are going through a mistrustful phase in your book, but I am pretty certain it is only because you have been working so hard at it. I have just had the same experience with the one I am doing now – *Laughing Gas* – a novel version of a short serial which came out in *Pearson's* last year – about the man whose soul goes into the body of the child film star. A few days ago it all seemed absolutely idiotic, but it looks quite all right again now.

Laughing Gas was the only long story he wrote with any pretension to a science fiction angle. *Honeysuckle Cottage* was a short story which touched on the paranormal, and there are those who would have us believe that *The Amazing Hat Mystery* was another such example. But neither had the interesting history or period of development enjoyed by *Laughing Gas*.

THE GIRL IN BLUE *MANUSCRIPT*

The manuscript of *The Girl in Blue*, which was sold in 1998 at the auction of the late Jimmy Heineman's Wodehouse collection, consisted of more than 180 pages, some two-thirds of which were typed with extensive hand-written alterations in black or red pen, while the remainder was hand-written in its entirety, again either in black or red.

Plum had himself suggested a number of alternative titles for the book, including;

ALL ABOARD FOR MELLINGHAM

DO NICE GIRLS STEAL THINGS?

DO NICE WOMEN STEAL THINGS?

NICE GIRLS DON'T STEAL THINGS

The manuscript is self-evidently not the final work which was submitted to the publishers and printers. Although one can see that the changes made in the first third or so are relatively insignificant, redolent of the normal polishing exercise which Wodehouse said he enjoyed so much, the remainder of the book reflected major deviations from this draft. The order in which events were reported was changed in some degree, but the content of parts of the plot was altered, which necessitated a significant rewrite of substantial portions of the draft.

A simple example can be used to illustrate this. In chapter 11 part 2, one paragraph of the published book reads:

> Willoughby was in his study, a cigar between his lips and a refreshing whisky-and-soda at his side. He was re-reading a letter which had come for him that morning from his nephew Gerald. He had read it twice in the course of the day, and each time, except for the postscript, with the same feeling of satisfaction. It is always gratifying to an executive to know that the subordinate to whom he has entrusted a delicate commission is proving himself worthy of his confidence.

This had evolved from a rather different draft:

> When she arrived, Willoughby was in his study. There was a cigar between his lips, a refreshing whisky-and-soda at his side, and he had urgent need of both these comforters, for he was in the grip of a severe depression. He had been reading for the third time a letter which he had received that morning from his nephew Gerald, and its contents had darkened the day for him It was a hard verdict to pass on anyone, but he had formed from the missive the definite impression that his nephew Gerald was going to be about as much use as his brother Crispin.

There were a number of minor alterations to locations and the names of characters, which should be mentioned in a *Concordance*. They can be summarised as follows (the use of bold type in the section below implies that an entry can be found in the main text of this volume):

Book Name | ## Manuscript Name

Book Name	Manuscript Name
Benedict Arnold (ch 11 pt3)	Hitler or Benedict Arnold
R B Chisholm (ch 8)	R B Wix
Bernadette Clayborne (generally)	Nicole Wicker
Marlene Hibbs (ch 8)	Marlene Higgins. Note this is a name brought forward from *Jeeves in the Offing*, in which she was a young lady of Brixton whom Jeeves had selected as the winner of a Bathing Belles competition.
Pliny (ch 9)	Francis Bacon
Homer Pyle (generally)	In just one place, he was given the surname 'Carlisle'. It was also stated that he had been to Harvard.
Duane Stottlemeyer (ch 1)	Raymond Stottlemeyer
Gerald Godfrey Francis West (generally)	Gerald Fothergill West

Name of Place in Book | ## Name of Place in Manuscript

Name of Place in Book	Name of Place in Manuscript
Hunstanton, Norfolk **(ch 8)**	Hayward's Heath, Sussex
Mellingham Hall (eg ch 11 pt2)	Mellingham Hall was in Norfolk according to the manuscript. This might have been changed since a house of the same name, in Sussex, had been rented for the season by Grayce Llewellyn in *Pearls, Girls and Monty Bodkin*.
Salisbury (Cathedral) **(ch 12 pt2)**	Norwich (Cathedral)
Savoy (for lunch between **Jerry West** and **Willoughby Scrope**) (ch 3)	Originally scheduled for Barribault's

Other Relevant Matter in Book	*Other Relevant Matter in Manuscript*
In chapter 5, a bookseller suggested to **Homer Pyle** that as an alternative to *Daffodil Days* he might like to try *My Life on the Links* by **Sandy McHoots** or *Theatre Memories* by **Dame Flora Faye.**	In the manuscript there was a third suggestion: *Nudes I Have Met* by Kenneth Tynan.
In the following paragraph we learn that **Homer Pyle**'s life had been singularly free from beautiful women, a corporation lawyer's chance of seeing anything in the **Helen of Troy** class being limited.	In the manuscript we also learnt that Homer Pyle did not subscribe to *Playboy*.
In chapter 11 part 2, **Jane Hunnicutt** thinks **Jerry West** has scruples about marrying a rich girl of the type you find in stories in women's magazines.	In the manuscript, the scruples are identified as those in Rosie M Banks stories.
Band of Hope (ch 11 pt 5)	Temperance League
Shakespeare statuette (ch 11 pt 5)	Gladstone statuette

We must conclude that this is not the final version of the story. Amongst the extensive alterations there are some strange occurrences, such as words or sentences being amended in handwriting or even fully deleted but still appearing in the final book in their original form. Without access to the copy from which the book was set, it is possible to guess how and why certain alterations were made, but not to fully understand the time at which the various parts were written or amended. To add to the difficulty, no part of the manuscript is dated, even on the final, signed, page.

THE INFLUENCE OF GEORGES COURTELINE

Two of P G Wodehouse's post-war novels, neither belonging to one of his 'series', have a partially or wholly French setting. Anne-Marie Chanet, a Wodehousean in Paris, has identified the source of a number of characters and incidents from the works of Georges Courteline (1858-1929). The lead she followed had been provided by PGW himself in the *Preface* to the 1974 edition of *French Leave*, but the extent of her discoveries is perhaps surprising.

Frozen Assets (referred to in the Concordance as 'FRA')

The opening of this book is set in a Parisian police station, where Jerry Shoesmith had gone to report the loss of his wallet, money and keys. Whether his dialogue with the Sergeant was or was not in any way realistic, it certainly reflects the popular impression today (let alone that prevailing in the 1950s) of the adhesive qualities of French bureaucracy. Anne-Marie Chanet reports:

> Chapter 1 has a strongly Courtelinesque flavour. I haven't found a passage that exactly mirrors it, but there is a short theatrical work, *La Lettre Chargée* (1898), from which Wodehouse may have drawn some inspiration. The theme is similar: a hapless member of the public is trying to recover his property from a French post office clerk and fails because of nonsensical red tape. Courteline's mislaid goods, a *lettre chargée* (ie a registered letter containing money) also differs from the wallet and key-ring in *Frozen Assets*, but there remains a striking resemblance.

French Leave (referred to in the concordance and below as 'FRL')

It is in this book that the similarities are both more extensive and more specific, Wodehouse having borrowed not only many of Courteline's characters' names, but several of their personalities, some of their exchanges of dialogue and a number of plot situations. Anne-Marie Chanet cites four sources from Courteline's work:

1   *Messieurs les Ronds-de-cuir* (1893, novel, referred to as 'MRC')
2   *Monsieur Badin, scène de la vie de bureau* (1897, one-act play, 'MB')
3   *Le gendarme est sans pitié* (1899, one-act play written with Edouard Norès, 'GSP')
4   *Le Commissaire est bon enfant* (1900, one-act play written with Jules Lévy, 'CBE')

The characters utilised from Courteline's work in FRL are as follows:

i   *M. de la Houmerie*, who in MRC is *chef du bureau des Legs*, a department head within the *Direction Générale des Dons et Legs*, a department which was itself borrowed for FRL.

ii   *M. Soupe*, who in both MRC and MB is a rather pitiful employee of 36 years' service, compared to the 41 years completed in FRL.

iii   *M. Letondu*, whose condition in MRC deteriorates from mere madness to homicidal mania and culminates with his stabbing M. de la Houmerie to death. In FRL Letondu contents himself with hitting de la H with a hatchet (ch 6(3)), the sloppiness and incompetence expected of the French civil service causing his hand to slip and little harm to be done.

iv   *Ovide*, who in both MRC and MB was a *garçon de bureau*, the lowest form of life in any office.

v   *M. Floche*, whose name in CBE was used by Wodehouse, though he had attributed to him (FRL ch 6) the character of the anonymous *'le monsieur'* (also from CBE), in particular his request for permission to carry a revolver to protect himself on the streets.

vi   *M. Boissonnade*, who in GSP was *procureur de la République*, endeavouring to spread sweetness and light. Wodehouse gave the name to *le commissaire*, who acted very much as did the anonymous holder of that office in CBE. Anne-Marie emphasises that Wodehouse's specific use of the far-from-befitting expression "I am *bon enfant* . . ." (FRL ch 6(1)) implies a clear acknowledgement of the character's source.

vii   *M. Punèz*, who in both CBE and FRL was a humble police employee, relentlessly bullied by the Commissaire. Anne-Marie explains that *Punèz* is pronounced exactly like *punaise*, whose literal meaning is 'bug' or 'beetle', but whose figurative equivalent is 'unpleasant person, the dregs of society'.

viii   The name of the Marquis de Maufringneuse et Valerie-Moberanne, affectionately known as 'Old Nick' may emanate from the same stable as some of those used in *The Play's the Thing*, when Plum's objective was to give an unpleasant character as many problems as possible in committing to memory a number of French names. Old Nick's character in FRL, though, bears some resemblance to M. Badin from MB, the expression 'badinage' offering a strong clue as to both their characters. Neither M. Badin nor Old Nick had visited the office in the two weeks previous to their appearances in their respective stories. Courteline himself was famous for real-life absenteeism from the lowly position he held of 'expéditionnaire à la Direction Générales des Cultes'.

No description of the similarities would be complete without mention of the dossier Quibolle. It was a thin file when slipped into Old Nick's pocket (FRL ch2) as he left the Ministry for the last time, causing M. de la Houmerie to pursue him to Roville (ch 6(2)). But though in MRC it was much larger (*'un dossier gigantesque'*), in both stories it related to (in Wodehouse's words in FRL) "the gift to the Ministry of a museum or something of that sort by the mayor of some rural community". In fact, in MRC we have the whole story. It referred to a legacy of binoculars and a pair of candlesticks to the museum at Vanne-en-Bresse (not the whole of the museum to anybody), by a native citizen named Quibolle. In MRC, the file relating to the legacy had been filched and almost destroyed by a mentally unbalanced employee named Van der Hogen, and as a result the museum curator endlessly wandered down dusty corridors searching for news of the legacy.

In real life, too, Wodehouse was to imitate Courteline, for the latter was a dedicated animal-lover, and when he was living in a house in Montmartre used to shelter cats and dogs. He took this generous nature to extremes, perhaps, when keeping a pig in a rather large but messy ground-floor dining-room, a step which was beyond Plum and Ethel. Plum merely made a heroine out of one of the species.

A number of other situations in Courteline's work, and specific exchanges of dialogue, were reproduced in FRL either precisely or with modifications. The following two examples provide convincing evidence for points (v) and (vi) above:

In CBE, Courteline uses his trademark expression 'bon enfant' in several places, eg in conversation Le Commissaire says

- to 'le monsieur': "Vous avez de la chance que je sois bon enfant. ..."
- to M. Punèz: "Taisez-vous! Je veux bien être bon enfant, mais j'entends ne pas être dupe!"
- to 'la dame': "Je suis bon enfant d'écouter vos sornettes!"

and mad M. Floche returns the compliment to Le Commissaire: "Silence! Ou ça va mal tourner. Je suis bon enfant, mais je n'aime pas les fous!"

IN FRL, chapter 6, we find the following passages:

- One – of which he was the sole representative – thought him a good fellow, a *bon enfant*, and in his dealings with the general public courteous and obliging almost to a fault.
- as if asking Heaven why it allowed a good man and a bon enfant to be persecuted like this.

[Commissaire Boissonade to Mrs Pegler]: "You exasperate me, madame. I am *bon enfant*, but when women come wasting my time –"

The second example concerns an conversation between M. Floche and Commissaire Boissonade in FRL, chapter 6, based on an exchange between 'le monsieur' and 'le commissaire' in CBE

[M. Floche]	"But I desire a permit to carry a pistol. You can give it to me, can you not?"
[C. Boissonade]	"No."
[M. Floche]	"Why not?"
[C. Boissonade]	"Because I don't want to."
[M. Floche]	"But I live in a dangerous part of town. . . . It is not safe there after dark, and my profession makes it necessary for me to be out late at night. ... "
[C. Boissonade]	" ... Adopt another profession."
[M. Floche]	"Find me one."
[C. Boissonade]	"This is not an employment agency."
[M. Floche]	"And if some apache attacks me?"
[C. Boissonade]	"I shall then authorize you to carry a pistol."
[M. Floche]	"After I have been massacred by the apache?"
[C. Boissonade]	"Precisely."

In CBE the original read:

Le monsieur :	Vous pouvez bien m'autoriser à porter une arme sur moi!
Le commissaire :	Non.
Le monsieur :	Qu'est-ce que ça vous fait?
Le commissaire :	Ça me fait que je ne le veux pas.
Le monsieur :	Le quartier n'est pas sûr. . . . Or la profession que j'exerce m'oblige à rentrer tard chez moi.
Le commissaire :	Exercez-en une autre.
Le monsieur :	Je veux bien. Trouvez-m'en une.
Le commissaire :	Vous voulez rire, j'imagine. Est-ce que vous vous croyez dans un bureau de placement?
Le monsieur :	Et si on m'attaque, moi, cette nuit?
Le commissaire :	Vous viendrez le dire demain.
Le monsieur :	Et alors?

Le commissaire :	Alors, mais seulement alors, je vous autoriserai à sortir avec un revolver sur vous.
Le monsieur :	En sorte que j'aurai le droit de défendre ma peau après qu'on me l'aura crevée?
Le commissaire :	Oui.

Wodehouse said in his introduction to the 1974 edition that he had studied the Courteline plays in the early 1930s. They evidently made a lasting impression, so much so that the suspicion lingers that he may have started an adaptation of one of those plays, as this was his prime period for playwriting.

A PRINCE FOR HIRE

Readers who have a copy of *Wodehouse With Old Friends*, volume 7 of the *Millennium Wodehouse Concordance*, will be familiar with the notes regarding *The Prince and Betty* which constituted *Appendix 4*. Since they were written, there has been a significant development of considerable importance to which this note is addressed.

This is no less than the discovery that the American version of *The Prince and Betty* was completely rewritten for *The Illustrated Love Magazine*, an obscure American magazine in which it appeared in five instalments in 1931. This was not a mere tinkering with the plot, or an edited version to meet space restrictions but a fully-blown revision, introducing a number of new characters and eliminating a number of others. Unfortunately, at the time these notes are being written, the first two instalments have still not been traced, and for these all there is to go on is a synopsis of the 'story so far' provided at the beginning of the third instalment, and summarised below. The analysis in this note is thus necessarily incomplete.

The newly discovered version is entitled *A Prince for Hire*. The following characters, for whom notes were provided in *Volume 7*, appear to play more or less the same roles in both versions, although in most cases their involvement in the plot and dialogue changed:

Edwin Crump	Scobell's secretary
Dude Dawson	Rival gang-leader
Gooch (now W)	Rent collector at the Broster Street apartments
Bat Jarvis	Gang-leader and cat-lover
Pugsy Maloney	*Peaceful Moments* office boy
John Maude	Hero, friend of Rupert Smith
Jane Oakley	Extremely wealthy, eccentric aunt of Benjamin Scobell
d'Orby	President of Mervo
Martin Parker	Agent for the owner of the Broster Street apartments
General Poineau	Royalist army leader in Mervo
Spider Reilly	Rival gang-leader
J Brabazon Renshaw	Permanent editor of *Peaceful Moments* on vacation

Benjamin Scobell	Betty's step-father, financier
Marion Scobell	Benjamin Scobell's sister
Betty Silver	Heroine
Rupert Smith	Temporarily, editor of *Peaceful Moments*

The previously anonymous young Italian boy about to be evicted from his Broster Street apartment because his father, in jail for a short period, could not pay the rent, is given the name Tony in *A Prince for Hire*.

A few active characters were omitted from the revised plot, the most important being Kid Brady, who not only contributed to *Peaceful Moments* with a weekly article, but also won a professional bout, saw off an attack by Jack Repetto and others, acted as the paper's security guard and helped rescue Rupert Smith from an awkward moment when he was being kidnapped. Jack Repetto was himself a casualty of the rewrite, as was Long Otto, Bat Jarvis's principal assistant.

A number of minor characters from the book do not appear in instalments 3 to 5 of *A Prince for Hire*, but may be in the earlier ones:

Mr Archer-Cleeve	Citizen of Mervo
Cyclone Dick Fisher	Boxer
Colonel Finch	Citizen of Mervo
Elsa Keith	Friend of Betty Silver
Herr von Mandelbaum	Citizen of Mervo
Mr Pugh	Citizen of Mervo
Martin Rossiter	Elsa's fiancé
Spiller	Clerk at Westley, Martin & Co
Andrew Westley (deceased)	Brother of John Maude's mother

There are at least nine new characters in *A Prince for Hire*:

Angelo	One of Bat Jarvis's henchmen
Miss Bronson	Replacement stenographer for Betty Silver
Butch Casey	One of Bat Jarvis's best men
Mr Cook	Scobell's agent, who was instructed to sell *Peaceful Moments* to the first bidder
George Hastings	Reporter who took over as editor of *Peaceful*

	Moments while Rupert Smith visited Scobell
Maitre Laboudeux	French lawyer who had acted as Paris man-of-affairs for the Princes of Mervo
Prince Maurice	Restored as Prince of Mervo, but plotted with d'Orby to have Scobell, his mentor, exiled
Mr Smathers	Bank cashier who paid out John Maude's $ 10,000

and an interesting law firm, Abernathy, Ronald, Fish, Brewster, Abernathy and Smythe, of 120 Broadway, New York, who provided Crump with news of the Princes of Mervo. Ronald Fish had, of course, been a leading character in *Money for Nothing* (1928) and *Summer Lightning* (1929).

We learn an important new fact about the previous Prince Charles of Mervo. Instead of having been deposed in 1891 for absenteeism, he was now reported to have been deposed in 1914 (ie after the original story was published) in a rebellion fomented by the Allies who suspected him of pro-Germanism.

Finally, there were two new pseudonyms. John Maude and Betty Silver took the names Jason Maxwell and Edna Schuyler respectively when they were arrested and bailed, charged with violating the *Volstead Act*.

Although *The Prince and Betty* is itself not a very common book, it is possible to locate copies at reasonable cost. The following synopsis of the plot of *A Prince for Hire* will show that there are many major differences between the two. As explained above, we cannot be sure exactly what the differences are, but major scenes from *The Prince and Betty* which do not, to the best of our knowledge, appear in *A Prince for Hire* are summarised below:

1   Since the Prince whom Scobell restores to the throne is not John Maude but Prince Maurice, there is no need for John Maude to abdicate in a revolution in order to follow Betty to America

2   The scenes with the *Peaceful Moments* contributors

3   Betty, not Smith, restored the cat to Bat Jarvis

4   The Kid Brady contributions to *Peaceful Moments*

5   The Kid Brady *v* Cyclone Dick Fisher boxing match

6   The fight between Smith, Maude and Brady on one side, and the Three Points with Jack Repetto on the other

7   Smith's arrest for resisting the police after a raid

8   The scene on the roof at Broster Street

9   Parker's visit to John Maude, during which he kidnaps him and takes him for a ride in a taxi before he is rescued by Kid Brady

The knowledgeable reader might well say "But surely that is most of the plot!" And the reader would be almost right. The revised version covers much new ground. John Maude was traced by Crump in chapter 4 of *The Prince and Betty*, for example, but not until chapter 18 of *A Prince for Hire*. Betty falls out with John not because she thinks that he is Scobell's lackey, but because she believes he has been 'bought' by Parker and his unknown principal. But a more detailed review is needed:

Synopsis of the first two episodes

1   Benjamin Scobell went to Mervo and financed a revolution to restore Prince Maurice to the throne

2   He proposed to build a casino and make Mervo a rival to Monte Carlo

3   He cabled Betty Silver to go over to meet Maurice, with a view to marrying him for the publicity which would ensue

4   Betty arrived in Mervo, met Maurice, and took the next boat back to New York

5   On the advice of Jane Oakley, and with her assistance, she obtained a job on *Peaceful Moments*

6   John Maude, with whom she had previously fallen in love, had also been hired by his friend, Rupert Smith, to work for the paper, but he was away from the office when Betty arrived

7   Smith, though only temporary editor, had made major changes to the magazine's content

8   Betty found and fed a cat belonging to the gang-leader, Bat Jarvis

9   Betty wrote a series of articles about conditions in the Broster Street tenements

10   Parker, representing the owner, offered Smith a bribe to drop the series, which Smith refused

11   John Maude returned to the office but as he was talking to Smith the pair were attacked, bound and gagged by Bat Jarvis and his gang, preparatory to being taken for a ride

The story continues:

Ch 10   Betty and Pugsy Maloney returned from a further visit to Broster Street. Pugsy went home, and Betty met Jane Oakley, who had come to New York to see if the tenements were as bad as had been stated. She promised Betty that when she found out the name of their owner he would never be able to borrow money again. Betty was given the opportunity to scrounge off Jane Oakley but impressed her by not trying.

Betty went into the office and found Bat Jarvis and his gang had tied up Miss Bronson, Smith and John Maude. Bat recognised her as the girl who had fed his cat, set them free and agreed to give *Peaceful Moments* protection instead.

Ch 11   In Mervo, Benjamin Scobell had been puzzled by Betty's desertion, for although he enjoyed making money, he did not understand how to enjoy using it. He paid no attention to his sister Marion's description of Prince Maurice as 'a nasty little toad of a man'. Scobell told Crump to arrange the sale of *Peaceful Moments* if an offer was received. Crump warned Scobell that Prince Maurice was planning a double-cross with d'Orby's assistance: that when Scobell had completed his investment in the island he would declare that the contract was terminated, confiscate the casino and other property, and expel Scobell with no compensation.

Ch 12   John Maude, Rupert Smith and Betty went for a meal. John and Betty agreed to go and meet the rent collector, but before they did so, John proposed. The building exploded, the lights went out, Betty accepted and as they left by the fire escape they were held up at gunpoint.

Ch 13   Crump was sent to track down the legitimate heir of Mervo, and arrived in New York via Paris.

Ch 14   Though Smith had harboured ideas of his own concerning Betty, he put them aside when he realised John's position. Bat Jarvis brought news of the explosion, before John called from the police station to say that an illegal still in the basement had exploded and he and Betty were under arrest and needed bail. John returned Betty to her hotel where she found a message from Crump. On arriving at his own hotel he found that he too had a message from Crump.

Ch 15   Betty had discussions with the Broster Street rent collector, Gooch, as John Maude came up, threatened him and forced him to reveal the name of the owner of the tenements. John did not tell Betty immediately, saying she would be upset. As they spent time together before leaving, Gooch came back with a gang of thugs, and John was knocked unconscious.

Ch 16   John Maude was taken to hospital, concussed, and suffering partial amnesia. Parker brainwashed him, and Smith and Betty thought he had betrayed them. Betty decided to return to Mervo via Paris (for

341

shopping) and would marry Maurice if her stepfather still wanted her to. Smith was also summoned to Mervo, to discuss with Scobell the position of *Peaceful Moments*.

Ch 17   John Maude was sacked by Smith, rejected by Betty, and discovered to his horror that his bank account contained $ 10,000 less than he had expected. The bank cashier confirmed that it was he who had drawn the cheque.

Ch 18   John returned to his hotel to find Crump awaiting him. Crump told him he was Prince John of Mervo, and was to be reinstated on the throne at a salary of $ 100,000 per annum.

Ch 19   d'Orby and Prince Maurice prepared to seize Scobell's property. Betty returned to Mervo and explained her position to Scobell, but realised that even though she did not trust him, she still loved John. Smith arrived on the same boat, but Crump and John Maude had missed it.

d'Orby told Scobell his contract was terminated, but Gen Poineau pulled a gun on d'Orby and war was threatened.

During the skirmishes, John Maude arrived with Crump and a group of sailors and policemen shouting for Prince John. He was again struck down by a stick, which caused his memory to return as did, a few moments later, Betty. It transpired that Jane Oakley had financed a special boat and come with them, and she told Scobell that there was to be no more fighting, but that Mervo should be turned into a winter resort. John said he would abdicate, made it clear to Scobell that he knew he was the owner of the tenements, revealed to Smith that he had bought *Peaceful Moments* and wanted Smith as its editor. Scobell said he had not realised how badly run down the tenements were and would repair them. John and Betty went off to get married.

A not untypical Wodehouse plot, though with rather more violence than usual, which betrayed the story's pedigree. Twenty years additional maturity and writing experience shows itself in some of the phraseology, as these three extracts demonstrate:

"Take a memorandum to Prince Maurice. Tell him he's got to appear in the Casino every night for at least two hours and be affable. It's part of his contract. He can entertain his chorus girls from Paris in his own time, not in mine." (Chapter 11)

[Crump] had not . . . up to this time had much to do with French lawyers. He knew that all lawyers, in general, were secretive and greatly given to stressing matters of *punctilio*. But he didn't know that in these respects the average French *avocat* excels; that he makes a simple transaction for the sale of a piece of property a thing of mystery and endless complexity. (Chapter 13)

The thickness of the average human skull is a manifestation of the wisdom of nature, difficult though it is at times – when one is arguing with a traffic policeman, for instance, or an income tax inspector – to bring oneself to admit it. (Chapter 17)

A final footnote to this topic concerns a paragraph which appeared in *The Alleynian* for November 1936, five years after *A Prince for Hire* was published. It read as follows:

Meet the Prince, a musical comedy based on one of his stories was adapted for broadcasting and given from the National station.

One has to wonder whether this was an adaptation of either *The Prince and Betty* or, more likely, *A Prince for Hire*. If any reader has access to the *Radio Times* for mid-to-late 1936 and is able to provide any information, please contact the author, via the publisher if necessary.

MATRIMONIAL SWEEPSTAKES

Neil Midkiff recently identified significant differences between the American story, *The Matrimonial Sweepstakes*, and its British equivalent, *The Good Angel*. Each was published in February 1910, in *Cosmopolitan* and *Strand* respectively, the British version being included in the short story collection *The Man Upstairs*.

Keggs, an English butler, appears in both versions, and the problem of how many different Keggs there were in Wodehouse's canon has been considered in *Plum Stones, Book 4*, and the *Millennium Concordance, Volume 7 (Wodehouse with Old Friends)*. Only in *The Matrimonial Sweepstakes* (which was published five years before the first Blandings Castle story appeared), though, did Keggs reveal that he was once butler to a Lord Emsworth.

Furthermore, he mentioned that Lord Emsworth's heir was the Hon Claude Havant, though he also referred to him as 'Mr John', and mentioned his fondness for whiskey. This raises the question of how this Lord Emsworth fits into the Threepwood family tree. As an 'Hon' title indicates a younger son, it might in theory be possible that he was the younger brother of Clarence, our ninth Earl's, but older than Galahad, and thus heir to Clarence until the birth of Lord Bosham. The application of basic arithmetic and genealogy leads to the conclusion that for this to be the case, the eighth Earl would have had to be over 50 when Clarence was born, and while not impossible, bearing in mind the troupe of younger sisters, it is unlikely. This conclusion is reinforced by the fact that we never hear about him again, which we surely would have done even if he had suffered an early demise as a result of alcoholism or some other scandal. It would also add a complication to the question of how many Keggs there were, as although we don't know how long Beach actually acted as butler at the Castle, as opposed to his total length of service, we don't really see him as footman under Keggs. For one thing, he would have learned an awful lot of bad habits. (We do know, of course, from Ronnie Fish, that Beach has been butler for quite a long time.)

So can we look elsewhere? John Fletcher solves one of the problem, that of the apparent inconsistent family name ('Havant', rather than 'Threepwood') by suggesting that the 'Havant' may have been an additional Christian name donated at the font by a godfather such as the Duke of Havant. The Duke would appear offstage in *A Gentleman of Leisure* when his wife had her diamonds stolen, and in *Something Fresh*, Beach referred to 'the Havant affair' in the context of a breach-of-promise scandal as though all present would know of the family. John then threw a spanner in the works by drawing attention to Clarence's comment in *Company for Gertrude* that his cousin Claude died at the age of 84. In arriving at his preferred solution, he proposed that Claude might have been the younger brother of the seventh Earl and a full cousin of Clarence. He added that if both Claude and the seventh Earl died childless, Clarence's father could have inherited the title from an elderly nephew.

While this may be plausible, the mathematics make it unrealistic, especially when you consider that Clarence is himself in the mid-fifties, and his father had at least a dozen children (Constance, *a* senior if not *the* senior sister, was described in one story as a handsome woman in her forties). So if the cousin Claude is the Hon Claude Havant, John's theory needs refinement.

This can come from a wide reading of the term 'cousin' as used by Clarence to describe Claude. In popular parlance, cousins can be first (or 'full'), second, and so on, and can be removed through generations. All are likely to be referred to in everyday speech as 'cousin'. If we explore this route, we can speculate that Clarence's grandfather might himself have been a younger son of say the seventh Earl, his elder brother being father to two sons, of whom the younger was Claude. Claude is then a second cousin once removed to Clarence, or a 'cousin' as he would say in conversation. Of course, Claude and his elder brother would have had to remain childless. It is even plausible that one of them, or their father, inherited the title, in which case Clarence's grandfather would have been the younger son of the sixth Earl. So that relationship may work in principle. What about the problem of ages?

We know that Clarence was in his late fifties. If it is assumed that his cousin Claude died at age 84 about twenty years earlier, when Clarence was a slip of a lad of say 39, the oldest his father could realistically have been at that time, bearing in mind his later fecundity, is 69. His grandfather, had he still been alive might well have been 95 or more, and his great-uncle, Claude's father, 105 or 110. Which brings us quite reasonably to Claude, as a younger son, at 84.

So, mathematically, if Claude is the 'cousin' referred to by Clarence in *Company for Gertrude*, the 'Lord Emsworth' whom Keggs introduced might have been either Claude's father or brother. But even this is not the end of the story, since an heir to an Earldom who was an elder son would not have the title 'Hon', but would take the secondary title, in this case Viscount Bosham. 'Hon' is reserved for younger sons. The probable solution to the problem can thus be narrowed down to the Lord Emsworth who was Keggs's employer having been Claude's elder brother and a second cousin, once removed, of Clarence, the ninth Earl.

346

OVERALL INDEX TO REFERENCES USED IN THE TEXT

This index provides a trail from a reference given in the main text of this volume to its source: either a novel, a short story in a book collection or a short story in a magazine. Readers should bear in mind the order of priority used by the compiler of the text:

1   UK first edition
2   US first edition
3   Magazine

This implies that information given in a magazine or US book version which also appears in the UK first edition will generally not be referenced separately. It also means that in the *Concordance* references to material from magazines should not be found in the book versions of the story. In this index, though, for completeness the title of generally the UK book, if any, containing the story is also given.

Readers are reminded of the unique treatment given to magazine appearances of the constituent stories of *Indiscretions of Archie*, for details of which see the *Introduction* on page ix.

Concordance Reference	Short Story Title, or *Novel*	Magazine Source	Book Featuring Short Story
Ainslee-RIE	*Ruth in Exile*	Ainslee	The Man Upstairs; The Uncollected Wodehouse
Ainslee-RUP	*The Romance of an Ugly Policeman*	Ainslee	The Man with Two Left Feet
Aldin-GOW	*Gone Wrong*		The Cecil Aldin Book
BurrMcK-MIS	*Misunderstood*	The Burr-McKintosh Monthly	The Uncollected Wodehouse
Century-BTB	*Bill the Bloodhound*	Century	The Man with Two Left Feet
Colliers-HOW	**Hot Water**	Colliers	
Colliers-JOW	*A Job of Work*	Colliers	None
Colliers-PAP	*The Pitcher and the Plutocrat*	Colliers	None
Colliers-PTR	**Phipps to the Rescue**	Colliers	
Colliers-SAG	*Sir Agravaine*	Colliers	The Man Upstairs
Colliers-TAS	**The Adventures of Sally**	Colliers	
Colliers-TLW	**The Little Warrior**	Colliers	
Cosmo-DFB	*Doing Father a Bit of Good*	Cosmopolitan	Indiscretions of Archie
Cosmo-DSQ	*Dear Old Squiffy*	Cosmopolitan	None

Cosmo-FAL	*First Aid for Looney Biddle*	Cosmopolitan	Indiscretions of Archie
Cosmo-FFD	*Franklin's Favorite Daughter*	Cosmopolitan	None
Cosmo-MMH	*The Man who Married a Hotel*	Cosmopolitan	Indiscretions of Archie
Cosmo-MMM	*The Man, the Maid and the Miasma*	Cosmopolitan	The Man Upstairs
Cosmo-MUP	*The Man Upstairs*	Cosmopolitan	Lord Emsworth and Others
Cosmo-SCH	*The Sausage Chappie*	Cosmopolitan	Indiscretions of Archie
DBB	***Do Butlers Burgle Banks?***		
Ellery-DAE	*Death at the Excelsior*	Ellery Queen	None
Ellery-MBD	*Mr McGee's Big Day*	Ellery Queen	None
FRL	***French Leave***		
GOB	***The Girl on the Boat***		Nothing Serious
Grand-COL	*The Colour Line*	Grand Magazine	None
Grand-JTR	***Jill the Reckless***	Grand Magazine	
HOW	***Hot Water***		Plum Stones vol 10
IOA	***Indiscretions of Archie***		Plum Stones vol 12
JohnBull-FRL	***French Leave***	John Bull	
JTR	***Jill the Reckless***		
LAG	***Laughing Gas***		
LHJ-FKA	*The Fatal Kink in Algernon*	Ladies' Home Journal	The Man Upstairs
McClure-AST	*A Sea of Troubles*	McClure	The Man with Two Left Feet
McClure-BRF	*Brother Fans*	McClure	The Man with Two Left Feet
McClure-GOF	*The Golden Flaw*	McClure	None
MLF-AST	*A Sea of Troubles*		The Man with Two Left Feet
MLF-ATG	*At Geisenheimer's*		The Man with Two Left Feet
MLF-BFL	*Black for Luck*		The Man with Two Left Feet
MLF-BIS	*The Mixer - II- Breaking into Society*		The Man with Two Left Feet
MLF-BTB	*Bill the Bloodhound*		The Man with Two Left Feet
MLF-CRH	*Crowned Heads*		The Man with Two Left Feet

348

MLF-HMV	The Mixer - I-He Meets a Very Shy Gentleman		The Man with Two Left Feet
MLF-MOM	The Making of Mac's		The Man with Two Left Feet
MLF-OTN	One Touch of Nature		The Man with Two Left Feet
MLF-RUP	The Romance of an Ugly Policeman		The Man with Two Left Feet
MLF-TLF	The Man with Two Left Feet		The Man with Two Left Feet
MOS	**Mostly Sally**		
Nash-MIS	Misunderstood	Nash	The Uncollected Wodehouse
NGW	**Nor George Washington**		
NSE-HTU	How's That, Umpire?		Nothing Serious
PallMall-MLB	Mike's Little Brother	Pall Mall	None
Pan-TMM	**Three Men and a Maid**	Pan	
Pearson-EDO	The Education of Detective Oakes	Pearson's Magazine	The Uncollected Wodehouse
Pearson-LAG	**Laughing Gas**	Pearson's Magazine	
Pearson-SAG	Sir Agravaine	Pearson's Magazine	The Man Upstairs
Pearson-SUM	**Summer Moonshine**	Pearson's Magazine	
PicRev-DOH	A Dinner of Herbs	Pictorial Review	The Uncollected Wodehouse
PicRev-PAW	Parted Ways	Pictorial Review	The Man with Two Left Feet
PicRev-TFD	Three from Dunsterville	Pictorial Review	The Man Upstairs
Playboy-GCS	A Good Cigar is a Smoke	Playboy	Plum Pie
PLP-GCS	A Good Cigar is a Smoke		Plum Pie
QUS	**Quick Service**		
Red-BCL	A Black Cat for Luck	Red Book	The Man with Two Left Feet
Red-BIS	The Mixer - II- Breaking into Society	Red Book	The Man with Two Left Feet
Red-HMV	The Mixer - I-He Meets a Very Shy Gentleman	Red Book	The Man with Two Left Feet
Red-ROM	The Romance of Mac's	Red Book	The Man with Two Left Feet
SatEvePost-ATG	At Geisenheimer's	Saturday Evening Post	The Man with Two Left Feet
SatEvePost-QUS	**Quick Service**	Saturday Evening Post	

SatEvePost-SUM	*Summer Moonshine*	Saturday Evening Post	
SatEvePost-TLF	*The Man with Two Left Feet*	Saturday Evening Post	The Man with Two Left Feet
SatEvePost-TSP	*The Spring Suit*	Saturday Evening Post	None
SPF	*Spring Fever*		
Strand-BFL	*Black for Luck*	Strand	The Man with Two Left Feet
Strand-BTB	*Bill the Bloodhound*	Strand	The Man Upstairs
Strand-BTG	*Back to the Garage*	Strand	None
Strand-COI	*Creatures of Impulse*	Strand	None
Strand-HMV	*The Mixer - I-He Meets a Very Shy Gentleman*	Strand	The Man with Two Left Feet
Strand-JOW	*A Job of Work*	Strand	None
Strand-LSC	*The Love-r-l-y Silver Cup*	Strand	The Man with Two Left Feet
Strand-MMH	*The Man who Married a Hotel*	Strand	Indiscretions of Archie
Strand-MWD	*The Man who Disliked Cats*	Strand	The Man Upstairs
Strand-PAW	*Parted Ways*	Strand	The Man with Two Left Feet
Strand-PWM	*Paving the Way for Mabel*	Strand	Indiscretions of Archie
Strand-RUP	*The Romance of an Ugly Policeman*	Strand	The Man with Two Left Feet
Strand-TSF	*The Spring Frock*	Strand	None
SUM	*Summer Moonshine*		
Sunday-IDK	*The Idle King*	Sunday Magazine	None
TAS	*The Adventures of Sally*		
TGI	*The Girl in Blue*		
ThisWeek-LAG	*Laughing Gas*	This Week	
Throne-KHE	*The Kind-Hearted Editor*	The Throne and Country	None
TLW	*The Little Warrior*		
TMM	*Three Men and a Maid*		
TMU-BAC	*By Advice of Counsel*		The Man Upstairs
TMU-INA	*In Alcala*		The Man Upstairs
TMU-MMM	*The Man, the Maid and the Miasma*		The Man Upstairs
TMU-MUP	*The Man Upstairs*		The Man Upstairs

TMU-MWD	*The Man who Disliked Cats*		The Man Upstairs
TMU-POM	*Pots o' Money*		The Man Upstairs
TMU-RIE	*Ruth in Exile*		The Man Upstairs
TMU-SAG	*Sir Agravaine*		The Man Upstairs
TMU-STW	*Something to Worry About*		The Man Upstairs
TMU-TFD	*Three from Dunsterville*		The Man Upstairs
TMU-TGP	*The Goalkeeper and the Plutocrat*		The Man Upstairs
TMU-TTM	*The Tuppenny Millionaire*		The Man Upstairs
TMU-WDD	*When Doctors Disagree*		The Man Upstairs
TOR	***The Old Reliable***		
TUW-BSA	*The Best Sauce*		The Uncollected Wodehouse
TUW-DAE	*Death at the Excelsior*		The Uncollected Wodehouse
TUW-MIS	*Misunderstood*		The Uncollected Wodehouse
TUW-TDH	*Tom, Dick and Harry*		The Uncollected Wodehouse
TUW-WPS	*When Papa Swore in Hindustani*		The Uncollected Wodehouse
USDBB	***Do Butlers Burgle Banks?***		
USFRL	***French Leave***		
USHOW	***Hot Water***		
USSUM	***Summer Moonshine***		
USTGI	***The Girl in Blue***		
USTOR	***The Old Reliable***		
VanFair-AAI	*Aubrey's Arrested Individuality*	Vanity Fair	None
WHC-TMM	***Three Men and a Maid***		
Windsor-CPB	*Cupid's Paint Brush*	Windsor	None
WTT	***William Tell Told Again***